THE MANY LIVES OF
TOMWAITS

PATRICK HUMPHRIES

OMNIBUS PRESS

LONDON / NEW YORK / PARIS / SYDNEY / COPENHAGEN / BERLIN / MADRID / TOKYO

Cover designed by Fresh Lemon

ISBN 978.1.84772.509.7
Order No: OP52558

Exclusive Distributors
Music Sales Limited,
14/15 Berners Street,
London, W1T 3LJ

Music Sales Corporation,
257 Park Avenue South,
New York, NY 10010, USA

Macmillan Distribution Services,
56 Parkwest Drive,
Derrimut, Vic 3030,
Australia

Every effort has been made to trace the copyright holders of the photographs in this
book but one or two were unreachable. We would be grateful if the photographers
concerned would contact us.

Printed by Gutenberg Press Ltd, Malta

A catalogue record for this book is available from the British Library.

Visit Omnibus Press on the web at www.omnibuspress.com

CONTENTS

To Thomas Dylan Brooke, for growing up . . .
and Laura-lou for arriving just in time.

INTRODUCTION

"Wasted and wounded . . ." a bowed and battered figure, bent by the wind, scuffs around, then huddles on a street corner. A lamp-post his only friend. Neon rips the city sky. There's a moon like a cuticle up there, patiently watching, and waiting . . .

The scene shifts constantly, while remaining, somehow, the same: The symphonic city sound made up of subway, streetcar and siren runs on an endless loop; the backdrop . . . traffic jam, crumbling tenement and subway steps; the cast . . . panhandler, whore and drunk. And only the bar stool, isolation and alcoholic haze can help.

What the hell: one will prick his memory . . . two'll numb the nostalgia . . . and three might just help him forget. Memories, hell. A couple of shots will make them as faded as the photo of a fiancé on a stripper's mirror. He flicks a match beneath his thumb-nail and fires a cigarette. All the snatched, corroded and unwarranted memories are exhaled bitterly and moonwards in the smoke. He tugs the collar up around his neck and moves towards the bright, beckoning light . . .

"When everything's broken . . ." From inside looking out, it's an urban hell out there. Like desolation row with a zip code. A place where the steam rises through the subway vents and makes every street look like it's auditioning. Round the corner, beneath a street lamp, rain dogs howl at the moon, and the fire hydrants pump their useless water out onto a pavement that glistens and gleams like polished linoleum. The store fronts recoil from the neon glare, like an ageing hooker that can't bear the inquisitive light. From some tenement, a listless, crackling radio pumps out the tunes that no one bothers to hum anymore. Yesterday's songs, spluttering and cutting out, as the radio fails to make a connection.

"And no one speaks English . . ." Here's where Spanish Harlem seeps onto 42nd Street. "You're going out there a nobody," Warner Baxter warns Ruby Keeler, as the first ten rows mouth along, "but you've *got* to come back a star!" Here's where bedlam gets into bed with squalor and celluloid dreams. This ain't bling bling town; this is where the hoods from *West Side Story* slunk off, to open all-nite drugstores, so that when times got really hard, they could rob themselves. On that far corner, beatniks

vii

click fingers in synchronised cool, and stand, waiting for The Man. Nerves are played out through endless plumes of cigarette smoke. Blind brown-stones huddle together. There's gotta be something more than *this* . . .

★   ★   ★

There are two coasts, East and West, with 3,000 miles worth of real life separating them. London is nearer to New York than New York is to Los Angeles. No wonder 90 per cent of Americans don't even have passports – it's a damn big country, why do they need to travel abroad? Who wants to cross an ocean? You stick your thumb out at the New Jersey Turnpike, and take Horace Greeley's advice . . . You hitch a ride out west.

West is the frontier: the far end of everything. It's where characters from John Ford films still cling to the edge. The raising of every wooden church and timber school marking the birth of a new community, carving civilisation out of the endless sprawling wilderness. And each small but determined step echoes to a mighty swelling chorus of 'Shall We Gather At The River'.

Today, it's easier . . . You can follow the long, snaking highway that bleeds across America. Soon the scabby blocks of New York are far behind; ahead lie wheatfields and mountains; desert and forest . . . This is a terrain mapped in your mind's eye by James Fenimore Cooper, John Steinbeck, Mark Twain and Jack Kerouac. These are the heartlands – the soul and steady heartbeat of the nation, dismissed by the elite of either coast as "fly-over states".

But inside the car, it's always night. Everything viewed at one remove, through the filters of shades, windshield, dust and the fug of cigarette smoke. The floor of the car is littered with Coors cans, burger wrappers and crumpled packets of Kents. The beat-up Buick eats up the miles, hurtling you nearer and nearer to the Pacific. Until, suddenly, you're out of the desert, and on the horizon palm trees stand sentinel. Then the neon takes over.

The shades stay on for a reason at Heartattack & Vine. The streets collide like a car crash – and all the while, on every Hollywood corner, dreams live and die, seeping slowly down plugholes and into the sewers. Lives are worn through, beneath the sign that for nearly a century has offered hope, illusion and immortality – Hollywoodland. A place where the good die young and the bad crumble under the weight of their broken dreams.

Los Angeles offers sun, palm trees and a limitless blue ocean. That's what makes the city even more mysterious. It's the collision, and collusion, between the bright open space and the dark wickedness that lives behind the blinds of those big old mansions, crumbling along the low thousands of Sunset Boulevard. A cheap dick opens an eye: he sees empty cigarette cartons; cold coffee in Styrofoam cups; paperback novels with their spines shattered like the limbs of a war vet. In the corner, an unwatched television set howls endlessly, with nothing to say. A neon sign competes with the static from the radio and the hum of the refrigerator. Because he's on expenses, he blinks an eye out of the blind. Something blurred and vast registers. Outside, it's America . . .

Welcome to the theme ride of your imagination. Welcome to life lived behind the shades. Welcome to Waitsworld . . .

Here are the ricocheted romantics bent out of shape by a broad who should have known better; the twisted psychotics; the loners; the losers . . . Here's where the hobos ride the rails all their lives, because it's the nearest thing they got to home. This is where a certain faded grandeur is de rigeur; you may be at the bottom of the pile, but you've still got to keep your shoes dry. And perhaps – just *perhaps* – shoes are the key to all this . . .

Here are realists and romantics; pragmatists and poets; the dupes and the dreamers. A world where even the piano has been drinking, and the old guy slouched in the corner is hammering those 88s – but wait a minute, he's not *that* old, though he looks mighty used – is weaving a barfly's tale of mystery and romance and poetry and imagination. He's taking us to the heart of a Saturday night. His tender little trip inspired by a Sinatra-style reverie, a bruised and beaten soul, with a wisecrack and a tune for every bum in every bar from Manhattan to Malibu.

Then suddenly the tempo changes . . . as if the mutant children of Kurt Weill and *Guys & Dolls* got trapped inside a dustbin, alongside a midget with a penchant for Howlin' Wolf, armed with a baseball bat, hammering at the sides to get out. That was the soundtrack in Tom Waits' mind after he got married – and it steered him towards the most remarkable rebirth since Paul Simon left Scarborough Fair far behind, and went all the way to the townships of South Africa to find Graceland . . .

Waits doesn't go in much for compromise. And it doesn't much worry him what you think of him – you just gotta take him as you find him . . . And that might be the gravel-voiced grouch of the Seventies: a hung-over Fifties hangover, soused in bebop and Kerouac, out of step and out of time with the times. Or the fearless musical pioneer of the Eighties, taking what you might call rock'n'roll out for a joy-ride somewhere, slipping it into a bag like a dead cat, and throwing it into the fast-flowing river. In his trilogy of Island albums, Waits was recklessly intent on shredding his past. As if he wished he could take the "old Tom" out to a little-visited bar of his acquaintance, buy him a couple too many Martinis, and let him go play in the traffic.

Then Waits pulled up sticks and went West. Bitten by the movie bug, he sat on a bar stool at Schwab's and waited until he was picked up by Hollywood. Though by no means a conventionally handsome leading man, over the years Waits has found himself starring alongside the likes of Jack Nicholson, Meryl Streep, Winona Ryder, Robin Williams, Lily Tomlin . . .

Whatever else changes though, one thing stays the same, there's always Waits the Wit. And this one was a godsend for rock journalists: all they had to do was turn up, switch the cassette on, and leave Waits to do the rest. He gave great lip from the hip; he *was* the hip, a scattergun of innuendo, wit and sublime quote. While others of his profession were struggling with the tricky ramifications of "What's your favourite colour?", Waits was dispensing wit ("I'm so broke I can't even pay attention") and wisdom ("Something like 43 million tons of meteor dust fall from the heavens every day").

Pithy and priceless, Waits was a walking one-liner just waiting to be quoted. "If I had a good quote," Bob Dylan once wearily responded, "I'd be wearing it." But Waits wore his all the time – with dignity and timeless irreverence: "I'm not a household word, I'm just a legend in my own mind."

★ ★ ★

The songs poured out of him: broken narratives and bleary-eyed ballads, populated by a cast of ne'er-do-wells, drifters and incurable romantics. Then he got bored . . . Movie roles and stage librettos, a growing family . . . other distractions took him out of play. But Waits found himself glued to his own past, a past that stuck to him like treacle.

He was pushing ahead with challenging new work, but all *they* wanted to talk to him about was . . . oh, the usual cocktail of jazz . . . and the drink . . . and Kerouac . . . But Waits knew it was time to move on, and so, for much of the Nineties, he kept a fugitive profile. The increasingly rare live shows had fans flying from all over the world; his profile found him stalked by U2 and The Pogues; and gradually, belatedly, the A-list – from Johnny Depp to Jerry Hall – all came out as Tom Waits fans.

For most of his career, Waits has steadfastly refused to be interviewed in a serious vein. He has never sanctioned a biography. And, so far, he has shown no inclination to write his own story. When I became his first biographer, back around the time Reagan was trying to find the War Room in the White House, I thought he might be quite flattered. Rock biography back then was still a fledgling craft – Elvis, Beatles, Dylan and, uh, that's it.

But elevation into the pantheon of printed biography cut no mustard with Waits. There was no growled answerphone message saying "well done", or hand-written note with a curt "thanks". But much later I did get to hear on the grapevine, that during one of his *many* court battles – when Waits was claiming that he was an internationally known performer and therefore using a soundalike to impersonate him in a commercial was damaging to his reputation – the judge, looking most severe, said: that's all very well Mr . . . Waits, but how do we *know* that is the case, we on the bench have never heard of you! Aha, says Waits, and with a flourish produces my book as a witness for the prosecution!

In the intervening years, phones shrunk and TV screens grew; movies got FX-ed and Imax-ed; and music became digitalised and duller . . . and ol' Tom just kept rolling along. His audience grew, and he became *the* cult name to drop. In 2004, at his first London shows in 17 years ("I know, I *know* . . ." he acknowledged as he came onstage), £65 tickets were swapping hands for £900.

What follows is very much a picture of Tom Waits from a European perspective. He epitomises so much that *is* America – and that we this side of the Atlantic are beguiled by: a cocktail mixed by Edward Hopper and Steinbeck, filmed by Coppola, and heavy on the Kerouac . . . The music, an abstract of bleary-eyed Sinatra fused with a heady dash of Dylan, Howlin' Wolf, Ethel Merman and James Brown . . .

To European ears, Waits' early albums served up the promise of the American Dream, with a side order of fries and a shake. He offered up the vast, sweeping expanses of America, complete with sombre crevices and dingy cracks. And he did it all with the deft hand of a poet, and the caustic wit of a vaudeville trouper.

Later still, Waits ran away and joined the carnival; living out his creative life on the midway – like the Elephant Man, out of Tod Browning and *The Greatest Show On Earth*. The megaphone-toting ringmaster took his songs to the circus, keeping the past at bay like a lion-tamer wielding his chair.

All along though, whichever hat he's wearing, Waits has been consistently entertaining. At a time when most "rock stars" could be measured on a Richter scale of dreary pretentiousness, Waits continued to deliver. In his sleevenotes for 1973's *Tales From Topographic Oceans*, for example, Jon Anderson of Yes found himself "leafing through Paramhansa Yoganada's autobiography of a Yogi" and getting "caught up in the lengthy footnote on page 83 . . .". I love that casual "leafing through . . ." Others recall Frank Zappa's tried and tested, but nonetheless acute, observation that: "Rock journalism is people who can't write, talking to people who can't talk, for people who can't read!" But Waits in interview, offered an object lesson in vaudeville ("Make like a hockey player and get the puck outta here!").

But critics, especially rock critics, are notorious for wanting to have their cake, and eat it. And so there was a lotta brouhaha one time 'bout how Waits was a lips-movin' type of phoney . . . Word was that Thomas Alan from Pomona was a teachers' boy, and that the drunken Boho bum on disc was just a character he'd Fed-Exed in from Central Casting. Critics carped that "Tom Waits" was a costume he put on when venturing out into the limelight.

'Twas ever thus . . . Even today, the undeniably middle-class, grammar school-educated John Lennon is popularly characterised as a "working class hero"; and Julie Burchill wasn't the only one to spot the irony of a man who wrote "imagine no possessions" devoting an entire room in the Dakota to the storage of fur coats. And Bob Dylan? The early image of a rollin' railroad bum outta Texas 'n' the South, hoppin' off at a carny an' pickin' up tunes from Cisco an' Blind Boy . . . Whereas, in fact, the rap should have run: "Good evening. My name is Robert Zimmerman. I am the eldest son of middle-class, store-owning Jewish parents from Minnesota, up near the Canadian border . . ."

Tom Waits was, in a sense, what critics and his audience *wanted* him to be. He certainly gave good quote, the sort of good-natured, bibular W.C. Fields-type you wouldn't mind being buttonholed by in a bar – though perhaps not every night . . . "An inebriated good evening to you all . . ." ushered in an evening of fun and frolics from a word-weaver and spell-binding storyteller.

As his success consolidated itself, and marriage and parenthood pleasantly enveloped our hero, Waits became ever more opaque and evasive. If a question got too close to home, the Waits eyes would narrow, the chin tilt, and a defiant, almost truculent tone would enter the interview. But Waits was such a seasoned practitioner of the interview scenario that even if the section headed "Private Life" came away blank, there was always page after page of feisty one-liners and enough fascinating facts and quotable quips to keep even the most demanding editor happy.

Persistent enquiries would be stonewalled. Waits was a past-master at obfuscation, battering you down instead with a litany of facts and tantalising trivia – disconcerting Barney Hoskyns in 1999, for example, with news of a nearby Banana Slug Festival ("Gelatinous gastropods, ten inches long. People cook with them. You find them in your yard about six in the morning. And this is the season of the banana slug.")

Such techniques cloaked an essentially reticent man. For all his flamboyant lip and showmanship, once coaxed "out of character", Waits proved reflective and surprisingly shy. The switch to film acting seemed like a natural progression. But "the real Tom Waits", the happily married man, the proud father, remained always at arm's length. For interviews, the public persona was switched on as routinely as a Pontiac's headlights at twilight.

"Talking about what you do is always so difficult," Waits once admitted. "It's like a blind man trying to describe an elephant. You usually make most of it up."

Perhaps it is, in any case, unfair to expect an artist to reveal himself – after all the play's the thing. And since he became a father, Waits seems doubly determined to keep it like that. Which possibly explains the evasive techniques he has mastered over the years, for eloquently deflecting awkward questions, and shielding the Waits he doesn't want the world to see from all those prying eyes and probing questions.

"Do you *always* lie?" Waits was once asked. "No, no. I always tell the truth . . . except to policemen. It's an old reflex."

Contrary and truculent, wayward and perverse, Tom Waits has nevertheless provided many people with much pleasure over the years. He operates in a shadowy world, a skew-whiff world, a world out of whack. It may not be somewhere you want to live, just somewhere you like to visit occasionally. But it is a unique and fascinating place, fashioned by a man with an imagination as big as Wyoming, a facility for words as impressive as the Grand Canyon, and a creative vision that twists and turns like the Mississippi.

This is, after all, Tom Waits' world. You know you are only along for the ride, but what an exhilarating, disorientating and wayward ride it is. It's a ghost-train ride, viewed through smoke and mirrors. Tom has an apartment here, his name's in the phone book and he's known at the local 5&Dime. But, like us, he doesn't live here all the time. It's just some place he drops by when the mood takes him.

Dipping into the life of Tom Waits is a bit like being in a fairground, playing one of those crane machines. Those impossible to manoeuvre, hard to handle games with the claw. What you *really* want is the big prize: the watch, the silver necklace, the gold medallion. But what you end up with are the novelty items: the charm bracelet, the tatty plastic choker . . . And in the end they're enough, those shabby little souvenirs: a broken radio, a rusty jackknife, patent leather shoes . . . oh, and a medal, "for bravery . . ."

Precious memories, all for a dollar; you scoop 'em into your pocket and take them home. It's dark now. The lights are on all over town. You pull down the shade, flick the switch, and it's time again for *that* voice to fill the room. "Wasted and wounded . . ."

There have been many other Toms: Tom Traubert; the piper's son, who learned to play when he was young; Tom Thumb; Tom, Dick and Harry; Uncle Tom (and his cabin); Tommy Gun; Tom Sawyer; Tombola; Tom Cat; Tom Dooley; Tommy rot; Major Tom; Tom Brown (and his schooldays) . . . Brewer lists Tom Fool; Old Tom; Tom Foolery; Poor Tom. And Tom O'Bedlam, a mendicant who levies charity on the plea of insanity . . .

But there's no one else quite like our Tom. Never has been. Never will be. So, even though you know he doesn't touch the stuff, raise a glass, and drink a toast: To "the crown prince of melancholy . . ." To the shadow spokesman of song noir. To Tom . . .

Patrick Humphries, London, January 2007

PART I

Shiver Me Timbers

CHAPTER 1

THE car turned down Lambeth Road and I pointed out the Imperial War Museum, site of the original Bedlam. It was here that the gentry in the eighteenth century used to go transpontine. They'd cross the Thames, making the treacherous journey a few hundred yards south of the river, and pay to gawk at the lunatics in their asylum.

Then the aristos would make their way back to their Mayfair mansions, to have their wicked way with easy-going, orange-selling courtesans, prior to having their portraits painted by Gainsborough and Reynolds. Later in the evening, over the port, they'd congratulate themselves on their cleverness in having avoided a Revolution, unlike those dreadful French people. Bedlam was, for those lucky aristocrats – heads still *in situ* – just a place to take an hour or so's diversion, laughing at those less fortunate than themselves.

"So," growled Tom Waits, from beneath a battered fedora, squinting out of the grubby passenger window at the elegant building on the far side of Lambeth Road, "this part of town's called Bedlam?" It was more than an idle question. This, after all, was the man who had once claimed to have rented an apartment on the corner of Bedlam and Squalor.

Sadly, I had to disillusion him, and admit that it was just called Lambeth. You know . . . 'The Lambeth Walk'? I sort of hummed a few bars. Waits sort of nodded. And the silence sort of filled the car.

One of the buildings opposite the museum was graced by a blue plaque, signifying that someone great or good had once occupied the property. This, I pointed out, keen to fill my passenger in on more details of Lambeth life, had once been the residence of William Bligh. You know, Captain of *The Bounty*? The ship that played host to the most infamous mutiny in naval history? This also struck a chord, and set Waits off growling again . . . some long, mumbling anecdote about Charles Laughton.

And he really *did* growl. The voice came from beneath a hat that had seen better days. Come to that, so had the voice. It was low and rumbling, and seemed to work its way up from the soles, like a stock car revving up on a distant track. It was exactly how you wanted Tom Waits to sound: if

3

they re-dubbed *The Lost Weekend*, and gave Ray Milland's hangover a voice, Waits would be a shoo-in for the part.

This was turning into one of the odder days of my life, chauffeuring the man who once claimed to have been "a legend of my own imagination" around London. And all the while pointing out places of interest, while also trying to conduct a probing, professional interview with one of America's finest post-Dylan singer-songwriters.

It had all begun ordinarily enough. Waits was in London for a handful of concerts. I was a journalist on *Melody Maker*. It was happily inevitable that our paths would cross. I had admired Waits' work for half a decade; *Melody Maker* was one of the four rock weeklies. I wanted to talk. He needed the coverage. This was in the days before glossy rock monthlies, back in the days when Fleet Street was still *in* Fleet Street – and paid little attention to "pop stars". So the only place where Tom Waits – or indeed almost any pop "star" – could find a platform was in one of the inkies.

The London of 1981 was a different place to the high-rise, buzzing Britpop capital of the twenty-first century. The pubs dutifully closed their doors for the afternoon at three every day (and at two on Sundays, reopening at 7.30). You could still smoke on the top deck of London buses. And for home entertainment, you could choose between not one, not two, but *three* television channels. Although opinion was still divided about which was the best home-recording system, VHS or Betamax.

There were no gates defending Downing Street; no concrete blockades around the Houses of Parliament or the American Embassy. I was still able to place an April Fool's piece in London's *Evening Standard* claiming – quite implausibly – that, one day, you would be able to make calls from telephones installed in the back of London taxis! It was all a very long time ago.

Docklands was not the Brave New World of today, but still the gleam in an ambitious architect's eye. It had only recently stopped being a place where ships docked – and its transformation to a glittering metropolis was way ahead. Maybe Waits' press officer thought he would enjoy seeing some of "olde London". So our rendezvous was arranged for lunchtime, at a themed pub called The Charles Dickens out by St Katharine's Dock. Waits came in, hat jammed over his forehead, wearing a long, long coat. He was wary, and surprisingly shy. He nodded as we were introduced, and extended a hand in cordial greeting. We shook. His hand was extraordinary – long, spindly fingers; they appeared double-jointed, pale and white, and inordinately long.

It turned out that the pub had about as much to do with Charles

Dickens, as the creator of *David Copperfield* had in common with Spandau Ballet. Waits was disappointed, as if he had hoped that by meeting here he was going to get the inside track on *The Mystery Of Edwin Drood*. But you didn't need to be a Dickens scholar to discern that the lackadaisical Filipino waitresses and corny themed menu bore little relation to the author of *The Old Curiosity Shop*.

However, on learning that we weren't far from the site of the Jack the Ripper murders, Waits suddenly perked up. And when he discovered that we weren't *that* far from the London Hospital, where the Elephant Man's skeleton was believed to be stored, I began to worry that I'd be finishing lunch on my own.

Before an interview proper can start, there's a certain sounding out process that takes place between the interviewer and his subject, between the matador and his bull. There is a circling, a convivial "How-ya-doin?" "Mustn't-grumble . . ." "Been-in-town-long . . .?" kind of ineffectual waffle as you set the cassette player up, and check that the battery is working and the tape is rolling.

Both protagonists are usually wary, on tenterhooks. Interviewing is a strange and unnatural act: you are hoping to establish a rapport, build a relationship, all within a matter of minutes. There are distractions too, often people literally looking over your shoulder, PRs windmilling an end to the conversation, ushering their charge out of your reach.

You particularly want this man to open up to you, because you like his work so much. You want him to remember you, to single *you* out from the parade of eager new friends which will be periodically wheeled in before him. He knows there is a game to be played, rules to be obeyed: he must sit politely and listen to questions he has heard a hundred times before. He is required to respond, to answer with a suave politeness that suggests: "Goodness me, what an original topic; let me give that penetrating and original line of questioning my earnest attention . . ."

There is more of a problem with interviewing people whose work you have admired – I draw the line at "idolise". But Waits was undeniably an impressive talent, one whose work I appreciated, and wanted to know more about. I was keen to press him on certain lyrical left-turns, some musical obfuscation; I was keen to glimpse behind the mask. I also wanted some of that Waits' bob and weave, a fist full of original quotes to cherish; an anecdote to take home, dust down and polish as the occasion required.

Tom Waits, though, was there to sell tickets for his upcoming London shows; he was there to talk up the album he had most recently been working on. He was practised at the process, engaging as he was, Waits was not sitting with me in order to go on a lengthy and rambling jaunt down Memory Lane.

Waits hunched down in his chair opposite, squinting at the menu. There was a lot of fish. Prawns prompted a memory of "a coupla bad experiences in Ireland". Whitebait somehow got us onto a meandering discussion about English licensing laws and the First World War. I tried for plaice, but it was off the menu, prompting a "What kinda plaice is this?" from my bemused guest.

My mind back on fishy business, I noticed a dish of "John Dory" featured on the menu. Having learned from a recent album by the Albion Band that the fish was a Biblical favourite, I conveyed this knowledge to Waits. The marks on the side of a John Dory are said to have been made by Christ's hands. The story goes that when He was with the fishermen in Galilee, He picked up a John Dory to illustrate a parable, and His fingers literally left their mark on that fish for ever more.

Waits nodded, and turned his attention to the menu once again . . . "So, John Dory, grilled in butter and parsley? You reckon it was *grilled* by the Son of God?"

The waitress at The Charles Dickens had obviously graduated with honours from the Less Co-operative School of Catering. Waits was edging towards lemon sole, but it came on the bone – and the waitress was reluctant to have these removed for the benefit of a mere customer. Waits asked if there were *many* bones. The waitress nodded enthusiastically. Waits averred he'd prefer something "that'd never had a bone in it". After some delicate negotiations we managed to hook a fish with just one bone, only to find that it too had swum off the menu. "Sea bream?" inquired Waits. "Oh, a *lot* of bones," the waitress gleefully concurred.

Worried that we might never progress beyond studying the menu Adrian Boot, the *MM* photographer, and I put our heads together to try and remember the "fish with few bones" lessons from school. Dover sole was an early favourite, but eventually we all settled for a de-boned lemon sole. That first huge hurdle overcome, we allowed waves of relief to wash over us, imagining that the rest of the meal might settle down into an easy canter. That lasted for several seconds until the subject of potatoes reared its problematical head . . .

"Chips?" pleaded Waits. But the waitress, now warming to the challenge, was quite emphatic that they only served "big potatoes". "No scallop potatoes?" "Big potatoes only!" Vegetables too proved as impenetrable as nuclear fission. It was not auspicious. But we finally settled on starters and determined to let the rest of the meal take its wavy course. The ordering complete, you could watch Waits almost physically unwind.

Masticating, Waits eyed my tape recorder like an unwelcome condiment. While I was still mesmerised by his hands and long, snake-like fingers: surely those of a strangler . . . or a pianist. In a couple of years' time, you'd see fingers just like that on a million movie posters, advising ET to "phone home".

As the meal took its aquatic course, a wide-ranging discussion ensued: at the time, Anna Ford was the talking point, her breathless beauty making news-time a treat. Waits nodded, he was familiar with the phenomenon: "People always prefer bad news coming out of a pretty mouth." (In later years, he would be equally fascinated by the emergence of topless news readers in the former Soviet Union.)

Before lunch, Waits had been hunched and wary, but now he let his limbs relax and spread. His conversation too was becoming more expansive, talking with a degree of pride about the recently completed *Heartattack & Vine* album. He was particularly enthusiastic about working with Francis Ford Coppola on *One From The Heart*. This was heady stuff, with *The Godfather, Part II* a recent memory, and in the immediate wake of *Apocalypse Now*, Coppola's reputation was at its zenith. And here I was talking to the man who had just completed the score for Coppola's *next* film.

Waits particularly admired Coppola's ability to bring "a child's wonder" to the process of movie making; and the way he could come straight out of an executive board room and then onto the set to work with actors. He marvelled at the director's unbridled enthusiasm, and the trust he had placed in Waits, who at that time, was a largely unknown quantity, with a shaky reputation.

It was all going swimmingly, then along came the inevitable interruption from the press officer – Tom had *really* enjoyed the lunch, but time was pressing. He had to get back to his hotel, so many more interviews to undertake; such a tight schedule you understand, Tom needed to relax . . . At least I was spared the excuse one journalist colleague had been offered – that the Beach Boys' Mike Love had to return to his hotel so he could *meditate*!

I grumbled and growled: barely had time to get to know the man; not enough on tape; hardly touched on *shoes* . . . when Boot, the *Maker*'s resident chirpy photographer had a brainwave: why didn't we give Tom a lift back to his hotel? Then we could have a little longer to conclude the interview, and Tom would get a chance to see some of London's historic sites.

Within minutes, Waits was whisked away into the front of my Fiat Strada, while Boot was bundled into the back with terse instructions on how to operate a cassette recorder. To get as much out of Waits as possible, the journey from St Katharine's Dock to Waits' hotel, some- where in Kensington, was somewhat . . . leisurely.

It was like one of those old Hollywood-comes-to-London traveleramas: in which even to get from Heathrow to west London, you have to go via Buckingham Palace, the Tower of London, Big Ben, the White Cliffs of Dover . . . It was a meandering journey, but there was a reality check: I knew I couldn't keep Waits in my car indefinitely. Despite my scant legal knowledge, I was vaguely familiar with the concept of "kidnapping".

At journey's end, Waits emerged undoubtedly stirred, but not too shaken, and offered a courteous acknowledgement for the lift. He adjusted his hat and made his way through the hotel doors. And for me it was home, dinner, pub . . . A Sunday spent transcribing the tape and writing the feature . . . And on Monday morning the double-spaced, typewritten sheets were delivered to the paper.

Back in the office, the rest of the week was absorbed by a *Melody Maker* meltdown: Bruce Springsteen's first UK shows in six years had just been cancelled. I was sent back home to bash out something – anything, *every-thing* – about "The Boss" to help fill the acres of space the weekly had allocated for the long-promised interview and gig review.

The Waits piece appeared in the *Melody Maker* of March 14, 1981 – " 'Heart Of Saturday Morning', Desolation Angel: Patrick Humphries; Dharma Bum: Adrian Boot." It is illuminating to see what else was pre-occupying the *Maker*, one of four music papers then published every week in the UK. Waits was on a cover dominated by Jools Holland and his new band, the Millionaires, and alongside Judas Priest, John Lydon and Queen in Brazil.

Try as they might to convince you that the Eighties are rock'n'roll's "great lost decade", a flick through that week's *Melody Maker* gives it the lie. The world was still reeling in the aftermath of John Lennon's senseless murder just three months before: Roxy Music's cover of 'Jealous Guy' was the UK's number 1; Lennon's own 'Woman' was number 1 in the USA; while his final album, *Double Fantasy*, was Top 5 on both sides of the Atlantic.

Meanwhile, the big new name in American rock'n'roll was . . . Christo-pher Cross, who had just swept the Grammy board with 'Sailing'. In the UK, New Romantic acts like Visage and Classix Nouveaux were shaping up for their nanosecond in the limelight.

Otherwise, there were ads for the Who's *Face Dances* LP (remember, this was before Compact Discs); and Island were advertising their "revolutionary new concept 1+1: one side a complete album – plus a bonus – one side a blank tape" (remember, this was before burning your own discs). The legendarily indecisive Lynden Barber could be found selecting his nine – 9! – Singles of the Week (Heaven 17, the Passage, Altered Images, Simple Minds . . .)

That week's *Maker* also carried an advert for Waits' UK concerts – two dates at London's Apollo Victoria Theatre ("tickets £3, £4 and £5") as well as the Edinburgh Playhouse and Manchester Apollo. A third London date had been added, according to a breathless news story, "due to the high ticket demand".

Waits was on a cusp back then. He was already emerging as a singer-songwriter favoured by the knowing few; and just over the horizon his songs would start to be covered by Bruce Springsteen. Still, to think that the shy tourist opposite would one day be acting alongside Jack Nicholson and Meryl Streep, was simply fanciful. But Tom Waits was about to go on a roll, and the more famous he got, the more elaborate his stories got. As his profile rose inexorably, so the tales grew more and more fantastic; the deceits more colourful; the truth an ever more distant land.

Back then, in that restaurant, on that particular day, I thought we had edged up fairly close to something approximating the truth. But that was a long time ago: back when Ronald Reagan was in the White House; Princess Diana was still single; and Tom Waits had yet to become practised in the art of deception. But hell, let him tell the story . . .

CHAPTER 2

"I WAS born in the back of a Yellow Cab in a hospital loading zone and with the meter still running. I emerged needing a shave and shouted 'Times Square, and step on it!' "[1]

Well, yes . . . up to a point. In actual fact, Thomas Alan Waits first emerged on December 7, 1949, the only son of Mr and Mrs Waits of Pomona, California. And with a pleasing sense of timing, young Waits was born eight years to the day after that other "date which will live in infamy" – December 7, 1941, when Japanese planes roared out of the skies over Pearl Harbor, sank the US Pacific fleet, and dragged America reluctantly to war.

"Nearly every American alive at the time can describe how he first heard the news," Walter Lord wrote later. "He marked the moment carefully, carving out a sort of mental souvenir, for, instinctively, he knew how much his life would be changed by what was happening in Hawaii.

"Sociologists point to December 7, 1941 as the beginning of the break-up of the American family unit; doctors point to the medical revolution wrought by it – new drugs to treat wounds, new methods of surgery; one might find the 'beat' and 'hip' generations began December 7, 1941 . . ."

Born under Sagittarius ("the sign of the archer"), young Thomas Alan Waits shared his birthday with fellow singer-songwriter Harry Chapin, and a clutch of actors: Eli Wallach, Ellen Burstyn and Hurd Hatfield, cinema's definitive Dorian Gray. And as Waits was coming into the world, Huddie Ledbetter, better known as the great Leadbelly, was leaving it.

"He died the day before I was born," Waits later recalled, "and I like to think I passed him in the hall and he banged into me and knocked me over."[2]

Leadbelly was born the son of slaves in 1889, and his grandparents were killed by the Ku Klux Klan. It's been estimated that of his 60 years, 13 were spent in prison – and it was while serving a stretch in Texas, that Leadbelly came to the attention of the legendary song-collectors, Alan and John Lomax. For Tom Waits, "Leadbelly was a river . . . a tree. His 12-string guitar rang like a piano in a church basement. The Rosetta Stone for much of what was to follow . . . Excellent to listen to while driving across Texas, contains all that is necessary to sustain life, a true force of nature."[3]

In 1999, just as he was facing up to turning 50, Waits delivered another encomium to Leadbelly: "I marvel at Leadbelly, who just seems to be a fountain of music. When he started working with Moses Asch, he told Huddie he wanted to record anything – nursery rhymes you remember, whatever . . . They were like concept albums . . . kind of like photo albums, with pictures of you when you're a kid. I love the way the songs unfolded . . . The stuff he did with Alan Lomax is . . . like a history of the country at that time."

Waits was not alone in his admiration, Lonnie Donegan, Paul McCartney, Van Morrison, Janis Joplin, Robert Plant, Ry Cooder and Nirvana, all went on to record Leadbelly songs. Strangely though, the world had to wait until 2006 to hear Waits interpreting the mighty Leadbelly, when the triple CD package *Orphans* included 'Ain't Goin Down To The Well' and the anthemic 'Goodnight Irene'.

Unlike his rock peers Robert Zimmerman (Dylan), David Jones (Bowie), Thomas Miller (Verlaine), when Tom Waits turned professional he had no need to adopt a hipper surname. His only significant musical namesakes were the southern gospel singer "Big Jim" Waits, who was big in the 1960s; and jazz drummer Freddie Waits, who played behind Ella Fitzgerald.

The family name was of British derivation; appropriately enough, "waits" was the name given to parties of singers and musicians. The word is thought originally to have come from the watchmen of medieval times, who played to commemorate the passing of the hours. Washington Irving wrote, in *The Sketch Book*, in 1820: "I had scarcely got into bed when a strain of music seemed to break forth in the air just below the window. I listened, and found it proceeded from a band which I concluded to be waits, from some neighbouring village."

Along with the end of World War II, 1945 had brought with it the baby boom. The GIs had vanquished Hitler and Tojo, and when they returned home victorious to the sprawling suburbs, all they wanted was stability and domesticity. Though still young, they'd had their fill of travel, excitement and danger; now all they wanted were the steady pleasures of a regular job, a loving wife and a healthy family.

Tom would remain the Waits' only son, although he has two sisters. And with both parents being teachers, he grew up in a household where the written word still took precedence over television and radio. "I read a lot because I didn't want to be stupid," Waits later admitted, somewhat pugnaciously.

His father taught Spanish at Belmont High School in Pomona, but soon after Tom's birth, the Waits family were on the move. They spent much of the Fifties shuffling around southern California. Towns like San Diego, Laverne, Pomona, Silver Lake, North Hollywood, which were predominantly blue collar, white picket-fence places. This was the territory where the Okies from Steinbeck's *The Grapes Of Wrath* had come to settle; where the nineteenth-century German immigrants had put down their roots. While Waits would later express a fondness for all things Spanish and Mexican, his adolescence was spent in predominantly white towns and suburbs, where few black or Hispanic faces were seen.

For a while, the Waits family settled in Whittier, a town chiefly famous as the birthplace of one Richard Milhous Nixon. On his elevation to the White House, Whittier began planning for a Richard Nixon Museum. Six years later, when he quit 1600 Pennsylvania Avenue in disgrace after Watergate, the land was turned instead into a public park.

The Waits' peripatetic existence gave Tom a taste for travel, but more importantly it gave him a flavour of the exoticism of America and Americana – a rich heritage in which he later came to revel. There was something in the vastness and diversity of the country which impressed him from an early age. That sense of the landscape was at the heart of one of Waits' earliest memories: "of getting up in the middle of the night and standing at the doorway by the hall in the house and having to stand there and wait while a train went by . . ."[4] Like Paul Simon once wrote so acutely: "*Everybody* loves the sound of a train in the distance."

"There were trains in all the places I grew up. My grandmother lived by an orange grove and I remember sleeping at her house and hearing the Southern Pacific go by. That was in Laverne, California. My father moved from Texas to Laverne and worked in the orange groves there. I also have a memory of wild gourds that grew by the railroad tracks, and putting pennies on the tracks."[5]

Pomona is where Waits claims to have been happiest as a child: "It had horses and a train that went through the backyard," he told *NME*'s Jack Barron. "There was laundry hanging up and vines down by the railroad tracks . . . and a creek. A pretty normal, all-American environment . . ."

A small town, located about 40 miles east of Hollywood on the fringe of the Angeles National Forest, Pomona was so far removed from the Los Angeles urban sprawl that it even hosted its own rodeos. Pomona, along with El Monte, Claremont and Cucamonga, was part of a suburban network known as the Inland Empire – which also provided a home for Ry Cooder and Waits' later *bête-noire*, Frank Zappa. For all its security, there was an anonymity in the familiar stretch of fast-food outlets, garages, bars, motels and gas stations. Those suburbs offered little more than somewhere to leave and something to kick against.

As a child, Waits had a clear ambition: "I wanted to be an old man when I was a little kid. Wore my grand-daddy's hat, used his cane and lowered my voice. I was dying to be old."[6]

The Waits family background was rich in European blood. There was a Norwegian strain on his maternal side, although his mother Alma's maiden name was McMurray, and she was born in Oregon. His father's people came from Scottish and Irish stock, but Tom's father was born in Sulphur Springs, Texas and christened Jesse Frank Waits, after the notorious nineteenth-century outlaw brothers, Jesse and Frank James.

The first song Tom remembers hearing as a child was the traditional Dublin street ballad 'Molly Malone' – the song came from his father, and it proved to be the beginning of a lifelong love of Ireland and all things Irish. But also deep in the genes was a love for all those towns huddled under what Waits would later call the "dark, warm narcotic American night . . ." As a kid, Tom remembered loving songs like Marty Robbins' 'El Paso', Bobby Bare's 'Detroit City' and George Hamilton IV's 'Abilene' that he heard on the radio. ("I just thought that was the greatest lyric ever," Waits fondly reminisced: " 'Women there don't treat you mean, in Abilene.' ")[7]

Tom's father played guitar, while he remembers his mother singing "in some kind of Andrews Sisters quartet". Church visits were an obligatory part of growing up in the cosy, conservative America of the Fifties. "Those are my earliest musical memories," Waits would later reflect to Phil Freeman in *The Wire*, "being in church and wishing I was somewhere else, like in a donut shop or on a camel."

There was also "an uncle, who played church organ. They were thinking of replacing him, because every Sunday there were more mistakes than the Sunday before. It got to the point where 'Onward Christian Soldiers' was sounding more like 'The Rite Of Spring', so they had to let him go."[8]

Rarely reflective about his own adolescence, Waits did admit that 'Pony' from 1999's *Mule Variations* had its roots in his own reality: "My Aunt Evelyn . . . was my favourite aunt. She and my Uncle Chalmer had ten kids, and raised prunes and peaches. They lived in Gridley, and there have been a lot of times when I've been far away from home and I've thought about Evelyn's kitchen."

Growing up, Waits reflected: "There were a lot of preachers and teachers in my family. In fact, my father was more than a little disappointed when he found out that I was going to be neither."[9] To Robert Sabbag, Waits admitted that "all the psychopaths and all the alcoholics are on my father's side of the family. On my mother's side, we have all the ministers."[10]

But then the young Thomas Alan was often a worry to his parents. It wasn't just his hair, which would *never* stay flat on his head, it was the *sounds* he claimed to hear in his head . . . Waits later claimed he heard sounds the way Van Gogh painted colours. "It was a frightening thing," Waits admitted over half a century later, while talking to Sean O'Hagan. "I've read that other people, artistic people, have experienced it too. They've had periods where there was a distortion to the world that disturbed them."[11]

A solitary child, Waits sought refuge in his own vivid imagination and lifelong love of stories – he swears that when on holiday in Mexico as a child, he saw a ghost ship while he was splashing in the surf. Close enough to touch, the ship and all its ghostly crew sailed right by him and away into the mist. "There were dead pirates hanging on the mast . . . skull and crossbones, the whole thing." His parents though, were unimpressed ("pirate ship, huh?"). The young Tom was equally convinced that he had made contact with Extra Terrestrials, via the short-wave radio sets he had constructed for himself in his bedroom.

In interview, Waits is endlessly entertaining and thoroughly diverting on his antecedents and upbringing. But more recently, as his fame has grown, he has worked hard – and successfully – at covering his tracks. When I met him in 1981 though, it was before he felt the need to embellish his adolescence: "My own background was very middle class. I was *desperately* keen to get away," he frankly admitted.

As a card-carrying member of the baby-boom generation, Tom Waits was born into a world of relative tranquillity and prosperity. Having vanquished Germany and Japan, America was between wars. Korea was still undivided; Vietnam and Iraq just distant place names in a rarely read atlas. Closer to home, radios, resembling mahogany sideboards, played sentimental favourites such as 'Buttons And Bows', 'Tennessee Waltz', 'Goodnight Sweetheart' and 'Now Is The Hour'. Those were the days . . . dull and dreary; safe and sweet . . . the days before rock'n'roll.

Superficially it was still a conservative era of conformity and cosy family values. Though in 1948, the year before Waits was born, America had been disturbed by *The Kinsey Report*, which revealed that half of all

American husbands admitted to having committed adultery. Eyebrows were raised even further by the revelation that one in six American farm boys confessed to copulating with farm animals.

That same year also saw the publication of Norman Mailer's ground-breaking war memoir, *The Naked And The Dead*. Such were the strictures of the era that Mailer was obliged to censor the soldiers' language, resorting instead to the verb "to fug" (as in "fugger", "motherfugger", etc.). "Ah yes," observed Tallulah Bankhead archly, when introduced to the author, "you're the young man who can't spell 'fuck'!"

Queues still lined up outside movie theatres to see the latest releases. In 1946, the first year of peace, cinema attendances were at an all-time high. Three years later, in the year of Waits' birth, the box-office hits included Bob Hope's *The Paleface*; Fred Astaire reunited with Ginger Rogers in *The Barkleys Of Broadway*; John Wayne being taken seriously as an actor with back to back performances in *Red River* and *She Wore A Yellow Ribbon*; while Gene Kelly and Frank Sinatra helped liberate the film musical from its studio limitations in Stanley Donen's exuberant *On The Town* . . .

Yet even while Hollywood wallowed in colourful fantasy, a new realism was emerging in the aftermath of World War II: topical titles like *All The King's Men*, *Gentleman's Agreement*, *The Best Years Of Our Lives*, *Pinky*, *White Heat* and *The Third Man* were all on release during 1949.

But if it was to survive at all, cinema needed the full brash, lavish, wide-screen hyperbole of films such as Cecil B. De Mille's *Samson And Delilah* to battle the small but insistent menace of black-and-white television. In 1949, there were barely a million TV sets across the whole of America – but, still, cinema admissions were down, from 90 million a week to 66 million.

In deep contrast to all the escapist optimism dished up by Hollywood, New York was offering a very different take on the American Dream with Arthur Miller's *Death Of A Salesman*, which opened on Broadway in 1949. In writing of Willy Loman and his life, Miller also wrote a requiem for the American Dream. Suddenly, it became frighteningly clear that the cosy family behind their white picket fence could not rely on the security which generations had taken for granted. Like Willy, many of them were out there on their own, "riding on a smile and a shoeshine. And when they start not smiling back – that's an earthquake."

Amid Willy Loman's despair and disillusion lay the seeds for the beat generation, the bohemians who would exert such a powerful pull on the young Tom Waits. In tandem with Miller's iconoclastic play, the year of Waits' birth was also marked by the publication of George Orwell's bleak prognostication, *Nineteen Eighty-Four*. As well as giving the world Big Brother, Orwell's novel contained the terrifying, totalitarian message: "If you want a picture of the future, imagine a boot stamping on a human face – forever!"

Besides the unimaginable shadow of the atom bomb and nuclear Armageddon, there was now the double-headed threat of Stalin's Russia and Mao's China. Despite being wartime allies, within a few years Communists had become the new enemy. As early as March 1946, Churchill was warning of the danger of "an iron curtain" descending across Europe. And the fear soon spread. Just three years later, across the Atlantic, Americans were reporting the first unidentified flying objects or UFOs – already there were 50 or more sightings every month. It was as if a maggot had begun to eat away at the very core of America's apple-pie complacency.

American baby-boomers like Tom Waits were nevertheless growing up in a land of plenty, and in an era which on the surface offered enormous stability. A great war leader was in the White House and the world had been saved for democracy. It was a comfortable and contented era that historians later called "the Eisenhower siesta", the period flanked by the end of the Korean war in 1953 and the launch of Sputnik in 1957.

Waits' parents separated in 1959, while he was still at school. "My parents divorced when I was 10 years old," Waits told me. "My father's been married about three times, and my mother finally remarried a private investigator." But, for future reference, it is worth recalling that Tom Waits' father was known to all as Frank, the name his son later adopted for the central figure of his key album trilogy of the Eighties.

"He was really a tough one," Waits would later reflect of his father Frank. "He slept in orange groves . . . a rebel raising a rebel."[12] Much, much later, Tom Waits recorded a song on his *Real Gone* album called 'Sins Of The Father'; asked if it was about his father, Waits replied in suitably Biblical tones: "My father. Your father. The sins of the father will be visited upon the son. Everybody knows that."[13]

Following his parents' divorce, Tom moved away with his mother and sisters, settling in National City, a suburb of San Diego dominated by a vast naval air station – which ensured thousands of servicemen permanently in transit. Otherwise, San Diego was a prosperous, industrial town, famous in certain circles for seafood canning. It was also home to an aircraft manufacturing factory run by Lockheed, the nation's largest military contractor, which employed the bulk of the local population.

Situated right on the Mexican border, the city was linked to Tijuana by a 16-mile transit line. The Waits' new home was not far from the Rio

Grande, where a century before, during the Spanish–American war of 1846, invading American troops had crossed over into Mexico to quell a rebellion. The song those Americans sang . . . and sang again . . . and then kept on singing . . . was the traditional 'Green Grow The Rushes O'. In fact, they sang it so often that the Mexicans borrowed it to coin a name for the invaders – "Gringos".

Waits has fond memories of visiting Mexico as a kid with his father: "It was such a place of total abandon and lawlessness, it was like a Western town, going back 200 years – mud streets, the church bells, the goats, the mud, the lurid, torrid signs. It was a wonderland, really for me, and it changed me."[14]

He also had some striking memories of one particular childhood visit to the cinema. "At the Globe Theatre, they had some unusual double bills. I saw *The Pawnbroker* [a harrowing account of a concentration camp survivor] and *101 Dalmatians* when I was 11. I didn't understand it, and now I think the programme director must have been mentally disturbed, or had a sick sense of humour."[15]

As Tom Waits grew up in the Fifties, America was undergoing a series of seismic changes. The young Americans polled in 1950 had been a curiously conservative bunch, who named their heroes as Franklin D. Roosevelt, General Douglas MacArthur, Joe DiMaggio and Roy Rogers . . . By 1956 though, the consensus was splintering. The same age group (now renamed "teenagers") had begun to follow a different drummer, jiving to the heady rock'n'roll rebellion of Elvis Presley . . .

In 1950 Baltimore had become the first city in the world in which more people watched television than listened to the radio . . . Soon they were watching as Senator Joe McCarthy's vicious "witch hunts" to name and shame Communist sympathisers – the more well-known, the better – further polarised the nation. It was the era of "better dead than Red" and the hula hoop; civil rights and Davy Crockett hats; but at the same time it was a now strange and distant world, where jazz was hot and folk was not; where Miles and Dizzy, Bird and Chet were cool, but 'How Much Is That Doggie In The Window', 'Hernando's Hideaway', and 'The Yellow Rose Of Texas' clearly were not. In 1956, Harry Belafonte's *Calypso* became the first long-playing album ever to sell a million copies. But jazz still held sway as the hip alternative to the mainstream – and the folk revival was still waiting in the wings.

Tom Waits was among those who felt inexorably drawn back to that incandescent era. He once famously claimed to have "slept through the Sixties – and believe me, I didn't miss a thing."[16] Like so many of his generation though, he remained very much enamoured of the decade in which he grew up.

Smiling fondly, he told me: "The Fifties gave us Joe McCarthy, the Korean war . . . and Chuck Berry!" However, it was not until 1956 – when Elvis Presley exploded onto the American psyche – that rock'n'roll became more than simply a Negro slang term for sexual intercourse. Until then, Julie London, Tony Bennett and Mario Lanza had been the big singing stars. But in the wake of Elvis's 'Heartbreak Hotel' the floodgates opened, and on came Chuck Berry, Buddy Holly, Fats Domino, Eddie Cochran, Gene Vincent, Jerry Lee Lewis and Carl Perkins . . . the golden age of rock'n'roll.

With his parents separated, Waits travelled a lot. He spent hours shuttling between them for visits – and still has fond memories of being driven by his father, to the accompaniment of Mexican music playing on the radio. As they barrelled along the freeways, clocking up the miles, Waits got a taste for life on the road. "The first car I had was when I was 14. It's kind of an American tradition. Getting a licence is kind of like a Bar Mitzvah. It's nice to have a car, but in winter you gotta have a heater, especially when it's colder than a Jewish-American princess on her honeymoon."[17]

On an early trip to London, Waits lovingly recalled his automotive history to the British fanzine publisher Peter O'Brien. Scrolling through the list of models he had driven, he carefully recited the litany, lingering over each name like he was going through an address book of old girl-friends: "Had a '56 Mercury, a '55 Buick Roadmaster, a '55 Buick Special, a '55 Buick Century, a '58 Buick Super, a '54 Black Cadillac four-door sedan, a '65 Thunderbird, a '49 Plymouth, a '62 Comet . . ."[18]

As recently as 2006, a similar list appeared as a narrative track on his *Orphans* collection. On 'The Pontiac', Waits lovingly evoked a fleet that included the Fairlane, the Tornado, the Ford, the Buicks, the Thunderbird, but above all, the Pontiac.

Aching to escape, and armed with little more than fond memories of driving trips with his father and a vague teenage awareness of Jack Kerouac, Tom Waits set off on the road. After all, this was still America: the frontier may have been tarmacked over and Monument Valley turned into a parking lot, but out there, just over the horizon, or round the next bend, lay the endless and enticing unknown.

For Waits the road spelt freedom, and in later life, he would speak fondly of driving and flicking the radio dial. Eating up the miles, to the sounds of Hank Williams, Ray Charles, Howlin' Wolf, Charlie Rich,

James Brown, Leadbelly, Frank Sinatra and Little Richard. To Tom Waits, Motown, R&B, soul, country, jazz, swing, gospel, blues, all meant a lot more than the newly emerging sounds of Lothar and The Hand People or the Strawberry Alarm Clock.

"I think [it's] exhilarating, especially when you set out in the morning in a late model Ford and you're leaving California, driving to New York. It's thrilling to know that the country is big enough, that you can aim your car in one direction and not have to turn the wheel for seven days. I think there's a great feeling of flight there."[19]

And somewhere out there, as he chewed up the miles, Waits caught glimpses of a different kind of life: a world beyond the end of his road; beyond school; and a long, long way away from the well-kept white picket fence.

One particular highway image remained with Waits well into his adult life: "Burma Shave is an American shaving cream company," he explained to Brian Case. "They advertise on the side of the road, and they have these limericks which are broken up into different signs, like pieces of a fortune cookie. You drive for miles before you get the full message. 'Please don't . . .' five miles. 'Stick your arm out so far . . .' another five miles. 'It might go home . . .' another five miles. 'In another man's car – Burma Shave!' They reel you in. So when I was a kid, I'd see these signs on the side of the road . . . and I think it's the name of a town, and I'd ask my dad: 'When we gonna get to Burma Shave?' "

In terms of brand recognition, the message had got through – and it stuck . . . Twenty years later, Waits would use the name of that same shaving cream for a track on his *Foreign Affairs* album. But he was not the first songwriter to be transfixed by the product. In 1962 Roger Miller, author of the immortal 'King Of The Road' and 'England Swings', also wrote a song called 'Burma Shave', later recorded by the Everly Brothers.

Despite – or perhaps because of – both his parents being teachers, at school Waits studied with no particular distinction; his lacklustre academic record not helped by the family's frequent moves. One long spell was spent at the Robert E. Lee Elementary School in south Los Angeles, where the boy Tom picked up the trumpet – one of the few instruments on which he ever had formal lessons. One memory remained lodged: "I played the bugle at school, when the flag was raised in the morning and lowered in the afternoon. That happens every day at every school in America. I can still remember the smell of that bugle case: bad eggs and a stale t-shirt."[20]

He did well at Spanish, and at English. Otherwise, Waits – like any other teenager – was chafing. He may not have succumbed to the charm of The Beatles when they conquered America early in 1964, but he was 15 years old and painfully aware that there was *something* out there that he wanted to be part of.

NOTES

1 *Street Life*
2 *Observer* Music Monthly
3 *Observer* Music Monthly
4 *NME*
5 Kristine McKenna, *NME*
6 Sylvie Simmons, *Mojo*
7 *Innocent When You Dream*, Ed. Mac Montandon
8 *NME*
9 Gavin Martin, *Uncut*
10 *Innocent When You Dream*, Ed. Mac Montandon
11 *Sunday Telegraph*
12 Sylvie Simmons, *Mojo*
13 Jonathan Valania, *Magnet*
14 *Innocent When You Dream*, Ed. Mac Montandon
15 Gavin Martin, *NME*
16 *Street Life*
17 John Platt, *Zig Zag*
18 *Zig Zag*
19 Kristine McKenna, *NME*
20 Richard Rayner, *Time Out*

CHAPTER 3

FOR Tom Waits, the epiphany occurred somewhere in California, sometime during 1962. The Sixties were a convulsive decade, too often eulogised for the benefit of those who weren't there, by those who can't really remember. But something undeniably did shift during that decade. For many, it proved to be a vibrant, exciting and life-altering period, simply by the scope of the changes being wrought – and many of those changes came about through music.

Of course, Waits was not alone as a teenager having his life changed by a musical phenomenon. But in his case, the turning point was witnessing James Brown & His Famous Flames: "It was like you'd been dosed, or taken a pill. I didn't recover my balance for weeks. When you're a teenager, music is a whole other thing. You're emotionally fragile and the music is for you, it's talking to you. It was like a revival meeting with an insane preacher at the pulpit talking in tongues. To have that *and* Bob Dylan, who I saw during the same period playing in a college gym, it set me reeling."[1]

Those moments left their mark on the teenage boy, and years later Waits still felt Dylan was "a planet to be explored". (In return, Bob namechecked Tom as one of his "secret heroes".) Like young Bob, the teenage Tom also went on musical odysseys. He sought out musical legends like the Reverend Gary Davis, Ramblin' Jack Elliott and Mississippi John Hurt, while they were still performing. Another formative moment that Waits never forgot was seeing Lightnin' Hopkins play at a local club called the Candy Company: "It was like watching birds land on a wire and take off again. Simple and very moving."[2]

Another Waits favourite of the time was less well known: "I used to listen to a lot of records by a guy called Lou Short," he told Mike Flood-Page in 1976. "He made a lot of albums in the Forties, and nobody knew who he was. He used to have to pay to have them made. But everybody in Baxter, Putnam County knew who he was. And he was the town hypochondriac. I mean, there's a breeze coming up, and he's got a little sniffle . . . Anyway, the town hypochondriac finally upped and died, and on his tombstone . . . it said 'Lou Short Died' and on the bottom it said 'I told you I was sick!' "

Waits joined his first band at the age of 15, soon after that James Brown moment. The System was a high school band that covered the popular surfing instrumentals of Link Wray, the Surfaris and the Ventures. But despite being a native Californian, Waits would have none of that: "I disavow any knowledge of the world of surfing," he told Peter O'Brien. "I don't know the first thing about surfboards – which way you ride it, or what side is up . . ."

Luckily for Waits – who played rhythm guitar and sang – The System was not exclusively a surf-band. They also played the Motown and R&B hits of the day, as well as songs by The Temptations, Smokey Robinson and Waits' very own hero James Brown . . . Indeed, the highlight of the System's short-lived career was, by all accounts, a full-on cover of the Godfather of Soul's 'Papa's Got A Brand New Bag'.

A lifetime later, Waits still remembered the impact of witnessing James Brown play at the peak of his powers: "It was like putting a finger in a light socket. He did the whole thing with the cape. He did 'Please, Please, Please'. It was such a spectacle. It had all the pageantry of the Catholic church. It was really like seeing Mass at St Patrick's Cathedral on Christmas and you couldn't ignore the impact of it in your life . . . And everybody wanted to step down, step forward, take communion, take sacrament, they wanted to get close to the stage and be anointed with his sweat."[3]

Music occupied a pivotal place in the firmament of young Tom. He took lessons on the piano and found his own way around the guitar. But Waits would later insist that his first professional engagement was as a teenager, playing first accordion with a Polish polka band, back home in Pomona.

"I was at home with these three women," Waits told me, "my mother and two sisters, I grew up without a father, and although they were there, I was on my own a lot." By all accounts, young Thomas Alan was an isolated child, who later rather poignantly admitted that his childhood role model had been Pinocchio! "After my father left, we struggled a little bit," Waits admitted to me. "And I was the man of the family."

That solitary childhood, in a house dominated by women, left the boy Tom shy and withdrawn. And even today, for all his bravura stagecraft and impressive interview routines, at heart Tom Waits retains that shyness and a tendency to stay away from the spotlight.

Growing up in the cloying, post-war comfort of America during the late Fifties and early Sixties, music offered the fastest highway out of suburbia. Like Waits, countless other teenage Americans, living thousands of miles apart, all found succour in the sounds coming from the radio. Some of them had names that would later become known around the world – like Bob Dylan, Bruce Springsteen, Tom Petty, Lou Reed, James Taylor and Paul Simon; many more would remain unknown outside their immediate circles . . . But back then, they were as one: ears glued to the wireless, riveted by the sounds emitted by all those mysterious and romantically initialled stations, pouring out their beguiling jambalaya into the anonymous night.

"I listened to Wolfman Jack every night, the Mighty 1090, 50,000 watts of soul power," Waits would later recollect. "My dad was a radio technician during the war, and after he left the family . . . I had this whole radio fascination. He used to keep catalogues, and I used to build my own crystal set, and put the aerial up on the roof."

Robert Weston Smith, aka Wolfman Jack, cultivated an air of mystery, which he maintained even after appearing as himself in the 1973 film of *American Graffiti*. But along with Alan Freed, Wolfman was certainly the most influential American DJ of the rock'n'roll era.

"The first station I got on these little two-dollar headphones was Wolfman. And I thought I had discovered something that no one else had. I thought it was coming in from Kansas City or Omaha, that nobody was getting this station, and nobody knew who this guy was and nobody knew who these records were. I'd tapped into some bunker, or he was broadcasting from some rest-stop on a highway thousands of miles from here, and it's only for me. He was actually broadcasting from San Ysidro near the border. What I really wanted to figure out is how do you come out of the radio yourself."

As a teenager, Tom Waits was out of step with current trends, and had few friends among his contemporaries. In the wake of America's drooling obsession with The Beatles and the knock-out blow of the British Invasion, 15-year-old Tom Waits dared to be different: instead of partaking of Beatlemania, he was listening intently to his parents' brittle old 78 rpm records, and working his way through the songbooks of Duke Ellington, Johnny Mercer and Jerome Kern.

One album that stands out as having had a tremendous impact on Waits at that time, was Thelonius Monk's 1964 *Solo Monk*. And years later, Waits still remembered its impact: "Monk said, 'There is no wrong note, it has to do with how you resolve it.' He almost sounded like a kid taking piano lessons. I could relate to that when I first started playing the piano, because he was decomposing the music while he was playing it. It was like demystifying the sound, because there is a certain veneer to jazz . . ."[4]

In an early press release Waits acknowledged he was "musically pulling influences from Mose Allison, Thelonius Monk, Randy Newman, George Gershwin, Irving Berlin, Ray Charles, Stephen Foster, Frank Sinatra . . ."

On a lighter note, Waits also had a fondness for the digital dexterity and musical lunacy of Spike Jones & His City Slickers. Big in the Forties, Spike's material was sufficiently zany to appeal to anyone from eight to 80 with a working sense of humour – after all, who could resist such songs as 'All I Want For Christmas Is My Two Front Teeth' or 'Never Hit Your Grandma With A Shovel, It Makes A Bad Impression On Her Mind'?

Nowadays, Waits admits picking over the bones of the past, though he denies being a teenage curmudgeon: "I loved the music of the Sixties – The Beatles and the Stones, lots of people," he told Nigel Williamson in 2002. "But when you're trying to find an original voice, you look in a lot of different places to discover who you are and find something that's uniquely you. And to do that you take a little bit of something from whatever you can find."

With his fondness for soul and R&B, Waits was in his element in the mid-Sixties. Motown and Stax were hitting their peak; Waits had a real thing about Dusty Springfield's sexy rendering of 'Son Of A Preacher Man'; and Otis and Martha and Marvin and Smokey and Aretha . . . were all burrowing into the hearts, minds, and pockets of teenage America.

By the time he left school, it was just about conceivable for someone like Tom Waits to make a career in pop music. There were booths waiting in the Brill Building for hard-working songwriters; and in the wake of Bob Dylan, it was possible for the likes of Paul Simon, Donovan, Phil Ochs and Tom Paxton to express themselves through their own words and music.

Further up the California coast, San Francisco was undergoing one of its periodic renaissances. In the Fifties, the city had played host to the Beat poets, who had clustered around the City Lights bookstore on Columbus Avenue. Revelling in the freewheeling atmosphere of San Francisco, which made it seem – along with New Orleans – one of the least American of all American cities, the Beats congregated in the bohemian coffee houses to listen to cool jazz, score dope and dig poetry. One poem, from City Lights owner Lawrence Ferlinghetti, gave a flavour of the times: 'Tentative Description of a Dinner to Promote the Impeachment of President Eisenhower'.

By the early Sixties, the coffee houses of San Francisco were starting to give floor space to a new generation. The Kingston Trio was among those discovered at the Hungry i, which also showcased irreverent comic talents such as Tom Lehrer, Mort Sahl and Lenny Bruce. Though frequently derided nowadays, back then it was the clean-cut Kingston Trio who singlehandedly launched the "folk revival" with their hit 'Tom Dooley'.

At the same time as Tom Waits was leaving school in San Diego, 500 miles away up the California coast, San Francisco was flourishing – and this time around, the epicentre was at the intersection of Haight and Ashbury. Post-beat, a new generation of hip young things were filling the San Francisco streets. A powerful – and in 1966, still legal – hallucinogenic drug was being taken widely and sacramentally. Welcome to the age of Aquarius.

It was LSD that fuelled Ken Kesey's Merry Pranksters – a travelling circus of misfits and mischief-makers who specialised in crossing boundaries, causing outrage and challenging the establishment. This band of hippies was a quintessentially Sixties phenomenon, but the driver of their magic bus provided a fascinating link with the previous generation of San Francisco rebels – he was none other than Neal Cassady, the real-life 'Dean Moriarty' who had been immortalised in Kerouac's Fifties Beat Bible, *On The Road*.

Besides Ken Kesey and the Pranksters, San Francisco was home to Timothy Leary, the self-anointed high-priest of LSD. Where Kerouac had offered a beguiling blend of gentle euphoria, fuelled by alcohol, Huckleberry Finn and Zen, those following Leary's dictum were advised to: "Tune In. Turn On. Drop Out".

But for Waits, drugs were never the key to anything. Certainly not LSD, and not marijuana – which at the time was floating everyone else off into their own personal kaleidoscopic Disneyworlds. For Waits it was always drink, not drugs . . . "I discovered alcohol at an early age, and that guided me a lot."

By 1966 San Francisco was home to the bands who would provide the impetus for the whole hippie movement. Bands like The Charlatans, The Chocolate Watchband, The Mystery Trend, Country Joe & The Fish, Quicksilver Messenger Service, Big Brother & The Holding Company, Jefferson Airplane and, most durable of them all, The Grateful Dead. But Waits felt little in common with their acid-inspired, lengthy improvisational jams; and for blues, he preferred the authentic voices of Ma Rainey and Bessie Smith to the frustrated howlings of Janis Joplin.

Back at home, the soundtrack was likely to be somewhat different. What with his peripatetic school background, and his father's penchant for talking Spanish, mournful Mexican music was more likely to feature in the Waits' household. But as Tom told Sylvie Simmons in *Mojo*, it was mariachi music that was his father Frank's big love: "If you went to a restaurant in Mexico with my dad, he would invite the mariachi to the table and give them two dollars for a song, and then *he* would start to sing with them."

Unlike many of his generation, Tom did not rebel against his parents' tastes; rather he embraced them. Indeed, the combination of his father's preoccupation and the proximity of the family's home to the border, resulted in Waits retaining a fondness for the music of Mexico throughout his life. "I've always thought that in Mexican culture, songs lived in the air," Waits reminisced to Mark Richard in 1994. "Music is less precious and more woven into life. There is a way of incorporating music into our lives that has meaning: songs for celebration, songs for teaching children things, songs of worship, songs to make the garden grow, songs to keep the devil away, songs to make a girl fall in love with you . . ."

Despite both his parents being teachers, Tom himself was academically undistinguished – and he made no secret of the fact that he couldn't wait to escape the education system. He left school at 16 and took his first job, washing dishes, servicing toilets and grilling pizzas at Napoleone's Pizza House in National City, California, a period Waits would recall on his second album *Heart Of Saturday Night* – the closing track of which was called 'The Ghosts Of Saturday Night (After Hours At Napoleone's Pizza House)'.

Napoleone's core business was catering for the thousands of sailors, soldiers and airmen who busted out of San Diego's military base on Saturday nights. Situated on the city's Mile of Bars, Napoleone's, Waits would recall later, with relish, was "just across from Iwo Jima Eddie's tattoo parlour . . . Club 29 and Phil's Porno".[5]

Like so many of the navy men who passed through Napoleone's, the teenage Tom Waits took the opportunity to get himself tattooed – which must have given him something to talk to his mother about when he returned home. "I got a map of Easter Island on my back," Waits told Barney Hoskyns, "and I have the full menu of Napoleone's Pizza House on my stomach. After a while they dispensed with menus; they'd send me out, and I'd take off my shirt and stand by the tables."[6]

Clearly feeling much more at home at Napoleone's than he had ever done at school, Waits spent five formative years at the restaurant, gradually being promoted from washing dishes to cooking pizzas. But the mundane work did nothing to stifle the teenager's love of music – and in between pushing and pulling the margaritas out of the oven, Waits listened and learned.

"I knelt at the altar of Ray Charles for years," Waits would recall many years later. "I worked at a restaurant, and that's all there was on the jukebox . . . 'Crying Time', 'I Can't Stop Loving You', 'Let's Go Get Stoned', 'You Are My Sunshine', 'What'd I Say', 'Hit The Road Jack'. I worked on Saturday nights, and I would take my break, and I'd sit by the jukebox and I'd play my Ray Charles. It was just amazing what he absorbed, and that voice . . . !"[7]

But although he appeared happy enough where he was, Waits was not devoid of ambition. Already, he was intrigued by the music business, and busy figuring out how you get from here to *there*. "I can remember working in a restaurant," he told Kristine McKenna years later, "and hearing music come out of the jukebox, and wondering how to get from where I was, in my apron and paper hat, through all the convoluted stuff that takes you to where *you're* coming out of that jukebox."

NOTES

1 Gavin Martin, *Uncut*
2 *Mojo* 74
3 *Observer* Music Monthly
4 *Observer* Music Monthly
5 Mick Brown, *The Word*
6 *Mojo* 65
7 *Observer* Music Monthly

CHAPTER 4

"I WAS in a small town," Waits told Ian Walker, "and I saw my friends go working in an aircraft factory, joining the navy or working in the bars. And I really wanted wings out of there. So, from a very childish point of view, you make these little songs, and then it's like Jack and the Beanstalk. I woke up, and I'm in New York, backstage in a nightclub, and knock, knock, you're on in five minutes. Then I'm in *Japan* . . ." at this point Waits paused in his recollection, "I'm leaving a lot out of course."[1]

Between the pizza house and the big break, four or five years of Waits' life were spent scuffing around in a long run of dead-end jobs. "I once worked in a jewellery store, and when I quit, I took a gold watch. I figured they weren't gonna give me one 'cause I'd only been with 'em six months anyway."[2] He also did the ring-a-ding thing as an ice-cream man ("Hardest thing about driving an ice-cream truck was getting the little bell out of your head at night.")

Somewhere along the way, Waits began writing his own songs – initially on the beat-up old piano his father had acquired, then on a girl-friend's Gibson guitar. Though in later years Waits would disavow these fledgling efforts, the long, late-night shifts, cooking pizzas and eavesdropping on customers' conversations, had clearly provided the raw material for these early songs.

Taking full advantage of the anonymity afforded him by his job, Waits made sure he didn't miss a thing, squirrelling away the odd scraps of dialogue and strange drunken ramblings for future use. He had unwittingly found himself a background character in an Edward Hopper painting; in the foreground were the lonely servicemen, determined to cram a lifetime into a 48-hour pass, who flocked to the cosy, brightly lit pizzeria – an oasis of warm, welcoming neon in the otherwise all-embracing night.

It was while washing dishes and serving pizzas at Napoleone's that the teenage Tom Waits picked up the nuances and influences, characters and situations, that would infuse his early work. It would be nice to think he absorbed these things subconsciously – as if by osmosis – but as it happens, the process was less accidental and more artful: "I started writing down people's conversations as they sat around the bar. When I put them together, I found some sort of music hiding in there."

Sailors on "shore leave" – an evocative phrase heavy with nostalgia, which later became a track on *Swordfishtrombones* – would pour into town, looking to get liquored-up, lucky, and laid. But at the time Waits was working at Napoleone's, there was an added edge to the frenzy of the off-duty servicemen who found their way into San Diego of a Saturday night – the dreadful knowledge that the war in faraway Vietnam was sucking in tens of thousands of American personnel. By the time Tom was 16 in 1965, President Lyndon B. Johnson had taken the decision to escalate the war in Vietnam with the ominously named Operation Rolling Thunder – an attempt to pound North Vietnam into submission with indiscriminate carpet bombing. But it would still take a further eight long years, and 60,000 young American lives, before the war in Vietnam was aborted.

Hanging out, biding his time, pushing pizzas onto plates, Waits watched and listened. There wasn't much romanticism evident in his surroundings: Napoleone's was just a place where kids on their way to war came to line their stomachs before moving on to the bars and brothels. But Waits had a good ear, and a sense that one day he would need all this. So he'd store away the dreams and ambitions, the dirty talk and wordplay of the customers, during those long, hot pizza and beer nights. Waits proved himself to be a very good listener. And he was lucky.

Waits himself managed to avoid the draft: "I had a very low lottery number," he told Sylvie Simmons in *Mojo*. "I wound up being a fireman for three years, in the forestry service . . . on the border between Mexico and California. I learned how to dig a hole in the ground and bury myself so the fire would burn over me. Never had to use it yet, but I'm ready!"

The "explanation" he gave Gavin Martin of how he avoided the draft was both more far-fetched and more facetious: "I was in Israel on a kibbutz. No, I wasn't, that's a lie. I was in the White House as an aide. I got excused the way anyone would from school: 'Dear Mr President, Tom is sick today and won't be able to come along.'"[3]

Before he ever made it onto disc, Waits' CV already made for colourful reading. As well as his residency at Napoleone's and serving his nation as a fireman (or a White House aide – take your pick), the boy Thomas had a stint in a Bible factory, spells as a newspaper delivery boy, short-order chef, car-wash attendant, salesman, toilet attendant, truck driver, jewellery salesman, bartender and doorman. No wonder he once described himself as a "jack-off of all trades".

If he had any thoughts at all about his future, Waits may vaguely have envisaged a future in the catering business, running a café, or as a restaurant owner. "I think that when children choose something other than a life of crime," Waits told Mark Rowland, "most parents are encouraging."

Despite his parents' best efforts at encouragement, Tom's light had not burned bright at school. But while working nights at the pizza parlour, the high school dropout began to read voraciously. Top of Waits' reading list – of course – was Jack Kerouac, that "strange, solitary Catholic mystic" who had singlehandedly launched the Beat Generation with the 1957 publication of *On The Road*.

Unsurprisingly, Waits' bookshelf found space for fellow beats such as Gregory Corso and William S. Burroughs. But he also devoured the writers of the South, those elegant, graceful prose maestros Carson McCullers and Flannery O'Connor; that sombre chronicler of middle-American despair, Eugene O'Neill; and that deft biographer of the gang that couldn't shoot straight, Damon Runyon.

This was the Sixties – and for many of Waits' contemporaries, the only point of reading a book was to lose themselves in the long haul through the other-worldly landscape of Tolkien's Middle Earth. *The Lord Of The Rings* was intended to take you there, and back again; further worlds within worlds were provided by Mervyn Peake's *Gormenghast*; and to try and get inside the military madness of the times, there was always Joseph Heller's *Catch-22*. But for maximum cool, it was necessary to ensure that the suitably battered grey spines of Penguin Modern Classics were visible – Camus' *The Outsider*; Hesse's *Steppenwolf*; Huxley's *The Doors Of Perception* . . . And, uh, that was about it.

Musically too, Waits was time-locked in a far-away country. Reflecting on his formative musical influences, Waits later equated his fondness for those from an earlier era to searching for a parent substitute. The British Invasion also, largely passed him by. Not for Tom Waits anything as trivial as a weakness for Freddie & The Dreamers or a hankering after Herman's Hermits. "I think I looked up to older musicians like father figures. Louis Armstrong or Bing Crosby or Nat King Cole or Howlin' Wolf . . ."[4]

Perhaps unsurprisingly, he admitted to spending more time with his friends' fathers than with his own contemporaries – and, should you wish to, you could read a lot into the teenage Tom's search for a "father figure". His fondness for *their* music rather than that from his own era . . . his young desire to be *old* . . . all this tied into his deeply felt separation from the biological father who had walked away, leaving him at home with his mother and two sisters. But while it might seem like a textbook case for

Freud, Waits Junior made it through apparently unscathed – and, arguably, the sense of being different and something of a loner suited him better than a more average life may have done.

Like the lettering in a stick of Blackpool rock, there is also an undeniably sentimental streak running throughout Waits' work. Much as he would deny it, the comfort he had found from those early songwriters would find its way into his own music. And it was that style, and substance, which the young Tom Waits would later try to emulate: "I was always backwards in a lot of ways," he told Sylvie Simmons in *Mojo*. "When I was a teenager I tried to get a job at a piano lounge at a golf course in San Diego. It was a little pathetic. I put on a suit . . . I learned some Frank Sinatra and Cole Porter. But it was interesting that that was the world I wanted to be part of, plaid pants and golf."

This is a strangely touching image: the young Thomas Alan Waits, endeavouring to penetrate the conservative world of Southern California's golf clubs. While the rest of teenage America was going Beatle-crazy, or scratching their heads at the convoluted rebellion of Bob Dylan, Waits sat at his golf club piano, earnestly rendering Gershwin's 'Summertime', Berlin's 'Blue Skies' or Bernstein's 'Somewhere': a strange variation on the theme of a misspent youth – the young Tom Waits, wilfully old before his time.

"It might be a rebellion against the things all your friends are listening to," Waits admitted to Nigel Williamson. "I listened to Frank Sinatra for a long time. That really made them mad . . . I'd end up sitting in the den talking to their dads. Eventually they'd start putting on records, so I was listening to old-timers' stuff. I felt like an old man when I was about 12, and I couldn't wait to grow old."

Waits' later claim that he "slept through the Sixties" was no idle boast. All around him in California, the culture was primed to explode. At the time Waits was slinging hash in a San Diego slop house, in Los Angeles, Jim Morrison was sorting out his Oedipal complexes, writhing through early performances with The Doors on Sunset Strip. And Arthur Lee was fusing together all manner of influences into the band whose name epitomised the flavour of the times . . . Love.

It was around the time that the first draft cards were being burned; when the Los Angeles suburb of Watts went up in flames; and President Johnson was pouring more and more young American troops into Vietnam. It was a decade on the cusp of change, but Waits chose to keep his head down and his powder dry, glancing backwards to a tradition that embodied a safer and more stable America.

31

Amid the hectic hedonism of the mid-Sixties, Tom Waits was more interested in trying to connect with the soul of Jack Kerouac and the musical heart of *Songs For Swingin' Lovers* than the fledgling sounds of Frumious Bandersnatch. He found more vitality in the freewheeling wordplay of Lord Buckley than the music of Quicksilver Messenger Service; and lionised the irreverence of Lenny Bruce rather than the surfers' paradise promised by The Beach Boys.

Talking to Fred Dellar in 1977, Waits admitted: "I was a bit of a misfit in the Sixties. I'd always had an early subscription to *Downbeat*. I had to do some research, and I became a curator I guess . . . I didn't find a whole lot of meat to carve throughout the Sixties on that rock'n'roll scene . . . I don't see anything that I do being nostalgic or having anything of a vicarious thrill, because I feel contemporary. I may be a little sentimental, but I'm not nostalgic."

"I was kinda lost in the Sixties," Waits would later elaborate. "I didn't go to San Francisco until the whole love and flowers bit was over, and when I did go, I was looking for the City Lights bookstore and the ghost of Jack Kerouac."[5] Later, when he was asked about his musical influences, Waits would reply with relish: "Vocabulary is my main instrument." And it was the influence of Lord Buckley and Lenny Bruce that helped Waits plug the gaps in his dictionary.

Richard Myrle Buckley (who thought, with good reason, that "Lord" suited him better) was born in California in 1906. A raconteur of fearsome ability, Buckley got his early break in the clubs and speakeasies of Chicago in the roaring twenties, where, it was said, Buckley flourished by virtue of being the only man who could make Al Capone laugh.

Blessed with the best waxed moustache this side of Hercule Poirot, Buckley's gravel voice parlayed black jazz argot to the patrons of chic West Coast supper clubs in the stultifying Eisenhower autumn of the Fifties. His raps coincided with the rise of the beats and bop; there was jazz in his every utterance.

Rapping from beneath a giant pith helmet ("so necessary in a night club, dear boy"), for Buckley there were no limits. The Son of God was reborn as "the Naz" – who was, Buckley reminded all you non-believers: "the coolest, grooviest, swingin'-est cat that ever stomped on this jumpin' green sphere . . . And when the Naz laid it down – *wham!* – it *stayed* there!"

His Lordship also took time to rewrite the Bard's well-known take on little Caesar, addressing his audience in the style of "Willie the Shake": "hipsters, flipsters and finger-poppin' daddies, knock me your lobes . . .".

Even when the rest of the joint was drippin' with sweat, Buckley was cool as a frozen margarita.

But Buckley was more than a comic turn; his fondness for jazz had led to a love of black culture, and a profound loathing of the racism then so prevalent in his homeland. Buckley's trenchant take on racism, 'Black Cross', was later picked up by a young Bob Dylan. And a few years down the line, Dylan featured a Lord Buckley LP sleeve on the cover of his own transitional album, *Bringing It All Back Home*. Thanks to his closeness to the subterranean world of jazz, Buckley was also no stranger to its illicit pleasures ("If I wasn't working this joint, I'd be smoking it!")

Worn out by booze, dope, and public indifference, Buckley pegged at 54 in 1960. Aside from fans like Frank Sinatra and Robert Mitchum, few mourned. Later though, Frank Zappa and Cheech & Chong would help pass Buckley's name on to a new generation – one of whom was the young Tom Waits. Waits knew Buckley's routines – and though, wisely, he didn't lift the pith helmet, he did model his own vocal mannerisms on his Lordship, and was certainly influenced by Buckley's remarkable onstage raps.

Literally watching in the wings, as Buckley rapped, was the young Lenny Bruce. Like Buckley, Lenny flourished in the jazz clubs; but unlike his Lordship, Lenny wilfully courted controversy, fascinated to see just how far he could go. By the end, Lenny was harassed by the cops every time he broke cover. What you can now hear on prime-time terrestrial TV is what Bruce was busted for. They were, indeed, different times.

Branded a "sick comic", Lenny's rise coincided with the liberating influence of jazz and rock'n'roll. His verbal dexterity found him tearing into pornography, racism, organised religion, drugs, politics . . . It also ran him consistently into trouble. The America for whom Peyton Place was a taboo address just could not handle Lenny Bruce.

Alongside Kerouac (and Lord Buckley), Lenny Bruce soon joined the Waits pantheon. Lenny liberated language. His early routines were perfect for jazz clubs, improvised routines which swooped and soared like saxophone solos. On the sleeve notes for the posthumous album, *The Sick Humor Of Lenny Bruce*, esteemed journalist Ralph J. Gleason noted: "Bruce improvises the way a jazz musician does. His routines . . . are never done the same way twice, but move like a soloist improvising on a framework of chords and melody . . ."

Despite all the furore, Lenny always maintained that his humour wasn't sick; just honest. All he did, he claimed, was to hold a mirror up to a sick society ("If the whole world were tranquil, without disease and violence,

I'd be standing in the breadline – right back of J. Edgar Hoover.") Lenny recognised the risks he was taking – in confronting the establishment and challenging the status quo – but he persisted. He simply figured that somebody *should* be saying this stuff. And if not him – then who?

Sadly, the few clips that survive of Lenny Bruce performing all come from late in his life, when he became obsessed by the persecution he was suffering, and his "act" consisted almost exclusively of reading aloud the transcripts of his recent trials. On disc though, there remains enough of Lenny's freewheeling, associative humour to give a sense of him at his peak.

Lenny Bruce's verbal dexterity found a willing fan in the young Tom Waits – and along with Tom Lehrer and Mort Sahl, Bruce also paved the way for other performers, like Robin Williams, Richard Pryor and Bill Hicks. Lenny knew the risks he ran with his routines, and with his drug taking – but he just couldn't stop. Playing it safe held no attraction for him – in public or in private. Acknowledging his heroin addition, he confessed: "I know I'll die young, but it's like kissing God."

In 1966, at the age of only 43, Lenny Bruce died of a drug overdose. Tom Waits was just 17. On hearing of Lenny's death, his friend Phil Spector observed that he had "died of an overdose of police". Over the years, Lenny Bruce was commemorated in song by Bob Dylan, Paul Simon and Phil Ochs, while Dustin Hoffman brought him to life again, on screen, in the 1974 biopic Lenny.

Forty years on, artists continue to namecheck him as an influence. But in truth, *every* comedian with a routine that reaches beyond "a funny thing happened to me on the way to the theatre . . ." owes a debt to Lenny Bruce – just as every rock'n'roll band owes thanks to Bob Dylan for helping liberate their lyrics from forever asking 'How Much Is That Doggie In The Window?'

Another ingredient that helped spice up the formative Waits chowder was Slim Gaillard. A jazzman who came out of vaudeville, Slim popularised jive talk on disc and radio during the Forties – "vout o-reenie?" was his most-asked question. After wartime service, Slim turned up in the company of Dizzy Gillespie, Charlie Parker and Miles Davis. He also makes a saintly appearance in Kerouac's *On The Road*.

With such a heady, old-fashioned – and eclectic – brew, no small wonder that the teenage Tom Waits felt somewhat disconnected from the joss-stick-scented peace and love vibe which was beginning to emanate from San Francisco. While acknowledging the talent of Bob Dylan – who in 1965 had already embarked on the startling volte-face of turning folk into rock – at the time, Waits found little to admire in Dylan's long, word-spinning songs of the period such as 'Subterranean Homesick Blues' and 'Like A Rolling Stone'.

It was that determined search for his own peculiar identity that led the young Tom Waits to keep Dylan at arm's length. Even later, when he emerged under the dispiriting umbrella of "the new Dylans", Waits remained cautious in his praise. Only much later, did he acknowledge that "for a songwriter, Dylan is as essential as a hammer and nails and a saw are to a carpenter."[6]

Back then, it was back . . . back . . . and yet further back . . . that Waits went: to field recordings by Alan Lomax, albums by Howlin' Wolf, and the songs of Stephen Foster. In 1967 though these were not names to drop. You were expected to endure a whole side of *In-A-Gadda-Da-Vida*, rather than 'One For My Baby'. But the past was where Waits' true musical heart lay – although, back then, listening was the nearest he got to music. Napoleone's paid the bills well enough, and the prodigiously unambitious Waits was happy just making it with the margaritas and biding his time.

However, if we prise away the layers of obfuscation from which Tom Waits has constructed his life "story", we find that at some stage the teen-ager began writing his own songs, which he picked out on a big, old, acoustic Gibson guitar.

He soon reverted to the piano, though. And seated at the keyboard, Waits found that as his long, bony fingers covered the keys, they could help him in the development of his songs. A girlfriend had donated the piano – albeit one which "had been left out in the rain for a year, and only played F-sharp". But Waits persevered, unperturbed, perhaps comforted by the knowledge that Irving Berlin, America's most revered composer of popular music, had composed on a specially built piano, which could also only play in F-sharp.

From early on, Tom Waits adored and respected the discipline which classic songwriters such as Irving Berlin, Cole Porter, George Gershwin, Sammy Cahn and Lorenz Hart had brought to their work. These were the men whose songs had mapped the landscape of the twentieth century, through war and peace, love and depression; whose songs went out to the whole world – a whisper of musical magic courtesy of the radio waves and cinema screens. But though he sensed the magic as well as the next man, Waits was also capable of appreciating the skill and pragmatism of the songwriters' craft. Sinatra's favourite, Sammy Cahn, was once asked which came first, when he was composing, the music or the lyric? His answer was not only funny, but honest too: "The phone call!"

"I don't know when I started writing really," Waits told Peter O'Brien in 1977, "I was . . . filling out applications and stuff real early. Last name first, first name last, sex . . . 'occasionally', stuff like that. Then I was writing letters, filling out forms, writing on bathroom walls . . ."

Eventually, while still in his teens, Waits teased some songs out of himself. His earliest compositions were broken-down ballads and heart-broken lullabies. They were autobiographical pieces, with titles like 'Ice Cream Man', 'Frank's Song' and 'Virginia Avenue'; stories of some daunted and dashed dream – 'Looks Like I'm Up Shit Creek Again' and 'I'm Your Late Night Evening Prostitute'; and there were songs which would later people his early albums – 'Ol' 55', 'Hope I Don't Fall In Love With You', 'Shiver Me Timbers', 'Diamonds On My Windshield' . . . These were early works – songs from a writer literally trying to find his voice.

"I guess I was always interested in music," Waits told Mike Flood-Page. "Actually, I sent away. On the back of a matchbox it said 'Success Without College. Send $5 to PO Box 1531, New York, New York'. And they had a whole list of occupations on the inside – TV repairman, washer and dryer salesman, insurance agent, banker, musician . . . draft-dodger, homicidal maniac, axe murderer. I just liked the sound of being a musician. So I'm a living example of success without college. The rest is history."[7]

Waits regarded his early songwriting efforts with little real affection; they were written as much as an exercise, as an opportunity for escape. But many of those early songs were recorded, in Los Angeles while Waits was barely out of his teens. And they were later released in two volumes: *Tom Waits: The Early Years*, which came out between 1991 and 1993.

The albums came about when Waits' first manager, Herb Cohen, decided to reactivate his Sixties Bizarre label. Waits, still bound by an early, pre-Warner Bros contract with Cohen, was powerless when the demos were released over 20 years after they were first recorded. So he did his best to resign himself to the situation: "You make mistakes when you're a kid. My oldest records belong to somebody else, so I can't determine a lot about them."[8]

"I'm not allowed to comment on those [songs] in a derogatory manner," Waits grumbled to Gavin Martin. "I was in litigation over that for a long time. I was very naive when I made them. Those songs are baby pictures. You know when you look over your baby pictures and you go Jesus! But you gotta have baby pictures, you know?"[9]

At other times, Waits was more dismissive: "I don't listen to my older stuff," he told Bill Forman in 1987. "It's like looking at old pictures of yourself. It's like 'My ears are too big in that one. And God, the lighting is terrible and I've got a double chin. And Jesus, look at that shirt. What did I think I was? Who is this guy?' "[10]

However dismissive of them he might later have been, those early songs did at least act as a motivating force for the young Tom. With them under his belt, he began to shape his character and persona for the next decade. And by the end of the tumultuous Sixties, Tom Waits had hung up his apron for good.

"When I was 21, I was just happy to be on the road," Waits told Adam Sweeting. "Away from home, riding through the American night, y'know, out of my mind, wild-eyed about everything."[11]

NOTES

1 *Time Out*, 1987
2 Fred Dellar, *NME*
3 *NME* 1985
4 Sylvie Simmons, *Mojo*
5 Steve Lake, *Melody Maker*
6 *Observer* Music Monthly
7 *Street Life*, 1976
8 *Sounds*, 1987
9 *NME*, 1992
10 *Music & Sound Output*
11 *Guardian*, 1992

CHAPTER 5

GRADUALLY, Waits – like untold millions before him – drifted up the California coast, to try his luck in the City of Angels. It was a long drive, from Waits' home in San Diego, to Los Angeles.

"I rolled around in the bowels of a small folk music circuit in the Los Angeles area," Waits would later recall, "picking up music from Mississippi John Hurt, Reverend Gary Davis, Utah Phillips, Zoot Sims and Ray Charles recordings."

Every Monday night, the 22-year-old Tom Waits would get up on stage and perform at what were basically live auditions at LA's prestigious Troubadour club. There was barely enough room for Waits, let alone a piano, on the Troubadour stage, so the fledgling performer accompanied himself on his large acoustic guitar.

The Troubadour was located on Santa Monica Boulevard, parallel to the more jostling Sunset Strip – and at the club's Monday night hootenannies, up to a dozen upcoming folk acts were showcased. During the folk revival – between The Kingston Trio and Bob Dylan's electric defection – the Troubadour was very much the place to be seen. Owner Doug Weston remained true to his folk roots, not even allowing electric instruments on the stage until 1967! Monday nights at the Troubadour were a platform, an open microphone night, when unsigned performers could get up and perform for industry figures. This was the musical equivalent of Schwab's drugstore.

Record company executives, A&R men, artist managers . . . all could be found milling around, drinking and schmoozing at the Troubadour on a Monday night. This was one of the clubs where Judy Collins, Phil Ochs and Tom Paxton had cut their teeth. Later, the Troubadour was where Elton John made his storming American debut, "flabbergasted" to have David Ackles as his opening act. It was also where Steve Martin performed an unforgettable stand-up routine, which according to opening act Richard Digance, involved Martin taking the entire audience out onto Santa Monica Boulevard, and showing them how to steal a car.

In 1970, the Troubadour was the venue for Fairport Convention's American debut, although they played to a largely indifferent crowd – that is until some old Midlands mates of bassist Dave Pegg, known as Led Zeppelin, joined them on the tiny Troubadour stage to jam the night away. It was also the club from which John Lennon was unceremoniously evicted during his "lost weekend", for heckling the Smothers Brothers and hitting a waitress. ("It's not the pain that hurts," she was later quoted as saying, "it's finding that one of your idols is a real asshole.") Even in decline, the Troubadour still held fond memories. 'The Sad Cafe', the final track of *The Long Run*, the Eagles' follow-up to *Hotel California*, was written as a reflective valediction to Doug Weston's club.

"If you sold out the Troubadour, that was it," Waits told Barney Hoskyns. "At the Troub they announced your name and picked you up with a spotlight at the cigarette machine and then they'd walk you to the stage with the light. Then Doug would go out on stage naked and recite 'The Love Song Of J. Alfred Prufrock'."

However left-field the club appeared, the Troubadour had also become an important cog in a hugely lucrative business. During its glory days, it was not uncommon to see moguls like David Geffen, Lou Adler, and even Dylan's manager, Albert Grossman, hovering, arguing and listening. While stars such as Kris Kristofferson, James Taylor, Joni Mitchell or Graham Nash would often just drop by.

One Troubadour regular, Eve Babitz, recalled those starry starry nights: "Gram Parsons and Mike Clarke [of the Byrds] drinking champagne and Wild Turkey, or Arlo Guthrie falling in love with one of the waitresses . . . Janis Joplin would sit in her nightgown with a pink boa, all by herself, drinking . . . Van Morrison glowered in corners and Randy Newman was all innocence and myopia."[1]

By the early Seventies, the folk wagon had rolled on, but the Troubadour still held its hootenanny nights. The record company executives had had their eyes opened wide by the multi-platinum success of singer-songwriters Carole King and James Taylor when *Tapestry* and *Sweet Baby James* had both gone ballistic. And now – with The Beatles broken up and Bob Dylan in absentia – everything was once again up for grabs: anyone who could strum'n'sing might well be the next big thing.

The Troubadour was where all the young pretenders made a beeline for when they came in from the sticks. Just like Linda Ronstadt, Jackson Browne and the Eagles, you could get up on stage an unknown, and pour your heart into the microphone. In the Hollywood version, a gnarled mogul removed the cigar from his mouth, took you to one side, and confided: "Kid, I've seen 'em all . . ." And quickly signed you to a binding seven-year contract.

Except that it wasn't just a Hollywood fantasy. At the rock and rolling Troubadour back in the 1970s, dreams really *did* come true. Founder member of the Eagles, Don Henley fondly remembered: "The Troubadour was the first place I went to when I got to LA. I had heard about how legendary it was, and all the people who were performing there. The first night I walked in I saw Graham Nash and Neil Young, and Linda Ronstadt was standing there in a little Daisy Mae kind of dress. She was barefoot and scratching her ass. I thought, 'I've made it. I'm here. I'm in Heaven!' "[2]

Tiring of the long round-trip up from Orange County, Waits secured a job as doorman at another Los Angeles club, the Heritage. "It was . . . fashioned after Gerde's Folk City," Waits told Peter O'Brien. "They dealt mainly in traditional music, a lot of guitar players, blues and bluegrass mainly . . . I got bluegrassed to death . . . the only thing I hate is bluegrass played poorly. I guess the only thing I hate more than that is bluegrass played well!"[3]

Unfortunately, Waits was not well suited to his new "career": "I got bounced every night. They gave me the arm of a chair to defend myself with and said 'good luck'," Waits told Fred Dellar. "One night, 25 Hell's Angels come into town, and they all want to come into the club to break skulls and furniture. And I'm there with an arm of a chair to keep them out. It was like a toothpick to a Hell's Angel."

It was while keeping Hell's Angels at bay at the Heritage that Waits got a glimpse of his own future: "One night, I saw a local guy on stage playing his own material. I don't know why, but at that moment I knew that I wanted to live or die on the strength of my own music."[4]

And it didn't take too long. At the age of 21, while still a doorman at the Heritage, Tom Waits made his professional debut. He appeared one night at the club, sometime during November 1970, and was paid the grand sum of $25.00.

Even after he quit manning the door at the Heritage, Waits still made the journey across town to appear at the Troubadour. He had become a familiar sight there, but it was still a nerve-wracking experience. "You arrive at the Troubadour at 10 in the morning and wait all day," Waits told Todd Everett. "They let the first several people in line perform that night. When you finally get up there, you are allowed four songs – you can blow it all in 15 minutes. I was scared shitless."[5]

The doors opened at 6.30 on Mondays for hoot nights, but queues were forming outside for hours before. Everyone carrying a guitar knew that if they made their mark at the Troubadour, there was a chance of making it in the wider world, beyond Santa Monica Boulevard.

The way Waits tells it, his breakthrough happened in one of three ways:

The Big Break Number 1 . . .

Herb Cohen is tired. He has a full-time job running Frank Zappa's Bizarre record label; but he is also busy managing Zappa, as well as other Bizarre acts, like Captain Beefheart, the GTOs, Wild Man Fischer and Alice Cooper. Still, Cohen is drawn along to the Troubadour hoots. You never know just who might turn up . . . Well, one Monday night in the early summer of 1971, Tom Waits is who!

Cohen is impressed by the boy's laid-back jazzy style. Perhaps because, in Waits, he sees someone of a similar style to his client, the singer-songwriter Tim Buckley. Maybe another of Herb's clients, Linda Ronstadt, will be gracious enough to cover one of this new boy's songs. Herb's not sure, Waits is veering a tad towards jazz, when all the signposts point towards Laurel Canyon. But Herb signs Waits up anyway.

The Big Break Number 2 . . .

Back then, Ben Frank's coffee shop was the place to be seen on Sunset Strip. This was where cool cats like Lord Buckley, Harry 'the Hipster' Gibson and Lenny Bruce all hung out. It was where Arthur Lee and Bryan MacLean formed Love. It was no accident that when TV producers were holding casting auditions for *The Monkees* in 1965, they advertised for "Ben Frank's types".

By the early Seventies though, Ben Frank's is emptier than a pimp's promise. But Waits is in there one night, when he falls into conversation with Herb Cohen over coffee. Cohen is so impressed that he promptly signs Waits, largely on the strength of his *shoes*.

(A brief digression: Shoes play a large part in the iconography of Tom Waits. One of his earliest UK press interviews, with Fred Dellar in *NME* in 1976, had Waits rhapsodising about shoes: "Muckalucks are carpet slippers with fur all over them; Stacey Adams once were a very prestigious shoe – 'Hey, you got your Stacey's on' . . . You can still get them on the South Side of Chicago, there's a store there and it's all they serve . . . The shoes I'm wearing are called Ratstickers." Waits was intrigued by English winklepickers ["We call 'em Puerto Rican fence-climbers."]. And while he may not have had much respect back then for Neil Young's *songs*, Waits was struck by the Canadian's shoes. Waits even claims to have quit Los Angeles for New York because the Big Apple was "a great town for shoes". Digging even deeper into his own profession, Waits theorised to Gavin Martin: "I think it's a good time for music when it's a good time for shoes." And it gets even weirder: In 1991 Waits was made an honorary salesman for the Mason Shoe Corporation ["They make really good farm shoes, with quality workmanship."]. The testimonial came complete with a plaque, and a citation commending Waits' "unceasing efforts to promote American footwear".)

The Big Break Number 3 . . .

"Herb came up to me by the phone booth at the Whisky A Go-Go," Waits later joked, "and asked if I could lend him ten bucks!"

Whatever . . . and however . . . he was on his way. And during 1971, 22-year-old Tom Waits took his first step on the ladder of a professional career: he had himself a manager. Herb Cohen was a long-time mainstay of the West Coast music scene. Although born in New York, Cohen had drifted to San Francisco during his Army service in the Fifties, and it was here that he latched onto the city's burgeoning folk scene. Cohen stayed, and began booking acts in the clubs, forming a close liaison with Odetta. Then, in the late Fifties, he moved down the coast to Los Angeles, where he opened the Purple Onion, and then the Unicorn, both venues that showcased the up-and-coming folk acts of the day.

In the still twitchy post-McCarthy America of the late Fifties, "folk" could easily be mistaken for "Communist", especially by the small-minded. But Herb Cohen courageously booked liberal folk acts like Theodore Bikel and Pete Seeger – at a time when Seeger was banned from television appearances. It was a risky strategy, and eventually Cohen ran foul of the law and was busted on an obscenity charge simply for booking a performance by Lenny Bruce.

After an extended four-year working holiday across Europe, Africa and the Middle East, Cohen made his way back to the States in 1963. Finding the Los Angeles scene unrewarding, he moved across country to New York – epicentre of the folk revival. By then, Bob Dylan had gone; but it was in Greenwich Village that Cohen first heard folk singer Fred Neil, whom he went on to manage.

Along the way, Herb couldn't resist taking a rather "shocking" new group under his wing. By 1966, Frank Zappa's Mothers Of Invention were, along with Andy Warhol's Velvet Underground, the most notorious new group in America. Herb got the Mothers a gig at LA's legendary Whisky A Go-Go club and into the Musicians' Union. "Almost overnight," Zappa reflected, "we had jumped from starvation level to poverty level." Cohen's most infamous client was unflinching in his praise for his erstwhile manager. In 1966, Zappa said of Herb Cohen: "He's a little Jewish man that nobody likes who always wears nylon shirts – the acme of bad taste . . . and has a terrible reputation coast to coast!"

While in New York, Cohen also managed the Modern Folk Quartet, who numbered one Jerry Yester in their ranks. It was Yester who would go on to produce Waits' 1973 debut album. But that was a long way down the pike from where Waits was standing in summer 1971.

His new manager swiftly put Waits under contract. "I got a songwriting contract," Waits told me. "I was sitting at a bus stop on Santa Monica Boulevard in the pouring rain, I'm scared to death . . . making $300 a month. I didn't feel qualified. I'm used to taking on more than I can handle, biting off more than I can chew, just so's I can find out how much it takes to break my back."

It was in Los Angeles, between July and December 1971, that Waits first went into a studio to record some demos of his own material. The sessions were produced by Robert Duffey, who was then road manager to Tim Buckley – another client of Waits' manager Herb Cohen. But these early efforts would not be released until more than twenty years later, when they surfaced, against the composers wishes, as *Tom Waits: The Early Years*. However, at the time, another young singer–songwriter, David Blue, heard something worthwhile in those early Waits demos, and was sufficiently impressed to ensure that his record label got to hear them.

David Blue is one of the saddest footnotes in the history of the many singer–songwriters who emerged in Dylan's wake. Born Stuart David Cohen, he made a handful of critically acclaimed but low-selling albums between 1965 and 1976. Out of favour, cash and luck, Blue was nevertheless one of the highlights in Bob Dylan's self-indulgent, and all but unwatchable, four-hour home movie, 1978's *Renaldo & Clara*. Four years later, Blue dropped dead while jogging in New York's Central Park. His body lay unrecognised and unclaimed for nearly a week.

To prove his credentials, Herb Cohen now had to land Waits a record deal. Reckoning that Bizarre would find too many similarities with their other "folk" act, Tim Buckley, Cohen had his eye on another label. It was a small, independent outfit, recently set up, which was run by a young man who was passionate about music.

David Geffen had talked his way out of the William Morris Agency's post-room and onto the fast track of rock music management in 1968, when he championed the precocious talent of Laura Nyro. Geffen landed Nyro a deal with the rapidly expanding CBS Records, then swiftly in the ascendant after adding Janis Joplin, Santana and Spirit to a roster that already boasted Bob Dylan, Simon & Garfunkel, and Leonard Cohen. While Nyro herself proved too intense for mass acceptance, her songs quickly found favour with fellow artists, including such big-sellers as Blood, Sweat & Tears, Three Dog Night, Barbra Streisand, and the Fifth Dimension. In 1970, Nyro would dedicate her album *New York Tendaberry* to David L. Geffen "Manager and friend".

Too mercurial a talent to be tied to one act, Geffen soon forged a fruitful alliance with Elliot Roberts. Together, by the early Seventies, the two men were managing a clutch of acts which epitomised the sound of young California: Linda Ronstadt, Jackson Browne, Joni Mitchell, the Eagles and – crucially – Crosby, Stills, Nash & Young.

Geffen's chutzpah, management tactics and industry knowledge had helped put the supergroup together – and by 1970, the former members of Buffalo Springfield, The Byrds and The Hollies were being hailed as "the American Beatles". They were later held to account for their superstar indulgence, battling egos, and their role as founding fathers of the "avocado mafia". But when Geffen handled them, Crosby, Stills, Nash & Young were so successful and popular that, as one insider remarked, "they could have founded their own religion".

By the early Seventies, David Geffen was reigning monarch of the "Laurel Canyon scene", which was then in the process of regrouping after the brutal murder of Sharon Tate by Charles Manson's family in 1969. Those chic Angelenos of the Seventies found feature films old-fashioned: the studios were still churning out big-budget blockbusters, but they came out already covered in dust. No one seriously wanted to watch groaning star-vehicles like *Tora! Tora! Tora!* or *On A Clear Day You Can See Forever*. No, what the fast-moving LA scene of the early part of that decade really took to its financial heart was rock'n'roll.

Old Hollywood embraced rock music with the wariness of a maiden aunt greeting her punk nephew. But for all their initial sniffiness, and even if they really couldn't abide the cacophony, what the Hollywood moguls did recognise was that these dope-smoking, bare-footed, long-hairs had the potential to generate *huge* sums of money.

And so it was, that the old-style movie makers and shakers let their hair grow down over their collars, ditched their suits and ties, and began smoking a little grass. Loot was always the lingua franca of Los Angeles. And one of the first to embrace that fact was the young David Geffen.

Barely out of his twenties, Geffen had successfully parlayed his way from the New York office of the William Morris talent agency to the West Coast. "Geffen had upped the stakes, turning back-porch folkies into Lear-jet superstars," Barney Hoskyns wrote in his book *Hotel California*. "He saw there were millions to be made here – maybe as many as in the film industry – and he fantasised about becoming rock's very own Louis B. Meyer, a biography of whom he'd devoured as a teenager."

Geffen recognised the growing cultural and financial importance of the rock industry; and he was very good at sweet-talking the talent, as well as the decision-makers. By 1971, he had established himself as one of the prime movers in rock management. But he was ambitious, and tired of playing second fiddle to record label executives. David wanted his own label. And, after rejecting the names Benchmark, Refuge and Protection, Geffen finally found one he liked: Asylum.

Now, with his own label up and running, Geffen could offer his acts just that: Asylum – a sanctuary from the money-grabbing world of corporate entertainment. In his trademark blue jeans, with curly Dylan-style hair, and a nice line in hip talk, Geffen was at ease rapping with the artists – not at all like some stilted businessman in a suit.

"He's one of us," David Crosby said of Geffen to a young Jackson Browne. "He's the guy who can deal with all the executives in the business world."[6] To prove the point, Geffen was once again acknowledged as "Agent & Friend" – this time on the sleeve of *Deja Vu*, the first number one album by the unstoppable Crosby, Stills, Nash & Young.

From the very beginning, following his nurturing of Laura Nyro, Geffen's Asylum label was a refuge for sensitive singer-songwriters – and he had soon marshalled an impressive roster, including such names as Joni Mitchell, Jackson Browne, Judee Sill, David Blue . . . and Tom Waits.

"By 'significant artist'," Geffen admitted to Barney Hoskyns years later, "I really meant singer-songwriters. People who were self-contained." Geffen had been "floored" after witnessing a Waits performance at the Troubadour in 1972, and was soon in negotiation with Herb Cohen. Within months, Waits had found his new home.

But Geffen was always a shrewd operator as well as a "good guy". And, despite all his persuasive talk of "us" and "them" at Asylum, within a year Geffen had sold the label to Warner Bros. There it was quickly absorbed into the parent company, which had itself recently become part of Kinney Enterprises, a funeral homes to car parks conglomerate.

In truth, there were always as many who loathed Geffen's business practices as there were those who embraced his relaxed blue-jean manner. "When David Geffen enters the California waters as a manager," Doors producer Paul Rothchild reflected bitterly in Fred Goodman's *Mansion On The Hill*, "the sharks have entered the lagoon. And the entire vibe changes. It used to be 'let's make music, money is a by-product'. Then it becomes 'let's make money, music is a by-product'."

A less brutal business strategy had been suggested by an early mentor of Geffen's, the wily and astute Ahmet Ertegun of Atlantic Records, who once offered his protégé this formula for success: "You walk very slowly. And maybe, by chance, you'll bump into a genius, and he'll make you rich!"

Tom Waits should worry though. At the time, all these chicaneries floated far above his head. He was blissfully unaware and unconcerned by all the business dealings. He was 23 years old, and at last he had a record deal.

"I caught that wave of songwriters garnering understanding and sympathy and encouragement," Waits told Barney Hoskyns, 30 years after he signed to Asylum. "For a while there, anybody who wrote and performed their own songs could get a deal. *Anybody*. So I came in on that."

While legend has Geffen's celebrated antenna first spotting Waits, it was more likely his partner, Elliot Roberts, who actually brought Waits to the label. Roberts had, by the time Waits came to Asylum, established a truffle-hound's ability at sniffing out promising singer-songwriters. Like Geffen, Roberts had sprung himself from the lowly ranks of the post-room at the William Morris agency, after championing the work of a young female singer-songwriter.

Having witnessed some early shows of the young Joni Mitchell, Elliot Roberts immediately became her manager. Like Geffen with Laura Nyro, Roberts brought a single-minded intensity to bear on Mitchell and her career ("I said I'd kill for her!" Roberts later confirmed.) When, in turn, Mitchell introduced him to another Canadian singer-songwriter, Neil Young, Roberts knew he had struck the mother lode.

"There were a lot of good writers we felt should have the chance to record," Elliot Roberts told Barney Hoskyns, "even though we knew they weren't going to be hugely successful. Waits was a little different, because he'd reinvented himself as a beatnik. He had the luxury of doing that in LA, because it was an empty white canvas."

NOTES

1 *To The Limit*, Marc Eliot
2 *To The Limit*, Marc Eliot
3 *Zig Zag,* 1977
4 *Record Collector*
5 *NME,* 1975
6 *David Geffen,* Tom King

CHAPTER 6

D EBUT albums . . . cha! They're like wild cats: you can keep kicking 'em out the way, back into the garden to scavenge; or just invite them home and learn to love them. Those first songs can be groomed, can win prizes, can become a member of the family. Or they can scratch the furniture, piss on the floor, and keep you awake all night with their wailing.

One way or another, that first album is always a distillation: you've had the whole of your life to write those first songs, but you shoot out of the traps a complete unknown. There may be some word of mouth among the loose-lipped cognoscenti, about *this one* being the one to hear, but more likely, it will slip out, completely unnoticed and remain that way.

Debut albums can set the world on fire, or dampen your enthusiasm for any future. The first releases of singer-songwriters are particularly intriguing: the first albums by Paul Simon, Bob Dylan and Bruce Springsteen, all sold in the low thousands. And all led to their respective acts being threatened with the curtailment of their contracts – unless things picked up.

Like so many thousand others, Tom Waits' first album was bound to be pivotal, drawing on the rich experiences of his life up to that point, with memories of a whole young lifetime full of fractured love affairs and big plans for the future, all distilled onto the two sides and 40-odd minutes of a vinyl album.

And this really is make or break time. If that first shot reaches an audience, then with the help of some diligent touring and selected radio play, the follow-up is well-placed to build on that success. Inevitably though, subsequent albums will find the author becoming further and further removed from their audience. Experience teaches us that the material starts to dwell on the isolating nature of stardom; the affairs you're having with other singer-songwriters, or the tragic and unreliable nature of room service.

That, by the way, was then; today, it's all very different . . . Nowadays, success is judged not on actual sales, but on the pre-release radio airplay of your first single. Reality TV chews up and spits out karaoke "stars" on a weekly basis – with little, if any, hope of them developing a real career.

And after that instant TV fame and subsequent hit record – there is rarely a third act. In today's frenzied, tabloid-led, celebrity-obsessed world, there is no real point in developing an act. After all, there's really no need: there'll be another one along any minute. In the fast-moving, cut-throat world of twenty-first century pop, the likes of Tom Waits, Ry Cooder, Elvis Costello and Van Morrison would have stood little chance of a cutting a deal.

Back in 1973 though, Tom Waits was in hog heaven. He had finally landed a record deal for his songs of sloppy joes, automobiles and, natch, old shoes. He was signed to Asylum, the hippest label in the land. And, at the time of release, along with every other first-time singer-songwriter, the world was his for the taking.

Closing Time hit the racks during 1973. The sessions at Sunset Sound in Hollywood (where Buffalo Springfield, Joni Mitchell, Neil Young, Love and the Doors had all recorded) were quick and efficient. Sure, Waits was nervous, but he was confident enough in his own material.

Asylum's designated producer was Jerry Yester, another client of Waits' manager Herb Cohen. Yester had been short-listed for The Monkees, then moved into the Modern Folk Quartet. Following their break-up, Yester replaced Zal Yanovsky in The Lovin' Spoonful, and on their split, he went into record production. As well as the clean-cut harmony singing of The Association, Yester also recorded a couple of albums with his wife Judy Henske.

In 1967, Yester had produced singer-songwriter Tim Buckley's masterpiece *Goodbye And Hello*, and two years later, his follow-up *Happy Sad*. The troubled Buckley was yet another client of Herb Cohen's, which is how Yester was eventually led to Tom Waits.

It was not to be the most cordial of relationships. Aware it was only his first album, Waits nonetheless had a clear idea of the record he wished to make. But while Waits had a jazz, piano-led album clearly in mind; Yester, with his background, inevitably veered more towards a florid, folk spectrum. In the end, Waits deferred to Yester's experience: "I was just a kid in the studio . . . I was just overwhelmed to be recording at all."

"We were pulling against each other," Waits reflected a few years later. "If he had his way, he would have made a more folk-based album, and I wanted to hear upright bass and muted trumpet . . . so that made it a little uneven."[1]

For all Waits' misgivings about *Closing Time*, and his producer's role in it, Yester did go on to work with him again, notably arranging the strings on Waits' fourth album – and his masterpiece – *Small Change*. Yester's abilities were particularly notable on the masterly, sweeping arrangement for the opening 'Tom Traubert's Blues'.

Looking back on *Closing Time*, Jerry Yester reflected: "It was done in . . . a week and a half. One reason it was good, I think, was we couldn't get the night-time hours that I was looking for, we had to come in from 10 to five every day. It took two days to get used to it, but once we did, it was great. Everyone was real alert and into it.

"Nobody was writing [the way] Tom was. His writing gift was huge. And the way he played the piano, it was like Hoagy Carmichael for Christ's sake!"[2]

The sleeve of *Closing Time* probably came closer to Waits' own idea of how the album should sound: the clock shows 3.22 – and that's a.m. bud, not afternoon time. The artist sits slumped at a battered bar-room piano, which supports a shot of rye, a bottle of beer and an ashtray overflowing with cigarette butts, smoked short for inspiration.

Three decades on, it's hard to reconcile the back sleeve photo with the artist we know today. Of course, at one time, Tom Waits *was* that young. Hey, at one time, we were *all* that young. But it isn't just the surprising youthfulness, it's the way he stares straight into the lens, head hunched into his shoulders, looking for all the world like an Aborigine terrified that his soul has been trapped by the camera lens. This fresh–faced troubadour sports a bushy head of hair and an unfashionable goatee. But still, on this evidence, here was a young singer-songwriter who could happily share a table with James and Carole and Neil and Joni.

And when you put the record on . . . where is the now familiar voice that sounds like it was hauled through Hades in a dredger? This young fellow sounds quite fresh . . . almost lively. Almost someone you'd have round to Sunday lunch. Someone who sounds like he's actually seen the dawn rise, rather than the sun set.

Closing Time is a confident debut, and one which already shows Waits pleasingly at odds with his contemporaries. His fondness for jazz, and the tradition of classic American songwriting styles is evident. And, already, with the weariness of his voice and the jaundiced nature of his material, Waits is well on his way to developing his familiar stage persona.

"I've always found it awkward to adjust to the studio," Waits later admitted. "You can go in and make a great album, or you can go in and suck raw eggs."

Well, sucking eggs wasn't on the agenda first time out. While *Closing Time* is in some ways flawed, there was enough promise to suggest a real future. 'Ol' 55', 'I Hope That I Don't Fall In Love With You', 'Martha',

'Old Shoes (And Picture Postcards)' and 'Rosie' are beautifully structured songs: poignant and heart-tugging, while managing to avoid the mawkish sentimentality and woeful self-indulgence which marred the work of so many of his contemporaries.

'Martha' is an achingly memorable song: Waits in character as an old man, reflecting on what might have been. He reconnects with his first love after a 40-year hiatus. It's a song that tugs at your heartstrings, while at the same time tugging the rug from under you. There were few others writing love songs about pensioners back in 1973. And certainly no one doing it so touchingly as Tom Waits.

Remember, at the time, *youth* was the key. Woodstock, hippies and *Easy Rider* were now in the past; and the year of *Closing Time* also saw such futuristic releases as Pink Floyd's *Dark Side Of The Moon*, David Bowie's *Aladdin Sane* and Roxy Music's *For Your Pleasure*. But 'Martha' is testament to Waits' incongruous wish to be born old. This is the 24-year-old's pitch at gaining admittance to the basement where the parents of his school friends hunkered down in Bermuda shorts, yakking over highballs to a wallpaper feast of unbroken Sinatra.

Closing Time opens with 'Ol' 55', surely the song for which the words "world" and "weary" were invented. This is Waits from the heart, a kid out riding "lickety splitly" in a battered, 20-year-old automobile. For Waits, like his near-contemporary Bruce Springsteen, the car offers a precious taste of freedom, the opportunity to escape . . . The song rolls beautifully on a mournful piano and guitar melody, like it's cruising smoothly in top.

'Old Shoes (And Picture Postcards)' is guitar-led, has a nice syncopated feel and a wistful lyric of adieu, with the highway beckoning. 'I Hope That I Don't Fall In Love With You' is tender while trying to be cynical. You can predict the twist in the song's tale, but that doesn't lessen its impact – which is buoyed by another beautiful melody, and Jerry Yester's production, which here is discreet and sympathetic. 'Rosie' is an atmospheric late-night vignette, Waits is up reflecting in the company of a midnight tomcat, beneath a *Night Of The Hunter* moon.

For all its initial promise, *Closing Time* is occasionally flawed. 'Grapefruit Moon' and 'Lonely' are both self-conscious and lacklustre; while 'Little Trip To Heaven (On The Wings Of Your Love)' is cloyingly sentimental. Waits' nervousness and uncertainty extends to too many of the album's 12 tracks. There are some tentative indications – 'Virginia Avenue', 'Midnight Lullaby', 'Ice Cream Man', 'Little Trip To Heaven . . .' – of Waits' future jazzier style. But here, he lacks the conviction and sureness

51

of touch to kick against the all-embracing singer-songwriter tapestry of patchouli and denim. *Closing Time* is the work of a novitiate, but nonetheless beguiling in all the right places.

"Okay," mumbles Waits, introducing the album's closing track, the instrumental 'Closing Time', "let's do one for posterity" . . . Well, hardly. *Closing Time* sold only to immediate family, and on release, attracted hardly any attention. It was probably the fact that the album appeared on David Geffen's Asylum label, more than any nascent talent in Tom Waits, which persuaded most initial purchasers.

Closing Time was up against some stiff competition when it was released, young LP-buying types had plenty of choice when it came to spending their record tokens. The year of Waits' debut also saw the release of Elton John's *Goodbye Yellow Brick Road*, Paul Simon's *There Goes Rhymin' Simon*, Wings' *Band On The Run*, Bob Marley's *Catch A Fire* and Led Zeppelin's *Houses Of The Holy* – as well as one further album from Elton John and *two* albums each from David Bowie and a young upstart called Bruce Springsteen.

"Harry Dean Stanton once told me he found a copy of my first album across a railroad track," Waits told Kristine McKenna. "He was in the middle of nowhere shooting a movie, and he found the record melted over the tracks. I kinda like that. Nicer place to end up than in a cut-out bin at a record store."

From early on, however, Waits has been financially well served by his peers. 'Ol' 55' became one of the first Waits songs to be covered, when in 1974 his Asylum labelmates, the Eagles, featured the song on their third album, *On The Border*. Waits, however, was unimpressed. "I don't like the Eagles," he grumbled to Fred Dellar in *NME*. "They're about as exciting as watching paint dry. Their albums are good for keeping the dirt off your turntable and that's about all."

Indeed, Waits was pretty withering about the whole country-rock scene – ironically, given that his label was pretty much home base for most of the music he claimed to despise. "Country rockers? Those guys grew up in LA – they don't have cowshit on their boots, they just got dogshit from Laurel Canyon. They wouldn't last two minutes in Putnam County [a favourite Waits location, and title of a track on his third album] that's for sure. If somebody gets shot and killed there on a Saturday night, the Sunday papers say he just died of natural causes."[3]

Years later, Waits admitted that his sneering punk lip was misplaced: "I was a young kid," he ruefully told Barney Hoskyns. "I was just corkin' off and bein' a prick. It was saying 'Notice me' . . . followed by 'Leave me the fuck alone', sometimes in the same sentence. I talked to Don Henley about that, and I apologised and I took it all back and we patched it up."

Unsurprisingly, 30 years on Waits rarely refers to *Closing Time*, and when he came to select material for his first songbook (1988's *Tom Waits: Anthology*), he chose only two songs from that album – 'Martha' and 'Ol' 55'.

Despite coming from the Asylum stable, *Closing Time* escaped largely unnoticed. There were no UK reviews, and precious few in the USA. But Waits did make it into the pages of *Rolling Stone*, the magazine that really mattered. After initial comparisons with Randy Newman and Frank Sinatra, Stephen Holden's thoughtful review of this "remarkable debut album" concluded: "Though many will resist Waits' sensibility as too self-indulgent, there is a consistent humour and sense of the absurd in his work that raises it above the level of banal 'kvetching' . . . Like Loudon Wainwright . . . Waits dances on the line between pathos and bathos without going too far in the wrong direction. Both singers know how and when to ham it up; both succeed on their instinctive acting ability as much, if not more than through musical intuitiveness."

Asylum were happy enough. They hadn't had particularly high expectations for Waits' debut, and their early signings, the Eagles, were now earning enough to subsidise less successful labelmates. David Blue, Waits' fellow Asylum singer-songwriter, and the man who had first alerted the label to Waits, enjoyed his biggest success when the Eagles covered his 'Outlaw Man' on *Desperado*.

Of his early relationship with the label, Waits confirmed: "They have a lot of faith in me . . . with the idea that sooner or later I'll do something significant." At the time, there was a lot of camaraderie among the labelmates – Joni and Glenn helped Jackson out on his 1973 debut; Jackson was there for Don [Henley] and Glenn [Frey] . . . But Waits warily kept them all at arm's length, remarking: "I don't invite them over to my house or anything."

It wasn't just the Eagles he didn't take to, Waits was generally dismissive of the whole laid-back California scene of the time: "You have to be a little bit of a private investigator to be a good songwriter . . . 'I rode through the desert on a horse with no name' . . . 'I almost cut my hair' . . . So what? . . . I mean, there's a sucker born every minute, and some of them have a lot of money and they spent it on 'A Horse With No Name'!"

What that most astute chronicler of the whole Asylum era, Barney Hoskyns, has called "a kind of denim apotheosis" occurred at the enormous Anaheim Stadium in Los Angeles on September 28, 1975. An estimated crowd of 55,000 took it easy while the Eagles, Linda Ronstadt, Jackson Browne and J.D. Souther serenaded the sun-drenched audience with their take-it-easy songs. Needless to say, Tom Waits was nowhere in view. He had other things than seven women on his mind.

The label had asked their boy to do what all labels at the time insisted every act do: go out on the road, and promote his album live, in front of real, live audiences who didn't do sympathy. "It was," Waits would tell me in London, still shivering after all those years, "a nightly experiment in terror."

NOTES

1   John Platt, *Zig Zag*
2   Barney Hoskyns, *Mojo* 102
3   Fred Dellar, *NME*

CHAPTER 7

AT the same time as David Geffen and Elliot Roberts were running Asylum records in Los Angeles, over in London David Betteridge was Chris Blackwell's deputy at Island Records. Island was then the best-known label for singer-songwriters in the UK, with a roster that included Cat Stevens, Richard Thompson, John Martyn and Nick Drake. Talking to me about the problems he had promoting Nick Drake at the same time Asylum were struggling with Tom Waits, David Betteridge emphasised: "Nick was definitely one of those artists . . . a worthy talent. But there was so much talent about then, so many things happening . . . There were always the questions: where's the single? And: is he on the road?"

The same two questions applied in America. The route was always the same: work up interest in your album by touring; along the way, try and pick up TV and radio play, but don't hold your breath.

For much of the Seventies Tom Waits maintained a base in Los Angeles, but most of the time, the highway was his home. In the competitive, cut and thrust world of rock'n'roll, Waits needed to be on the road alerting audiences to his existence. It was a long, lonely and frustrating road.

Let's just press pause, and remember how it was back then, back when Waits was beginning to fashion a career. The mistake people often make is imagining that the music scene of thirty years ago was in any way similar to today's twenty-first-century industry. Today, the moguls are dealing with declining record sales and the virtual anarchy of downloading. *Pop Idol*, *The X Factor* and *Fame Academy* are now seen as the arbiters of popular taste, not the pop charts. Television, radio, satellite television, digital radio, the internet . . . all have theoretically expanded the appetite for popular music. But, if anything, that vast breadth of choice has only served to diminish its impact.

Back when Waits was first tentatively venturing out on the road, music . . . rock'n'roll . . . call it what you will, was a relatively compact industry. It had only been 10 years since The Beatles conquered America, but they were now long gone. The Rolling Stones steamed across America every couple of years, to be hailed as "the greatest rock'n'roll band in the world", as did Led Zeppelin and The Who, but the multi-million dollar concept of sponsorship was still something out of a dystopian novel.

Bob Dylan hadn't toured in eight years, and it was far from certain that there was still an audience out there for him. Pink Floyd was perceived as an "underground" band. Crosby, Stills, Nash & Young had gone four ways to the wind. Simon & Garfunkel had split in the wake of *Bridge Over Troubled Water* – an overwhelming success which neither solo career could hope to match.

Jim Morrison, Jimi Hendrix and Janis Joplin were already dead. And nobody outside the pages of *Zig Zag* magazine had ever heard of Gram Parsons, The Velvet Underground or Nick Drake. Bob Marley's reggae was just that funny sort of music that skinheads danced to and David Bowie was a mere Glam novelty, to be filed alongside Gary Glitter, Slade and The Sweet. Even Bruce Springsteen was still an unknown, one of a dozen "new Dylans" who had yet to prove themselves.

In Britain, the weekly music press – *Melody Maker*, *New Musical Express*, *Sounds*, *Disc* and *Record Mirror* – were filled with new names and chart sensations. Hard to believe now, but every week of the year – all 52 of 'em – the inkies were filled with pop news, reviews and interviews. Whether you were a serious muso, or just moderately curious, that was where you went for your music info. There were no monthly magazines filling you in on the lustrous, 20-year background of rock history – because there *was* no "rock history". Elvis was still *in* the building, and once a month, regular as clockwork, there were fresh rumours that he was finally coming to play in Britain. And, just as regularly, reports that all four Beatles would be getting back together someday soon.

There were no websites to tell you just who all the people on the cover of *Sgt Pepper* were; none of the national television channels (well, there were only three) screened hour-long documentaries about the making of classic albums. No network would even consider devoting a whole evening to deliberating on The Greatest Single Of All Time. And you certainly couldn't attend The University At The Top Of My Road to undertake a degree course in Rock'n'Roll – so no dissertations about 'How To Write An Album Review', or lectures on 'Blagging Your Way Backstage'.

If your local library – and it was a very big "if" – had any pop books at all, they would be (a) Anthony Scaduto's Dylan biography, (b) Hunter Davies' Beatles book, and (c) Jerry Hopkins' life of Elvis. You couldn't do your own rock'n'roll research in 10-volume encyclopaedias – there weren't any in print. All in all, it seemed likely that the musical heritage of Wayne Gibson & the Dynamic Sounds, Holly Near and Vent 414 would remain, forever, a closed book.

For rock'n'roll radio, there was Radio 1. And, believe me, that was *it*. Radio 2 played Mantovani. The death knell of *Sing Something Simple* still sounded regularly every Sunday evening. There was no commercial or pirate radio. There was no digital radio. There was just Radio 1 . . . and its power was mighty.

The Breakfast Show was massively influential, because the last thing you heard before leaving for work was likely to be the song you hummed all day – and the record you bought at the weekend. You couldn't listen to music on your iPod on the way to work, because there were no iPods – not even a Walkman. You couldn't listen to music on a computer at work, because there weren't any PCs. The majority of computers that did exist were HAL-size, occupying whole rooms in purpose-built buildings, and tended by worried-looking men in white coats.

This then was the landscape rock music inhabited when Tom Waits released *Closing Time* in 1973. America did have FM radio and *Rolling Stone*, but otherwise remained equally hidebound. While 1969's Woodstock has become enshrined as *the* rock festival, it was the 1973 gathering at Watkins Glen that attracted the largest crowd ever, when 600,000 people turned up to see The Band, The Allman Brothers and Grateful Dead.

It was as if, following the excesses of the Sixties, the early part of the new decade took solace in less challenging artists: besides Tom's friends the Eagles, Chicago, The Carpenters and Neil Diamond were all absolutely massive.

And then there was Elton John . . . During his peak in the mid-Seventies, Elton accounted for an astonishing 3 per cent of *all* records sold around the world. America in particular, took the Pinner piano-pounder to its heart, and in 1975 Los Angeles even declared one week in November "Elton John Week". Coming offstage every night, after appearing before paying audiences of 70,000, Elton would literally bump into legends like Cary Grant and Groucho Marx. Multi-million selling albums like *Madman Across The Water* were exactly what record labels wanted from their singer-songwriters.

From the very beginning, Tom Waits recognised that it was going to be a hard slog for his brand of mournful whimsy to get attention. It was lonely in the middle. "Marcel Marceau gets more airplay than I do!" he joked, quite seriously, early on.

Waits knew that if he was to make his mark, he had to quit LA and travel, pack up his piano and walk. He'd have to go out on the concert circuit, selling his wares, each night and every night. From Atlanta to Poughkeepsie; Tupelo to Peoria . . . One night, New York's Bottom Line; the next, Passim's Club in Cambridge, Massachusetts. Next up, Bryn Mawr's Main Point, then on to the Shaboo Club in Wilamantic, Connecticut . . . And on and on and on . . .

Once on the road, Waits grew used to facing hostile audiences. Though their antipathy was as much to do with the incongruity of who Waits was wheeled in to open for. You might expect promoters to exercise a degree of sympatico when it came to putting concert bills together: Graham Parker & The Rumour warming up the Rainbow for Southside Johnny & The Asbury Jukes would have been heaven. An unannounced Elvis Costello, keeping the Brixton Academy crowd happy before Bob Dylan put in an appearance provided exceptional value for money. Elton John coming on strong before Sandy Denny's Fotheringay at the Royal Albert Hall drew few requests for refunds . . .

But Tom Waits' early gigs sound like they were put together in bedlam, by a bitter and broken-down promoter . . . "I opened a show once for Billy Preston," Waits cheerfully told me, "which was a *catastrophe.*"

As his manager, Herb Cohen, also handled Frank Zappa and The Mothers Of Invention, Waits was a shoo-in as opening act. Except that Zappa fans who'd come along for Frank's guitar pyrotechnics, subversive humour and challenging neo-classical rock'n'roll, really didn't want a stumble bum who looked and sounded like a hangover from a long-forgotten decade.

"On the road with Zappa," Waits chuckled when he recalled the tour, "it was one long emergency." As Zappa and his Mothers trawled through the auditoria of America, Waits was regularly given the raspberry. Sharing the same manager, Waits came cheap and easy as an opening act, but even he sensed early on that he was being used as a "rectal thermometer" on the partisan Zappa crowd.

Zappa was as dictatorial as any South American general when it came to his own band of Mothers – and his cordiality certainly didn't extend to his opening acts. Even his most recent and sympathetic biographer, Barry Miles, described Zappa as: "a confirmed misanthrope who treated the outside world with extreme cynicism and scorn and restricted his human relations to as few people as possible."

"I did three tours [with Zappa]," Waits told Todd Everett, "until I couldn't stand it anymore. It's very difficult for one man to come on in front of five or ten thousand people and get anything but visual and verbal insubordination from the audience . . . People will come and throw produce at you."

Thirty years later, with the Zappa wound evidently still smarting, Waits recalled the experience as a "really hard time, very disturbing, with 3,500 people united together chanting 'You suck' full volume, in a hockey arena."[1]

For Waits, the early shows, those years of struggle while he was cutting his performing teeth, were far from easy. Quite what fans of country superstar, and former Sun Records artist, Charlie Rich ("The Silver Fox") made of his somewhat incongruous opening act goes sadly unrecorded, although Waits quickly recognised Rich's talent: "sure can sing, that son of a bitch!"

Others who headlined while Waits licked his wounds backstage included Blue Oyster Cult, Jerry Jeff Walker, John Hammond, Fishbone, Billy Preston, Bonnie Raitt, Poco, Al Jarreau, Roger McGuinn, Martha Reeves (sans Vandellas), Mink DeVille, John Stewart and Leon Redbone . . . Now *that* must have been one hell of a confusing evening: a jazz-styled singer of indeterminate age, Leon Redbone was to have been the first signing to Bob Dylan's own Ashes & Sand label. Redbone specialised in ragtime, jazz and vaudeville covers; a Groucho Marx lookalike, he also sounded uncannily like his erstwhile opening act.

Waits recalled one other memorable early gig when he spoke to Nick Kent in 1978: "For some godforsaken reason, I'd been booked to perform at a Gay Liberation Benefit, and it was a real . . . uh, testy audience out there. The worst thing was, though, I had to follow Richard Pryor who'd just completed his act, screaming 'Kiss my rich black ass, you faggots' and storming off the stage.

"Well, I was in something of a quandary at that particular point, but I went on anyway, and started off with . . . well for some reason, I'd chosen to perform the old show tune 'Standing on the corner, watching all the girls go by . . .'!"

Then there was the show Waits lovingly evoked when we met: "I opened a show once for a guy called Buffalo Bob & the Howdy Doody Revue. He was like an American children's programme host. We went out on a tour of colleges, and I'd have to do like three matinees for the children and their mothers. He used to call me 'Tommy', I wanted to strangle the sonofabitch. He had that real vaudeville attitude to 'the business', the old veteran and the young . . . I hoped he'd die of bone cancer the entire week."

Later, Waits did grudgingly concede that "In cities like Minneapolis,

Philadelphia, Boston and Denver, I'm a very bizarre cultural phenomenon."[2]

Bizarre was the word. Just imagine: it's 1974, and you're going along to
see a concert. You've seen Led Zeppelin. And Peter Frampton. And
Fleetwood Mac. When you stay in nights, you listen to the open-heart
surgery of Joni Mitchell and James Taylor. You missed Woodstock – but
got the triple album and saw the movie, twice, so that was almost like
being there . . . By a cruel accident of birth you managed to miss the
Sixties, but the Seventies is shaping up nicely. Then on comes this guy
who sounds like a haemorrhage and looks like your uncle. This is definitely
not what you want on your big night out.

But whatever else he was, Waits was not a quitter. So he kept on
keeping on, spending the rest of the decade – the best part of seven years –
on the road promoting his first half-dozen albums.

Regardless of the time of year, 'Christmas Card From A Hooker In
Minneapolis' was always bookended by 'Silent Night'. And for good
measure, Waits would frequently include a snatch of the 1964 Little
Anthony & The Imperials hit, 'Goin' Out Of My Head'. It was a tender
performance, touching in its evocation of an imagined life – but like most
of his work at the time, it made little impact.

Life on the road all but destroyed his liver, he drank to conquer his
nerves before performing in front of threatening (and often openly hostile)
audiences. And his penchant for all-black outfits only emphasised the
ghostly pallor of his face. Onstage he was confident and in control, but the
years of touring were clearly taking their toll. It was this strict regime of
poor diet, too much booze and too many cigarettes that turned Tom
Waits from an almost unrecognisably sweet-voiced troubadour, into a
gnarled and grizzled old soak.

The endless, thankless, touring also gave him an appetite for trivia.
Playing all manner of dives, Waits became a walking repository of witnessed events and learned knowledge of a somewhat specialised nature. It
was while playing the bijou Dark Side Of The Moon club in East St Louis,
that Waits spotted his all-time favourite piece of graffiti: "Love Is Blind.
God Is Love. Therefore Ray Charles Must Be God!"

Desperate to reach an audience of his own, between 1973 and 1980,
Waits toured relentlessly; a grinding schedule of one-nighters, played out
to, at best, indifferent, and at worst, overtly antagonistic, audiences. They
were long, punishing years on the road, all over the highways and byways
of North America. Like fellow Californian John Fogerty, Waits would
have groaned more than once: "Oh Lord, stuck in Lodi again . . ."

Save when opening for Zappa, Waits was mainly playing dives, where the PA was dodgy and the lighting unambitious. Like the down-on-his-luck actor performing at a church hall in Scotland, he instructed the stage manager: "I'd like a single spot on me when I make my entrance; backlit for the soliloquy; then full flood for the finale!" Only to be met with the deflating question: "You want the switch up, or down?"

Austin City Limits was a cult public access television show which launched in 1974. Based, as you might expect, in Austin, Texas, it was designed to showcase the growing outlaw music scene of the state during the mid-Seventies. Guests like Willie Nelson, Townes Van Zandt and Lyle Lovett fitted right in with the maverick nature of the show.

Introduced ponderously as "music from the soul, with an edge that cuts deep," Waits appeared on *Austin City Limits* in 1978. Recordings of the show give a revealing vignette of just how he was in performance at the time, after spending the best part of five years on the road. A gentle reading of 'Summertime' ushered in a thoughtful 'Burma Shave', and demonstrated Waits' ability to hold an audience rapt with his raps.

In performance at the time, Waits switched between piano and guitar – his arms revolving like windmill sails; they'd lock at right angles behind his head, frequently wreathed in a plume of cigarette smoke. His onstage nerves were calmed by smoking, and by scratching, like he had nits. While Waits applied serious finger motion to his skull, his back arched, his torso contorted at weird angles – and now Tom had a new toy to play with . . . Bob Dylan had his harmonica holder; Bruce Springsteen had the E. Street Band; Tom Waits had a car tyre.

Onstage, Waits writhed, like the songs inside him were struggling to get out. And as he sang, those long white hands wrapped around the microphone stand, like they were sending out semaphore signals. Sometimes, Waits seemed in mid-seizure as he spasmed through a song. His stage wear was hat, black suit and a tie as thin as the sole of a hobo's boot. At times, Waits looks like a bookie, doing the tic-tac, with his arms flailing. At other times, he looks simply, sadly, like old man Steptoe – someone you'd likely as not cross the road to avoid.

Ever keen to accentuate the positive, Waits did recognise in hindsight that those thankless opening dates had helped him hone his stagecraft. Hecklers got short shrift: "Your opinions are like assholes, buddy, everybody's got one," and such confrontations did help turn a shy singer-songwriter into a confident performer. All that remained was for Waits to go out and find an audience that wouldn't throw produce at him.

NOTES

1 Sylvie Simmons, *Mojo*
2 Todd Everett, *NME*

CHAPTER 8

AUTHENTICITY was the big thing back then. But it was a bogus type of authenticity. By the time Waits arrived in 1973, everyone knew that New York Messiah Bob Dylan was on more than nodding terms with Minnesota's Robert Zimmerman. It was just more fun to believe that Dylan had grown up hopping boxcars, working in a circus and playing piano for Bobby Vee – except, actually, that last one turned out to be true.

Rock'n'roll was perceived by the critics as the authentic expression of young working-class angst. And, like *The Hitler Diaries*, it was something everyone *wanted* to believe. John Lennon's determination to cast himself as a "working-class hero" crumbled before the prim lace curtains of Aunt Mimi's proudly middle-class "Mendips". If you were looking for real working-class heroes among the Fabs, you needed to make your way to the Madryn Street birthplace of one Ringo Starr.

The heirs of Woody Guthrie were expected to be rollin', ramblin' types, for whom the highway was their home. But polite, well brought-up middle-class boys recognised the dichotomy. Paul Simon addressed it, when he spoke to David Hepworth about his decision to move to Britain in 1964: "I was just a Jewish kid from Queens; Paxton came from Oklahoma, Dylan was from Minnesota. I was simply not from far enough away to make it in the Village."

In the sleeve notes to his third album, *Outward Bound*, Tom Paxton rue-fully admitted: "Liner notes to folk albums traditionally reveal how Funky Fifthstring left the campus and hit th' road, bummin' from Coast t' Coast singin' in cow camp an' diner, livin' hard, growin', findin' dusty roads t' walk down. I *did* a little hitch-hiking, but only when I couldn't raise the bus fare . . ."

On the other hand, Waits' contemporary Bruce Springsteen was about as authentic as you could get: the only son of a working-class, New Jersey family, raised on TV and rock'n'roll ("I didn't hang around with no crowd talking 'bout William Burroughs"). "Blue-collar rock" hadn't yet been christened, but when it was, Springsteen was undeniably its authentic voice.

Neil Young was another who was venerated as an authentic voice, a maverick artist, a renegade who marched to the beat of his own drum. But though his lyrics spoke of massacring movie stars, in real life he soon ended up living with one. And as the voice of liberation and individuality, Young also displayed double standards: by 1972 he was pining in song for a woman "to keep my house clean, fix my meals and go away".

Tom Waits, incidentally, never took to Neil Young: "Another one who is embarrassing for displaying a third-grade mentality," he bitched to John Platt. "'Old man, take a look at my life' that's real good, 'it's a lot like yours' . . . that's great. If he'd come up with that in a bar and not had a pen, it would have been lost to the world."

This though was the early Seventies: a decade still looking for a direction. And for the likes of Tom Waits, it was an ideal time to be dipping a toe in the waters: singer-songwriters were likely to be to the Seventies what groups like The Beatles and Rolling Stones had been to the Sixties. James Taylor's second album, *Sweet Baby James*, attracted little attention on its initial release in 1970, but something in Taylor's engaging brand of "sweet melancholy" caught the national mood.

While Nixon consolidated his sinister court in the White House, war raged in Cambodia and Vietnam. GIs returned, hooked on heroin. City streets were unsafe, whole neighbourhoods unstable. Peaceful protest had given way to anger and Black Power. Acronyms and initials shielded terrorist organisations. It was a time of turmoil; the tranquillity of the Sixties toughening up for the grittier Seventies.

As if offering solace behind closed doors, *Sweet Baby James* quietly spun its spell on a million turntables. It stayed on the charts for two years, landed Taylor a *Time* cover, and alerted record companies to the reality that there was serious money to be made out of melodic introspection.

Taylor was friendly with Carole King, and played on her second solo album *Tapestry*. The whole album was cut in five days, but on its release, early in 1971, *Tapestry* went on to sell 24 million copies. For over 20 years, it remained the most successful album ever released by a female artist. The double whammy of Taylor and King made the moguls quiver with anticipation.

Better still, there were more where those two came from . . . Paul Simon had established himself as an effective solo act; Leonard Cohen's mournful poems continued to make their mark; while Elton John, Neil Young, Carly Simon and Cat Stevens all helped reinforce the financial possibilities of the solo singer-songwriter.

The success of the new breed would help fill a vacuum in rock'n'roll.

The Beatles had split bitterly at the onset of the Seventies, and given their pedigree, their solo careers so far had been patchy and largely unremarkable. The Rolling Stones were now lionised by the demi-monde of American society – Jackie Onassis' sister Lee Radziwell and Truman Capote were regular backstage visitors – but the Stones' latest album, *Exile On Main Street*, was deemed by critics to be a murky mess.

By 1973 Bob Dylan had lain largely dormant for three years, but sporadic sightings and occasional sessions had done little to diminish his standing. While his actual record sales were negligible in comparison with Elton John, Dylan was still regarded as the archetypal singer-songwriter. But his continued absence, coupled with the chart triumphs of *Sweet Baby James*, *Goodbye Yellow Brick Road* and *Tapestry*, had set cogs turning in executive boardrooms.

The record industry could hardly be considered an innovative business. Although there is a proud history of small independent labels striking out and following their hunches, like film companies, the large labels tended to bide their time, watch and covet their rivals' success, then immediately try and replicate it. This was a strategy which went all the way back to the Fifties, when Elvis Presley – "the Memphis Flash" – first burst out of the South and scandalised America.

Once the shockwaves had settled, Elvis himself was tamed, packaged and bowdlerised; and an army of clones were duly minted and marketed, quicker than you could say "Tutti Frutti". In the Sixties The Beatles breathed new life into the moribund American music scene, and almost immediately efforts were made to cash in on the phenomenon. Barely had they ceased to be lovable mop-tops than The Monkees were manufactured as a quick antidote to the increasingly wayward direction the original Fab Four were taking.

Similarly, the success of Bob Dylan's strident and thought-provoking songs of the Sixties had persuaded the suits that folk-rock was now the place to be. The initial success of The Byrds, Sonny & Cher, Simon & Garfunkel and Van Morrison came about as a result of the major labels quickly jumping onto the folk-rock bandwagon.

The record sales of Dylan's Sixties peers – singer-songwriters such as Phil Ochs, Joni Mitchell, Fred Neil, David Blue, Tim Hardin, Randy Newman and Tim Buckley – were negligible compared to the cornucopia of the early Seventies. It did little harm for any label to have a low-selling, "prestige" singer-songwriter on its books – but with the success of King and Taylor, there was also the hope that one of their quirky troubadours might, one day, hit the financial jackpot.

It was on the back of this quest for the a new Dylan that Tom Waits first motored into town. Anyone with curly hair who could hold a note and find a rhyme for "Watergate" could land a deal. And by 1973, the year Tom Waits made his recording debut, singer-songwriters were the currency: Bruce Springsteen, Jackson Browne, John Prine, Kris Kristofferson, David Ackles, Loudon Wainwright, Harry Chapin, Steve Goodman and David Blue . . . all had made their debuts by the time Waits first appeared on the scene.

Each of them was branded as the "new Dylan" – and, just as inevitably, damned by the comparison. Sure, there were similarities with their mentor: this new breed all applied a tougher, more focused sensibility to their writing. They had learnt that honesty and open-heartedness had a market. Their best work was vivid: short stories in song; scenarios full of identifiable characters; the ability to translate the universal into something personal and more intimate.

As a group, they spoke of an America keen to reconnect with itself during one of the most turbulent times in its history. Songs such as James Taylor's 'Sweet Baby James', Kristofferson's 'Me And Bobby McGee', or Goodman's 'City Of New Orleans', recalled the rolling sense of freedom evoked by Kerouac. David Ackles wrote with economy and poignancy on 'His Name Is Andrew'; John Prine's 'Sam Stone' was a heartbreaking account of a Vietnam vet plunged into heroin addiction and early death; while Jackson Browne's 'Before The Deluge' remains a bittersweet epitaph for the era.

These then were the "new Dylans". But as Kris Kristofferson remarked at the time: "I never thought there was much wrong with the old one."

The furore surrounding all these newcomers owed as much to their wordplay as their persona – an early ad for Springsteen's debut album ran: "This man puts more thoughts, more ideas and images into one song than most people put onto an album."

As for Bruce Springsteen and the rest of the Class of '73, for Tom Waits, the word was the message. Lyrics were of paramount importance in those days – even those, like Kristofferson or John Prine, who struggled to hold a note, were revered as lyricists. And early on, Waits came into his own as a low-life chronicler; a bar-room balladeer; even, some said, a poet!

Waits was forever shucking that dog-tag of poet. Asked at the time if he saw himself more as a poet or a singer, he deadpanned: "I'm a Methodist." (Asked later, "Are you prolific?" Waits responded, "Well, I was *raised* a Catholic . . .")

More seriously, in 1975 he told Todd Everett: "I call what I'm doing an improvisational adventure, or an inebriated travelogue . . . If I'm tied down and have to call myself something, I prefer 'storyteller'."

The old Dylan, asked in 1965 if he saw himself primarily as a singer or a poet, replied blithely and without missing a beat, "I think of myself as more a song and dance man . . ." But with the "new Dylan" lasso roping everybody in, it was inevitable that Waits should be cast as a new type of urban poet.

Like Bob, he is a great poet of the American place name, a celebrator of the byways: Burma Shave; Potter's Field; Elkheart, Indiana; Johnsburg, Illinois . . . But Waits himself remained wary: "Most people, when they hear the word 'poetry'," he told Todd Everett, "think of being chained to a school desk memorising 'Ode To A Grecian Urn'. When somebody says they're going to read me a poem, I can think of any number of things I'd rather be doing."

Despite the witty and whimsical veneer that overlays his songs, Waits likes to think of them as vignettes, rooted in real life. As a writer, he told me, he saw himself as a "professional eavesdropper"; an observer rather than a poet. "I can't stand writers that just varnish something and then put it out. I like to know that there was gum under the table . . . how many cigarettes were in the ashtray, little things like that. You have to be a little bit of a private investigator to be a good songwriter."

Although hungry for appreciation of his work, Waits was also wary of the recognition it might bring. "Keeping your anonymity is important as a writer," he told me. "So that you can go anywhere, any part of town, sit in a corner. Anytime you're swimming around in the American public . . ." He became suddenly animated, quoting Dylan: "'Well, people just get uglier, and I have no sense of time . . .' you know?"

Warming to his theme, he paused before continuing: "*The Devil's Dictionary* described being famous as 'conspicuously miserable'. I've never been particularly comfortable with the idea of 12 million people sitting down and enjoying *anything* at the same time."

CHAPTER 9

O N the road and with no direction home, for Tom Waits most of the Seventies was spent out on tour. When he wasn't trawling the highways of America, Waits' off-duty hours were spent lodging at the Tropicana Motel in Los Angeles. Located on Santa Monica Boulevard, along from the Troubadour, and owned by a former baseball star, for the remainder of the decade the Tropicana was the place where Mrs Waits would send Christmas cards to her errant son.

Waits happily paid his $9 a night, sawed up the breakfast bar and installed a piano in his room. Then he was off on tour again . . . "You go away for three months, and come back to a fridge that looks like a science experiment." Such a life hardly suggested domestic bliss, and boy was he eating badly. For Waits, food just got in the way of "more liquid libation" – and his stove at the Tropicana was little more than "a large cigarette lighter".

There was a camaraderie in the flop houses Waits frequented which he found winning: "If you get hungry at 3 a.m.," he remembered of the Tropicana, "you can go downstairs and the desk clerk will give you half his sandwich. They won't do that at a Hilton."[1]

Waits adapted quickly to the LA lifestyle, though he offered a couple of cautionary notes to Peter O'Brien in 1977: "Watch out for 16-year-old girls wearing bell bottoms who are running away from home and have a lot of Blue Oyster Cult albums under their arm . . . Don't go to the Compton drive-in on a Saturday night and announce over the loudspeaker that you are responsible for the death of Malcolm X."

The Tropicana is where Andy Warhol's *Trash* had been filmed in the late Sixties, so its seedy credentials were already secured by the time Waits took up residence. Much beloved of rock'n'roll bands, the Tropicana had also been a favourite haunt of those recently deceased rock revellers, Jim Morrison and Janis Joplin; and had played host to Alice Cooper and Iggy Pop. The owners were tolerant of the rock fraternity's high jinks, reckoning that the rest of their dissolute clientele wouldn't notice if the swimming pool was clogged with debris – so long as the rates remained cheap. Waits fitted right in – and the Tropicana was soon to acquire another regular, who could drink as good as she got.

Rickie Lee Jones was born in Chicago in 1954. The child of a broken home, she began writing songs at the age of seven, and soon after began living the life of a bohemian tearaway. She made a beeline for Los Angeles while still a teenager, and worked spells as a waitress at an Italian restaurant in the city while simultaneously honing her songwriting skills.

Like Waits, five years her senior, Jones was a regular at the Troubadour's Monday night hootenannies – which is where, in 1977, Waits first clapped eyes on his future girlfriend. "The first time I saw Rickie Lee," Waits told Timothy White, "she reminded me of Jayne Mansfield. I thought she was *extremely* attractive, which is to say that my first reactions were rather primitive – *primeval*, even."

For the next few years, Waits and Rickie Lee Jones were an item in the close-knit community, centred around the Tropicana and the bars along Hollywood and Vine. It was here that Waits, when not out working, would stroll for a preprandial sherry, or the occasional glass of stout. Later, he might dally awhile at the Traveller's Café, or hang around in Bud's coffee shop, or take in a show at the Troubadour.

Poor diet, endless cigarettes, overwork, and too much booze – this was the Tom Waits' Workout. While the rest of Los Angeles celebrated the tie-dyed, bright-eyed enthusiasm of the Eagles, Waits and the Tropicana gang kept vampire hours. Hard liquor rather than soft drugs was their fuel.

For all his tales of beatnik glory and wild-eyed bohemian adventure, much of Tom Waits' persona was mere mythologising. But Rickie Lee Jones really had lived the life: running away from home at 15; stealing a car and driving from her home in Phoenix to San Diego; getting booted out of three schools within a year . . . "She's much older than me in terms of street wisdom; sometimes she seems as ancient as dirt . . ." Waits admitted.[2]

Waits and Jones forged a firm alliance, though it was constantly interrupted by Waits' touring. *Closing Time* had pricked up a few ears, and Waits was accruing a reputation of sorts as a performer. Asylum were keen to get him back in the studio, and capitalise on his growing reputation with a second album.

On its release in 1974, *The Heart Of Saturday Night* hinted that Waits really might be a talent to cherish. Here was an individual voice, a writer shining a spotlight down into the mean streets and dark alleys of America. This was the album where Waits found a voice, and his characters found a platform.

The songs on *The Heart Of Saturday Night* capture the feeling of filching the final dregs from a cup of cold coffee as the jukebox plays 'Stand By

Your Man' for the very last time. Waits, of course, is the guy curled up in the corner of the diner, making maps out of the cup stains on the counter, scrabbling round for "the last bent butt from a packet of Kents". He's about to leave, but afraid to commit to the morning. And something tells the waitress that he's the type of guy who'll be back inside in a quarter of an hour, mumbling about a watch he thought he'd left there. Or a lighter. "Oh, and while I'm looking, any more Java to be squeezed out of that baby . . .?"

From the cover painting in, it was clear that here was a new style: a head-scratching, still-smoking Waits, soused outside a bar, being eyed up by the kind of night-time companion the Mother Superior warned you against. *The Heart Of Saturday Night* is where you need to begin if you go looking for the ghost of Tom Waits – here are songs which ooze booze, love and loss, shrouded in a jazz style that speaks of Waits' enduring fondness for the Fifties.

The opening 'New Coat Of Paint' was a sassy, piano-led shuffle, which had Waits sounding wearier and more scuffed than he had on his debut – like all that hard living had etched itself onto his vocal cords. 'San Diego Serenade' further celebrated the "new" Tom Waits: the gnarled observer, the jaundiced jazzer. Lines like "never saw the morning 'til I stayed up all night . . ." brought to mind the Stones, swaggering with junkie bluster on *Exile On Main Street*: "sunshine bores the daylight outta me".

With 'Diamonds On My Windshield', accompanied solely by a tautly plucked stand-up bass and lightly brushed drums, Waits was edging towards the sound that would soon define him on disc. A finger-clicking highway odyssey, the place-names flashing by, as if glimpsed from the warm cab of a 16-wheeler. As a trucking anthem, 'Diamonds On My Windshield' is right up there alongside Little Feat's 'Willin''. Inside the cosy haven, shielded from the rain, Waits is wrapped in radio waves. Outside – in a much-quoted line – "it's colder than a well digger's ass".

The sound of a truck rolling, a car horn tooting, ushers in 'The Heart Of Saturday Night'. The title track is an early classic, with a melody as steady as the Oldsmobile of which Waits sings. Here, in a few scant lines, Waits conveys the hope and anticipation which Saturday night offers up. ("One of the most haunting, exquisite songs ever written about the cruel myth of eternal youth," *Rolling Stone* wrote later of the song.)

A gentle, enticing song, 'The Heart Of Saturday Night' concludes what was side one of the original vinyl album, while side two wraps with 'The Ghost Of Saturday Night'. *The Heart Of Saturday Night* is by no means a concept album, but it is a series of linked, sharply observed snapshots, centring round that night of nights . . . You're all gassed up and ready to party, you got a six-pack and your best girl by your side, and you don't have to work on Sunday.

Above all, Saturday's the night you get to be yourself: the hours that you can savour as your own. Saturday night is what sustains you the rest of the week, as you labour through your dead-end job on dead-end street. Waits' own best reflection on the subject, 'The Heart Of Saturday Night' echoes all those other "Saturday night" celebrations by Sam Cooke, The Drifters and The Bee Gees.

There is a wonderful performance of 'The Heart Of Saturday Night' by Mary Elizabeth Mastrantonio in John Sayles' frustrating, but under-valued film *Limbo* (1999), which perfectly captures all the poignancy and anticipation of the original.

Maybe it was life on the road, maybe it was the acuity of Waits' eye, peeping out from beneath the fedora, that turned his songs into a leathery kind of poetry. *The Heart Of Saturday Night* is hard and shiny, with songs that are beginning to breathe. 'Fumblin' With The Blues' fashions the now-familiar Waits character: that hard drinkin', pool shootin' guy, known by name to all the local bartenders. Musically, meanwhile, he's scatting and edging further and further away from his Laurel Canyon contemporaries.

'Shiver Me Timbers' is a grand song on a sweeping scale, a musical trawl through maritime history, a veritable sea-shanty for the Seventies; with young Tom, press-ganged in a sea-front tavern by a leering Robert Newton, one moment high as a crow's nest, and next, cast down full fathom five. Namechecking Jack London's *Martin Eden* and Melville's unforgettably driven Captain Ahab, there is a mood of world-weary understanding, as Waits the sailor quits port, abandoning family and friends as he goes selfishly off, sailing away. At the time, I was struck by the vividness of images such as: "The clouds are like headlines, on a new front page sky." When we met though, Waits admitted: "I've never been particularly knocked-out by that song."

The album's concluding track, 'The Ghosts Of Saturday Night (After Hours At Napoleone's Pizza House)' was a further indication as to where Waits was heading. It's little more than a recitation against a slow blues backing. But the subtitle clearly tells where Waits got his inspiration – these are the memories of that young short-order chef who dreamed of being a contender.

Waits casts his short-story eye over solitary sailors, and Irene, the waitress "with Maxwell House eyes" is as cold as the Sacrament to your lips; the night, as spent as a used cigarette. You're limbering up for a bleak and unrewarding Sunday morning. The coffee's lukewarm and the dawn's bleary-eyed. It's time to be moving on . . .

Way back in the Sixties, there was a theory – one of many – that the concluding track of every Bob Dylan album prefaced the next, thus 'Restless Farewell' was a signpost to *Another Side Of* . . .; 'I'll Be Your Baby Tonight' ushered in *Nashville Skyline*, etc., etc. In Waits' case, it was certainly true that the thread of 'The Ghosts Of Saturday Night' would run through into the jazzy narratives of *Nighthawks At The Diner*.

The Heart Of Saturday Night was not perfect – 'Semi Suite', 'Please Call Me, Baby' and 'Drunk On The Moon' do little to enrich the Waits palette. But in hindsight, the overall feel of the album is the sound of someone beginning to find his way.

On *The Heart Of Saturday Night*, Waits got to sit up at the bar in excellent company. Producer Bones Howe had begun engineering jazz records in the Fifties, behind the dials for such giants as Ornette Coleman and Ella Fitzgerald. By the early Sixties, he was scoring for Mel Torme and Frank Sinatra. Moving into pop, Howe worked as an engineer with Lou Adler on the classic Mamas & Papas hits of the mid-Sixties.

In 1965, Bones' first production credit gave him a number one, with The Turtles' cover of Dylan's 'It Ain't Me Babe'. A lucrative association with The Association, The Fifth Dimension and Laura Nyro followed. And by the time of the Summer of Love, Bones Howe was one of those responsible for the sound at the world's premier rock festival, 1967's Monterey Pop.

David Geffen, who knew Howe through his work with The Association, and was now established at Asylum, gave him a call about a new act he thought would be of interest. "He told me he had an artist who had made this one record for him [*Closing Time*] and he thought because of my background in jazz and pop that we'd make a good pair," Howe remembered when talking to Dan Daley for an exhaustive *Sound On Sound* interview in 2004.

Neither Waits nor label boss Geffen had been happy with the way that *Closing Time* sounded – Geffen felt that Waits was being pushed in a "Bob Dylan direction", when his true instincts favoured a jazzier style. With an astute eye on the singer-songwriter success of James Taylor and Carole King, Geffen wondered whether, by emphasising Waits' jazzy penchant, he couldn't cover both ends: tapping into the vogue for singer-songwriters, at the same time as marketing his artist as a fresh sound, distinctively different from the myriad of guitar-wielding, folk-rooted contemporaries.

Talking to Barney Hoskyns, Howe recalled the day that Geffen called and told him about Waits. "He said . . . 'Waits has a lot of jazz and beat influences that didn't really come out on his first album' . . . He played me 'Martha' and a couple of other things that sounded unique." It would turn out to be an inspired piece of matchmaking. Steeped in the Fifties jazz scene, and with a consummate knowledge of pop, Bones Howe would go on to work with Waits for the remainder of his career on Asylum.

Howe later recalled his first meeting with Waits: "I told him I thought his music and lyrics had a Kerouac quality to them, and he was blown away that I knew who Jack Kerouac was. I told him I also played jazz drums and he went wild. Then I told him when I was working for Norman Granz, Norman had found the tapes of Kerouac reading his poetry from *The Beat Generation* in a hotel room. I told Waits I'd make him a copy. That sealed it."[3]

The two men clicked right away, and at the time, Waits professed himself happy with the direction Howe took on *The Heart Of Saturday Night*. During recording breaks, Waits would pump Howe for anecdotes about the jazz names he had worked with – like how Ornette Coleman was working as an elevator man in a Hollywood department store while at night cutting his renowned *The Shape Of Jazz To Come* album.

"Pre-production always took place in some dumpy restaurant talking about songs and music and people . . ." Howe remembered. "The first record we made together [*The Heart Of Saturday Night*] was probably the most 'produced' album we did, partly because I wanted to take him out of the folk/singer-songwriter thing."[4]

Like Paul Simon, Bob Dylan, Richard Thompson and many others, Waits is often critical of his own early songs – "a sentimental guy belly-aching", is how he once characterised them. But when we spoke, he was at pains to point out how lucky he had been: "There are songs on each album . . . some of my early stuff I'm a little embarrassed with. People think that you do most of your growth before you begin to record. There's the moment where downbeat, the drum roll, the fanfare, and now you're baptised. For me it happened *during* and I felt like I snuck in when I was about 22."

He was, however, his usual loquacious but oblique self when it came to pinning down just why: "It's like looking at old pictures of yourself," he told Bill Flanagan. "'Here I am with that funny hat on. I didn't have the beard, and Ruth was overweight. She's trimmed down now. Was that the DeSoto we had? No, it's the Plymouth . . .'"

With the release of his second album, Waits thoughtfully gave the hard-working hacks a press release, to save them the trouble of writing anything themselves. In his own words, here's the 1974 model Tom Waits describing himself: "I drink heavily on occasion and shoot a decent game of pool and my idea of a good time is a Tuesday evening at the Manhattan Club in Tijuana. I reside now in the Silver Lake area of Los Angeles and am a dedicated Angeleno, and have absolutely no intention of moving to a cabin in Colorado. I like smog, traffic, kinky people, car trouble, noisy neighbours, crowded bars and spend most of my time in my car going to the movies."

Looking back on his second album, Waits reflected: "*The Heart Of Saturday Night* was very ill-formed, but I was trying. There was spoken word on there. I don't know, in those days I think I really wanted to see my head on somebody else's body."

Then it was back on the road, to tour, and promote, and talk-up his new product. It was gruelling work – and Waits met resistance all down the line. But, as he told Sylvie Simmons in 2004: "I think I *wanted* some resistance. So that I could really be genuinely committed to what I wanted to do. I didn't want it to be too easy. It wasn't!"

NOTES

1 *Innocent When You Dream*, Ed. Mac Montandon
2 Timothy White
3 Dan Daley, *Sound On Sound*
4 Barney Hoskyns

CHAPTER 10

TOM WAITS' third album, 1975's *Nighthawks At The Diner*, was Bones Howe's attempt to capture the chatty nature of Waits in concert. "Tom was a great performer onstage," Howe recalled, "and Herb Cohen and I both had a sense that we needed to bring out the jazz in Waits more clearly."[1]

Howe was keen to recreate the intimacy of a club venue, which he thought would be ideal for a vinyl Polaroid of Waits on stage. He felt that a small jazz combo and a friendly audience was bound to be more receptive to Waits' style than the antipathetic Frank Zappa crowd.

"Herb gave out tickets to all his friends, we set up a bar, put potato chips on the tables, and we had a sell-out, two nights, two shows a night . . ." Howe remembered of the *Nighthawks . . .* sessions. "I remember that the opening act was a stripper. Her name was Dewana . . . it put the room in exactly the right mood. Then Waits came out and sang 'Emotional Weather Report'. Then he turned around to face the band and read the classified section of the paper while they played. It was like Allen Ginsberg with a really, really good band."[2]

Nighthawks At The Diner opens with our hero wishing: "An inebriated good evening to you all." This was, in itself, one of the things that put Waits firmly *outside* the pack. After all, one of the defining characteristics of mid-Seventies rock'n'roll was the drugs. Long before there was Slash, Shaun Ryder or Primal Scream, there was Keith Richards, whom God preserve . . .

Drink was what your dad did when he got in from work; drunk was what your parents got at the weekend. The bright young things sought their Nirvana at the end of a joint, or searched for Shangri-La on a sugar cube . . . They certainly didn't choose anything so staid as looking at life through the bottom of a bottle.

In the Seventies, with the concept of an "alternative lifestyle" almost as important as the music, drugs were the key to opening *The Doors Of Perception* – not for numbing you against the dull reality of the everyday. Drugs were rock'n'roll. Their world, even their language, was a closed book to workaday society. Narcotics could transport you to a land of "tangerine trees and marmalade skies"; allow you to set the controls for the heart of the sun; offer a fully paid passage to the strange, brightly lit new new worlds of *Sgt Pepper* and *Their Satanic Majesties*.

Drugs allowed you access to secret, hidden worlds your parents hadn't even dreamed of. With a little help from your friends (and their dealers) you could take a trip in the company of The Rolling Stones' basement jinks on 'Dead Flowers'; snigger along on the road with Jackson Browne's 'Cocaine'; or visit the haunted landscape of Dylan's 'Mr Tambourine Man' . . .

Drink was old-fashioned, and – worse still – legal. It was what "straights" used to relax themselves, to blunt their fears; to help their workaday selves escape for a brief few hours from the pinched reality of their suburban lives. Alcohol was for Sinatra and his crumbling Rat Pack buddies, not for the new messiahs of rock'n'roll. But then, from early on, Tom Waits had far more in common with Frank than, for example, Blue Cheer.

Waits' reputation preceded him. So his audience knew exactly where he was coming from, when he cracked the now familiar: "I don't have a drink problem, 'cept when I can't get a drink." It was becoming clear that this was no "new Dylan"; this was, if anything, a slightly more sprightly Dean Martin. But if there was not a drink problem, there was still an image problem. Tom Waits was simply not *cool*. Journalists sat and watched as glasses were raised, bottles were emptied and endless toasts made: "Raise up the bottle and throw back the rum," Waits would roar, "look out liver, here I come!" It was not an image that many found endearing at the time.

For a while back there, Waits' sales had been running neck and neck with another of the "new Dylans" so beloved of the mid–Seventies record industry. But Waits' third album, *Nighthawks At The Diner*, did little to spread his appeal to an audience outside of those cloistered in the Tropicana Motel. Bruce Springsteen's third album, on the other hand, was *Born To Run*.

Nighthawks At The Diner really should have been a better souvenir of Tom Waits live in concert. On stage, Waits is a consummate performer, a raconteur of the recherché, and a genuine wit. He commands the stage, hugs the spotlight, and connects with his audience. *Nighthawks At The Diner*, though, just missed the basket.

Waits seems to be trying just *too* hard here – like he's trying to convince you he's as hard-boiled as Leadbelly, as reckless as Kerouac, as lived-in as Woody Guthrie. He certainly looked the part – his stage suit gave off the hum that it had been squatted in by Munchkins. He sounded different too, the warm-edged balladeer of 1973 had gone, replaced by the voice of a grouchy, grubby, nicotine-stained old uncle.

Throughout the set – a double album on its original release – Waits tosses one-liners at the boisterous audience like firecrackers: "I'm so goddam horny the crack o'dawn better be careful around me . . . make like a hockey player, and get the puck outta here . . . plant you now, dig you later . . ." And then there was the old favourite: "She's been married so many times, she got rice marks all over her face."

The crowd, peppered up on free beer, lap it up and whoop at every Angeleno reference. But many of the references are lost on anyone outside the immediate Los Angeles area. Waits chuckles at his own one-liners, but this was a self-indulgent set and a mite contrived. The whole affair was just too laboured. Too little, too early . . .

Musically, Waits was happily ensconced in the sax, piano, bass and brushed drums territory that would preoccupy him for a further five years. But for all its flaws, *Nighthawks At The Diner* did offer glimpses of a nascent originality, as when a lyric found it "colder than a ticket taker's smile at the Ivar Theater on a Saturday night". And the songs *read* better than they *sounded*: the lengthy impressions of 'Nighthawk Postcards' are rich in tangible detail: the El train, rumbling across the trestles, sounding "like the ghost of Gene Krupa"; "the whispering brushes of wet radials on wet pavement"; or the asthmatic riffing as you quit a bar in "Putnam County": through the "warm narcotic American night" on your homeward journey.

But 'Better Off Without A Wife' sounded half-formulated, like an out-take from his second album. And, even this early on in his career, 'Warm Beer And Cold Women' already seems like self-parody. While Waits' scat interludes sound like what they are: a po' little white boy trying to make himself seem ol' and black.

Ironically, Waits' best performance on this set came with the only cover. 'Big Joe & Phantom 309' was a 1967 hit for the country singer Red Sovine – actually written by Tommy Faile, not Sovine as Waits says on the record. It is, even by country and western standards, a spectacularly glutinous example. A mawkish hitch-hiker's tale of schoolchildren saved by the sacrifice of a ghostly truck driver. Trucking songs were all the rage that year, on the back of C.W. McCall's 'Convoy'; and Waits relishes the telling. He plays it straight, to a stand-up bass and his own guitar backing.

Describing the clientele in 'Eggs & Sausage', Waits was clearly pinpointing his own audience too: "nighthawks at the diner . . . strangers around the coffee urn . . . gypsy hacks, insomniacs". These were the same characters who peopled the black-and-white photographs of Diane Arbus – and, of course, they were the bleakly coloured protagonists of Edward Hopper's best known painting, from which Waits' third album borrowed its title.

Hopper began painting *Nighthawks* in January 1942, and for many, it remains a defining image of alienation. In 2004, A.A. Gill wrote of *Nighthawks* that it was "one of the most famous and familiar images of the twentieth century". It's night time, and four figures sit separately, spread around the counter of a New York diner. Outside it's big-city dark; inside it should be cosy and warm, but there is something about the distance between the diners in which the artist suggests menace. Something sinister, almost Hitchcockian, about the hunched figure mysteriously sitting with his back to the painter. Although nominally together, the positions of the grey-hatted man and his companion in the red dress, convey dislocation and separation. Mesmerising and somehow deeply touching, *Nighthawks* is about loneliness, lack of communication and a sense of isolation – in the midst of a city of millions.

Waits' album cover half-heartedly mocks the Hopper painting, with the singer slouching in a diner, staring at the camera. As double live albums of the Seventies go, *Nighthawks At The Diner* is nowhere near as involving as Van Morrison's *It's Too Late To Stop Now* or Bob Dylan & The Band's *Before The Flood*. For all its faults though, it is demonstrably superior to Crosby, Stills, Nash & Young's *4 Way Street* and offers up a lot more laughs than *Frampton Comes Alive*.

The sound Waits had in mind for *Nighthawks At The Diner* was that conjured up on the 1957 album *Kerouac/Allen*: "It's Jack Kerouac telling stories, with Steve Allen playing piano behind him. That album sort of sums up the whole thing. That's what gave me the idea to do some spoken word pieces myself."[3]

The impact and influence of Jean-Louis Lebris de Kerouac on Thomas Alan Waits cannot be overestimated. Still in short trousers when *On The Road* was first published, as a teenager Waits, like untold thousands of others, absorbed Kerouac's freewheeling texts as if his life depended on it. In image, style and influence, Waits was clearly and seriously enamoured of the man from Lowell, Massachusetts.

Along with Elvis and James Dean, Jack Kerouac offered a generation chafing against the stifling conformity of Fifties middle America, the tantalising prospect of liberation. Sure, the United States was still basking in the security and stability of the Eisenhower presidency, which ran from 1952 to 1960. But, for many of those cradled at the bosom of consumerism, there just felt like there should be . . . *more*.

Americans of the Fifties were a whole new breed . . . While accounting for just 6 per cent of the world's population, Americans drove 60 per cent of the world's cars, chattered away on 58 per cent of the world's telephones and listened to the newfangled rock'n'roll on 40 per cent of its radios. And – chafing or not – American teenagers were not above enjoying this new-found prosperity: in 1959, it was estimated that they had $400 a year each to just fritter away – and teenage girls spent $20 million a year on lipstick alone.

There was just so *much* to spend it all on – and so much *choice*. Cars that looked like spaceships; television sets built like mahogany cathedrals; machines that did the washing-up for you; crisp white shirts which would never need ironing . . . There were record players . . . refrigerators . . . washing machines . . . vacuum cleaners . . . all tumbling off the production line. There were even restaurants, banks and cinemas that you could visit without leaving your car!

But for all the temptations of this consumer paradise, many felt there was something missing at its core. And for some, not wholly seduced by the complacent prosperity of life under Eisenhower, nagging, corrosive doubts began to surface. Deep below the shiny wipe-clean surface, there was a slippery snake of uncertainty slithering through this drive-thru Eden.

In 1957, those who had already felt that uncertainty found their holy writ in Kerouac's *On The Road*. In its crazy, capering odyssey were found echoes of other American revolutions of the era – of the cocksure rock'n' roll, epitomised by Elvis, and the confused teenage rebeldom of James Dean. Kerouac's bop-inspired, Benzedrine-fuelled prose sounded a clarion call of liberation.

On The Road offered up sexual emancipation, drug experimentation and mystical searching – all wrapped up in a heady literary frenzy. While the sales of *On The Road* could not match those of Grace Metalious' near-contemporaneous steamy, suburban saga *Peyton Place*, its impact was seismic.

While he was not the first "beat", nor the genre's longest lasting exemplar, Jack Kerouac – like Scott Fitzgerald – could be said to have "invented a generation". Not long after *On The Road* was published, *Playboy* magazine was offering its readers the opportunity to purchase "a beat generation sweatshirt".

While Kerouac couldn't wait to get out of Lowell, Charles Dickens, a century earlier, had been quite charmed of the place. Lowell was a nine-teenth-century model town, its cotton mills the very acme of modern technology. On his first visit in 1842, Dickens said his time spent in the Massachusetts town was "the happiest day" of his journey. But what the author of *Bleak House* found so appealing, the author of *On The Road* couldn't wait to get away from.

"The beat emphasis was on escape," Margaret Drabble wrote in *The Oxford Companion To English Literature*, "from conventional, puritanical, middle-class (termed 'square') mores, towards visionary enlightenment and artistic improvisation, approached via (Zen) Buddhism and other echoes of religious confessional, such as Red Indian and Mexican Peyote cults; also through drive and accelerations charged by wheels, drugs, sex, drink or talk."

It was that intoxicating sense of freedom offered by Kerouac that chimed so well with the American psyche. The anti-heroes of *On The Road* – Sal Paradise (Kerouac) and Dean Moriarty (Neal Cassady) – are adventurers, explorers and dreamers in the tradition of Hawkeye, Huckle-berry Finn and Melville's Ishmael.

For many at the time, including the teenage Bob Dylan – and later for Tom Waits – *On The Road* was a sacred text. Kerouac's inspired riffing appeared to offer an alternative to that stifling suburban existence. Comfortable and consoling as mid-Fifties America was to those of their parents' generation (not least because they had lived through World War II), their children were now rebelling against the dullness of a life already mapped out to mirror those of their parents. Their resentment of a mundane nine-to-five future was given exhilarating voice in *On The Road*.

"My own background was very middle class," Waits wistfully told me, while reflecting on Kerouac. "I was desperately keen to get away . . . I loved Kerouac since I first discovered him, he really helped me decide what I wanted to do. I discovered him at a time when I could have ended up at Lockheed Aircraft, or a jewellery store or a gas station, married at 19 with three children, lying on a beach . . . a lot of Americans went off on the road, just to be able to get into a car and drive for 3,000 miles, east or west . . ." Although, ironically, it wasn't until he heard Kerouac *reading* his best-known work that Waits "suddenly got it, and I went back and I read that and *The Subterraneans*, and I understood".

On The Road tapped into the zeitgeist of the bored and disillusioned mid-Fifties young American, hungry for life and fresh sensation. "They go on wild parties or sit in joints listening to hot trumpets . . . always moving, drinking, making love, determined to say Yes to any new experience . . ." ran the novel's original blurb.

The success of *On The Road* sent Kerouac into meltdown. Overnight, he became known as the spokesman of the beat generation. Even now, half a century on, the power and impact of *On The Road* remains undiminished. Kerouac's subsequent novels, however, were an unsatisfactory melange of Buddhism, alcoholism and cynicism. He died in 1969, aged only 47, back with his mother in his childhood home of Lowell, Massachusetts – a bitter, broken, forgotten drunk. It was reported that he died with less than $100 in his bank account; a few years ago, the original manuscript of *On The Road*, typed on its infamous 120-foot scroll, was sold at auction for $2.4 million.

Brian Case once asked Waits if Ann Charters' iconoclastic biography of Kerouac hadn't pricked the myth of the King of the Beats? "No," said Waits, "I actually prefer to see the other side. He wasn't a hero who could do no wrong. He saw a lot, got around. He wasn't nearly as mad and impetuous as Neal Cassady."

The Kerouac myth still endures, nearly 40 years after his death and half a century since the publication of *On The Road*. Though, typically, San Francisco's City Lights bookstore, the centre of much beat activity, has more biographies *of* Kerouac in stock than books *by* Kerouac.

Hailed as the King of the Beats, Kerouac was also a walking contradiction (partly truth and partly fiction, Kris Kristofferson might add): a Buddhist who was vehemently anti-Semitic; a liberated bohemian who was madly misogynistic; the man who sent a generation out on the road, but always returned to his mother's side . . .

On The Road provided a template for the next generation, the baby-boomers who in the Sixties found themselves liberated but adrift. Kerouac scorned the hippies who idolised him, and who went on to commemorate and venerate Kerouac in song. Van Morrison, Paul Simon and 10,000 Maniacs are among the many who, over the years, have namechecked the beat guru. In 1997 a CD *kicks joy darkness* had Michael Stipe, Steven Tyler, Patti Smith, Jeff Buckley, Joe Strummer et al. adapting Kerouac texts to music. Waits himself got to put some atmospheric music behind Kerouac later: long-lost acetates of the author reading from *On The Road* were found amongst Kerouac's papers, and subsequently released on a 1999 CD, *Jack Kerouac Reads On The Road*, which featured a Waits collaboration with cult band Primus.

Following in the footsteps of Bob Dylan – as seen in *Renaldo & Clara* – I went looking for Kerouac's grave when I visited Lowell. Unlike Dylan, though, I couldn't find it. Mind you, Bob did have Allen Ginsberg on hand to help him find Jack's final resting place. When I was in Lowell, looking for the cemetery, my request for information was relayed to the barman thus: "Any idea where they buried that sonofabitch Kerouac?" I never found the grave to pay my little homage – it would have been so much easier, my companion remarked, if they buried them alphabetically.

Waits was luckier; he made his own pilgrimage to Lowell and found the grave, where he paid his tribute. His impressions of the place though were not so favourable: he described Lowell to me as "dark . . . like Liverpool".

After the release of *Nighthawks At The Diner*, it was back on the road again for Tom Waits, to try and generate interest in his current product. It was during 1976 that Waits undertook a famously "disastrous" week-long residency at Reno Sweeney's in Manhattan. But then Waits was no stranger to tough gigs: "I've played places where the average age was deceased," he once admitted.

Now, though, touring was beginning to take its toll, as Waits told David Wild in *Rolling Stone* at the time: "I was sick through that whole period . . . I'd been travelling quite a lot, living in hotels, eating bad food, drinking a lot – too much. There's a lifestyle that's there before you arrive, and you're introduced to it. It's unavoidable."

When he wasn't out on the road, Waits was back at the Tropicana Motel, hunkering down with Rickie Lee Jones. "I love her madly in my own way," Waits admitted. "You'll gather that our relationship wasn't exactly like Mike Todd and Elizabeth Taylor – but she scares me to death."[4]

Another beatnik resident of the Tropicana, Chuck E. Weiss, was soon to be immortalised in song by Waits' girlfriend. A native of Denver, this was the man of whom Waits once said: "Chuck E. Weiss is the sort of guy who'd sell you a rat's ass as a wedding ring – and I'm the sort of guy who'd buy a dozen of 'em!"

Chuck E. was working in the kitchen of the Troubadour while Rickie Lee was performing there, and it was he who introduced her to her soon-to-be beau Tom. The three quickly hooked up, dodging out of the Tropicana to hop freight trains and sleep beneath the Hollywood sign. Waits later namechecked Weiss on 'Jitterbug Boy' and 'I Wish I Was In New Orleans'; and Weiss also got a co-writing credit for 'Spare Parts' on Waits' *Nighthawks At The Diner*.

But it was sometime around 1979, that immortality finally came the Weiss way: "There was a telephone call from Denver one day," Rickie

Waiting… (LFI)

The "new Dylan", just after signing to
Asylum in 1973. (MICHAEL OCHS ARCHIVE/REDFERNS)

Waits on his first trip to London, 1976.
(MICHAEL OCHS ARCHIVE/REDFERNS)

On the road. (MICHAEL PUTLAND/RETNA)

Waits (left) at book launch, New York, 1975.
(RICHARD E AARON/REDFERNS)

Waits in Portobello Road, London, May 1976.

Waits at the Bottom Line, New York, December 1976. (RICHARD E AARON/REDFERNS)

Still smoking after all these years… New York, 1977. (EBET ROBERTS/REDFERNS)

Waits, 1978. (ALAIN DISTER/REDFERNS)

Telling tales, 1978.

(HULTON ARCHIVE/GETTY IMAGES)

Closing time, sometime in the Boho 70s.

(GEMS/REDFERNS)

Waits with Rickie Lee Jones.

(ADRIAN BOOT/URBAN IMAGE.TV)

Waits in the studio, LA, 1980. (HENRY DILTZ/CORBIS)

Guitar Man, onstage in London. (BARRY PLUMMER)

'You can't keep singing like that;
you'll end up like Frank Sinatra.'…
'What? Rich and powerful?'. (BARRY PLUMMER)

With his wife Kathleen at premiere of
One From The Heart, New York, 1982.
(TIME & LIFE PICTURES/GETTY IMAGES)

Waits in Rotterdam, February 1983.
(ROB VERHORST/REDFERNS)

'Time is a funny thing…', Waits in *Rumble Fish,* 1983. (UNIVERSAL/THE KOBAL COLLECTION)

Waits recovers after meeting with biographer, London 1981. (ADRIAN BOOT/RETNA)

Lee remembered, "and it was Chuck E. And Waits hung up the phone and said 'Chuck E.'s in love.' I just made the rest of the song up."[5]

Rickie Lee Jones could be spotted on the cover of Waits' album *Blue Valentine*, when it was released in 1978 – and that same year, a four-song demo she had recorded found its way to Warner Bros. The esteemed Lowell George of Little Feat took a shine to 'Easy Money', one of the songs from Rickie Lee's demo, and decided to cut it for his only solo album, *Thanks I'll Eat Here*. That led to Rickie Lee signing to Warner Bros . . . which led to her 1979 hit, 'Chuck E.'s In Love' . . . which in turn resulted in a Grammy for the 25-year-old.

It all happened very quickly – and by the end of the Seventies, in commercial terms, Rickie Lee was streets ahead of her boyfriend.

On the back of his 1979 infamy, Chuck E. Weiss recorded an album, *The Other Side Of Town*, which came out in 1981 but is now long-deleted. He then undertook an 11-year residency at West Hollywood's Central nightclub. Located on Sunset Strip, the club was later renamed the Viper Club by its new owner Johnny Depp.

In 1998 Chuck E. released his second album, *Extremely Cool*. The imprimatur of Tom Waits was all over the album – and his influence could also be felt when Chuck E. put down the 18-year absence between albums, saying simply: "I was distracted." Waits collaborated on two new songs with Weiss, 'It Rains On Me' and 'Do You Know What I Idi Amin'. "Chuck E. Weiss sings like the devil is chasing him," Waits admiringly observed.

Back in the Seventies, 'Chuck E's In Love' sounded so different to everything else that was around that, on its release, Rickie Lee was hurled immediately into the spotlight, her career quickly eclipsing that of Waits. The press seemed only vaguely aware of a boyfriend, who was also "in the business".

"I get compared a lot to Tom Waits," Rickie Lee told Timothy White, "and I can understand it only from the point of view that we're both writing about street characters. Our writing and our singing styles have nothing in common, I think. But we walk around the same streets, and I guess it's primarily a jazz-motivated situation for both of us. We're living on the jazz side of life, the other side of the tracks, and it's a real insecure, constant improvisation."

However, there was some professional cross-over: Waits wrote the beautiful 'Rainbow Sleeves' for Rickie Lee – and though he has never recorded it, her version enhanced the soundtrack to Scorsese's *King Of Comedy*. In the end, the main reason given for the sundering of their relationship was said to be the usual incompatibility of two artists maintaining separate careers.

Their split coincided with another change in Waits' domestic arrangements. Though, typically, when Waits' residence at the Tropicana Motel also came to an end in 1979, he insisted that the reason was: "They got tired of cleaning it. It's like black socks, you never have to wash them." Cleaned or not, the Tropicana managed to stumble along without Waits and his compadres for almost another decade – until in 1988, it was finally demolished.

By then, though, Tom Waits was long gone.

NOTES

1 Dan Daley, *Sound On Sound*
2 Dan Daley, *Sound On Sound*
3 Todd Everett, *Melody Maker*
4 Timothy White
5 Timothy White

CHAPTER 11

THROUGHOUT much of his 26 years, Tom Waits had heard vague but disturbing rumours of a world outside the Tropicana Motel, beyond Hollywood and Vine. Midway through 1976, he went looking for it.

There had been a modicum of interest from the UK in Waits' "emotional weather reports", so Asylum decided to run the risk of letting him loose in London. Actually, it was Warner Bros that paid the bill, as Asylum was now part of the mighty WEA (Warner-Elektra-Asylum) conglomerate. The sales of Waits' first three albums wouldn't even have covered the label's chiropody bills, but they should worry. During 1975–6, Warner-related labels had enjoyed number one albums from the likes of Led Zeppelin, Linda Ronstadt and The Rolling Stones; there were also a couple apiece from the Eagles and Fleetwood Mac, both of whom chalked up multi-platinum sellers. *The Eagles Greatest Hits, 1971–1975* remains the best-selling album ever released in North America – and that was before *Hotel California* – while the Anglo-American Fleetwood Mac's *Rumours* wasn't far behind.

So, one way and another, there was enough pocket money rattling around Burbank to send young Tommy off on a trip abroad. Waits had never left America before, but he was soon ensconced at the President Hotel in London's Bloomsbury – it proved an appropriate location, with one visiting journalist describing it with relish as "sleazy".

For his British debut, Waits was booked to appear at Ronnie Scott's Club, at Frith Street in the heart of Soho. In 1976, Soho was still considered sufficiently sordid to raise an eyebrow. For many years, the bohemian colony at the centre of London, Soho had been the slash of vermilion lipstick across the grey face of the capital.

Back in 1976, British licensing hours still restricted daytime drinking to between 11 a.m. and 3 p.m. – lest there should be another sudden outbreak of World War I. But Soho was known as the place where you could quench your thirst in various subterranean shebeens when the pubs were shut. Strip-clubs also boasted their neon wares above ground; and there were adult bookstores, coffee shops and bars. For many Soho spelt "exotic": from the ladies of the night, who still went out on parade, to the lingering – and rather un-British – aroma of freshly ground coffee. And Waits just loved it.

Ronnie's was the premier jazz venue in London. Since opening in 1959, the club had played host to every leading jazzer over on a visit – from Duke Ellington to Count Basie. It was also where The Who premiered *Tommy* – and, in 1970, the location of Jimi Hendrix's last-ever appearance. Scott himself still played host on occasion, immortalising his club with his droll wit: "This place reminds me of home – filthy, and full of strangers."

There are a feast of Scott stories that Waits would have relished, but I cannot resist retelling my favourite: at saxophonist Tubby Hayes' funeral, jazz critic Benny Green was having terrible back problems. He could hardly walk, so his wife got special dispensation to drive their car up to the graveside. The only way Green could get out was to have his wife pull him, feet first, through the hatch-back. Observing this elaborate procedure as he passed on his way to the internment, Ronnie Scott murmured dryly: "Hardly seems worth going home, does it?"

The section of the UK music press that turned out to greet Waits on his inaugural trip was, by and large, favourably impressed. Although by 1976, most music writers had made the transatlantic hop, visiting Americans were still greeted with respect, if not as the rare and exotic creatures from a faraway country they were before the arrival of the jumbo jet.

Waits was particularly appealing – and particularly welcome. He arrived on the shores of England's green and pleasant at a time when rock was going through one of its periodic flaccid moments, and Waits didn't disappoint. Looking like the sort of man who'd rather disembowel himself than enter a disco, and sounding like a freight train . . . here was someone soused in the America of Jack Kerouac and Chet Baker.

Back home, even *Newsweek* was beginning to sit up and take notice; though a 1976 profile of Waits found him looking "more like a guest in a fleabag hotel than a rising new singer with three popular albums".

For the pinched and starved UK market, however, that down-at-heel authenticity was a big part of Waits' charm. British journalists of the baby-boom generation were enchanted by the very idea of beat culture. Many who had read *On The Road* following its publication in 1957 cherished Kerouac's novel as a fabulous fantasy. Meandering in the family's Morris Minor on a B-road to Paignton for donkey rides somehow lacked the urgency of gunning a '56 Chevy over the Mexican border to crash a Tijuana bordello. And here, at last, was a real live dharma bum.

Lenny Bruce had made it to Soho before Waits, but he was deported after insinuating, among other things, that Prince Charles was really a 40-year-old midget. A baffled Peter Cook remembered trying in vain to score heroin for Bruce, and having to settle instead for some aspirin he cadged off Dudley Moore.

For British journalists, Waits' character was immediately appealing, and – better still – he was eminently quotable . . . For far too long during the Seventies, rock stars had used the pages of *Melody Maker* or *New Musical Express* as a platform for their half-baked philosophies. It was all so very *earnest*. Then Waits flew in, firing – most entertainingly – on all cylinders, and a good time was had by all. There were some dissenters who accused him of being a sham, a poseur; but, for the most part, they soon got over it.

Certain people, however, still had reservations about his relevance. In particular, a number of rock critics, exhilarated by the raw power of punk rock which was just beginning to manifest itself when Waits made his UK debut, considered his shambling Boho chic contrived. At a time when, once again, "authenticity" (in this case, the street cred of the punks) was venerated, there was also a tendency to believe that, musically, anything American, contemporary and on a major label was tainted by bland super-ficiality, whether it was Fleetwood Mac, the Eagles or disco. "I'm so *bored* with the USA . . ." The Clash were singing, as Waits' plane touched down on British soil.

Still, the new kid in town patently didn't give a shit. He was glad to be working, on parole from the Tropicana, and keen to find out as much as he could about London life. I remember the late John Platt of *Zig Zag* telling me of his experiences when he interviewed Waits on that first UK trip. The American – plainly plastered, but extremely convivial company – apparently spent a convoluted 45 minutes shaggy-dogging an unrepeat-able joke about the country stars Hank Snow and June Carter. Platt, in turn, found himself convincing Waits that he was the model for Ralph the Dog on TV's *The Muppet Show*. Waits had never seen the hugely popular programme, which was actually made in the UK, but he was nonetheless enchanted by the idea of being the role model for a puppet dog.

Peter O'Brien remembers one particular encounter, which consisted of accompanying Waits on a pub crawl through Soho, while the visiting American declared himself singularly impressed by the variety of beer on tap. Waits was also fascinated by English slang, diligently noting any that caught his attention ("You call 'em French letters here?")

Another tale of the time had an infatuated Joe Strummer turning up at Ronnie Scott's after Waits put his name on the guest list. When summoned to greet his guest, Waits appeared in a knee-length black coat, and according to Pete Silverton in *Vox*: "stared hard and blank at Strummer, then reached into his coat and pulled a pint of freshly poured Guinness from an inner pocket, drank it right off and told the doorman to let Strummer in". The timing was certainly right; Strummer later admitted a fondness for Waits' work. But did it actually happen, Waits was later asked. "Gee, it's a *great* story . . ." the visitor concurred, "I go more for a great story than what really happened."

At a time when Frampton was coming alive, Tom Waits was slumped into Ronnie Scott's, half-dead. His London debut was memorable as much for what he said, as what he sang. Taking to the tiny stage at Ronnie's, Waits took in the small but appreciative audience, and nodded. As if confirming a fact to himself, he acknowledged to the happy breed: "I've been riding on the crest of a slump lately."

Those early shows demonstrated a genuinely maverick talent. But it was, as yet, unfocused and rambling. The songs had their moments of originality and insight, but Waits was still sounding out the songs for his masterpiece, *Small Change*, while relying on the *Nighthawks At The Diner* repertoire. But it was the image which was the most striking element of his performance, and that veered somewhere between sham and shambolic.

There were also problems with the venue. ("Most nightclubs are more concerned with serving lager than putting a spotlight on you, or giving you a decent sound system.") But overall, Waits enjoyed the experience, and being in one place long enough to change clothes was a welcome novelty.

It was while in London during 1976 that Waits wrote what many regard as one of his defining songs, 'Tom Traubert's Blues'. It was a song of dislocation and transient exile, written on the run. Indeed, much of what became *Small Change* was fashioned in London, following Waits' European dates in Scandinavia, Holland, Belgium and Germany.

The incessant touring in the States, and the nightly appearances before unsympathetic, and sometimes openly aggressive, audiences had left their mark on Waits – particularly because he had found no time to write ("always someone pulling on your coat"). Now, in the comparative isolation and anonymity of Europe, he could lock himself away and write. In London, Waits fashioned 20 new songs, eleven of which (including 'Tom Traubert . . .') made it onto *Small Change*.

Talking to *NME*'s Fred Dellar, Waits admitted to new songs called: 'A Briefcase & The Blues', 'Frank Is Here' (a decade before *Frank's Wild Years*), and 'Whitey Ford', though he conceded: "A lot of them haven't been written yet, but I got the titles!" Thirty years on, it appears they're still just titles.

Most of the British critics were willing to give Waits the benefit of the doubt during his debut at Ronnie Scott's. But he was plainly still an unknown quantity – indeed, the *New Musical Express* review even credited the artist as "Tom Wits". There were hecklers, but Waits loyalists duked it out. Reviewing the show in *NME*, the ageless Fred Dellar noted "a suit . . . straight from the great LA misfits sale of '48 . . . a cap that's more worn than a Ronnie Scott joke".

Fronting a band of tenor sax, double bass and drums, Waits himself did pithy from the piano stool. He was cheerfully disparaging about his own playing abilities: "I'd never cut it as a sideman," he told Fred Dellar. "I just accompany . . . I'm glad to have my band with me, they're a real hi-voltage bebop trio."

The set at Ronnie's drew from his three albums, with a frenetic 'Diamonds On My Windshield' proving a notable highlight. Waits quit the stage with the tried and tested "plant you now, dig you later", apparently more interested in reading the racing form than the audience response. But he didn't need to worry. "The fans and hecklers unite in their applause," Dellar noted, "the low-life loser's won again."

Beguiled by Soho, though disturbed by what he called the nation's "sandwich crisis", Waits returned home to begin recording, leaving behind a few more hard-won fans. In his mind was an album, which he had provisionally titled Pasties & A G-string. "I'm going back to Los Angeles to get as drunk as a skunk and stay that way for three days, then I'm going right into the studio."

It was while he was visiting here on that first trip in 1976 that I first saw Waits perform; sadly, not at Ronnie's, but making his UK television debut. At the time, there were only two TV pop programmes – hell, there were still only *three* channels. Pop fans had to wait for Thursday night's *Top Of The Pops*; while the, uh, "serious" *MM* and *NME*-reading types found succour on *The Old Grey Whistle Test*, scheduled whenever BBC2 had an empty insomniac slot.

Waits made his *Whistle Test* appearance on May 3, 1976, in a show that also boasted a live set from Roger McGuinn's Thunderbyrd – which was more to the taste of genial host, "Whisperin' " Bob Harris.

Punk had yet to intrude on the cosy world of *Whistle Test* – even Elvis Costello didn't make his debut on the programme until 1983. So, for the moment, *Whistle Test* was populated by three distinct types of act: power trios . . . bass and drums supporting a guitarist whose solos went on longer than the last European land war; American bands with long hair . . . all of them masking their misery at not being in the Eagles, while enjoining us to "boogie" at periodic intervals; and "Art Rock" outfits . . . collections of doleful looking individuals, all of whom had been in Gong, who failed to recognise either melody, rhythm or song structure.

Then Waits slumped on to perform 'Tom Traubert's Blues' – and I was mesmerised. It was late – I was probably just in from the pub – but here was genuine pathos. Here was real *wit*. Rock, back then, was dreadfully serious and straight-faced. There was no place for laughter listening to a Pink Floyd album; no time for levity while reflecting on the wisdom of Genesis. But the very look – and *sound* – of Tom Waits immediately set you chuckling. Here, at last, was the sort of cove you could imagine sharing a pint of porter with.

As Waits moved on to 'The Piano Has Been Drinking', he seemed to stumble into his stride. He sounded like he hadn't slept since 1959, and looked like the kind of guy who'd picket an Emerson, Lake & Palmer concert. From memory, though, Waits went down about as well as a cardiac arrest in a lift.

Waits was more shabby thrift-store than shiny new, but he was, at least, refreshingly different from everything else around. Watching Waits that night, way back in the Seventies, was in Vivian Stanshall's immortal comparison, like "being handed a saveloy, blindfold at a gay party".

CHAPTER 12

B Y the time of its release in 1976, Tom Waits had settled on the title *Small Change* for his fourth album. And, for the first time on disc, he was threatening to match up to the talent that critics, his manager and Waits himself had promised for so long. Bones Howe was once again behind the board, and *Small Change* also found Waits in some new good company – most notably, drummer Shelly Manne. Over the years Manne had worked with most of the jazz legends, listing Coleman Hawkins, Stan Kenton, Woody Herman and Chet Baker on his CV.

Recorded in a five-day blitz during July 1976, *Small Change* testified to every claim ever made on Waits' behalf. It was also the album which proved, beyond doubt, that Waits was more than just a hangover from the Fifties. On this evidence, here was a major talent of the Seventies, more than ready to stand in his own right.

The Waits voice was finding its own level, descending into the familiar gravelly timbre that we now associate with the man. But back then, it was a jolting experience. After the detour of *Nighthawks At The Diner*, he was also back at home with a good tune: 'Tom Traubert's Blues' and 'I Wish I Was In New Orleans' remain two of Waits' loveliest-ever melodies.

Bones Howe later recalled the *Small Change* sessions, all recorded on two-track at Wally Heider's studio in Hollywood. It was a time when bands like Fleetwood Mac, the Eagles and Pink Floyd were determined to build their albums up, using an increasingly large number of tracks to enable them to nip and tuck to their heart's content. Not so Waits and his producer: "Jazz is more about getting a good take, not about having a lot of tracks to mix . . ." Howe pointed out. "We set up at Heider's for that record the same way I used to make jazz records in the Fifties. I wanted to take Tom back to that direction of making records, with an orchestra and Tom in the same room, all playing and singing together. I was never afraid of making a record where the musicians all breathed the same air."[1]

The success of *Small Change* was particularly notable at a time when many of Waits' fellow "new Dylans" were in all kinds of trouble. The hype surrounding 1975's *Born To Run* had left a sour taste, and immediately afterwards Bruce Springsteen found himself locked in a legal quagmire that would keep him out of the recording studio for the next three years. By 1976, Rita Coolidge had married Kris Kristofferson – and they had started making albums together . . . While John Prine, Steve Goodman, Loudon Wainwright and Steve Forbert just hadn't carried through on their initial promise.

And, to make matters even worse for the "new Dylans", the real Bob had come back with a bang. The back to back albums *Blood On The Tracks* and *Desire* had seen him effortlessly recapture his crown in the singer-songwriter stakes; his extensive 1974 tour with The Band had been the most successful in rock's 30-year history; while 1975's guerrilla Rolling Thunder Review had helped Dylan maintain his air of mystery.

But if there was one crucial element that allied Waits to Dylan, it was that increasingly rare quality in pop music: a good sense of humour. While Dylan was rightly venerated as the conscience of a generation, for every 'Blowin' In The Wind' or 'The Times They Are A-Changin'' there was the deft satire of 'Tombstone Blues' or 'I Shall Be Free'. Waits too enjoyed a good joke.

Others, including Waits' favourite Martin Mull, had tried – but, for the most part, they had failed. *National Lampoon* were poking fun at rock icons on *Lemmings* (their John "I'm a fucking *genius*" Lennon; their "Hi, I'm Bob Dylan. Remember those fabulous Swinging Sixties . . .?"). But by 1976 the rock fraternity were taking *themselves* very, very seriously indeed. With the Bonzo Dog Band split, there was precious little to laugh at (save for solo albums from David Crosby or Graham Nash; or [teehee] *joint* albums from David Crosby and Graham Nash) – and the funniest thing about Alberto Y Lost Trios Paranoias was their name.

Even Waits' nemesis, Frank Zappa, had gone from being a witty, iconoclastic social commentator to an increasingly serious neo-classical dullard. You couldn't help but smile as the punk bands demolished such Sixties shibboleths as 'Help!' and 'Nights In White Satin'. But the humour there was largely amphetamine inspired and lager fuelled.

Small Change, though, was rich in wit and humour. 'Step Right Up', 'Pasties & A G-string', 'Bad Liver And A Broken Heart' and, particularly, 'The Piano Has Been Drinking' all emphasising the ready wit of the former pizza chef.

Even now, these songs – and Waits' delivery of them – are *funny*. 'The Piano Has Been Drinking' inhabits that late-night Hades, the club where you can't find a waitress, "even with a geiger counter"; where "the spotlight looks like a prison break" and the owner has "the IQ of a fence post". It was a song Waits regularly included in his sporadic concert appearances, and for many, 'The Piano Has Been Drinking' is the archetypal Waits song: the laconic, bar-room philosopher delivering pithy lyrics, in a voice that sounds like a garbage crusher.

'Jitterbug Boy' was a routine Waits had been ruminating over for some time, trying it out on hapless visiting journalists. The song was a loose-lipped farrago, 'bout the man resting on his laurels, who'd slept with Monroe, and taught Rocky Marciano and Louis Armstrong and Minnesota Fats everything they knew.

On 'Step Right Up' ("lyrics obtainable from 'Young Tom Waits, c/o the Tropicana Motor Hotel, Hollywood, California'", Waits helpfully advised on the sleeve) the composer offers a universal panacea. Delivered in Waits' engaging scat style, whatever "it" is: "entertains relatives" and "turns you into a nine-year-old Hindu boy"; it mows the lawn and picks up the kids from school. The song concludes with the sage advice: "the large print giveth, and the small print taketh away."

When we met, Waits had spoken at length of his affection for New Orleans, calling it fondly "the bosom of American music". This was the city they call the Big Easy, the birthplace of jazz. And the affection Waits felt was evident on 'I Wish I Was In New Orleans'. The singer hears a tenor saxophone calling him home, hears the band strike up 'When The Saints Go Marching In' beneath a Dixie moon. When I visited New Orleans' Preservation Hall, the home of jazz, it had a sign above the stage: "Requests $5. 'The Saints' $10!" New Orleans, where you weave your way across the French Quarter, and then, like a dream, see the streetcar with 'Desire' illuminated on the front, swaying along the tram tracks.

New Orleans, that most un-American of cities; where, as Kerouac wrote, the air "was so sweet . . . it seemed to come in soft bandanas". "There are a lot of places I like," Bob Dylan said recently, "but I like New Orleans better!" With so much of the history and culture of the city woven into the fabric of American life, the devastation of Hurricane Katrina in 2005 – and the criminally careless botched "clear-up" – seemed all the more tragic. Waits responded to the tragedy by donating a song – 'A Little Drop Of Poison' – to an album released to benefit the victims of Katrina.

For all its apparent flippancy, *Small Change* was also shot through with the songwriter's weary depiction of the low-lifes and bar-flies who populate the album. It's a shadowy, melancholy world where "the dreams ain't broken . . . they're walking with a limp"; a landscape where "the moon ain't romantic", but rather, "intimidating as hell".

'The One That Got Away', which recalled the menace of Elvis Costello's 'Watching The Detectives', was a Cadillac ride through film noir – but it wasn't alone. Indeed, required reading for *Small Change* rounded up all the usual suspects: Raymond Chandler, Nelson Algren, Dashiell Hammett, Mickey Spillane, Damon Runyon . . . You know how to read, doncha?

This was Tom Waits wishing he'd been out of short pants in time to play in the film of Runyon's *Guys And Dolls*, back of Marlon and Frank. Waits would have played the sort of cheesy character Brando's daddy warned him about: "Son, no matter how far you travel, or how smart you get, always remember this: some day, somewhere, a guy is going to come to you and show you a nice brand-new deck of cards on which the seal is never broken, and this guy is going to offer to bet you that the Jack of Spades will jump out of this deck and squirt cider in your ear. But son, do not bet him, for sure as you do, you are going to get an ear full of cider!"

Small Change has Waits sounding like the sort of guy who is happier sifting through yellowing back issues of *Modern Screen* than keeping abreast of the current scene via *Rolling Stone*. 'Bad Liver And A Broken Heart' opens and closes with a snatch of 'As Time Goes By'. On 'Invitation To The Blues', Waits' heroine is obviously modelled more on Rita Hayworth's *Gilda* than Stevie Nicks' white witch. The song is a mournful requiem, the sort of thing at which Waits excels: the waitress who's been abandoned by her sugar daddy, who never loved her anyway ("'cept at night"). But she's determined to claw her way up and out.

Waits sounds as grizzled as the city coroner on 'The One That Got Away' – a song from the wrong side of the tracks, where the undertaker casts a professional eye over the corpse and closes the casket. And it all ends on the nice euphemism for coffin – wooden kimono. The song is an embittered postcard to Los Angeles. Like a dismal screen test for all the failed actors who've lost their equilibrium, their car keys and their pride; for all the pianists who could have got the Dooley Wilson role in *Casablanca,* but didn't.

The album is littered with characters whose dreams have been hammered out on an anvil; dreamers who've left behind the small Texas town where the entire population turns out to watch the traffic lights change, and beelined that Greyhound straight for the City of Angels. And then when they get there, after a while, there's the growing, chill appreciation that this is *it*. Whatever tricks you turn, whoever you service and however desperate you get, you are never going to be anything more than a waitress, whose ambition is sagging as inexorably as the rest of her.

Los Angeles is a city built on dreams, and the movies were its foundation: "The girls come in from Nebraska," Waits told Brian Case, "wanna be in motion pictures. Where I live, I hear a lotta them stories. They end up on their backs in one of the rooms . . . there's a lot of sadness. I see a lot from where I'm living. I don't see much hope. Can't go any further West . . ."

No wonder then, that Waits shot *Small Change* through with all those broken motel dreams. No wonder that he made it a black-and-white world culled from the movies. And nowhere more so than on the title track, 'Small Change (Got Rained On With His Own .38)'.

"I even kinda impressed myself with that one," Waits admitted around the time of his film noir nightmare, citing as his source the Jack Webb film *Pete Kelly's Blues* ("The story of a jazz man of the wide-open twenties . . . caught in the crossfire of its blazing .38s!" shrieked the film's poster). The 1955 film starred Peggy Lee, Edmund O'Brien and Janet Leigh; a fast-moving tale of jazz musicians and gangsters, it was a kind of B-movie forerunner of *The Cotton Club*.

As a song, 'Small Change (Got Rained On With His Own .38)' is an atmospheric monochrome trailer, the story and back-story unfolding quickly, thanks to the keenness of Waits' eye for detail . . . You can just picture the hard-bitten cops (William Bendix and Arthur Kennedy, probably) "cracking jokes about some whore house in Seattle" while the body of the victim (John Garfield, almost certainly) lies next to the jukebox on the bloodied linoleum floor. But it's the racing form sticking out of his pocket, with Blue Boots circled for the third, that completes the poignant scene. The whores (Clare Trevor and Barbara Stanwyck, no strangers to such roles) have mouths "like razor blades and their eyes are like stilettos". Outside, in the yellow bargain-store light of the night, "naked mannequins with their Cheshire grins" stand silent as a siren splits the night, hauling itself into the distance, like some great wounded mastiff crawling off to die.

But come the penultimate verse, this familiar celluloid tale dissolves into a truer – and more personal – tragedy as Waits writes the teenage victim's epitaph, comparing his gravestone to a chewing-gum machine, the end of dreams and the washing down of a blood soaked pavement.

'I Can't Wait To Get Off Work' is a disappointingly downbeat end to a remarkable record. Aside from its inclusion of the word "copacetic", there is little of note about the concluding track. After what has gone before, it seems half-hearted, a mere afterthought – and one wonders why Waits didn't finish, instead, on the narrative peak of 'Small Change . . .'.

Copacetic as that title track was, the truly outstanding song on the album is to be found right at the beginning. At first acquaintance, the real shock of 'Tom Traubert's Blues' was hearing *that* voice. When Tom Waits hit a note, there was scant chance of it surviving intact – but on 'Tom Traubert's Blues', Waits sounded positively tubercular, and the notes he was hitting were all pleading the fifth.

There was something quite majestic though about 'Tom Traubert's Blues': perhaps it was the incongruity of Jerry Yester's lush strings ushering in that noble, cracked-foghorn voice. Hearing Waits boom out effortlessly evoked all the pain of urban despair and big city isolation, without ever sounding maudlin or pathetic. It's all summed up succinctly and movingly in Waits' economic devastating description of desolation, as a place where "no one speaks English, and everything's broken".

As Waits sings of whisky-stained shirts and lost St Christopher medals; of night watchmen and strippers, soldiers and sailors; of soaking wet shoes and midnight dragnets . . . Both performance and lyric speak of the ties that bind, the common bond of humanity, and those last clinging vestiges of dignity.

Another element in the timeless appeal of 'Tom Traubert's Blues' was Waits' memorable utilisation of the unofficial Australian anthem 'Waltzing Matilda' as his song's chorus. Written in 1895 by 'Banjo' Paterson (1864–1941), the song has been dogged by controversy ever since. It has been claimed variously by the Socialist left (who have it inspired by the death of a trade union organiser in 1894), while others claim it came to Australia with the German immigrants who were lured by the gold rushes of the late nineteenth century.

The tale itself is hardly epic: an itinerant travelling with a sack on his back, stops by a water hole and waits for his kettle to boil. He stuffs a passing sheep into his sack, and avoids apprehension by the troopers by drowning himself! But there is something resonant in the juxtaposition of the unfamiliar language ("billabong", "coolabah", "jumbuck") and that rousing melody, which has ensured the enduring popularity of 'Waltzing Matilda'.

Even where Paterson picked up the melody from is an issue shrouded in mystery and controversy: one possible source is the age-old Scottish ballad 'The Bonnie Wood Of Craigielea', while the eighteenth-century military marching song 'The Bold Fusilier' has also been cited.

With just the sort of eye for linguistic detail that Waits relishes, the Victorian critic Henry Lawson helpfully notated: "Travelling with swag in Australia is variously and picturesquely described as 'humping bluey', 'waltzing matilda', 'humping matilda', 'humping your drum', 'being on the wallaby' . . ." Sadly, though, only one of those variations made their way into 'Tom Traubert's Blues'.

Over the years, 'Waltzing Matilda' has seen frequent and noble service; the Paterson original has been recorded by untold thousands over the years – from Liberace to Warren Zevon. And virtually every act who makes the trip over to Australia feels honour bound to make mention of the "jolly swagman". Scots composer Eric Bogle reckons there have been over a hundred covers of his own poignant 'The Band Played Waltzing Matilda' alone, including one by The Pogues – one of Waits' own favourite bands.

In 1984 'Advance Australia Fair' was finally chosen as the nation's official anthem, just beating 'Waltzing Matilda'. As late as 1995 though, 'Waltzing Matilda' was still courting controversy: just where in Queensland was the centenary of the song to be celebrated . . . Dagworth, the location which inspired "Banjo" Paterson? Winton, where 'Waltzing Matilda' was first heard in public? Or Kynuna, which historians claim is where the song's "jolly swagman" was executed?

Talking to Bill Flanagan in 1987, Waits admitted that: " 'Tom Traubert's Blues' goes over real well in England." He went on to describe the strangely universal impact of the chorus of that archetypal Australian song – reconfigured by a Californian, in exile in London: "When you're 'waltzing matilda', you're on the road. You're not with your girlfriend, you're on the bum. For me, I was in Europe for the first time, and I felt like a soldier far away from home and drunk on the corner with no money, lost. I had a hotel key and I didn't know where I was. That kind of feeling."

Breaking the good news to the composer that Rod Stewart had taken his 'Tom Traubert's Blues (Waltzing Matilda)' into the British Top 10 in 1992, Warner MD Rob Dickins was surprised to hear Waits grumble: "I wrote that song so no one would cover it!"

The cover of *Small Change* showed Waits comfortably at home, looking exactly like the kind of guy Central Casting would send when someone wanted a bum, or a ne'er-do-well. There was Waits, scruffily backstage in a stripper's dressing room. The nominal star scratching his head, while the stripper carefully avoids eye contact. The cover's seediness seemed to permeate the whole album. Waits was like Woody Allen in *What's New Pussycat?*: "What do you do?" Peter O'Toole asks. "I help the strippers dress and undress," admits Woody. "What's the pay like?" "$20 a week." "That's not much . . ." "I know, but it's all I can afford."

Small Change was the album where Tom Waits made it straight to the top. That was the set which got him into the *big* time – all the way to number 89 on the *Billboard* chart!

In his review for *NME*, David Hepworth noted wryly that: "This paper was no slouch in numbering him as a hollow pretender, seemingly because of his refusal to court rock'n'roll or its preening future . . . If you're expecting *Small Change* to show him taking the advice of his critics and toning it down, playing it a bit straighter, writing another tune for the Eagles, then you get counted out by the fourth bar of 'Tom Traubert's Blues' . . . That voice has not been gargling honey and lemon, more like it's been regularly oiled with paint-stripper straight from a broken bottle and caressed by fumes of uncut Turkish rolled in sandpaper."

To gather an audience for his new album, Waits was back in harness. He toured extensively around the time of its release, keeping himself "busier than a one-armed bass player". But even for Waits the wanderer, life on the road was beginning to lose its appeal. He had reached a stage in his life, he admitted, where "the uncontrollable urge to play Iowa has finally left me".

NOTE

1   Dan Daley, *Sound On Sound*

CHAPTER 13

BY now, Waits was accruing something of a cult reputation. He was actually appearing on television, rather than repairing them. But though Waits dutifully did the rounds of local radio and TV – he wasn't always what they were expecting.

They were probably hoping for the likes of Elton John, with his breezy songs about crocodiles rocking and honky chateaux, or piano-led singer-songwriters like Billy Joel or Barry Manilow. One look at Waits told nervous chat-show hosts to fasten their seat belts for a bumpy ride alongside this grizzled and grumpy bad-tempered souse, with his songs about pimps, G-strings and billabongs.

The format was that guests appeared, modestly plugged their latest "product", made a few self-deprecating remarks about themselves, and talked a bit about golf. They then strolled to the piano, played their hit, returned to the comfy chair to run through a tried and tested series of anecdotes concerning their celebrity friends in showbiz – and, out . . . But not Tom Waits.

On the *Fernwood Tonight* television show in 1977, for example, he managed to convince the baffled hosts that the only reason he was there was because his van had broken down on the way to somewhere else. He even claims to have succeeded in borrowing $20 off one baffled interviewer ("but I had to leave the four-year-old as collateral").

So convincing was Waits as a down-on-his-luck Boho bum, that arriving at the television studio to appear on *The Mike Douglas Show*, Waits was refused entry, because the guard was convinced he *was* a down and out.

Even when he did manage to get inside the studio, he was not particularly co-operative, and did little to ingratiate himself . . . ("I've always maintained that reality is for people who can't face drugs"). Heads were scratched as Waits demonstrated his "new dance number 'Do The Breakfast In Jail' "; and on another occasion, host and audience were left none the wiser when he announced that his new album went by the snappy title: *Music To Seduce A Divorced Waitress By*.

And one can only imagine Middle America's bafflement in 1976, when Waits appeared ("as himself") on the top-rated chat show, *The Dinah*

Shore Show – sandwiched incongruously between the clean-cut delights of The Monkees and Andy Williams. By and large, American TV audiences were not seduced – and Waits was soon back off on the road.

His TV antics had done little to expand Tom Waits' US fan-base, but – if possible – he was even less appealing on British television in 1983. In town to talk up *Swordfishtrombones*, Waits was booked to appear on *Loose Talk*, Channel 4's new late-night "yoof" chat show, hosted by journalist Steve Taylor. It seemed like the perfect forum for a maverick talent like Waits – except that Waits took greatly against Taylor, mumbling and grumbling, as the hapless host struggled not so much to interview his guest, as to comprehend him.

Taylor: "You've lived in some dives, haven't you?"

Waits: "I don't know if I translate in my language. Do you mean a place with a pool?"

Taylor: "No, not really . . . Low rent? Is that an American expression?"

Waits: "Low rent? You mean like Rangoon?"

Taylor: "I'm thinking of the seedier parts of LA . . ."

Waits: "You mean like a *farming* community . . .?"

Taylor: "No, not *that* kind of seed. Have a go, have a guess. Try and guess what I'm getting at . . ."

Waits: "I think what you're trying to ask me is, have I ever lived in a cheap hotel?"

One of Waits' fellow guests was future *Private Eye* editor Ian Hislop, who was equally baffled by the American's strangulated mannerisms. "I'm terribly sorry," Hislop interjected, as he tried to grasp just what Waits was on about, "could you speak up a little?"

"I'll talk anyway I damn well please," Waits retorted sulkily.

When he wasn't out and about provoking chat-show hosts, Waits was safely ensconced at the Tropicana. But by the end of Seventies, he was in pretty bad shape. Touring had chewed him up; he was losing sleep and drinking too much; and Waits' motel coterie of Rickie Lee Jones and Chuck E. Weiss weren't the type to ensure he was getting his five daily portions of fruit and veg.

"An inebriated good evening to you all," wasn't just Waits' snappy onstage opening line. Offstage too, he was viewing the world mostly through the bottom of a bottle.

Of course, there is a grand tradition of the "professional eavesdropper", the bar-room bard, the pissed poet . . . and perhaps Waits was simply trying to live up to this image of the artist or writer as a "doomed romantic". But if you didn't know that he was an eminent practitioner of his craft, you might just have mistaken Waits for the type of barfly you'd be less than enchanted to find yourself standing next to at a bar.

Waits hung out in the sort of dives that had signs behind the bar, courtesy of Nelson Algren, which read: "I've been punched, kicked, screwed, defaulted, knocked down, held up, held down, lied about, cheated, deceived, conned, laughed at, insulted, hit on the head and married. So go ahead and ask for credit. I don't mind saying *NO!*"

And he looked and sounded like the type of guy who'd buttonhole you all night, bending your ear, yakking that he'd once bumped into Al Pacino – at least, he *thought* it was Al Pacino, sure looked like Al Pacino – right outside this very bar. And, hey, wasn't that barmaid the spit of Lana Turner . . .?

Waits was gradually becoming as much a victim of myth, as he was myth-maker. The jazz musicians he was increasingly drawn towards were heroic figures, and Waits was irresistibly sucked into their legend. He wanted to believe that they played until they dropped, slept in their clothes, flopped in $4 rooms, and drank cheap booze for breakfast; when actually, "all these guys wear pantyhose, sit out by the swimming pool and play golf in the afternoon".

Most interviews with Waits at that time took place in a bar. And in stark contrast to the TV debacles, these encounters were rarely less than entertaining. Trouble was, having lovingly fashioned the character of soused singer-songwriter, dripping hip from the lip, Waits was now expected to live up to it, both onstage and off.

Brendan Behan and Dylan Thomas were the obvious precedents – fine examples, both, of inimitable literary stylists who preferred the boisterousness of the public bar to the silent seclusion of the writer's study. Drink does, however, tend to make even the most talented, somewhat repetitive – while in his cups, Dylan Thomas once observed: "Somebody is boring me – I think it's me!"

By now, Waits too was in severe danger of allowing the image to overpower the man. And in May 1977 he was arrested in a restaurant, along with Chuck E. Weiss. Accused of disturbing the peace and being drunk in public, the pair were hustled into the back of a pickup truck, where Waits had a gun pressed to his temple, while a cop explained in graphic detail that, fired at close range, the bullet would explode his head "like a cantaloupe". Waits was banged up for a night, and on release, sued. When he got his day in court five years later, he was cleared and awarded $7,500 compensation – but it was, nonetheless, a timely warning.

Increasingly aware of his unappealing image and the dangers of his precarious lifestyle, Waits knew he was skating on thin ice. Discussing 'Bad Liver And A Broken Heart' from *Small Change*, he admitted at the time: "I put a lot into that; I tried to resolve a few things as far as the cocktail-lounge, maudlin, crying into your beer image that I have. I ended up telling myself to cut that shit out. On top of everything else, talking about boozing substantiates the rumours that people hear about you, and people think that I'm a drunk. So I directed that song as much to the people that listen to me and think they know me, as much as I directed it to myself."[1]

For the benefit of journalists, Waits still made the effort to give great copy – his interviews as much of a performance as any paid gig. But thanks to the steady flow of liquor, Waits began to display all the hallmarks of the classic inebriate: boring to the sober, and repetitive. And repetitive: "Had an Indian meal last night . . ." he told Mike Flood-Page three times in two hours, "didn't know whether to eat it or drive it home."[2]

Not that there was that much call on Waits' time in 1977. Musically, Fleetwood Mac's *Rumours* and the Eagles' *Hotel California* personified "Adult Oriented Rock"; while, at the other end of the spectrum, John Travolta strutted his white-suited stuff in *Saturday Night Fever*, and put disco firmly on the map. But for many, 1977 was simply year-zero: the year that saw debut albums from The Sex Pistols, Elvis Costello and The Clash, who sang: "No Elvis, Beatles or The Rolling Stones . . ."

Like many others, Tom Waits was left in limbo. So he just carried on doing what he had always done: making records, touring and drinking. Fortuitously, he could combine at least two of those activities.

Foreign Affairs was recorded in Hollywood during the summer of 1977. Waits had toyed with *Ten Dollars* or *Stolen Cars* as titles, but the sense of distance suggested a foreign perspective. "I'm writing some stuff right now," Waits told John Platt prior to recording, "I'm trying to get darker in my writing . . . I can't avoid comic relief, I need it for my own mental health, but I also want to be able to display myself as a lyricist and writer of stories and tall tales."

The cover photos for *Foreign Affairs* were taken by George Hurrell, a photographer famous for his work with Hollywood icons (most notably Marilyn Monroe) during the Golden Age of the Forties and Fifties. Fashioned, once again, while he played Europe, the album was imbued with Waits' impressions of his distant homeland. From 'Burma Shave', an evocation of childhood drives with his father; through 'Foreign Affair', which offered a unique perspective on home; through to 'Potter's Field', a lengthy detour back to the territory of 'Small Change (Got Rained On

With His Own .38)' – this was a typically Waitsian take on home thoughts from abroad.

Musically, *Foreign Affairs* had Waits back on home turf. Here he was again, an inebriated companion wreathed in a fug of cigarette smoke, basking in cool jazz backings, as he thumbs his cheap paperback of lurid pulp fiction for inspiration.

'I Never Talk To Strangers' was a diversion, which saw Waits duetting with Bette Midler, then at the height of her popularity. The 'Divine Miss M' had shocked middle America with her off-colour act in the mid-Seventies, but by 1977 she was on her way to becoming a gold-plated star.

Her duet with Waits was a joy, a close bar-room encounter of the torch-song kind. Waits growls and Midler coos, and it all added up to some fine Adult-Oriented fun. "Bartender, I'd like a Manhattan please . . ." chirps Bette seductively, then Waits slumps in with a clumsy pick-up line. The two go through the whole four-in-the-morning-and-there's-no-one-in-the-bar-but-me routine, and Bette kisses Tom off with a conciliatory: "You don't look so much of a chump."

'Muriel' and 'A Sight For Sore Eyes' were bittersweet love songs, played out against some of Waits' most enticing melodies. As with the earlier 'Tom Traubert . . .', Waits was not afraid of seeking inspiration from wherever and whenever – and 'A Sight For Sore Eyes' is ushered in by a snatch of 'Auld Lang Syne' played on the piano. But at the core of the album are the three lengthy narratives: 'Jack & Neal', 'Potter's Field' and 'Burma Shave'.

'Jack & Neal' finally paid a belated, full-on tribute to Kerouac & Cassady, the freewheeling spirits of the Fifties who had been such a formative influence on the solitary, homebound Thomas Alan Waits. In truth, 'Jack & Neal' was a tad disappointing: a less than spellbinding narrative played out against a non-existent tune. Although there is the striking image of a landscape that's "lonelier than a parking lot when the last car pulls away". Waits' tribute segued into 'California, Here I Come', a song popularised by Al Jolson more than half a century before – as if also acknowledging the musical heritage that had so inspired him. It was almost as if, with those songs, Waits was unwittingly bidding adieu to a formative part of his past, and was set to move on.

"He had a stool at the bar, and nobody sat there except Jack," Waits wistfully remembered to Kristine McKenna, as he vividly recalled Kerouac's influence on him as a teenager. "He was writing his own obituary from the moment he began, and I think he was tragically seduced by his own destiny . . . I enjoy his impressions of America, certainly more than anything you'd find in the *Reader's Digest*. The roar of the crowd in a bar after work; working for the railroad; living in cheap hotels; jazz."

'Potter's Field' came at you, hard "from the edge of a maniac's dream". A tale of low-life hoods, with only sweet dreams of revenge to keep them warm, as they double-cross and, in turn, are betrayed. They'd sell their mothers "if it was whiskey that they payed [sic]". Their shadowy world of gunshots and ricochets, of punks and whores, was bordered by Riker's Island and the Bronx – but Waits also calls in Charon, the boatman of death from Greek mythology, "skipper of the deadline steamer". This was Waits in full flight: a tour de force of storytelling, rich in detail, and dripping with atmosphere.

But best of all was 'Burma Shave', a lengthy narrative inspired by the 1947 film, *They Live By Night*, starring Farley Granger, who Waits namechecks in his song. A *Bonnie & Clyde*-style romance, Nicholas Ray's debut was later hailed as a film noir classic – and in 1974 it was remade, as *Thieves Like Us*, by director Robert Altman, with whom Waits would later work on *Short Cuts*.

Waits fashioned 'Burma Shave' as an edgy, restless piece, dealt from the same deck as James M. Cain's *The Postman Always Rings Twice*. With admirable economy, he paints a picture of the small, dead town of Marysville ("nothing but a wide spot in the road"), as the trucks thunder past on the highway, and "everybody's got one foot in the grave".

And over there's the girl who wants, more than anything, to get out – pinning her hopes on leaving town with the just-passing-through "Presley", who looks just like Farley Granger. Stifled by the smallness of the town, she's someone for whom the very idea of a place called Burma Shave, just over the horizon, is intoxicating. For her, it's Shangri-La . . . enticing, beckoning down the highway, offering hope to those suffocated by life in the small dreary backwater. She jumps her parole, keen to take her chances out in Burma Shave – and you share the elation of escape as, together, they "count the grain elevators in the rear-view mirror", with each one leaving Marysville further and further behind.

But fate had other ideas. On the way out of town a blown tyre cruelly kills their hopes and dreams. Death comes to the nameless girl from nowheresville – but at least she died cool, and still wearing her shades.

Waits' song, inspired by the childhood journeys with his father, makes a haunting companion piece to Springsteen's 'Wreck On The Highway'. Waits admitted that his song was autobiographical: "I have a lotta relatives in this little town called Marysville," he told Brian Case soon after the album's release, "and a cousin . . . Corinne Johnson, and every time I'd go up there from Los Angeles . . . she was like, 'Christ, man, I've gotta get out of this fucking town. I wanna go to LA.' She finally did. She hitch-hiked out and stood by this Foster Freeze on Prom Night, got in a car with a guy who was just some juvenile delinquent, and he took her all the way to LA, where she eventually cracked up."

Like Anarene, the dying Texas town in *The Last Picture Show*, Marysville was a typical small, black-and-white place, off the highway, and cut off from the mainstream. These were the sort of locations that fascinated Waits. Talking to me, he spoke softly and fondly of his homeland, particularly enchanted by the sad, small towns where there was nothing for people to do, but dream.

Waits' imagined towns were the kind of place that Malcolm Muggeridge arrived at, late one night in 1958: "Driving . . . into the town of Athens, Ohio (pop. 3,450) four bright coloured signs stood out in the darkness – 'Gas', 'Drugs', 'Beauty', 'Food'. Here, I thought, is the ultimate, the logos of our time, presented in sublime simplicity. It was like a vision in which suddenly all the complexity of life is reduced to one single inescapable proposition. These signs could have shone forth as clearly in Athens, Greece as in Athens, Ohio. All the world loves Lucy."

Foreign Affairs was the lead review in the *New Musical Express* of February 11, 1978, written by Nick Kent. Mind you, it was a thin week – a double-live Ted Nugent; the latest from Gallagher & Lyle; Paul Morley on Judas Priest; and Julie Burchill on Munich Machine . . . Ironically, these journalists are now better known than the acts they once reviewed.

Kent identified Waits' flaws, but was impressed by the strengths displayed on this, his fifth album: "There's something truly righteous glowing from these grooves that finally places this trashy genius in just the right perspective." He concluded: "A true subterranean, he won't come to you so you'd better make the effort to come to terms with him . . . And remember – make Tom Waits a superstar and you'll be making the world a better place."

In the all-important *Rolling Stone*, Fred Schruers was obviously a fan, though with reservations – finding Waits repeating "some mistakes from his last two albums: the chief sin he can't shake is an over-abundance of the facile, researched-and-rehearsed jive talk that is meant to dazzle but in fact fatigues the listener . . ." But, in the end, he granted him the benefit of the doubt: "Tom Waits is never less than intent and honest – he pushes to his own slow, heartfelt beat. Uneven though *Foreign Affairs* may be, it shows that Waits is still the kind of performer who can make us say 'you must be reading my mail.'"

Ultimately though, *Foreign Affairs* barely limped to the bottom of the pole. Half a decade into his professional career, Tom Waits was still failing to connect with an audience. Even with Bette Midler on board, the highest the album registered was number 113 in America.

Undeterred, Waits ploughed on . . . He was chafing at the lifestyle of the touring musician, but to liven things up on the road in 1978, Waits had a local stripper as his opening act – dutifully auditioning each applicant himself.

Waits' sixth album was cut in a week-long burst in Hollywood during the summer of 1978. Waits was at the time running a 1964 Thunderbird, the fin of which featured the name of the car, and the album: *Blue Valentine*. The car was featured on the album's back sleeve, as was Rickie Lee Jones, whom Waits is seen straddling on the bonnet. Since that shot was taken, the pair had split – now, her career was in overdrive, while Waits was still busy chasing his.

Typecast as the Boho beat who'd "slept through the Sixties", Waits was generally seen as an off-track maverick: the singer-songwriter who revered Lerner & Loewe or Rodgers & Hammerstein in preference to Page & Plant or John & Taupin. So a cover of Bernstein & Sondheim's 'Somewhere', from *West Side Story*, shouldn't really have come as too much of a surprise. But this aural assault left listeners reeling, as the lush strings ushered in Waits, growling from the bottom of a hangover: "There's a place for us . . ."

Such was the song's shock value that Asylum felt there might even be novelty value in releasing it as a single. They went ahead, and in April 1979 'Somewhere' became Waits' first-ever 45. Though, with strong competition from Art Garfunkel ('Bright Eyes'), Village People ('In The Navy') and Sister Sledge ('He's The Greatest Dancer'), it was perhaps no real surprise that it failed to chart.

Bob Dylan once said that "fame is like a million invisible people pressing you against a wall"; while Tony Curtis likened celebrity to having Alzheimer's: "Everyone knows you, and you don't recognise anybody!" And Tom Waits remained largely indifferent to that sort of success.

"A hit single means that you make a lot of money and a lot of people know who you are, and I don't know that that's so attractive. I don't see the importance of having your face on a lunchbox in Connecticut. I don't see how that fits into the grand scheme of things as something to strive for

. . . A lot of people are looking for affection and acceptance in the form of this anonymous group of people thinking they're wonderful, people they don't even know. You don't want to choose your friends arbitrarily."[3]

Besides the somewhat startling 'Somewhere', the other surprise on *Blue Valentine* was that Waits was moving from piano to electric guitar. Otherwise, the album was full of echoes, like we'd all been here at least once before. 'Romeo Is Bleeding' (which later became the title of a 1993 Gary Oldman film) smacked of a rewrite of 'Small Change'; while 'Whistlin' Past The Graveyard', '$29.00', and the title track, all seemed like re-treads of familiar Waits themes and territories.

But while they may have had a familiar, weary feel, certainly no one else was writing songs with titles like 'Christmas Card From A Hooker In Minneapolis' and 'A Sweet Little Bullet From A Pretty Little Gun' – and *Blue Valentine* did have some redeeming elements.

Waits' voice was nowhere near as harsh as it had been on *Foreign Affairs*; the rasp was on hold, and the roughness had softened. A song such as 'Kentucky Avenue' was undeniably moving, a charming autobiographical fragment of childhood, with memories of snatched kisses, scabby knees and stolen cigarettes. But, true to Waits' world, this was no soppy, soft-focus memory: he plans to liberate the heroine from her wheelchair and leg braces with his daddy's hacksaw. "That one came over a little dramatic," Waits reflected later, "but when I was 10, my best friend was called Kipper, he had polio and was in a wheelchair – we used to race each other to the bus stop."[4]

'Christmas Card From A Hooker In Minneapolis' was quite spellbinding: a heartbreaking letter, recalling a romance bordered by filling stations, Little Anthony & The Imperials records, and used-car lots. The song had actually been sliced from the jauntily titled screenplay *Used Carlotta*, which Waits was fashioning at the time, but which was never produced. Open and affectionate, the sting of the 'Christmas Card . . .' is in the tail. It is all a sad fabrication, a total invention: there never was any husband; he never did play the trombone; and the attempt at rekindled romance is doomed from the start, as the heroine won't be eligible for parole until Valentine's Day! It's a communique from someone with no life and little future, pathetically trying to invent a past that never was.

From the undoubted highpoint of *Small Change*, both *Foreign Affairs* and *Blue Valentine* seemed like a falling from grace. Waits still registered as a unique voice on the late Seventies pop radar, but neither his fifth nor sixth albums were particularly remarkable. Like the repetitive drunk he was in danger of becoming, Waits' music was stuck in a groove. Handcuffed to a jazz yesterday and locked into a dead-end cycle of chronicling low lives, he seemed to have forsaken melody for ever.

The good news was that Waits had begun to bore himself . . . and even at the time, it seemed as though he acknowledged that *Blue Valentine* marked the end of a particular era. "I'll tell you one thing for sure," he emphasised to *NME*'s Nick Kent in 1978, "if I have to write one more song about booze and being drunk and all that, I'm going to throw up! Seriously! I've had enough of all that. It's all become played-out. There's changes due."

NOTES

1 *Record Collector*
2 *Street Life*
3 Kristine McKenna, *NME*
4 *Record Collector*

CHAPTER 14

WAITS spent much of 1979 in Paris, working with Guy Peellaert, the Dutch artist who had come to the pop world's attention with his book *Rock Dreams* – in which familiar rock music icons were infamously imagined in oil paintings (the Stones in Nazi uniforms, Ray Davies pushing a pram, etc. . . .). That project led to Peellaert designing the cover for The Rolling Stones' *It's Only Rock'N'Roll*, which would have been a first . . . except that Mick Jagger made the mistake of mentioning the commission to David Bowie, who jumped the gun by getting Peellaert to paint his controversial *Diamond Dogs* cover – literally, the dog's bollocks.

When Waits was first asked to supply the text for Peellaert's new book, it was to comprise a selection of his paintings of American icons and idols – though in the end, the pair focused on those who had passed through Las Vegas: Frank Sinatra, Howard Hughes, Liberace, George Raft, Marlene Dietrich, Muhammad Ali, Jimmy Durante, Pearl Bailey . . .

"Book's called *Vegas* . . ." Waits enthused to Nick Kent, "Guy's tribute to the great American heroes . . . it just so happens that all the ones he'd chosen had one thing in common, and that was that they had spent time in Las Vegas."

Sadly, and for no clear reason, the book failed to appear. ("It never happened," Waits told me, "I was going through a lot of . . . turmoil.") Though Peellaert did eventually publish the book in 1986, as *The Big Room*, with text supplied by Michael Herr – author of *Dispatches*, and scriptwriter of *Apocalypse Now* and *Full Metal Jacket*.

On his return from Paris, disturbing rumours started to circulate among Waits' friends that the City of Light – and fashion-capital of the world – had left its mark on the scruffy singer-songwriter . . . That he had binned the bohemian chic which had characterised his image thus far, and was favouring instead the work of an up-and-coming couture stylist. "Giorgio *who*?" Waits queried, still happily wearing his well-worn winklepickers, black pants and a shirt which could, at best, be described as "off-white".

Brian Case from *Melody Maker* ran into Waits on tour in Copenhagen during the early part of 1979. Jazz expert and one of the few journalists who could match Waits word for word, Case knew where Waits was coming from. And Waits knew, that Case knew, that he knew . . .

With Hamlet on the horizon, Waits was beginning his European jaunt in the capital of Denmark. It was, as Case remarked: "a curious joint to open a tour, and he has Vienna, the Palladium, Dublin and Australia yet to come, all of which sounds more like a B. Traven predicament than a tilt at the stars. A tricky talent to place, but this itinerary recalls the Palookaville Scenic, no offertory boxes or blood-bank credit accepted."

Waits and Case hit it off immediately, like Robert Walker and Farley Granger in *Strangers On A Train*. They swapped drinking yarns (Waits particularly liked hearing about the Durham miners' wives who decorated butcher's hooks, then stabbed them into the bar on Saturday nights to hang their handbags on). Why, they got on so well that 4 a.m. found Waits, Case and amiable *Melody Maker* smudge Tom Sheehan in a Copenhagen bar, alone – except for a solitary Mancunian drunk, and the All-Woman Eskimo Chapter of the Hell's Angels!

Surviving to tell the tale, Waits returned to the States, and later that year would relocate to New York from Los Angeles. He had spent his life in the Golden State, but there were now compelling reasons for him to up-sticks and move East. Waits was increasingly disillusioned with his career, his life and his lifestyle. He turned 30 in Salina, Kansas, although that didn't trouble him unduly: "The big ages are 16, 33 and a third, 45 and 78!" (One of Stiff Records' most imaginative campaigns, aimed squarely at post-war baby-boomers, ingeniously pointed out that: "Anyone born in 45 will be 33 in 78.")

Mick Farren caught Waits live in New York in 1979: "On stage, Tom Waits is a cartoon character . . . His shambling, hip-dancing, corkscrewing legs and seemingly double-jointed hands that appear to bend back on themselves while still gripping the cigarette between the tips of his first two fingers are all reminiscent of a rubber toy duck. Whereas the rubber drunk traditionally wears white tie, top hat and tails, Waits is a bopster's version in pork-pie hat and electric blue mohair. He is the jive, dapper drunk, but by incorporating so much humour into his act, he manages to retain the tattered dignity of the bum."

Away from work, there had already been big changes in Waits' life. As well as splitting with Rickie Lee Jones, Waits had quit the Tropicana. Tired of the occasional fan wanting to shoot the breeze in the dark hours with their hero, he had shifted to Crenshaw Boulevard, and then out to suburbia by Silver Lake, not far from the motel where Sam Cooke had met his grisly end.

Gone, too, were the Lucky Strikes. Approaching the big three-oh, Waits had decided to quit smoking: "I felt like I was caving in inside. I couldn't walk two blocks without coughing and wheezing . . . So I said, 'What am I doing killing myself?' I don't want to live hard, die young and have a beautiful corpse. I really don't."[1]

Then there were the movies . . . "Work with you in a *film*?" Richard Dreyfuss gasps in *The Goodbye Girl*. "Well . . . we could go and *see* one . . ." smirks Nicol Williamson's producer.

Waits' film career *almost* got off to an early start . . . Along with all his fellow "new Dylans" – indeed, with every singer-songwriter who could hold a plectrum – Waits was on the list to play Woody Guthrie in the 1976 biopic, *Bound For Glory*.

Tim Buckley got the closest, but he died. Woody's son Arlo was rejected. Bob Dylan wouldn't do it. Tim Hardin was too strung out on heroin. So instead they cast . . . David Carradine, the high-kicking, wandering philosopher star of TV's *Kung-Fu* series . . . And Tom Waits, having finished *Foreign Affairs*, took a role in *Paradise Alley*, which marked his film debut when it was released in 1978.

Perhaps hard to believe now, but back then, Sylvester Stallone was seriously considered the "new Brando". By the time he came to write, direct and star in *Paradise Alley*, Stallone already had a clutch of undistinguished features under his belt. But in 1976, in true Hollywood star-is-born fashion, he hit big with *Rocky*; the inspiring story of a punch-drunk, coulda-bin-a-contender boxer. Ahead lay the whole *Rocky* franchise, and the Eighties jungle jingoism of *Rambo* – but at the time of *Paradise Alley*, on the back of the original, bracing *Rocky*, Stallone was seen as the perfect antidote to the slick, homogenised Hollywood hokum.

The story of three wrestling brothers living in the Hell's Kitchen of the 1940s, *Paradise Alley* recalled the Warner Bros dramas of that period: John Garfield as the palooka from the wrong side of the tracks; Spencer Tracy as the priest who packed a mean right-hook; James Cagney, the gangster who always remembered Mother's Day; Virginia Mayo, the dame who could still find some good in the rottenest apple . . .

Besides Stallone, *Paradise Alley* had Anne Archer, a decade before she got stalked by a bunny boiler in *Fatal Attraction*; Armand Assante, prior to becoming a *Mambo King*; and Waits, who found himself cast as Mumbles, an "inebriated, slovenly bar-room pianist".

He did have a little scene with the star ("When was the last time you were with a woman?" Stallone asks Waits, "Probably the Depression . . ."), but most of his role ended up on the cutting room floor ("five weeks of work for three lines of dialogue"). Still, it was good experience ("interesting to see the bowels of the film industry"), and film was certainly an area Waits was keen to explore. Though he wasn't going to take anything and everything that was flung his way; he did decline to appear (as a Satanic cult leader) in an episode of TV's *Starsky & Hutch*.

By the end of Seventies, Waits was pragmatic about his chances in the movie business – and already wary of becoming typecast: "The thing is, once you've gotten any kind of image . . . I've gotten countless calls to play a drunk Irish piano player, which is . . . not very challenging. I'd much prefer to play an axe murderer."[2]

In real life, too, he saw the dangers of becoming stuck in a rut.

On December 31, 1979, Waits made a New Year's resolution. It was another switch, this time crossing coasts from Los Angeles to New York. A lifelong Angeleno, Waits packed three suitcases and went in search of a "new urban landscape". He made a beeline for West 23rd Street, where all the Big Apple artists, poets and beats ended up at one time or another.

The Chelsea Hotel had first opened its doors in 1884, and soon became a haven for all and any artistic types. The bohemians felt at home in the Chelsea, its rooms had thick walls, and the management turned a blind eye to pretty well everything. Although they did shut off the balconies, after one too many residents had jumped off, and hit the sidewalk of West 23rd.

The hotel's air of gently decaying nineteenth-century grandeur and faded glories held wide appeal. Early residents included Mark Twain and Eugene O'Neill; Arthur Miller and Thomas Wolfe; Arthur C. Clarke and William S. Burroughs. During the Fifties, poets like Dylan Thomas and Allen Ginsberg roomed there. And throughout the Sixties, poets continued flocking to the hotel – one resident remembers Ginsberg and Leonard Cohen taunting each other by shouting out details of their respective royalty statements across the Chelsea's bar.

"Once I hit the Chelsea Hotel," Leonard Cohen remembered, "there was no turning back." Indeed, during the Sixties the hotel became the prime location for rock'n'roll royalty: as well as Cohen, the Chelsea played host to Kris Kristofferson, Janis Joplin and Jimi Hendrix. The Velvet Underground's Nico was a Chelsea Girl; Joni Mitchell was struck by a 'Chelsea Morning'; and Bob Dylan famously wrote 'Sad Eyed Lady Of The Lowlands' while in residence at the hotel.

During the Seventies, the Chelsea's rock'n'roll residents included the Stooges, Patti Smith, Sam Shepard and various Ramones. But by the time Waits got there, the Chelsea had surpassed even its earlier seedy reputation: it was in Room 100, in October 1978, that Sid Vicious murdered his girlfriend Nancy Spungen.

In the event, Waits only called the Chelsea home for a matter of months. He'd had to leave his Blue Valentine Thunderbird behind in LA ("She went out without me one night and got in a fatal accident," he mourned). And having seen most of his film debut consigned to the cutting room floor, Waits had resigned himself to the fact that – for better or for worse – his entire future was mapped out. All there seemed to be on the horizon was the familiar routine of album, tour, album, tour . . . played out to the same loyal, but barely expanding, audience.

Waits had famously observed that he "slept through the Sixties", so I asked him how he'd coped with the Seventies: "I was on the road throughout the Seventies. I was really living out the whole dream: travelling, playing clubs with my band, working, living in hotels . . . the Seventies for me were . . . I lived in hotels for 10 years."

It was the end of the decade. He had just turned 30, quit smoking, switched coasts . . . and Tom Waits was edgy and rootless. Looking back at the period when we met a few years later, Waits admitted: "I was totally disenchanted with the music business. I moved to New York and was seriously considering other possible . . . career alternatives."

He elongated every word, plainly still bitter at the way his career had seemed to be spiralling downward at the time: "The whole Modus Operandi" – the way Waits mouthed it made it sound like a particularly threatening branch of the Cosa Nostra – "of sitting down and writing and making an album, going out on the road with a band . . . Away for three months, come back with high blood pressure, a drinking problem, tuberculosis, a warped sense of humour. It just became . . . predictable."

Despite his reluctance, Waits dutifully began fashioning a new album, provisionally entitled *White Spades*. But by chance, one of the songs from 1977's *Foreign Affairs* album, 'I Never Talk To Strangers', had alerted a stranger to his existence. And though he didn't know it at the time, this happenstance would shift Tom Waits' life and career into a whole new direction.

NOTES

1 Stephen X. Rea, *Ampersand*
2 Stephen X. Rea, *Ampersand*

PART II

Shore Leave

CHAPTER 15

FRANCIS FORD Coppola is up-river, way, way out in the jungle, the director is marooned in the Philippines and things are slipping explosively, expensively out of control. The sky is flapping, full of helicopters. The air is sticky with the imagined smell of napalm. Gasoline explodes and scorches the sky . . . And Coppola watches helplessly as the not inconsiderable profits from his two *Godfather* films literally go up in smoke.

Steve McQueen, Al Pacino and Gene Hackman had all declined to star in the film Coppola is now fashioning, far, far away from the studio security of Hollywood. And, though not yet 40, Martin Sheen – the leading man Coppola eventually selected – has just suffered a heart attack.

The film's above-the-title star is Marlon Brando, who Coppola had rescued from ignominy with *The Godfather*. But having arrived on location in the Philippines to lend his inscrutable charisma to a climactic role, once on set, Brando refuses to read the script Coppola has specifically fashioned for him.

Attempting to film the Wagnerian opening – consisting of a squadron of helicopters razing the jungle with a napalm attack – Coppola is told that he cannot communicate with the airborne pilots from the ground. Then he is informed that a hurricane threatens to destroy every single location for the movie he is shooting. He is isolated, desperate, and very, very far from home.

Mud, blood and bullets are now closer to Coppola than his blood family. The economy of an entire third-world country is quickly being devoured by one film: the budget of his eagerly anticipated Vietnam epic now looks set to exceed $30 million. Coppola has been planning this for five years, and already 238 days have been spent filming. As he sweats it out in the fierce jungle heat, the pressures on him growing daily, and the future spinning chaotically out of his control, Coppola comes to appreciate three things with great clarity: (1) he is an artist; (2) he is going slowly crazy; (3) and, *still*, Charlie Don't Surf!

Later, in the equally frenzied, but slightly more comfortable environment of the Cannes Film Festival, when his movie was finally screened in 1979, Coppola stated emphatically: *"Apocalypse Now* is not a movie. It is

117

not *about* Vietnam, it *is* Vietnam!" Later still, he admitted: "We were in the jungle; there were too many of us; we had access to too much money, too much equipment. And, little by little, we went insane."

Madness was certainly in the air as Coppola attempted to capture on celluloid the hallucinatory, dislocated aspects of the Vietnam War. His wife Eleanor was on location, and she watched with horror as the madness enveloped her husband: "It is scary to watch someone you love go into the centre of himself, and confront his fears; fear of failure, fear of death, fear of going insane."

Comparisons were immediately made with another Hollywood wunderkind who got too big for his boots. As the framework for *Apocalypse Now*, Coppola was using Joseph Conrad's 1902 novella *Heart Of Darkness*. Forty years earlier, another brash young director had intended to shoot Conrad's story as his first film. But when budgetary considerations and production difficulties proved insurmountable, Orson Welles had been forced to fall back on his own resources, instead making his debut with a little film called *Citizen Kane*.

In the end, and against all expectations, *Apocalypse Now* did become a critical and box-office success. Coppola regained his sanity, and its success kept him afloat financially. But he had learned enough to know that his future films must never, ever be on that scale again. Coppola was now looking to downsize; to work on a small, intimate film that would recall his earlier acclaimed works, *The Rain People* and *The Conversation*.

The film he made next would certainly have to be studio based – that *had* to be a cheaper (and easier) option than filming on a jungle location. Except that, being Francis Ford Coppola, he ended up *buying* the studio. And the resulting film would once again familiarise him with the word "bankruptcy". Coppola really wanted to make a small-scale movie, and for his sins, he made himself one; one which would obsess him in the same way as *Apocalypse Now*, except that this one was from the heart . . .

Francis Ford Coppola had been honorary Godfather to a whole generation of directors: film-makers such as Martin Scorsese, George Lucas and Steven Spielberg, who would go on to revolutionise cinema, and equally significantly, cinema *admissions* during the Seventies. But Coppola was the first of the "movie brats" to get inside the studio system and make movies.

Having made his reputation with scripts such as *Patton* (President Richard Nixon's favourite film) and *The Great Gatsby*, Coppola was ready for the next step. And in 1968 – despite his beard – Warner Brothers decided to trust him with a big-budget project: the film of a popular

Broadway musical, *Finian's Rainbow*, which would boast a baffling cast that included Tommy Steele, Petula Clark and Fred Astaire.

For the film of Mario Puzo's 1969 Mafia novel *The Godfather*, however, Coppola was way down the list as director. Until, as is the way with Hollywood, all the other contenders were made offers they couldn't refuse . . . So Coppola found himself at the helm of Puzo's potboiler. And because he was of, duh, Italian descent, the studio reckoned he would be just the guy to get a handle on these hoods.

With his customary arrogance, Coppola quickly ditched the script and dissed Paramount's initial casting – can you really imagine Robert Redford or Ryan O'Neal as Michael Corleone? Then, with terrier-like tenacity, boundless ambition, and a vision at odds with any other mainstream director, Coppola proceeded to fashion *The Godfather* into one of the defining American films of the Seventies. Actually, make that *the* defining film of the Seventies.

Coppola (and co-writer Puzo) came up a classic script bristling with unforgettable lines: "I'll make him an offer he can't refuse . . .", "Tell Mike it was only business . . .", "Fredo, you're my only brother, and I love you, but don't ever take sides with anyone against the family again. Ever . . .", "Luca Brasi sleeps with the fishes . . .", "Keep your friends close, but keep your enemies closer . . .", "If history has taught us anything, it is that anyone can be killed . . ."

In hard, financial terms, *The Godfather* started the trend for films that operated in an independent financial universe. Within weeks of its opening in March 1972, *The Godfather* had overtaken *The Sound Of Music* as the all-time box-office champion. Coppola's film was taking in an unheard-of million dollars *a day* during its opening weeks. The delighted studio estimated that, within three years, 132 million paying customers had lined up to see Coppola's masterpiece.

Before there was *Jaws*, *Star Wars* or *The Lord Of The Rings*, *The Godfather* sent box-office takings ballistic. But in the immediate aftermath, Coppola had little opportunity to revel in his new-found fame, or to squander his millions. Barricaded inside a Parisian hotel room, the director could only hear at second-hand tales of the queues of people snaking round the block as they waited to see his movie. Coppola himself was already on to the next project, locked away in luxury, completing the script to *The Great Gatsby* – something he had committed himself to prior to commencing work on *The Godfather*.

Then Coppola began to party. And, as if to emphasise that he was of the rock'n'roll generation, rather than old Hollywood, Coppola nurtured and then produced *American Graffiti* – George Lucas' hymn to lost innocence. "Where were you in '62?" the poster for the 1973 film enquired.

It was inevitable, though, that the murky doings of the Corleone family would eventually draw Coppola back. And, if anything, *The Godfather, Part II* is an even better film than its illustrious predecessor. Al Pacino moves magnificently centre-stage, and the time-shifting, era-jumping three-hour sequel stands as a true cinematic triumph. At times, Coppola and Puzo struck an almost Shakespearian note in this tale of revenge, deceit, power and corruption; and, appropriately, in 1974 *The Godfather, Part II* became the only sequel ever to win a Best Picture Academy Award. As is often the way of these things in Hollywood, Francis Ford Coppola had gone, in a remarkably short stretch of time, from pariah to messiah.

As far back as 1969, the 30-year-old Coppola had expressed interest in running his own studio – as "a haven for young film-makers . . . run by creative talents, free of businessmen and bureaucrats". But it took his 6 per cent stake in the two *Godfather* films to make Coppola bankable – and nearly $7 million of that for his dream to become a reality.

The 10-acre site of the old Hollywood General Studios on North Las Palmas Avenue had been a studio since 1919, and at one time stars such as Mary Pickford, Mae West and Gary Cooper had worked there. Now, Coppola determined to breathe new life into it, and even financially successful peers such as Steven Spielberg and George Lucas could only look enviously on as he became a mogul, with his very own film *studio*.

In 1980, Coppola announced his plans for what he now called Zoetrope Studios. The "zoetrope" was a nineteenth-century cylindrical metal drum, with a series of slits around its sides, through which you could view the paper illustrations inside. When rotated quickly, the device gave the illusion that the picture inside was moving. The zoetrope marked the first time that a "moving picture" experience could be shared by a group of people. And after a hard day's Empire-building, a prosperous Victorian family could relax together in front of a flickering zoetrope, before settling down to read the latest instalment from Mr Dickens.

Modern-day audiences can be considerably harder to please, and those keen to carp, were quick to criticise the location Coppola had chosen for his Zoetrope. The studio was situated in Long Beach, nestling close to where the eccentric millionaire aviator Howard Hughes had built his *Spruce Goose* during World War II. At the time it was the largest aeroplane ever constructed, and it only ever made one flight: Hughes himself piloted the massive eight-engined plane across the harbour – a trip of no less than

70 feet! Many in the film industry now saw Zoetrope as Coppola's very own *Spruce Goose*!

After the bloated brilliance and jungle mayhem of *Apocalypse Now*, and the five years spent setting up his own studio, what Coppola needed now was a fast hit-and-run project which would get Zoetrope up and running. Quick and easy, that was the plan. Which was fine, until Francis Ford Coppola decided to build his own Las Vegas in Los Angeles, right there on the Zoetrope lot . . .

Attracted by a script submitted to the studio by Armyan Bernstein, Coppola had quickly been drawn into the Chicago-set "fantasy about romantic love, jealousy and sex", which had reminded him irresistibly of Las Vegas. By switching Bernstein's double-handed love story from Chicago to Las Vegas ("the last frontier of America"), Coppola opened up a whole host of visual opportunities for his movie.

Isolated in the middle of the Nevada desert, Las Vegas had always been seen as a town for passing through; if anyone ever did stop there, it was just to fill up with gas, and move on. It wasn't until the first casino, the Flamingo, opened in 1947, that the desert crossroads was almost literally put on the map.

To attract the high rollers to Las Vegas, and then get the gamblers to spend, spend, spend . . . the casino owners employed the best musical entertainers in the world. Vegas soon became a second home to stars like Frank Sinatra, and during the Fifties Vegas became the base for the legendary Rat Pack. Although when Elvis Presley first performed there in 1956, he died a death – *Variety* concluded its disparaging review with the words: "For teenagers he's a whizz; for the average Vegas spender, he's a fizz!"

It was Sinatra's links to organised crime, rather than his talent, that really helped give Vegas its sinful lustre. The Mob loved Vegas – owners there regularly skimmed the take, there was no closed-circuit television to monitor play, and no tax requirements on gambling profits . . . With all this *and* the unfeasibly high turnover of gambling cash generated by the desert resort, no wonder Las Vegas became the favoured place for the Mafia to launder its cash.

Situated just a short 300-mile hop from tinsel-town, Las Vegas could also boast an abundant supply of Hollywood glamour, with all the movie stars visiting the gambling capital to see shows by Sinatra and Dino and Sammy and even, improbably, Noel Coward. For the really big opening nights, names such as Marilyn Monroe, Humphrey Bogart, Shirley MacLaine, Cary Grant, Judy Garland, Tony Curtis, Kim Novak, Kirk Douglas and Lauren Bacall would all be ringside.

And when the US government tested 14 atom bombs in the Nevada desert during the early Fifties, Las Vegas wasn't slow off the mark to capitalise on *that* excitement either. The town hosted a "Miss Atomic Bomb" pageant and offered guests the chance to pay to witness the exploding mushroom cloud from the balcony of the Atomic View Hotel, while the gamblers sipped atomic cocktails and danced to the Atom Bombers!

Vegas was where JFK came to relax; Elvis returned to the gambling capital in triumph in 1969; and Howard Hughes died there . . . No small wonder that Las Vegas appealed to Francis Ford Coppola and Tom Waits.

Waits had already immersed himself in the city and its culture while working on the abortive Guy Peellaert book project during 1979. He later spoke of his fascination with the extraordinary town: "That is the only place where I've ever seen false teeth in a pawn shop window. And prosthetic devices. I've seen a guy sell his glass eye for just one more roll. It's in the middle of nowhere, a graveyard for performers, like a parody of the American Dream. All very confusing; you can be a shoe-shine boy in the morning, a millionaire by noon. More often it works the other way. It's insane."[1]

NOTE

1 Richard Rayner, *Time Out*

CHAPTER 16

FROM the very beginning, Coppola envisaged *One From The Heart* as more than just a movie with songs grafted on as an afterthought. It was while directing a stage version of Noel Coward's *Private Lives* that he had first become attracted to the idea of using songs not simply as background music, but as a direct commentary on the characters, their actions and their motivations. Ironically, one of Coward's most quoted lines – "extraordinary how potent cheap music is" – originally appeared in *Private Lives*.

Incorporating popular song within the framework of a major Hollywood studio movie was not an original idea. The breakthrough had come in 1967 when director Mike Nichols used the songs of Simon & Garfunkel to such great effect on the soundtrack of *The Graduate*. And that same year, Coppola himself had used John Sebastian's songs with The Lovin' Spoonful in his first major directorial project, *You're A Big Boy Now*.

But it was the overwhelming success of *The Graduate*, and its subsequent soundtrack album, that alerted movie moguls to the enormous spin-off potential of harnessing film to rock'n'roll. And by the end of the Sixties, with audiences drifting away from the bloated fare on offer from the major studios, the youth audience was being specifically targeted. The runaway success of *Easy Rider* in 1969 confirmed the profitability of deliberately marrying the movies to rock music.

Of course, for every successful effort like *The Graduate*, there were a dozen ripe-smelling turkeys (who now remembers *The Strawberry Statement*; *Getting Straight* or *The Landlord*?). Still, the moguls reasoned, the odds were in their favour: if Group A sold 10 million albums in America alone, there was already a vast potential audience for any film which showcased that band's music. But as with so many other theories in the history of Hollywood, the moguls got it wrong. The case for the prosecution would probably cite the Village People's *Can't Stop The Music*; the Bee Gees and Peter Frampton in the film of *Sgt Pepper's Lonely Hearts Club Band*; and Olivia Newton John and Electric Light Orchestra collaborating on *Xanadu*. And while we're talking turkeys, space should also be made for *Velvet Goldmine, Hearts Of Fire, Absolute Beginners, Under The Cherry Moon*, and so on, and so on . . .

The trouble was, that when it worked, the fusion really *was* a licence to print money – as the runaway success of soundtracks from *Saturday Night Fever*, *Dirty Dancing* and *The Bodyguard* proved. And the inevitable consequence was the "let's-write-the-film-after-we've-secured-the-sound-track-rights" explosion of the Eighties, when films such as *Top Gun*, *Footloose* and *Days Of Thunder* were routinely programmed with all the detached skill of an embalmer. Then there was the "let's leave 'em humming something as the end credits roll" bandwagon, which spawned such pairings as 'Love Is All Around' in *Four Weddings And A Funeral*; 'Everything I Do (I Do It For You)' with *Robin Hood: Prince Of Thieves*); and the sustained use of 'Unchained Melody' in *Ghost*.

There were, of course, inspired exceptions to the rule: films in which contemporary music was featured both sensitively and creatively. One thinks of Robert Altman's use of Leonard Cohen's songs in *McCabe & Mrs Miller*, which greatly enhanced the film's bleak location; Bob Dylan's moody and atmospheric soundtrack for *Pat Garrett & Billy The Kid*; and, later, Aimee Mann's score for Paul Thomas Anderson's *Magnolia*. And, in the right hands, even individual songs could be used to great effect: 'Everybody's Talkin'' in *Midnight Cowboy*; 'Then He Kissed Me' in *Good Fellas*; 'Tiny Dancer' in *Almost Famous* . . .

Originally, Coppola was keen to have Van Morrison score *One From The Heart*, but the reluctant, truculent Irishman would have none of it: "I'm not particularly fond of Las Vegas," he told Dermot Stokes, "and that's why I didn't do it. I didn't feel like I could be true to doing that kind of music – although I like Coppola a lot. I think he's a great film-maker." Al Stewart was another singer-songwriter who may have been angling for the gig, if his 1981 song 'Here In Angola' was anything to go by: "Take another sip of your cola/ You'll be the colonel of the cavalry/ I'll be Francis Ford Coppola."

In the end, it was Coppola's son, Gian Carlo (who died in a boating accident in 1986, aged only 23) who passed a copy of Waits' *Foreign Affairs* on to his father. "It had this beautiful duet," Francis Ford Coppola later recalled, "'I Never Talk To Strangers', with Bette Midler singing the female part, and I thought wow, that's a concept! I can have the male voice and the female voice and they can be involved in dialogue, working out issues in song, sort of paralleling the male and female pro-tagonists in the story."

During pre-production for what became *One From The Heart*, Coppola was full of enthusiasm about the ways in which a musical score could be utilised. He had it clearly in mind to fully integrate the songs with the narrative – with the songs being written in tandem with the script, rather than simply grafted on afterwards. Coppola spoke enthusiastically of doing away "with all the psychological motivation stuff, and placing people as part of the composition, in which scenery, acting, words, lyrics, colour . . . all come together with equal importance."

The luxury of having Waits on board from the very beginning allowed Coppola the rare indulgence of being able to direct the music, in tandem with his rich visual imagination. Looking back on *One From The Heart,* a quarter of a century later, Coppola admitted: "I originally told Tom, 'What I really want you to do is make an album called *One From The Heart,* and then I'll make a movie that goes with it!'" It was a two-way street: "*One From The Heart* was the most rewarding experience I've had since I started working," Waits told me while he was in London, on sabbatical from the film.

Work on *One From The Heart* would occupy Waits for the best part of two years. Until then, for each album Waits would write 20 or so songs for consideration, then he'd whittle them down to the requisite 12, to fill two sides of a 40-minute record. For a full film soundtrack, however, a very different technique was necessary.

By his own admission, Waits was "a very undisciplined writer until I began working with Francis". He remembered when we met: "The seasons when you're working for a major company aren't necessarily the same seasons which coincide with your own creative development."

Waits was still living in New York when he began the score for his first film soundtrack. "There's an opening tune, then it goes into a duet, an overture . . ." he told me, "and we come down into the city and there'll be a song about rain . . . I wrote about 12 different themes to be used wherever he wanted them, then I strung them all together like an overture for a musical."

Prior to his collaboration with Coppola and *One From The Heart,* Waits admitted that most of his writing owed a healthy debt to the odd libation. But for his new assignment a different method of working – and a lot more discipline – was required. "Film scoring is like writing songs for someone else's dream," he told David McGee of *The Record.* "Up till then, writing songs was something I did when I'd been drinking, and I wasn't absolutely sure I was capable of doing it in terms of being a craftsman. And being part of something very large, you have to discuss openly what it is you do and how it relates to a carpenter, a lighting guy and an actor. So it made me more responsible and more disciplined."

At the onset of filming, Coppola was equally responsible and disciplined.

Talking to Christopher Frayling for a BBC profile, he admitted that *One From The Heart* began as a very simple idea: "I wanted to do a story told all by song. It was basically stagecraft and a kind of musical parable about a couple being together, breaking apart, each having another affair, getting back together again – it was no more complex than that and it had a beautiful score and songs – it was a little musical Valentine." As with so many of his projects though, that elemental simplicity somehow got lost in its translation to the screen.

One of Coppola's cost-cutting innovations at Zoetrope while shooting *One From The Heart* was the use of video to provide instant playbacks. He was in awe of this pioneering technology, which he saw as the beginnings of "electronic cinema". Today, in a world awash with electronic everythings, it is hard to identify with Coppola's early enthusiasm; but back in 1981, while he was shooting *One From The Heart*, it was still long before home video recording was a widespread possibility, and Digital Versatile Discs were something you could only imagine in *Blade Runner*.

By first shooting a scene from the angle he wanted on video, Coppola could immediately see the results played back. Then, if he was happy with that, he could go ahead and film the master shot, thereby avoiding tedious, expensive and time-consuming delays while the film was processed and viewed the next day as rushes. Coppola estimated that just by watching instantaneous video playbacks he had saved in the region of $2 million.

The original budget for *One From The Heart* was an estimated $15 million, which was dependent on the shoot taking place on location in Las Vegas. Alas, the reality of the gambling capital in the Nevada desert failed to live up to the "heightened reality" the writer/director was looking for in his film. "We took the . . . truck to Las Vegas," Coppola told Chris Peachment in *Time Out*, "and then I looked down the street and, really, it's just another street, with a lot of trash in the gutter and a few tenements and a bit of neon here and there . . . and it was then I realised that I was much more interested in fantasy."

And so it was that any potential savings made by utilising the new technology were immediately blown by Coppola's determination to build *his* Las Vegas on the Zoetrope lot, rather than filming on location. That decision alone is estimated to have added a further $5 million to the budget. So, to try to keep costs down, the principal cast (Nastassia Kinski, Raul Julia, Frederic Forrest, Teri Garr) were drawn from a repertory company Coppola was establishing as part of the Zoetrope roster. Future star and Leonard Cohen muse, Rebecca De Mornay could also be glimpsed, delivering her only line in her film debut: "Excuse me, those are my waffles."

Humphrey Bogart famously concluded of *The Maltese Falcon* that it was "the stuff that dreams are made of". And in keeping with *his* dream, Coppola had enlisted Michael Powell and Gene Kelly as creative consultants at Zoetrope from the very beginning. Besides being Martin Scorsese's favourite director, Powell was the maverick Englishman behind some of Britain's most uncharacteristic and haunting cinema – films such as *A Matter Of Life And Death*, *A Canterbury Tale* and *Black Narcissus*. Aptly, *One From The Heart* was filmed on the same studio where Powell had shot his fantastic fable *The Thief Of Baghdad* – Coppola's favourite film – 40 years before.

Gene Kelly, cinema's most elegant and adept hoofer (just think of *Singin' In The Rain*, *An American In Paris*, and *On The Town*) was on hand to supervise the choreographic elements of *One From The Heart*. Though, in hindsight, Kelly recalled his *One From The Heart* experience ruefully: "It was a terrible shame the idea didn't work out because, for the first time in 20 years, here was a man who took the musical seriously."

In the end, *One From The Heart* (the film that began as Coppola's "little musical Valentine") is believed to have come in at a then staggering $26 million. Investors dropped out, loans were called in, and in order to get the film finished, Coppola had to pledge around $8 million of his own money from his *Godfather* proceeds.

Coppola's musical collaborator, however, remained unstinting in his admiration for the director: "Francis is always changing his mind when he gets inside a film, then he eats his way out," Waits told me. "He's a creative maverick who is distrusted by all the cigar-smoking moguls. He keeps morale up, like Orson Welles said, a movie studio is the best train-set you could ever want. Coppola keeps a child's wonder at the whole process, even after a business meeting."

As a songwriter, Waits clearly relished the opportunity of working alongside such a director – and the importance of *One From The Heart* in Tom Waits' career cannot be overstated. His involvement as composer of a multi-million-dollar film project, in the company of one of the industry's few real *auteurs*, led directly to Waits moving from cult (i.e. largely unknown) artiste to centre-stage.

Because Coppola was determined to make music such an integral part of *One From The Heart*, he had moved Waits into his own office on the Zoetrope lot. Complete with a Yamaha grand, tape deck, mahogany walls and a coffee table groaning with script revisions, Waits relished the "David Niven feel to the room".

Coincidentally, at the same time Waits was savouring his new role as film composer, in Hollywood Ry Cooder was finishing his first soundtrack, for *The Long Riders*, and Randy Newman was completing *his* first scoring commission, *Ragtime*. Like Waits, Ry Cooder was only too happy to slip the familiar album–tour–album routine. Talking to Barney Hoskyns in 2005, Cooder fondly recalled his experience working with Walter Hill on *The Long Riders*; sentiments which echo Waits' feelings on his relationship with Coppola: "If I wanted to airbrush 50 guitars tuned in unison," Cooder recalled, "and it took three hours to set it up for a 10-second cue, he'd never bat an eye . . . I had a great time. You earned respectable money and you didn't have to go on tour and go on the treadmill of horror."

One From The Heart was undoubtedly a turning point in Waits' career, but it would also mark the last collaboration between him and his long-time producer Bones Howe. The pair shared an office on the Zoetrope lot as, together, they fashioned the soundtrack. "I would come in . . . in tennis shoes and shirt and he would come in looking like he just got off Skid Row," Howe later recalled.

But it was while he was recording an orchestra made up of car horns, or supervising a percussive track entirely composed of hubcaps being pounded, that Howe began to sense a widening gap between himself and Waits. Tom had also just met his future wife Kathleen ("He was smitten," Howe recalled) which may have been another factor in their partnership sundering. But the actual parting was conducted without acrimony.

"He called me up and said, 'Can we have a drink?'" Howe told Dan Daley. "He told me he realised one night that he was writing a song, and found himself asking, 'If I write this, will Bones like it?' I said to him that we were getting to be kind of like an old married couple. I said I don't want to be the reason that an artist can't create. It was time for him to find another producer. We shook hands and that was it. It was a great ride."

As a music industry outsider, Waits had identified on a personal level with what Coppola was trying to do at Zoetrope. "Coppola is actually the only film director in Hollywood that has a conscience . . . who is selfless," Waits told Dermot Stokes of *Hot Press*, "in that he sees himself as a conduit and a part of something much larger. He's concerned with the future of the cinema . . . most of them are egomaniacs and money-grabbing bastards . . . He's concerned with developing not just an acting repertory company but also . . . a place where you can have a full emotional curriculum, dealing with every aspect of the fine arts. Francis is very musical, and one of the warmest, most open, vulnerable, and imaginative people I've ever met.

"He gave me an office with a piano, with Venetian blinds, wood panelling and a view of the gas station! And I got up in the morning, shaved, put on a suit and went to work."

Clearly a real culture shock had awaited him when he went to work on *One From The Heart*. Each of Waits' six albums had been recorded in little more than a week or so, but collaborating so closely with Coppola on a major film project, there was inevitably a lot of hanging around. Additional delays were caused by Coppola grappling with the new technology of "electronic cinema"; the persistent haemorrhaging of money out of Zoetrope; the problems arising from other films on the studio schedule . . . all of which left precious little time for Coppola to actually direct *One From The Heart*.

"It was constantly being changed," Waits told Neil McCormick in *Hot Press*. "What do they say? A camel is a horse designed by a committee! . . . It's a very involved process. It's like a city. Film staff, cast, crew, it's like you're all building this thing. Everything has to fit, so whatever you're doing has to be designed in with the overall fabric of the piece."

Waits himself can be glimpsed, playing a trumpet, in the crowd that fills the screen near the beginning of *One From The Heart*. But he was too preoccupied with the music to take a larger on-screen role. "Francis was shooting with a PA system on the set. When he's rehearsing, he plays the music and the actors can listen and grow accustomed to hearing the melody while they're working on a scene, and it's . . . put together much more like a theatre production than a movie.

"He wants to shoot it in sequence, so you get a real feeling for the story, and you see magic while you're making it, not months later, where people stand back and say it's great. But it was two years of hell. What he's trying to do is get everyone to enjoy the process and leave it open for new ideas. Francis loves somebody to tell him that something's not possible, and he'll make it possible."[1]

In his head, Coppola heard a man and a woman's voice permeating *One From The Heart*'s soundtrack ("What I originally wanted was something like a male and female *presence* . . . only they were up in Heaven!"). Waits' duet with Bette Midler, 'I Never Talk To Strangers' was clearly one of the models in Coppola's mind, but Midler's workload meant that she was unavailable for the shooting schedule Coppola originally had in mind. In the event, it was Waits himself who suggested his eventual – and somewhat incongruous – singing partner.

Crystal Gayle was already established as one of the leading divas of the country scene, having enjoyed her first hits on the country charts in 1970, while she was still in her teens. Hits such as 'Don't It Make My Brown Eyes Blue' and 'Talking In Your Sleep' subsequently helped her cross over onto the pop charts – and now Crystal was a Grammy award-winning singer. She could also lay claim to being the first female country singer to sell one million copies of an album, and to having the longest hair in showbusiness. Coppola was enchanted, later admitting to "having this respectful little crush on her".

There have been other incongruous vocal partnerships: Bing Crosby & David Bowie; Nick Cave & Kylie Minogue; Nicole Kidman & Robbie Williams; Kirsty MacColl & The Pogues . . . But Waits – who had come to represent the sybaritic excess at the bohemian edge of pop, and Gayle – the sweet-voiced younger sister of Loretta Lynn – represented a particularly striking juxtaposition.

The subsequent *One From The Heart* soundtrack album worked, to everyone's surprise, remarkably well. On paper, Waits and Gayle sound like a blind date gone horribly wrong; on disc, it was a marriage made in heaven. The purity of Crystal Gayle's voice contrasts breathtakingly with the spit'n'sawdust grumble of Waits' delivery. The odd couple play off each other perfectly, particularly on 'This One's From The Heart'. And undeniably, something about working on *One From The Heart* inspired Waits as a composer.

Fired by Coppola's enthusiasm and brio, the Waits songs really help in furthering the narrative, enabling the characters to develop by way of his music rather than lengthy expositions on screen. And even on disc, without the benefit of the director's lustrous images, the melodies Waits supplied are some of his most beguiling.

Crystal Gayle is simply enchanting on a song like the wistful 'Is There Any Way Out Of This Dream?' And because it's the movies, Waits reins in his customary husk and bark, and croons sensitively as required. Embracing late night jazz and neon-lit Broadway, the soundtrack crackles. There is verve and melancholy in equal measure – and a really moving quality in Waits' singing and writing, as for example, this line from 'Broken Bicycles': "Somebody must have an orphanage for all these things that nobody wants anymore."

'Old Boyfriends', 'Take Me Home' and 'Broken Bicycles' were among some of Waits' loveliest tunes to date. 'Little Boy Blue' operates on full steam, sounding like it could have sat happily on *Small Change*; while the fairground sound of 'Circus Girl' signposts the way towards *Frank's Wild*

Years. 'You Can't Unring A Bell' features some of Waits' deftest lyrics, and one of his most menacing vocals. The 2004 CD reissue of *One From The Heart* offered two bonus tracks, the sibilant jazz of 'Candy Apple Red', and the boozy 'Once Upon A Town/ Empty Pockets', which features the nice line, "I spill myself another drink."

It was while working on *One From The Heart* that Waits met his future wife. Kathleen Brennan was employed as a script editor for Zoetrope, and on those rare occasions when Coppola let Waits loose from his office, the two began walking out. According to Waits, it was an extremely colourful courtship. Certainly, eyebrows were raised at his claim that Kathleen had jumped the Grand Canyon alongside Evel Knievel and that she had seven kids from a previous marriage; or that true love had burgeoned between Waits and his bride-to-be while she was his parole officer. But there was no mistaking Waits genuine admiration for his intended, when he confided to Elissa Van Poznak in *The Face*: "She can lie down on nails, stick a knitting needle through her lip and still drink coffee, so I knew she was the girl for me."

The story of *One From The Heart* takes place one Independence Day in Las Vegas; and during the course of the ensuing 24 hours, the four characters weave in and out of each other's lives. They drift apart, and come back together, against the constant glare of the Vegas neon and the dusty sweep of the Nevada desert. Slight it may be, but stylish . . . very, *very* stylish.

One From The Heart is full of what Christopher Isherwood called "tarnished superlatives". It celebrates its artificiality, revels in its cinematic magic of fades and dissolves, and for all the weakness of the story, the heightened reality of *One From The Heart* pulls you along with its defiantly superficial style.

The film is also rich in striking imagery: Nastassia Kinski's high wire act; Teri Garr's walk down lonely street; Raul Julia's golden tango; Frederic Forrest, using a dipstick, conducting his "used carlotta" . . . But though the acting is sound, the real star of the film is Las Vegas itself – courtesy, in this reincarnation, of Zoetrope Studios.

One From The Heart was light on actual stars: Nastassia Kinski had starred in *Tess* in 1980, when she was only 20, but she was probably more famous for her off-screen relationships with Roman Polanski and Quincy Jones. Even the 42-year-old Raul Julia had only made one previous film, though he went on to stardom in *The Addams Family*, before dying in 1994, aged only 54. Frederic Forrest had worked with Coppola on *Apocalypse Now* and would star as the eponymous *Hammett*, also for Zoetrope while Teri Garr had appeared in *Close Encounters Of The Third Kind*, and was

Oscar-nominated for Best Supporting Actress in *Tootsie* the same year as she starred in *One From The Heart*.

Perhaps the story is somewhat flimsy, and the narrative less substantial than you might wish, but *One From The Heart* had an undeniably involving charm. And even a quarter of a century on, with computer-generated imagery an integral part of every major Hollywood product, *One From The Heart* still maintains its idiosyncratic and rather futuristic appeal. This was genuinely memorable magical-realism: a touching cinematic fairy tale starring Las Vegas as an adults-only playground.

The final credit of *One From The Heart* read: "Filmed entirely on the stages of Zoetrope Studios." And when the film premiered at Radio City Music Hall in New York, on January 15, 1982, the celebrity audience, which included Andy Warhol, Paul Simon, Norman Mailer, Martin Scorsese and Liza Minnelli, was stunned.

The critics, however, found faults aplenty: "Full of pretty-pretty imagery . . . but with characters so humdrum they are practically androids" (*Los Angeles Herald Examiner*). "Unfunny, unjoyous, unsexy and unromantic" (*New York Times*). "The picture comes from the same artistic impulses that inspire airbrush art, three-dimensional pop-up greeting cards and the deliberately beautiful new neon that illuminates LA shops" (*Los Angeles Times*). "With all his technological huffing and puffing, Coppola has thrown out the baby and photographed the bath water." (*Village Voice*).

Under the headline "Dazzling body, empty heart", *Variety* complained that Coppola's "giddy heights of visual imagination and technical brilliance are lavished on a wafer-thin story". The influential trade bible review did, however, also note that: "Underscoring and counterpointing the emotional tones is Tom Waits' bluesy-jazzy score and songs, with the composer and country balladeer Crystal Gayle warbling respective 'boy' and 'girl' roles."

On general release, *One From The Heart* stiffed. American audiences at the time were flocking to see Dustin Hoffman in drag in *Tootsie*; and welcoming new stars like Eddie Murphy (*48 Hours*), Richard Gere (*An Officer And A Gentleman*) and the ensemble cast of *Diner*. But at the box office, everything else succumbed to the all-conquering *ET* – directed, ironically, by Coppola's protégé, Steven Spielberg.

The film was better received in Europe – and in France, *One From The Heart* was rather charmingly titled *Coup De Coeur*. It took a year for *One From The Heart* to open in the UK, and though by then its reputation had preceded it, critics on this side of the Atlantic – always kinder to Coppola – gave it a far warmer reception. *Time Out* called it "a likable, idiosyncratic musical . . . the saving grace is a light heart", while Richard Cook concluded his *NME* review: "It's a cold heart that doesn't love this one."

Even so, *One From The Heart* struggled to find a cinema audience. That only came much later, with the subsequent video and DVD releases. The film's influence though was wider-ranging. There were obvious similarities in Jean-Jacques Beineix's *Betty Blue*, and the film of the long-running stage show, *Chicago*. But the most evident homage came in 2001, when Baz Luhrmann modelled his *Moulin Rouge* on Coppola's 1982 film.

Waits was nominated for 'Best Original Song Score', but lost out to Leslie Bricusse and Henry Mancini's music for the Julie Andrews cross-dressing vehicle which was *Victor/Victoria*. Coppola's most sympathetic biographer Peter Cowie later wrote: "Critics have not given enough credit to . . . songs in *One From The Heart*, which enhance the movie's mood indigo."

One From The Heart had proved, in many ways, a watershed for Waits. His 1982 Oscar-nominated score offered a new route, at the beginning of a new decade – and a new perspective. "As I turn the corner on 30, I'm fastly becoming concerned about personal hygiene. Drinkin' and smokin' and smokin' and drinkin' started slowing me down. One of these days I'll want to have a family, I've gotta think about that."[2]

At the age of 30, Waits discovered that he had turned into "a caricature of myself". As he told Mick Brown in 1981: "You have to be very clear about who you are and who it is you're projecting, but the two got very confusing. I got swept away with it, then felt I had to live up to something . . . I realised that a guy who writes murder mysteries doesn't have to be a murderer . . . I don't feel I have to live up to something anymore, which is not to say I have turned into Perry Como – although I still look up to Perry a lot."

NOTES

1   Dermot Stokes, *Hot Press*
2   Stephen X. Rea, *Ampersand*

CHAPTER 17

BENEATH his bohemian image and beat aspirations, Waits had always been more of a white-picket-fence kind of guy than you might imagine. It was that surprisingly conservative element that Rickie Lee Jones reacted against as their relationship drew to a close. She confided to the late Timothy White that Waits "really did want to live in a little bungalow with a bunch of screaming kids and spend Saturday nights at the drive-in".

Now turning 30, Waits' thoughts turned seriously to settling down. His two-year stint at Zoetrope had given him a base of operations, a life off the road, and something approaching a normal existence. As he revelled in that return to "normality", after the best part of a decade spent in self-absorption and self-indulgence, Waits and Kathleen Brennan enjoyed a "whirlwind" courtship. The couple were married in August 1980, just a matter of months after Waits began working at Zoetrope. The location, he told me with a twinkle, was the Always Forever Yours Wedding Chapel in Watts, Los Angeles.

When I spoke to him some seven months after his marriage, Waits was still in the first flush of romantic ardour. His bride, he told me, had been training to be a nun before she married him, "so you could say I've saved her from the Lord".

Kathleen's family background was Irish. But though she was born in Cork, the family moved to Johnsburg, Illinois when she was just a child. "My wife's from a small town in Illinois," Waits told me proudly. "It's all flat. It's where most of our great writers and creative thinkers and presidents come from." A spell at 20th Century Fox led her to Zoetrope, and the meeting with her future husband. One of the most moving songs in all the Waits canon is the dignified 'Johnsburg, Illinois', which he recorded on *Swordfishtrombones*, his first album after marrying Kathleen: "She's my only true love," Tom croons, "she's all that I think of . . ."

The wedding ceremony itself was not without incident: "I found the Marriage Chapel in the *Yellow Pages*," Waits told me, "right next to 'Massage'. The registrar's name was Watermelon, and he kept calling me 'Mr Watts'. My mother likes what I do, but I guess she's happier now that

I'm married. I think she was a little bit worried about me for a while." And not without reason . . .

In an early press release Waits had painted an empty picture of his bachelor lifestyle: "A cigarette dangles from his weary mouth as he mourns to an empty beer can, melancholia for lost loves and good times and bad times good enough to make the strongest weep for their loss. He cuddles up to himself better off without a wife, consoling his empty evenings by asking himself for a date."

The newlyweds honeymooned in Tralee, County Kerry – and in 2005, they celebrated their silver wedding anniversary. "If it wasn't for her," Waits confided recently, "I'd be playing in a steak house somewhere. No, I'd probably be *cleaning* the steak house."[1]

However, despite the new-found bliss of his personal life, professionally, his 1980 release *Heartattack & Vine* was the sound of Waits treading water – smacking of contractual obligation rather than artistic inspiration. Released while he was working on *One From The Heart*, his seventh album was more guitar-based, with a harder, R&B edge rather than the familiar piano-led jazz colourings.

The title track had Waits sounding a cautionary note to those flocking in from Iowa, all set for stardom, only to be swindled out of their dreams by the callous indifference of Hollywood. 'Heartattack & Vine' also included his much-quoted quip observation that: "There ain't no Devil, there's just God when he's drunk." The whole album teems with the madness of the City of Angels, the cautionary tales played out against the glare of bright neon and the scream of police sirens. 'Til The Money Runs Out' tells of craziness, fuelled by "a pint of green chartreuse", where "nothin' seems right"; the sort of place where "you buy the Sunday paper on a Saturday night".

Though not everyone shared his opinion that *Heartattack & Vine* was a catalyst, Waits himself characterised it as an attempt at breaking out of his own comfort zone: "Me trying to avoid using a knife and fork and a spoon. It wasn't 100 per cent successful, but it's usually the small breakthroughs that give you a tunnel to laterally make some kind of transition. The title track was a breakthrough for me, using that kind of Yardbirds fuzz guitar, having the drummer using sticks instead of brushes, small things like that. More or less putting on a different costume."[2]

For all its guitar-driven edge, *Heartattack & Vine* also displayed the softness of touch to which we had become accustomed; the album boasted two of Waits' most beautiful songs: 'On The Nickel' and 'Jersey Girl', while 'Ruby's Arms' was a heartbreaking adieu to the girl who lies sleeping while her lover disappears, taking only her scarf as a souvenir.

Elsewhere, we were in the territory of the first Crosby, Stills, Nash & Young album, *Deja Vu*. 'In Shades' was an unremarkable instrumental; 'Saving All My Love For You' was no marked improvement on *Foreign Affairs* material from years before; 'Downtown' little more than a rambunctious roar; 'Mr Siegal', another unremarkable subterranean trip among the low lifes . . .

However, the album did contain the lovely 'On The Nickel', a haunting ballad used as the theme for the 1979 film written, produced and directed by Ralph Waite. Best-known as the paterfamilias from TV's long-running series *The Waltons*, Waite had begun his film career acting alongside Paul Newman in *Cool Hand Luke*; now a director, *On The Nickel* was Waite's take on life among the bums of LA's Skid Row.

"I read about the film being made downtown," Waits told me. "I didn't know Ralph Waite, but it looked like something I'd like to be involved with. So I drove round looking for the location, but I couldn't find anything and a couple of weeks later I got a phone call from the film's composer who'd been asked by Ralph Waite to contact me with regards to writing a title song."

Made with actors from LA's Actors' Theatre, *On The Nickel* featured Donald Moffat, now familiar as one of Hollywood's most in-demand character actors. He appears as CJ's dad in *The West Wing*, for example; and that's him occupying the Oval Office in *Clear And Present Danger* – nowadays Moffat tends to play presidents rather than bums.

When you're down and out, and you can sink no lower, you go "on the nickel". Waits' song is a curiously touching nursery rhyme for these hopeless derelicts, a hobo's lullaby reminding us all that no matter how far down you slip, everyone began somewhere, as some mother's son. Skid Row, the song suggests, is the address of "all the little boys who never comb their hair". (The version of the song used in the film included an extra verse from Waits: "You never know how rich you are, you haven't got a prayer/ Heads you win, tails they lose, on the nickel over there.")

The film attracted respectful reviews on its release in 1979 ("What emerges is a rich slice of life we seldom see . . . filled with compassion and surprising amounts of humour . . . Its sense of truth is shattering," enthused *The Hollywood Reporter*). However, Waits' *Heartattack & Vine* did little real business at the time. It reached number 96 on the US album charts in October 1980, but the UK remained publicly indifferent. One song from the album did have long-term ramifications, though: 'Jersey Girl' was a powerful ballad and a shoo-in for the unelected representative for the garden state of New Jersey – Bruce Frederick Joseph Springsteen.

Way back in the Seventies, Waits and Springsteen had been rivals in the great "new Dylan" handicap chase. Springsteen was only a couple of months older than Waits, but since the success of 1975's *Born To Run*, his career had easily eclipsed that of his gravel-voiced contemporary.

Subsequent albums *Darkness On The Edge Of Town* and, particularly, 1980's *The River*, had consolidated Springsteen as the pre-eminent American rock star of the era – while, in Britain, his stature was barely less than mythic. Springsteen had only ever played a couple of London shows in 1975, but during the intervening six years, breathless accounts of his marathon American gigs had excited British fans to fever pitch.

Hardly surprising then, that Bruce Springsteen's six shows at Wembley Arena during 1981 were the most keenly anticipated of any visitor in living memory. Waits, meanwhile, was displaying a more modest hand, at the more intimate Apollo, Victoria. With Springsteen-mania tangible in the streets of the capital, Waits smiled as we passed the huge "Sold Out" posters boasting The Boss's London shows. "He's a nice guy," he smiled, "I sure hope that my shows don't detract from his ticket sales."

As we drove on through London, I remember asking if he secretly desired that level of fame. Waits shuffled down in his seat and stared out of the passenger window . . . "Nah, not at all. I've spent the last 10 years looking for something, now I'm married and I'm very happy."

Waits wrote 'Jersey Girl' as a love song to his wife Kathleen, who had spent some time living in New Jersey. It's a beautiful, affecting song, simple and direct, with Waits musing that everything's all right "when you're with your baby on a Saturday night". With a meandering guitar opening, sinisterly echoing 'The End' by The Doors, it is undeniably one of the highlights of *Heartattack & Vine*, and one of the clutch of truly great songs to which Tom Waits can lay claim.

It was during that unforgettable 1981 tour that Springsteen began to include 'Jersey Girl' in his set – and because he has always been so closely identified with New Jersey, many of his fans assumed that 'Jersey Girl' was a Springsteen original. Certainly Bruce loved the song, and he did write an extra verse to wrap the song up in concert, but he was always at pains to point out Waits as author. And at the giant LA Sports Arena during August 1981, the composer joined Springsteen and the E. Street Band onstage to sing 'Jersey Girl'.

Springsteen went on to dominate Eighties American rock. On its release in 1984, *Born In The USA* hurled him into a different dimension, spawning no less than *seven* American Top 10 singles from its dozen tracks. The second of these singles, 'Cover Me', featured a live version of 'Jersey Girl' on the B-side – which presumably enabled the newly married Mr and Mrs Waits to afford some nice new curtains.

There are many who believe Tom Waits has been marginalised over the years and never accorded the respect due to him as a composer, but financially that has never been the case – which is largely due to that one song, 'Jersey Girl', and that nice Mr Springsteen.

Following *Born In The USA*, and its 20 million-plus sales – just when you thought that Bruce Springsteen could never get any bigger, his fans took the whole Boss phenomenon a step further.

Though renowned as rock'n'roll's premier live act, Springsteen had long fought shy of a live album. After all, how could he possibly compress those magnificent and frenetic four-hour shows into one album? But in 1985, Springsteen and his manager Jon Landau finally sat down and began assembling a chronological record of Springsteen as a live performer.

Eventually, 40 tracks were squeezed onto five LPs and three of those newfangled compact discs, and released in time for Christmas 1986. The plan was to conclude the set with Bruce's own '10th Avenue Freeze Out' – until Landau felt that a more subdued song would make for a better conclusion. Springsteen concurred, and in the end they agreed on wrapping the marathon set with a dignified reading of Tom Waits' 'Jersey Girl'. "That's the same guy that's on the boardwalk in 'Sandy', back in the same place," Springsteen would later comment when asked why he had chosen to record the song. "The same guy in 'Rosalita' – you know, he got the Jersey girl."

The live, five-album Springsteen set became the first box-set ever to reach number 1 in America; it was also one of the very few albums *ever* to enter the chart straight at the top. And with worldwide sales in the millions, the inclusion of 'Jersey Girl' ensured Waits further substantial royalties.

He was duly grateful, and not just for the cash. Waits had long been a Springsteen fan, and genuinely appreciated the accolade from a song-writing peer. "Bruce Springsteen? Well, I've done all I can for him. He's on his own now! . . ." Waits joked to Bill Flanagan in 1987; but as he continued, his admiration for a fellow craftsman shone through: "God, I love his songs, I wish I had written 'Meeting Across The River'. His early songs are like little black-and-white films. Things like 'Wild Billy's Circus Story' were real well crafted. He's got a great visual sense, a great balance."

In a sense, Springsteen returned the compliment on his 2005 *Devils & Dust* album, particularly on 'Reno' – an adult account of a guy buying love from a hooker. It was a song that tipped its hat to Tom, and in the process, earned Bruce a ban from the Starbucks chain of coffee shops.

However different Waits had tried to make *Heartattack & Vine* sound, one thing that remained as distinctive as ever was his own voice. Ever since Bob Dylan burst on the scene, the idea of an orthodox "singing voice" had been ditched. Way back in 1961, in the breakthrough review that landed Dylan his recording contract, Robert Shelton had noted: "Mr Dylan's voice is anything but pretty. He is consciously trying to recapture the rude beauty of a Southern field hand musing in melody on his porch. All the 'husk and bark' are left on his notes . . ." In Dylan's wake came Randy Newman, Kris Kristofferson and John Prine, whose scratched and flaky vocals were whole city blocks away from what Tin Pan Alley expected from traditional pop singers. By now, critics and public alike had grown used to "distinctive" voices in pop – but Tom Waits' still took some swallowing.

In its review of *Heartattack & Vine*, *NME* commented: "Waits' voice no longer sounds like it's simply been lived in – more like it's been squatted in by 13 separate Puerto Rican junkie families with tubercular in-laws." In his *Melody Maker* review, Brian Case called *Heartattack & Vine* "Waits' best album since *Small Change*." But even he couldn't ignore the tubes: "His voice, that deformed instrument, happiest with words like 'bitch', and resembling the hacking up of stubborn phlegm . . ."

In passing, and on the subject of voices . . . Once, when asked: "Do you take steps to protect your voice?" Waits replied cheerfully: "Protect it from what? *Vandals?*" While in a 1987 profile, Robert Sabbag admitted: "Even now, telling many Americans that your favourite singer is Tom Waits is like telling them that your favourite actor is John Wilkes Booth."

Even for true believers, Tom Waits' singing voice can best be described as 'distinctive'. But . . . once heard, never forgotten. The sound growls through his mouth, as if rising painfully from the very sole of his shoes. It's not a voice at all really, it's a '56 Buick with a broken exhaust. A rasping reminder of former glories, a silencer, snapped somewhere out on the kokomo. Waits doesn't croak when he sings, he roars, just like that magnificent MGM lion. On disc, it's a bouncer grumbling come closing time. In concert, it's downtown: the city of Memphis given voice.

Waits' own favourite description of his singing voice was "Louis Armstrong and Ethel Merman meeting in Hell!" And Waits has a good ear for voices, and their nuances. Speaking of Marianne Faithfull, who took part in the 2004 production of his play *The Black Rider*, Waits mused: "She's the aunt offering you a cigarette at a wedding when you're 11. Her voice is spooky oil on a squeaky gate, baby powder meets gunpowder."[3]

The recording of *Heartattack & Vine* had been marked by an appearance from expatriate British jazzman Victor Feldman, who was to have a marked influence on the even more startling future sound of Waits' records. "He suggested instruments I wouldn't have thought of," Waits told Brian Case, "squeeze drums, Balinese percussion, marimba, things I'd always been timid about."

As a new decade dawned, Tom Waits was setting sail for as yet undiscovered new shores. Bobbing along in the distance was the "old" Tom Waits, with his familiar bar-room rambles and spindly piano ballads. While ahead, just over the horizon, were new sounds inside his mind. Strange, unsettling sounds . . .

NOTES

1   Richard Grant, *Telegraph* Magazine
2   David McGee, *The Record*
3   *Mojo* 135

CHAPTER 18

NEWLY married; on the wagon; no longer smoking; working in *an office* for Francis Ford Coppola . . . the early Eighties were a shifting time for Tom Waits. Though he denied that marriage had mellowed him, or that Kathleen was responsible for him cutting down on the booze, she had "just given me someone to share it with".

In truth, though Kathleen did help Waits straighten out, he already realised that was what he needed. The old lifestyle was draining him, and he knew it. Worse than that, he had been in danger of becoming a caricature – and coming off the booze undeniably helped him avoid that fate. But so insolubly linked to smoky bars had he been, that many found it inconceivable that Waits could ever go on the wagon. Years later, Ross Fortune asked Waits if he didn't miss the booze and the bars? "Nah . . . I heard better stories in the AA meetings to be honest with you."

Post-production work on *One From The Heart* ate up a lot of Waits' time in the months following his marriage, but he did tour to promote *Heartattack & Vine*. I caught him in London, in March 1981. He was a tiny, twisted figure onstage, welded to his piano – with stand-up bass and sax his only companions. Oh, and there was also a lamp-post . . . But what you remembered was Waits and his piano . . . it was jazz you could almost *taste*. At the end of the show, "rain" poured down on the solitary figure of Tom Waits. He raised an umbrella (in those far-off days few LA-based singer-songwriters appeared on stage without one) and sauntered off.

Live in concert, Waits was a loose-limbed figure, a puppet without strings. He spun words, like plates on a juggler's stick, casting high lines over low lives. Seated at the piano, a goatee apparently added as an afterthought, eyes closed on that Herman Munster-like face, Waits wore his hat at what Dylan Thomas called "a desperate angle". Standing, those long, spindly hands clutching a microphone, he cut a stick figure, like Eraserhead out on the town.

Poignant as the material – drawn from his seven albums – was, it was the between-songs patter that made the evening remarkable. Waits mumbled, muttered, rasped and growled. And 2,000 people hung on his every utterance like they were eavesdropping on a sleepwalker . . . What was that about someone fracturing a rib in Italy? And the connection between an ambulance siren and 'Over The Rainbow'?

With the chill of winter still holding sway, it was apt that Waits' 1981 visit coincided with a major Edward Hopper retrospective at the Hayward Gallery. There they were, the two great depicters of American isolation, in London at the same time.

Waits was visibly restless. Already twitchy from nicotine withdrawal, he got even more jittery anticipating the new music he wanted to make. He was feeling creatively stifled and sick of the no-hoper beat bum image, admitting "I was getting lazy."

Though he envisaged with clarity his new direction, it was still a frightening leap into the unknown. But he was encouraged by his new wife, Kathleen, who helped ease him into the next phase of his career. "She had the best record collection," Waits told Sylvie Simmons. "She thought I was going to have a really great record collection and was sorely disappointed . . . I was such a one-man show, very isolated in what I allowed myself to be exposed to . . . She helped me rethink myself . . ."

Unfortunately, some of his working relationships were not going so well. There was an acrimonious dispute with his manager Herb Cohen which led to their parting. And around the same time, after nearly a decade together, Waits quit working with producer Bones Howe.

His head was now spinning fast and furious, exploring bewildering new territories: trying to conjure up "a mutant dwarf community in a steam tunnel" was far removed from the simple touching romanticism of 'Jersey Girl'. In April 1982 Waits took three of his new songs ('Frank's Wild Years', 'Shore Leave' and '16 Shells From A 30.6') to Warner-Elektra-Asylum top-gun Joe Smith.

Waits regarded these as exhilarating proof of his innovative new direction, and he was looking for encouragement. Unfortunately, the label disagreed, and after seven albums Waits was off Asylum Records – and out of the whole Warner-Elektra-Asylum family.

"Record companies are like large department stores," Waits complained. "I was at Elektra for over 10 years, and while I was there, I spent a considerable amount of time on the road and blowing my own horn. They liked dropping my name in terms of me being a 'prestige' artist, but when it came down to it, they didn't invest a whole lot in me in terms of faith. Their identity was always more aligned with that California rock thing."[1]

A real rarity among the Waits' catalogue is the Asylum pressing of *Swordfishtrombones*. Although eventually rejected as having "no commercial potential" (a phrase beloved of Waits' old nemesis, Frank Zappa) Asylum did initially press up a number of copies of the album, the most striking feature of which is the cover, an abstract painting by Waits himself. A copy turned up in New Zealand in 2004; another, inevitably, on eBay.

With both himself and his record rejected by the suits, Waits was left shopping round for a new deal; but he remained philosophical: "A career's like having a dog you can kick," he remarked inscrutably to David McGee in *The Record*, "sometimes it jumps up on you when you're all dressed up and you have to scold it . . . And other times it runs away and you can't find it or it ends up in the pound and you have to spend all this money to get it out. So that's my dog. My career's a dog."

When I met Waits in London in 1981, between the end of the Asylum era and and the unveiling of his mysterious new direction, the clues were already there . . . Waits told me facetiously of his plans for a new album: "It's called *My Favourites*." So, bearing in mind Bowie's *Pin-Ups*, Bryan Ferry's *These Foolish Things*, and Lennon's *Rock 'N' Roll*, I asked if that was what Tom had in mind – an album of cover versions? New interpretations of much-loved material, with his own inimitable spin? "Nah, I'm just gonna take 12 songs by other artists and put them on a record. Stuff like 'Lady Of Spain', 'The Polonaise', 'Tutti Frutti', 'Ruby My Dear', The Rolling Stones' 'Just Wanna See His Face' . . . with a picture of me on the cover – listening to them!"

Swordfishtrombones was still two years in the future, but with hindsight it's clear that the foundations for it were already being laid. And if I'd followed Waits' lead, gone back to *Exile On Main Street* and played 'Just Wanna See His Face', I'd have got a couple of years jump on his next career move – and then *Swordfishtrombones* wouldn't have come as such a surprise.

Back then though, in the post-punk London of 1981, the Stones were themselves on the margin. Few paid any heed to the sprawling gumbo of their 1972 double album conceived as tax exiles in the South of France, a record that in future years would routinely be voted "best ever Stones album". Writing much later in Q, Mat Snow called *Exile On Main Street* "one of the very few double albums without a single weak link". But back in 1981, a decade after its release, *Exile* . . . was exiled from the pantheon.

Listening to it now, *Exile* . . ., and particularly 'Just Wanna See His Face', is a clear indication of where Waits was going. The song is a demented gospel gris-gris. Jagger sounds weirdly disconnected. He ruminates, drifting off-mike, then back again, with no discernible purpose. In the far distance, a girl shrieks, shadowing the Stone. There is a sheen of fractured percussion; an acoustic bass throbs purposefully. And you know something really weird is happening on a Stones album when Keith plays the *piano*.

Now, of course, we know that Waits was staking a claim in the same territory – staccato rhythms, unhinged percussion, demonic howlings floating over asylum walls.

"That song had a big impact on me," Waits confirmed years later, "particularly learning how to sing in that high falsetto, the way Jagger does. When he sings like a girl, I go crazy. I said, 'I've got to learn how to do that.' I couldn't really do it until I stopped smoking."[2]

Another ingredient that was stirred into Waits' new gumbo can be found on the 1968 album *Gris Gris* by Mac Rebennack, masquerading as Dr John, the Night Tripper. Heavy on percussion and dislocated New Orleans rhythms, the album is best known today for the heavily sampled 'Walk On Gilded Splinters'.

The songs Waits was fashioning now were so left field that his own label had let him go without so much as a backward glance. But with encouragement from Kathleen, Waits shopped what would become *Swordfishtrombones* around half a dozen labels – until it came to rest at Island Records.

Waits had a lot of time for Island's Chris Blackwell – "Blackwell is artistic . . . you can sit and talk to him and you don't feel you're at Texaco or Heineken or Budweiser. There's something operating here that has a brain, curiosity and imagination."[3]

A descendant of the family that produced Crosse & Blackwell preserves, he enjoyed a privileged upbringing divided between Britain and the Caribbean before settling in Jamaica, where he followed various careers, including aide-de-camp to the island's governor, real-estate salesman and water-skiing instructor. In 1961 Blackwell had also enjoyed a spell as location manager for a film based on a novel by a family friend. The friend was Ian Fleming; the film, the very first James Bond 007 adventure, *Dr No*.

Blackwell had been familiar with Jamaica's unique ska and blue beat music since childhood, and it was on his home island that he first launched Island Records. By 1962 though, the ambitious Blackwell brought Island to the UK, where the Jamaican recordings sold well to the West Indian immigrant communities in Birmingham and London.

The very first Island singles were delivered by Blackwell in his Mini Cooper – and it was this personal commitment, as well as his enthusiasm for all music, that saw Island branch out beyond its reggae roots. Blackwell made Island into one of the few labels you could trust. And as a result, the company flourished and continued to grow, until in 1989 Island was bought by the Polygram group for an estimated £200 million.

For a whole generation, Island – like Tamla Motown or Stiff – was one of the very few labels whose music you bought *because* of the label. A record released on Island virtually guaranteed quality. It was during the late Sixties that Island first became synonymous with particular strands of audacious and experimental music, with figureheads including such up-and-coming bands as King Crimson, Jethro Tull and Traffic – although they did miss out on Procol Harum, Queen and Led Zeppelin.

Island also provided house room for the very best folk-rock of the period: Fairport Convention, John Martyn, Fotheringay, Cat Stevens, The Incredible String Band and Nick Drake all graced the label during those years . . . But it was during the Seventies that Island really came into its own commercially, with Free, Roxy Music and Blackwell's championing of Bob Marley & The Wailers helping to put reggae on the world stage. By the end of the decade, Island had also enjoyed substantial chart success with Sparks, Steve Winwood and Robert Palmer.

It was a few years prior to Tom Waits' signing to Island, that the label snared what would become their biggest act. A tip-off led Blackwell to the Half Moon pub in Herne Hill, south-east London, where he witnessed one of the first UK shows by a young Irish quartet called U2.

For Waits, the journey to *Swordfishtrombones* was tortuous, but engaging. "I'm . . . interested in how your memory distorts things," Waits told *Sounds'* Edwin Pouncey around the time of the album's release in 1983. "It's like an apparatus that dismantles things and puts them back together with some of the parts missing."

Tom was already typecast, and the recent release of *One From The Heart* had only confirmed his reputation as a bar-room piano-player. Thus, on its release in 1983, the shock of his debut Island album was seismic. *Swordfishtrombones* was such an iconoclastic album that Waits was moved to articulate his inspiration: "Francis Thumm is an old companion of mine, he is a professor, and he also plays the Chromelodeon in the Harry Partch Ensemble . . . Partch was an American hobo and the instruments he made were all built from things that he essentially found on the side of the road, not literally but figuratively. He dismantled and rebuilt his own version of the whole concept of music and its purpose – but I just like the sound he makes."[4]

Harry Partch (1901–1974) lived and died in and around Waits' birthplace of San Diego, California. A typical Partch composition would be entitled 'Eight Hitch-Hiker Inscriptions From A Highway Railing At Barstow, California'. Partch began composing in his mid-teens, soon rejecting the standard 12-note scale for his own 43 tones to the octave system – which made his music nigh-on unplayable by anyone else.

During the Great Depression of the Thirties, Partch did ride the railroads and live the life of a hobo; and it was while on the bum that Partch – literally – picked up the idea of making his own musical instruments. The impenetrability of Partch's compositions wasn't eased by the unorthodox instruments on which he chose to fashion them. Among his own home-made instruments were the Gourd Tree, the Bloboy, the Chromelodeon, the Kithara, the Zymo-xyl, the Marimba Eroica, the Spoils of War, Cloud-Chamber Bowls and the Cone Gong. These he constructed from such unlikely sources as hub-caps, empty bottles and the shell casings from bomber aircraft.

Pretty much unheralded in his lifetime, Partch did have his admirers – jazzmen Gerry Mulligan, Gil Evans and Chet Baker all testified to the quirky appeal of his work. But it took Tom Waits to bring the name of Harry Partch to a wider audience with the release of *Swordfishtrombones* in 1983.

"It's a little arrogant to say I see a relationship between his stuff and mine," Waits told *Playboy*. "I'm very crude, but I use things we hear around us all the time, built and found instruments – things that aren't normally considered instruments: dragging a chair across the floor or hitting the side of a locker real hard with a two-by-four, a freedom bell, a brake drum with a major imperfection, a police bullhorn. It's more interesting. You know, I don't like straight lines. The problem is that most instruments are square and music is always round."

"I started wondering what would happen if we deconstructed the whole thing," Waits recalled, talking to Nigel Williamson 20 years after he took his first audacious steps into the unknown on *Swordfishtrombones*. "I like things to sound distressed. I like to imagine what it would sound like to set fire to a piano on the beach and mike it really close and wait for the strings to pop. Or drop a piano off a building and be down there waiting for it to hit with a microphone. I like melody. But I also like dissonance."

That brand of DIY musical experimentation was not unique to Waits. When Pink Floyd were struggling to follow-up *Dark Side Of The Moon* a decade before *Swordfishtrombones*, they laboured long over an album called *Household Objects*, which featured no musical instruments at all. Looking back, the Floyd's Roger Waters told me: "There was a lot of going into the studio and chopping wood, recording the noise. And you'd spend weeks and weeks recording a rubber band with some kind of schoolboy physics . . . And what you're actually doing is reinventing the bass guitar – just doing it incredibly expensively and laboriously. Weeks and weeks of wasting time."

Waits' efforts during 1982 and 1983 were rather more productive, and the instrumental line-up of *Swordfishtrombones* was undeniably intriguing: "Anthony Clark-Stewart played the bagpipes," Waits recalled, ". . . looked like he was trying to strangle a goose!"

It struck Waits as particularly significant that *Swordfishtrombones*, his ninth album, was the first not to feature a saxophone – and even the hall-mark piano was hard to hear. With this album, he was leaving "jazz" determinedly behind, and setting off on his own weird trajectory, trawling through the flotsam and jetsam of American music. "I started out complacent," Waits told David Fricke many years later, referring to his mid-Eighties transition, "and got more adventurous."

Initially uncertain what he'd discover on his shambling musical odyssey, Waits soon found he was as much intrigued by the sounds, textures and instruments that made up the album's sound, as by the songs. Firmly in the mix was Captain Beefheart, ironically a client of Waits' original manager Herb Cohen, but whose weird and dissonant music he had only come across after Kathleen introduced him to it. Of the good Captain, Waits later commented sagely: "The roughest diamond in the mine . . . enter the strange matrix of his mind, and lose yours."[5]

The finished *Swordfishtrombones* was the sound of Beefheart colliding head-on in a wind tunnel with Charles Ives, while Howlin' Wolf and Kurt Weill stood by, nodding their approbation. For Waits, it was listening "to the noise in my head and inventing some junkyard orchestral deviation".

Now he was really out there on his own. The musical climate of 1983, when Waits released *Swordfishtrombones*, was as conservative as the scene when his debut had come out a decade before. Overshadowing everything on the contemporary music scene was Michael Jackson's *Thriller*, which came out in time for Christmas 1982. *Thriller* soon became enshrined as the best-selling album of all time, with total worldwide sales reckoned to be in excess of 50 million – one million of those copies being sold in Los Angeles alone!

Around the time Waits was pushing the musical envelope off the edge of the table, a second British Invasion of the US was being spearheaded by Eurythmics, Duran Duran, Culture Club and David Bowie. Meanwhile, on the fringes, The Smiths and R.E.M. made their debuts; and in a move pregnant with irony given the nature of *Swordfishtrombones*, Waits' old boss

David Geffen sued his own client Neil Young for making records that were "not commercial in nature and musically uncharacteristic of his previous albums".

At first *Swordfishtrombones* sounded to many like a rag and bone man sifting through the detritus of a scrap-metal dealer's yard. Hub-caps banged and pipe organs wheezed on the songs, like they were the muzak of Dante's Inferno. And the timing . . . the timing . . . As rock music became increasingly androgynous and homogeneous, relied more and more on the impact of the promo video, and emphatically embraced style over content, Tom Waits was moving all alone, into territory that hadn't yet been mapped. It certainly didn't make for comfortable listening, but then records with bagpipes seldom do.

Swordfishtrombones is a nocturnal album, daylight does not intrude. The album opens with 'Underground', a percussive stomp that sounds like a Dr Goebbels-approved theme for a production of *Snow White and The Seven Dwarfs*. And the instrumental 'Dave The Butcher' referred, Waits claimed, to an acquaintance of his: "He worked in a butchery shop, so I tried to imagine the music going on in his head while he was cutting up pork loins."[6] But the album's defining song was '16 Shells From A 30.6': a song that sounds like it was fashioned on a blacksmith's anvil, with Waits wielding that hammer with relish. The initial impact of *Swordfishtrombones* was jarring and dislocating. Even today, after nearly a quarter of a century, it still doesn't make for an easy listen.

Despite the startlingly innovative flavour of *Swordfishtrombones*, for many the outstanding tracks are those which also retained some echoes of the "old" Tom Waits. 'Johnsburg, Illinois', as mentioned earlier, was a lovely little song Waits had written for his muse and wife, Kathleen. While 'Town With No Cheer' was both intriguing and faintly reminiscent of past glories. There was clearly something about Australia that resonated with Waits – he had already remodelled 'Waltzing Matilda' brilliantly to his own ends. And this time – struck by the potential of that other great alternative Australian anthem, 'A Pub With No Beer' – Waits had ventured fearlessly into the arid *Town Like Alice* territory of the outback ("the great bugger all", as the locals call it) and emerged clutching 'Town With No Cheer'.

'In The Neighbourhood' was perhaps the album's outstanding song. A nice slice of carnival mayhem, Waits waltzed his listeners through the sort of neighbourhood that was manifestly on the wrong side of the tracks. At a time when 45s were routinely lifted off LPs, 'In The Neighbourhood' became the first single from *Swordfishtrombones*; it also marked his grudging emergence into a different kind of alien territory: the world of the promotional video.

Submitting reluctantly to the latest industry gimmick, Waits employed Oscar-winning cinematographer Haskell Wexler (*American Graffiti, One Flew Over The Cuckoo's Nest*) to direct 'In The Neighbourhood'. The resultant promo was shot through a fish–eye lens in warm sepia tones, with Waits cast as a top-hatted carny barker leading a ragged band of ruffians and misfits through the neighbourhood. They may not all have been close friends of Waits, but they sure looked like they should have been . . .

'Soldier's Things' was another song that harked back to the past, this time inspired by Waits' memories of working nights at Napoleone's, back home in San Diego: "It was full of soldiers most every night," he remembered, "tattoo parlour next door, country and western dance-hall type place down the street, Chinese restaurant, Chinese laundry, pool hall, all real close, walking distance. So I called up some of my memories of that time. Sitting out on the sidewalk, wearing the apron, paper hat, watching the traffic go by . . . a rainy night at the pawn shop, all these sailors, and I looked around . . . I saw all these musical instruments, picture frames, and one of the sailors pawned a watch . . ."[7]

It is a dignified account of a typically Waitsian character sorting through the detritus of his life, noting all the little things, the fragments, that constitute an ordinary life. Mournful and evocative, it was nevertheless a rather baffling choice for clean-cut white soul boy Paul Young to cover on his 1985 multi-million selling *The Secret Of Association*. The subsequent royalty statement may not have made for quite such interesting reading as those bolstered by Bruce Springsteen, but Paul Young was then at the height of his popularity – so for him to record a Waits song (albeit one credited to "T. Waite") gave the composer a little extra financial security and a little more time for his own brand of musical archeology.

Listening to *Swordfishtrombones* for the first time, one was struck by how much Waits' recent cinematic experiences had informed the album. This is Tom's very own Zoetrope: a camera ducking and weaving over his own studio back-lot, the crane pulling back to reveal the neighbourhood, then panning in to Dave the butcher, hard at work, hacking meat. On the other side of the lot is the flaking wall of an apartment, personalised with a Quantas poster of the outback. And zooming right in close, we glimpse the postcard addressed to an intimate in Johnsburg, Illinois.

A wind-up gramophone has Kurt Weill croaking his way to the next whiskey bar. Dollying along, a stall outside a pawn shop has a battered box, full of the minutiae of a soldier's life. Pull back again, and there are sailors rampaging on shore leave, carousing along the Shanghai waterfront, while sneering lipsticked faces peer out from doorways and, forgotten music plays in an upstairs room . . .

On another continent, in another town, it's raining hard and the Sedan's wiper blades are plainly unable to cope. The only light comes from a blazing home, illuminating a mysterious minor character who Waits would get to know much, much better over the next few years . . .

And that title . . .? Well, according to Waits "*Swordfishtrombones* is either a musical instrument that smells bad, or a fish that makes a lot of noise." There was another theory though . . . The same year that Waits unleashed this pivotal album, he also became a father for the first time. In 1983 Kathleen and Tom became the proud parents of a daughter, Kellesimone. Interestingly, Jem Finer of The Pogues, who knew Waits at the time, remembers reading to his own daughter from an American illustrated alphabet book, in which 'Woodpecker' and 'Xylophone' were the examples spread over two pages. Finer is convinced that the selected illustrations for "S" and "T" were "Swordfish" and "Trombone".

As ever, Waits was happy to help clarify the direction in which he was travelling: "It's like you start with a few colours and a certain style and you kind of paint yourself into a corner. I didn't know how to break out, unless I just set fire to it all. And I was afraid to do that, because I didn't know where it would lead me."[8]

Waits realised that he was venturing into unknown territory with this album – and that there was no guarantee his loyal and devoted audience would follow him into the jarring and disconcerting purgatory of *Swordfishtrombones*. Certainly listening to that album on release was a shock – not unlike being knocked unconscious by a pile of 78s you'd forgotten you owned. But critically it was a triumph, and *NME* voted it Album of the Year.

Despite his brave protestations, even Waits himself was uncertain quite where he was headed. All he knew was that with his first Island album he was doing a rock 'n' roll Vasco da Gama. But the risky – some might say foolhardy – odyssey was undertaken with the full encouragement of Kathleen, who seemed to have no such doubts: "She encouraged me to look at songs through a funhouse mirror, and then take a hammer to them."

NOTES

1   Kristine McKenna, *NME*
2   *Observer* Music Monthly

Chapter 18

3   Gavin Martin, *NME*
4   Edwin Pouncey, *Sounds*
5   *Observer* Music Monthly
6   Edwin Pouncey, *Sounds*
7   Brian Case, *Melody Maker*
8   Bill Forman, *Music & Sound Output*

CHAPTER 19

THAT energetic hammering would continue over the next couple of years, while an incidental character gradually moved centre-stage in Waits' lurid imagination. Rather like the Rawlinson family – which preoccupied the late Viv Stanshall from the moment they were first mentioned in one line on The Bonzo Dog Doo Dah Band's 'The Intro and The Outro', and ultimately went on to occupy two full albums, a radio series, a book and film – Waits' character first appeared almost as an afterthought, in the middle of *Swordfishtrombones,* on a short, spoken-word narrative entitled 'Frank's Wild Years'.

With his dreams strangled by a clinging wife, a crippling mortgage and a scabrous chihuahua called Carlos ("never could stand that dog") Frank lit out. Even by Waits' outré standards, Frank Leroux was quite a guy. He torches the family home, incinerating all inside and laughs as it burns. Then he calmly tunes in to a Top 40 station, and heads north out of the San Fernando Valley, going God knows where.

Like Frank, Waits had struck out with *Swordfishtrombones* – and the experience was a liberating one. The album's warm critical reception, together with a burgeoning film career which now helped pay the bills, gave him the confidence to continue along his chosen path.

In the wake of his Island debut, Waits was determined to further explore that same territory. In the end, the track 'Frank's Wild Years' would grow into a huge and an all-consuming project that would pre-occupy Waits for much of the ensuing four years – resulting in both a stage show and the 1987 album *Frank's Wild Years.* There was just something about this guy . . . maybe it was his distaste for canines or his penchant for petroleum . . . that kept drawing Waits (and his wife) back to Frank.

Asked what Kathleen brought to his songs that wasn't there before, Waits replied: "A whip and a chair. The Bible. The Book of Revelations. She grew up Catholic, you know, blood and liquor and guilt. She pulver-ises me so that I don't just write the same song over and over again. Which is what a lot of people do, including myself."[1]

In conversation and during interviews, Waits was typically reluctant to discuss songwriting specifics; but he did admit that the overall theme of the play *Frank's Wild Years* was that good old Catholic standby . . . redemption. Kathleen had lived in Chicago, and the couple had been impressed by the work of the city's Steppenwolf Theater Company, co-founded by John Malkovich and Gary Sinise. In the end, it was the Steppenwolf ensemble that mounted the only-ever theatrical production of *Frank's Wild Years*.

What became a full-length theatrical experience had begun with Waits "just eavesdropping on an insurance investigator in California". From those small but promising *Double Indemnity* beginnings, Tom and Kathleen Waits fashioned not just an entire show – but an entire life.

It was a huge project, and an ambitious undertaking, to take the brief snapshot of Frank from an album and transform him into a fully rounded central character. "It's the story of a guy from a small town who goes out to seek fame and fortune," Waits elucidated to Brian Case in *Time Out*, "but he steps on every bucket in the road. Frank's no champion. We start him off on a park bench in East St Louis – despondent, penniless, freezing – but he dreams his way back to the saloon where he began."

Frank's Wild Years wove fantasy and fiction together with ambition and redemption. As Frank wakes and starts to tells his tale, the audience has to decide whether it is fact or fiction. "He's no hero, he is no champion, wasn't what he says he was . . . His friends kind of pull him out of it, tell him he's got plenty to live for. In the end, he wakes up on the bench, ready to start again."

F. Scott Fitzgerald famously wrote that "there are no second acts in American lives"; but Tom Waits' Frank (now renamed O'Brien) was out to prove him wrong. "It was," Waits rather poetically told Rip Rense, "the snowflake that didn't fall that saves him from hitting freezing point."

The human being responsible for incinerating Carlos the chihuahua was beginning to obsess the composer. Just why would Frank torch his family home? What was it that finally drove him over the edge? And where would he have wound up after the fire?

In New York, supposedly busy fashioning the follow-up to *Swordfishtrombones*, Waits was still distracted by his wild speculations on the fate of Frank: "Frank goes to Las Vegas and becomes a spokesman for an all-night clothing store. He wins a talent contest and some money on the crap tables, but then he gets rolled by a cigarette girl and . . . finds an accordion in a trash can, and one thing leads to another, and before you know it, he's onstage.

"Y'see, when he was a kid, Frank's parents ran a funeral parlour, and while his mother did hair and make-up for the passengers, Frank played accordion, so he'd already started a career in showbiz as a child."[2]

The whys and wherefores of what made Frank *so* wild, quietly obsessed Waits for the next few years, and together with his wife he started work on a stage play based on the song 'Frank's Wild Years'. In 1985 the couple also produced their second child, a son, whom Waits was keen to christen "Ajax". Keener still, ol' father Tom boasted proudly of political aspirations ("'Senator Waits' sounds good").

Warming to his role as a new-wave Joe Kennedy, he even claims that Kathleen wanted to name their second-born "Representative". But they settled instead on Casey Xavier, who was followed in 1993 by Sullivan – both boys would come to work alongside their old man in the twenty-first century.

The play of *Frank's Wild Years* opened in Chicago in June 1986, and ran for three months during the summer before a famously tough crowd. Hard-bitten novelist Nelson Algren characterised the denizens of the windy city as "the nobodies nobody knows, with faces cut from the same cloth as their caps, and the women whose eyes reflect nothing but the pavement". Chicago native David Mamet concurred: "Chicago audiences are difficult to fool. They like going to the theatre and having their socks knocked off."

Waits himself starred as Frank, and the production was overseen by Steppenwolf's Gary Sinise – who later went on to star in and direct an impressive adaptation of Steinbeck's *Of Mice And Men*; receive an Oscar nomination as Best Supporting Actor for *Forrest Gump;* and find television stardom in *CSI: NY*.

Prior to opening in Chicago, Waits was keeping his powder dry about what *Frank's Wild Years* was actually about. Nowadays, we are immune to hearing the latest add-water-and-stir celebrity talking-up their latest release by the endless treadmill of instantly forgettable promotion. Back then, it was rewarding and refreshing to hear Tom Waits titillating his potential audience. Publicising the Chicago run, Waits sold *Frank's Wild Years* as, variously: "a cross between Jacqueline Susann's *The Love Machine* and the New Testament . . ."; "it's got girls, it's got dancing, something for the children, even a dog act . . ."; "something bent and misshapen and tawdry and warm . . ."; and even "a cross between *Eraserhead* and *It's A Wonderful Life* . . ."

The seeds of *Frank's Wild Years* had been planted years before. It was the volubly Italian Francis Ford Coppola who first introduced Waits to the joys of opera, while they were working together on *One From The Heart*, thus inspiring Waits himself to go the Verdi and Rossini route a few years later.

"I heard 'Nessun Dorma' in the kitchen at Coppola's with Raul Julia one night," Waits was to recall. "I had never heard it. He asked me if I had ever heard it, and I said no, and he was like, as if I said I've never had spaghetti and meatballs – 'Oh My God! Oh My God!' – and he grabbed me and he brought me into the kitchen (there was a jukebox in the kitchen) – and he put that on and he just kind of left me there. It was like giving a cigar to a five-year-old. I turned blue, and I cried."[3]

When we met in the early Eighties, Waits spent quite a bit of time enthusing about *his* opera, *Used Carlotta*. The piece had begun life as a screenplay, *Why Is The Dream So Much Sweeter Than The Taste*, co-written with Paul Hampton in the late Seventies ("It's got a few songs in it," Waits admitted, "but it ain't no *Oklahoma!*").

The subject matter, he told me, concerned "a used-car salesman and a racetrack commentator who change identities". But despite Waits' palpable enthusiasm, the project was destined to remain stillborn, although elements of it would surface in his later work, including 'A Christmas Card From A Hooker In Minneapolis' ("Wish I had all the money we used to spend on dope; I'd buy a used car lot and I wouldn't sell any of 'em, I'd just drive a different car every day, depending on how I feel."). The influence of Waits' *Used Carlotta* also found its way into the scene in *One From The Heart*, in which Frederic Forrest waves a dipstick enthusiastically conducting in front of an orchestra of used cars.

It was Kathleen who came up with "Un Operachi Romantico" as the subtitle for *Frank's Wild Years*, a bastard collision between Italian opera and Mexican mariachi. Waits envisaged Frank on his travels as a kind of Don Quixote figure, tilting at run-down urban windmills. Stylistically, the album's 17 songs span everything from Frank Sinatra, through Rudy Vallee, to Marty Robbins' country morality; and from mariachi, through Vegas lounge, to Irish ballads.

But for contemporary audiences, more used to humming along with *Cats*, *Frank's Wild Years* was perhaps a tad too elliptical – and, perhaps unsurprisingly, a transfer to the Great White Way eluded Mr and Mrs Waits. For a while, there were plans to mount a touring production, but even that fell by the wayside when the costs proved prohibitive. So to claw some of the money back, Waits decided to take a scaled-down version of the ambitious *Frank's Wild Years* on tour – but not until he'd nailed the sucker on disc.

Once in the studio, Waits was unusually strict and severe; he admitted later that his behaviour had verged on the dictatorial. "I sing through a $29.95 police bullhorn, and once you've used one of those, it's hard to go back," he explained. "There's something about the power it commands and the authority it gave me in the studio over musicians."

Authority is all well and good, but Sergeant Major Waits seemed in danger of getting carried away: "Everybody has to wear a uniform with their name on it. If they're paid well, you can expect just about anything from them. It's an army. Runs on its stomach. Or we run on your stomach . . . The new band is all midgets, they share a room, they don't want to be paid for their work. They all have a basic persecution complex and they want me to punish them for things that have happened in their past life."

Munchkins were featuring predominantly in rehearsal, maybe they were cheaper to hire, but Waits did confess: "I did actually try and put together an entire band of midgets . . ." but he conceded, "I was probably approaching fatherhood."

As work progressed, Waits became keen to enrich the musical textures of the album. He wanted *Frank's Wild Years* to sound like Braille; but in this he was fighting a losing battle. Waits yearned for the grit in the oyster, the splinters from the wood. But in the brave new world of digital technology, with studios bulging with synthesisers and sequencers, Waits felt increasingly isolated. "I'm not in the music business . . ." he once reflected. "I'm in the salvage business."

The studio may have been equipped with all the latest gizmos, but the instrumentation Waits was utilising was archaic ("most of the instruments . . . can be found in any pawnshop"). Influenced by what Harry Partch had accomplished, and impressed by what he himself was achieving on his Island albums, Waits was becoming increasingly Luddite in his musical philosophy. "I haven't completely joined the twentieth century," conceded the writer-producer, who had incorporated accordion, pump organ and optigon on *Frank's Wild Years*.

Waits also retained a perverse fondness for the Mellotron, which his Eighties contemporaries had long regarded as superseded by the synthesiser – but then his influences were far from contemporary. "The Beatles . . . and Beefheart used the Mellotron a lot. They're real old, and they're not making them any more. A lot of them pick up radio stations, CB calls, television signals and airline transmitting conversations . . . So it's almost like using a wireless or a crystal set."[4]

When the album of *Frank's Wild Years* was released in 1987, it was, necessarily, a truncated version of the stage show – but it was enough to give Waits' fans the opportunity to relish what only audiences in the Chicago area had ever seen.

The character of Frank had developed a life of his own in the years since his first appearance, becoming a sort of blank canvas on which Waits and Kathleen could project all manner of hopes and desires, flaws and failures. Frank was Everyman – and nobody. His life was the American Tragedy and the American Dream.

During his odyssey, Frank passed through all manner of musical swing-doors. There was 'Hang On St Christopher' ("a depraved vaudeville train announcer . . . mutant James Brown"); 'I'll Be Gone' ("kind of a *Taras Bulba* number . . . Halloween music . . . part of a pagan ritual we still observe in the Los Angeles area"); 'Yesterday Is Here' ("almost like a Ray Charles number. All of a sudden we ended up with Morricone . . . the title was given to me by Fred Gwynne"); 'More Than Rain' ("a little Edith Piaf attempt"); and 'I'll Take New York' ("uh . . . Jerry Lee Lewis going down on the *Titanic*").

For Adam Sweeting, writing in the *Guardian*, the album, "was like a radio dial spinning between Memphis and Tijuana, Detroit and Havana".

As ever, it was Frank's sad decline that marked the album's finest songs. Waits is often at his best when chronicling the lowest of lives – and Frank obligingly sinks like a White Star liner on its maiden voyage. His voice is at its most wistful, and Waits is at his most heart-tugging on songs like 'Innocent When You Dream', 'Cold Cold Ground' and 'Train Song'.

For many, the train symbolises a means of escape, or a new beginning, but here Waits – in the persona of Frank – wearily recognises that "it was a train that took me away from here, but a train can't take me home". 'Train Song' stands as one of the most haunting songs in the Waits canon – and in those few pathetic lines lie all the broken dreams of a journey which began with so much promise, but ended with so much disappointment.

While many of the album's lyrics deal poignantly with the quality of dreams, there also is much sage Waitsian advice to be found among them. 'Telephone Call From Istanbul', for example, advises: "Never trust a man in a blue trench coat/ Never drive a car when you're dead."

'Straight To the Top' and 'I'll Take New York' are bleary homages to Hoboken's favourite son, Francis Albert Sinatra. For years, Waits had championed the singer – long before Sinatra was hijacked by the "cool" crowd. He even wrote a song, 'Empty Pockets', specifically for Sinatra; but the Chairman never got it. "I guess he's unlisted," Waits mourned.

"The worst mistake that Frank Sinatra ever made," Mick Brown wrote from the heart, in *The Word*, "was to ignore the producer who suggested he should cut an album of Tom Waits songs."

Frank's Wild Years closed with a reprise of its most beautiful song, 'Innocent When You Dream'. This second version was even more haunting and evocative than the first, thanks to the techniques Waits had used to replicate the sound of a scratchy, well-played, much-loved 78 rpm record. The song, in waltz time, also drew on Waits' father-in-law's fondness for John McCormack – an Irish tenor who was phenomenally popular during the early part of the twentieth century.

Although classically trained, it was McCormack who popularised such sentimental favourites as 'The Irish Immigrant', 'The Sunshine Of Your Smile' and 'It's A Long Way To Tipperary'. During a 40-year career, at a time before the long-playing record became widely available, McCormack managed to notch up sales of over 200 million – through a combination of sheet music, cylinder recordings and a smaller number of the newfangled shellac discs.

In Waits' hands 'Innocent When You Dream' is played out against soft green fields, bats in the belfry and dew on the moor, with a chorus that sounds as if it's drifting, like peat smoke, from the village bar. The song is poteen made vinyl, and it captures with great tenderness that moment when bonhomie hovers on the cusp of maudlin memory.

With a taste for melancholy, an Irish wife, a father-in-law with a penchant for John McCormack, and 'Molly Malone' as the very first song he remembered hearing, it was no small wonder that from early on, Tom Waits lost his heart to The Pogues.

The band roared out of London in the mid-Eighties, around the time Waits signed to Island, infusing maudlin Irish balladry and a love of the *craic* with the boisterousness of punk. Like Waits, The Pogues were reacting against the blandness of contemporary pop. They also featured a band member who banged an empty beer tray on his head. And Waits loved them.

"You have to give them awards for standing up first of all," Waits reported back, admiringly. "They're like something out of a Hieronymous Bosch painting . . . They're like the Dead End Kids on a leaky boat . . . the singer's got a smile like the South Bronx."[5]

Pogues bassist Cait O'Riordan (who would later become the second Mrs Elvis Costello) had sung with a north London outfit, Pride Of The Cross. They only ever released one single, 'Tommy's Blue Valentine', which was a tribute to none other than Cait's hero – Mr Waits. (In later years, a band called The Tom Waits Appreciation Society surfaced – and guess whose songs they sang . . .)

Waits himself had been beguiled by the second Pogues album *Rum, Sodomy & The Lash* – and he reported gleefully that his daughter

Kellesimone's favourite record was the band's cover of 'Dirty Old Town'. Waits remained entranced over 20 years later: "They are a roaring, stumbling band . . . They play like soldiers on leave. The songs are epic. It's whimsical and blasphemous, seasick and sacrilegious, wear it out then get another one."[6]

Some years after the release of *Rum, Sodomy & The Lash*, I interviewed The Pogues, and accordionist James Fearnley had vague and distant memories of the band on tour in Chicago, where Waits was starring in *Frank's Wild Years*. Following the show, the ensemble cruised a series of cheesy bars, with Waits' name opening all manner of dubious doors. Fearnley dimly recalls accompanying Waits as together they entertained drinkers with a lengthy interpretation of the theme from *Exodus*. Shane MacGowan later recalled that wild night in Chicago as "one of the best nights I've ever had". High praise indeed . . .

Waits himself had another, even stranger, memory of that night. As he remembers it, his mother was in town at the time – to see her only son on stage, and finally going legit. And somehow she too had been enticed along on the pub crawl. Years later he was still marvelling at the memory: "I can't believe it: my mother drinking in a bar, with The Pogues!"

When *Rum, Sodomy & The Lash* was reissued in 2004, Waits con- tributed an impassioned poem to the sleeve ("their music is like the brandy of the damned . . . pirates, full of malarkey . . . they're as old as treasure island . . ."). *Rum, Sodomy & The Lash* had originally been released in 1985, while Waits was filming *Ironweed* alongside Jack Nicholson and Meryl Streep. Waits had taken copies of the album along as presents for his co-stars – though, sadly, history does not record their verdicts.

Throughout 1985, Waits and Kathleen had been writing and recording what would become *Rain Dogs* in New York, while simultaneously fashioning *Frank's Wild Years* for its premiere in Chicago.

How, *NME*'s Gavin Martin wondered in 1985, had *Frank's Wild Years* turned into a musical? "The song was like a fortune cookie, after I wrote it I thought, what happened to this guy? Everybody knows guys like that, people you haven't seen in a long time. People go through these permuta- tions in different stages of their life, perceived by someone else it can look strange."

Waits clearly had the bit between his teeth, but his internal brake soon kicked in: "I imagined Frank along those lines, y'see my folks split up when I was a kid and . . . Hey, look, let me give you $100 and I'll lie down on the couch over there, you take notes, and we'll see if we can't get to the bottom of this!"

NOTES

1 Mick Brown
2 Barney Hoskyns, *NME*
3 *Observer* Music Monthly
4 Bill Forman, *Music & Sound Output*
5 *Melody Maker*
6 *Observer* Music Monthly

CHAPTER 20

INSPIRED by the Waits family moving back to New York, *Rain Dogs* was the first album that Waits had ever composed and recorded away from Los Angeles. The family's new home was conveniently situated somewhere between the Salvation Army, the National Guard recruiting office, and the New York State Armory. But Tom's internal compass was taking him somewhere quite different . . . For him the album became "kind of an interaction between Appalachia and Nigeria".

Waits revelled in it all. "Everything is heightened," he told Gavin Martin soon after his move back to the city. "You get picked up by a Chinese cab driver in the Jewish district, go to a Spanish restaurant where you listen to a Japanese tango band and eat Brazilian food. It's all blended." As a writer, Waits got off on the edge provided by city life. And despite now being a father, the 24-hour energy still lubricated him: "It's like an emergency ward, a magnet, a narcotic; it's like a language that's spoken only here."[1]

"You do develop certain skills that I found are completely useless anywhere else," Waits told Henry Beck and Scott Mehno in the *East Village Eye*. "Just being out on the streets, watching your change, watching your back, watching the traffic . . . just a certain street wisdom about getting around that in other communities is unnecessary. In fact, if you continued to conduct yourself in the same way, you'd be put in jail."

Even the city's legendary panhandlers found favour with the new arrival. "I met a guy one night," Waits told Chris Roberts, "came up to me with his hand out. I said, 'Oh no'. He said, 'Hey, listen, it's not what you think, I don't want any money, I just wanna be your friend. My name is Charlie. What's your name?' I said, 'My name's Tom.' He said, 'How ya doin' Tom? That's all I wanted, see ya.' He went all the way round the block, came all the way back, saw me coming round the corner and said, 'Hey Tom, it's your old buddy Charlie, can you loan me a coupla bucks?' I got a kick outta that."

But what was the *real* reason for the cross-country move Tom . . . ? "Well," he confided, "I came here for the shoes . . . it's one of the best times in American history for footwear."

Waits later admitted that *Rain Dogs* reminded him of "some kind of war movie starring Ernest Borgnine, Lee Marvin and Rod Steiger as Solomon the watchmaker"; but the album was originally called *Evening Train Wrecks*, before Waits, influenced by his new home-town, decided on a more canine title.

Apparently, rain dogs were unique to New York: "It's a phenomenon you'll find mostly in Lower Manhattan. After a rainstorm, the dogs get caught. Somehow the water washes away their whole trail and they can't get back home. So about four in the morning, you see all these stranded dogs on the street and they look at you like 'won't you help me, sir, please?'"

The look and sound of *Rain Dogs* was haunted and lashed by the visceral feel of Martin Scorsese's 1976 *Taxi Driver* – and in particular, Robert De Niro's belief that the rain will come and heal, and wash "all the scum off the streets".

The feeling of bleakness was compounded by the album's cover shot: a photo by Anders Petersen that had caught Waits attention: "It does kinda have that Diane Arbus feel . . . it's a drunk sailor being held by a mad prostitute. She's cackling and he's sombre. It did capture my mood for a moment."[2]

Rain Dogs was Waits' follow-up to *Swordfishtrombones*, but throughout its gestation he was simultaneously writing the songs for the stage musical of *Frank's Wild Years*. But in his mind, there was always a clear distinction: *Frank . . .* was for the stage; *Rain Dogs* for the turntable.

On *Rain Dogs*, Waits was dealing from a pack whose seal hadn't been broken. There were reverberations of what had gone before, but it was as much the sound and shape and *feel* of the music which enthralled its creator. "Texture is real important to me; it's like attaining grain or putting it a little out of focus. I don't like cleanliness. I like surface noise."

No surprise then, to learn that one of Waits' favourite locations in New York was the basement of Columbia Broadcasting. This was where magic was made, during the era when radio was king – before the upstart television muscled in and took over the nation's entertainment psyche. It was here that movie legends like Humphrey Bogart, Orson Welles and Bette Davis came to spellbind, telling stories across the airwaves. And it was here that whole worlds were created or – in Orson Welles' infamous 1938 production, *War Of The Worlds* – destroyed. Waits wallowed in the arcane technology: "They had all this stuff set up they'd used in the radio days. They had wind machines, and thunder machines, every conceivable device to create movies for the ears."[3]

Chapter 20

Working in the brave new world of sampling and sequencing, when shiny new compact discs were sliding into every home, bringing the illusion of perfect sound in their wake, Waits was fighting a lonely rearguard action. By the middle of the Eighties, the whole world seemed hungry for the shock of the new. But what Tom Waits was wilfully shelling out was the echo of the old.

Like the rain dogs themselves, his songs were crepuscular, prowling the rain-soaked city streets, like ghosts in the gloaming. They hung around the docks, howling at the big ships as they trawled out to Singapore. They lifted their legs at lamp-posts on the corner of 9th & Hennepin. They trotted, tails between their legs, to Spanish Harlem, staring at the hard-eyed Brooklyn girls, those "thorns without the rose" . . .

Rain Dogs sounded ancient and withered. Here were blues that had lain mouldering, abandoned in a damp bargain basement. Here was jazz, the like of which had not seen daylight since Armistice Day. Here was a record redolent of New Orleans funeral bands mournfully trailing a hearse with no name.

This was music that felt like it had escaped from the cabarets of Weimar Germany – and been in hiding ever since. It sounded real sleazy – stocking-and-suspender decadent – with strangely hypnotic rhythms. This was roistering, defiant music, like it had been oozing out from Kurfurstendamm basement clubs, only to be drowned out by arms heiled high and the crunch of jackboots.

Brecht & Weill; *Treasure Island* & "Ladybird, ladybird, fly away home . . ."; Armstrong & Leadbelly; *Have Gun, Will Travel* & 'The Clapping Song'; Springsteen & Crufts; Mad Hatters & 'The Rose Of Tralee' . . . In anyone else's hands, dangerously subversive stuff; with Tom Waits, just rounding up the usual suspects.

'Singapore' opened the proceedings, a swaggering fusillade of wharf rat yarns and boasts. It sounded like Waits had been listening to The Pogues while reading Lewis Carroll and H.G. Wells. For most singers, 'Clap Hands' would be the big audience participation number, for Waits it had the opposite effect – alienating listeners with its opaque lyrical turns and a Marc Ribot guitar-solo that sounded like it had been beamed down from a passing space station.

Waits had rarely sounded so despairing. But he was still a great storyteller. Maybe you couldn't catch all the words, the narrative was a little wayward, and the storyteller perhaps a bit confused . . . But, still, he held you utterly spellbound. On *Rain Dogs*, Waits came across as the type of crusty, barnacled mariner who'd buttonhole anyone with tales as tall as his mast.

And 'Time', well, time . . . the whirligig, the corridors, "the last syllable of recorded . . ." For Waits, on one of his most eloquent and impassioned songs, it's time that you simply love. On 'Time', drifting on a slow wave of accordion, Waits sings of being marooned, "east of East St Louis", and he somehow manages to make it sound like the most desolate, god-forsaken spot on the planet.

Waits returns to the Missouri city frequently, in song and interview. He told Jonathan Valania: "It's a good name to stick in a song. Every song needs to be anatomically correct: You need weather, you need the name of a town, something to eat – every song needs certain ingredients to be balanced. You're writing a song and you need a town, and you look out the window and you see 'St Louis Cardinals' on some kid's T-shirt. And you say 'Oh, we'll use that.'"

I continue to find something strangely affecting in Waits' rumination on 'Time', that "memory's like a train, you can see it getting smaller as it pulls away . . ." While, "the things you can't remember tell the things you can't forget . . ." seems to hold an almost biblical resonance. For me, that reflective sense of eternal mystery is slightly spoiled by the conclusion that, for some inexplicable reason, "history puts a saint in every dream" . . . but no matter.

The feel of 'Hang Down Your Head' was familiar to admirers of the late 'Tom Dooley', with Waits doing the decent thing, all in the name of love. The song also marked the first recorded collaboration with his wife, Kathleen. 'Blind Love' was arthritic country and western, 'Midtown' a staccato detour into 'Dragnet' turf. While Waits narrates '9th & Hennepin' with the menace of a stalker who'd watched *Rear Window* one time too many – though he later claimed that the song was inspired by a pimp war he witnessed in a Minneapolis doughnut shop. 'Gun Street Girl' sounded like it was hewn from chain-gang rock. The album closer, 'Anywhere I Lay My Head', tipped its titfer to Old Father Thames, before drifting off in swaying funeral-march style . . .

The best-known song on *Rain Dogs*, 'Downtown Train', was a rolling ride to the Battery and Staten Island, welded to a stop-go tune which Rod Stewart would later lock onto and take into the Top 10 on both sides of the Atlantic. The song was at various times both spiky and reflective, a ballad pierced by G.E. Smith's pistol-shot guitar. Even Waits' own ragged vocal couldn't dent the commercial appeal of 'Downtown Train', and it was released in 1985 as his second Island single.

So there you have it: mix in tangos from Batista-era Cuba; tarantellas that would have singed the King of Spain's beard; and some deftly fractured rock'n'roll . . . bring it all to the boil, sprinkle with chopped chorizo, garnish with fresh tarragon and leave to stand. And there's the finished dish: 54 minutes of soul food to warm you through on one of those rain-dog nights.

The video for 'Downtown Train' ("the greatest song Bruce Springsteen never wrote" in the opinion of *NME*) featured the real raging bull himself, Jake La Motta, in a cameo. Waits appeared too, gavotting along the street, leading a procession of ne'er do wells, hair sticking out as if escaping from the split in a horse-hair sofa.

With his tenth album, Waits had inched further forward, marking his card as one of the few genuine musical innovators of a distinctly dull decade. Waits knew that resting on your laurels got you nowhere. So it was heigh-ho, heigh-ho . . . and off into the unknown we go.

With *Rain Dogs*, Waits' creative audacity found favour in all the right circles: *Rolling Stone* critics named him Songwriter Of The Year; Michael Stipe of R.E.M. chose *Rain Dogs* as one of his albums of the year; in a 2003 retrospective of The 500 Greatest Albums Of All Time, *Rolling Stone* put *Rain Dogs* in at number 397 between ZZ Top's *Eliminator* and The Temptations' *Anthology*, calling it "his finest portrait of the tragic kingdom of the streets". While Bono accorded Waits the ultimate U2 accolade: "He should have been an Irishman!"

"When the records *Swordfishtrombones* and *Rain Dogs* came out, I thought it was a very brave move," Elvis Costello told me. "Because he had such a totally complete persona, based around this hipster thing he'd taken from Kerouac and Bukowski, and the music was tied to some beat/jazz thing, and suddenly it's exploring music that was something to do with Howlin' Wolf and Charles Ives.

"I think I was envious, not so much of the music, but his ability to rewrite himself out of the corner he appeared to have backed himself into. It was an audacious thing to do, and I think that everyone who can't recognise the quality of that music really doesn't have their ears on the right way round!"

Unfortunately, so far as the rest of the world was concerned, *Rain Dogs* simply took Waits further down an uncharted road. Waits himself evidently still found the exoticism offered by the music and ideas of Harry Partch liberating, and allied with his own dramatic musical developments, he really was setting sail on seas unknown. Asked by Gavin Martin if there weren't any more piano-led songs in the pipeline, Waits was dismissive: "It's firewood as far as I'm concerned. Slowly, I've started peeling the boards off until there's nothing left but metal, strings and ivory."

"I had a pile-driver by my window," Waits told Elliott Murphy in *Rolling Stone,* when asked about the creation of *Rain Dogs.* "It worked all day, every day, and Sundays, and I started making tape recordings of it, and my wife says 'Jesus Christ, not only do we have to listen to this unnatural sound, now at night, he finally knocks off, and you have to play *tapes* of it!'"

His 1985 tour on the back of *Rain Dogs* demonstrated just how far Waits had travelled in half a decade. *Rain Dogs* was the first Waits album ever to crack the UK Top 30 – in at number 29! His only previous chart entry, *Swordfishtrombones* had peaked at a lowly 62. The London dates found him playing a grand total of *six* sold-out nights at the Dominion Theatre, concerts which Waits fans still speak of with misty-eyed reverence. The European leg of the tour took in Oslo, Malmo, Copenhagen, Hamburg, Amsterdam, Frankfurt and Paris.

And while Waits played, the critics ransacked their dictionaries for superlatives. Even the uber-stylish *Elle* magazine decreed that "this month's ticket to credibility" was the opportunity to see Waits in concert. Not everyone succumbed to the old growler's spell though; *Record Mirror* reader Sean Coyne quibbled that Waits "seemed more like Frank Sinatra's grandfather than the hottest thing to cross the Atlantic in recent months".

Two years later, the release of *Frank's Wild Years* saw Waits touring again, this time exclusively in theatres. The set, this time round, was drawn almost entirely from Waits' Island trilogy, as if he was bidding adieu to all his errant illegitimate children pre-swordfish, rain dogs and Frank. In New York on that tour, Elvis Costello, Keith Richards, Billy Idol, David Byrne, Barry Manilow and Daryl Hannah trooped along to the Eugene O'Neill Theatre to see Waits weave his gruff magic. ("I went to a throat doctor," he informed the crowd between songs. "He said, 'You can't keep singing like that; you'll end up like Frank Sinatra.' I said, 'What? Rich and powerful?'")

Live in concert, Waits had always been a compelling performer. But now he no longer had to live up to an image he found artificial and out-moded, he could concentrate all his efforts on chronicling, with sympathy and real affection, the lives of the characters he'd created. Seated at the piano, or confiding conspiratorially into a microphone, Waits watched as his creations came to life like a scientist looking at a slide. It was clear that, thanks to his increasing film workload, Waits had grown in confidence as a performer.

The stage itself looked like the set for the unproduced *Used Carlotta*: a junkyard, with battered fridge featuring prominently. Not many bands during the Eighties incorporated a working refrigerator into their live sets. But, never one to follow the herd, Waits eschewed the more usual dry ice and lasers, and stuck with his fridge. Musically too, the shows were intriguing: powerhouse percussion was leavened by a colourful blend of sitar and accordion, while, weaving away from the piano, Waits wielded the bullhorn, lending all manner of vocal nuance to his already powerful voice.

Between songs, Waits remained as mesmerising as ever. He was a great performer. Not for him the usual "rilly great to be back in your wunnerful Hammersmith Odeon . . ." schtick; instead, he took his audience along with him. They laughed at the sight of Waits in a tuxedo, giving it his best Bobby Darin – of course, he knew that *they* knew that ol' Tom wasn't in the same crooning league, but at least he had the jacket.

The apparent contradiction was all part of the complex sleight of hand Tom was trying to pull off onstage. He was ingratiating himself with his expanding audience, while simultaneously taking one step back from the footlights. He wanted to be liked – adapting the old showbusiness mantra, he confided to the London crowd that they were "closer to me than my immediate family". But that was explicitly part of the act. Waits was constantly pushing the boundaries of live performance to see how far he could take it – you could hardly imagine Bryan Ferry singing through a police bullhorn!

Interestingly though, Waits was not the first to utilise the technique. Whispering Paul McDowell had employed a megaphone to great effect with The Temperance Seven in the early Sixties, and their 'You're Driving Me Crazy' was in fact the very first number one produced by a certain George Martin.

And then, after all the effort, and inventiveness – after playing with irony and exploring the tensions of live performance – that was it . . . Those 1987 performances would be his last full tour for nearly 20 years.

It seemed that Waits had too many bitter memories of lonely nights on the road in anonymous hotels, thankless support slots and rigorous touring schedules to gain any real satisfaction from live performance. "I couldn't even laugh at *Spinal Tap*," he told the *NME*. "It was too real for me. That film's every tour I've ever been on. I didn't laugh once. I wept openly."

Plus, he was now a father, and he wanted to watch his children grow. By 1987 the Waits family were back in Los Angeles: "For what I used to pay to park in New York, I bought an apartment in Los Angeles."

Way back in 1983, at the time *Swordfishtrombones* was released, Waits had reflected on the creative voyage that had brought him to that point:

"Things like 'Frank's Wild Years' worked, but sometimes a story can be too dry and alone. I'm getting where I want to see things where either the words are more concise so that the picture I am trying to create becomes more clear, or be more vague in description, and allow the music to take the listener to the place where you want them to go.

"I've been working in film recently, and there are so many departments, this enormous committee making decisions about illusion." That committee now reconvened to bring *The Cotton Club* to the screen. The film would reunite Waits with his cinematic mentor, Francis Ford Coppola, but for all concerned it was to prove as traumatic an experience as *One From The Heart* had been only two years before.

NOTES

1 Elissa Van Poznak, *The Face*
2 Chris Roberts, *Sounds*
3 Phil Freeman, *The Wire*

CHAPTER 21

ONE *From The Heart* had been stressful from the start, and its box-office failure had led inexorably to the subsequent decline and fall of Zoetrope Studios. But for all the problems associated with that film, Francis Ford Coppola had nonetheless been enchanted that it had given him the opportunity of working with Tom Waits. However, while Waits' standing had soared in the years since *One From The Heart*, the director's reputation was now in severe decline.

In an effort to down-scale following the expensive folly of *One From The Heart*, Coppola had re-learned the meaning of "small scale". During 1983 he found himself directing *The Outsiders* and *Rumble Fish,* back to back. Both were adapted from books the novelist S.E. Hinton had written as a 15-year-old, and both were shot in quick succession in Tulsa, during 1982.

In a move which might have come straight from a Hollywood movie, Coppola was alerted to the novels by a letter he received from the librarian of a school in Fresno County. She and her students ("representative of the youth of America") had enjoyed the Zoetrope production of *The Black Stallion*, and felt that the studio head might consider Hinton's books for the studio.

Alongside *The Magnificent Seven*, *The Outsiders* has one of the best "Wow, look what happened to *them* . . ." casts in film history. Tom Cruise, Patrick Swayze, Rob Lowe, Matt Dillon, Emilio Estevez, Ralph Macchio, C. Thomas Howell . . . But for all the dynamism that the youthful cast brought to the project, and for all Coppola's enthusiasm, his efforts at creating a *Rebel Without A Cause* for the Eighties ended up falling flat.

Waits had come back into Coppola's orbit for both films: "In *The Outsiders* I had one line: 'What is it you boys want?' I still have it down if they need me to go back and recreate the scene for any reason."[1]

More successful on all counts was *Rumble Fish*, which boasted one of Mickey Rourke's best-ever performances, at a time when he really *did* look set to inherit James Dean's mantle. Matt Dillon also scores as his hero-worshipping younger brother, and the cast is bolstered by strong performances from Laurence Fishburne and Dennis Hopper, both of whom had featured in *Apocalypse Now*. *Rumble Fish* also marked the debut perfor-mance by Coppola's teenage nephew, Nicolas Cage.

Describing *Rumble Fish* as "Camus for 14-year-olds", Coppola's aim with both these films was to try and entice teenage audiences away from the likes of *Rambo* and *Conan The Barbarian*. He felt that it was important to alert them to wider issues than those posed by *Return Of The Jedi* or *Flashdance* and that the way forward was to make more substantial and thought-provoking teenage dramas – "art films for kids" as Coppola characterised them. "They don't have to be *Porky's* . . . *The Outsiders* and *Rumble Fish* are heroic epics for 14-year-olds."

Waits was particularly partial to his role in *Rumble Fish*. "I play Bennie, of Bennie's Pool Hall. I'm like Doc at the Malt shop," he told Brian Case of *Melody Maker*. "It's where the kids hang out. It's my joint – keep ya feet off the tables; knock it off; watch ya language . . . I got a chance to pick my own costume and write my own dialogue. Got a nice scene with a clock . . . 'Time is a funny thing. Sometimes you wish you could take time when you have the time, put it somewhere, save it, because there's times when you haven't got time. Spend it there. Ahhh – you kids. Gotta full life ahead of ya. I've had 35 summers. That's all. Think about it.'"

Waits was moving up the movie ladder and, finally, shifting away from Typecasting Central. Each performance was a little more demanding than the last, and his work responded by becoming more measured, more disci-plined. Waits was not yet in the same quiet scene-stealing league as William H. Macy or Gene Hackman, but he was edging slowly towards it. Asked at the time about the challenges of making the transition between musician and actor, Waits reflected, "It's like going from bootlegging to watch repair."

And when it came to getting help to make that tricky transition, Waits knew exactly where to turn: "I don't think there is anyone quite like Francis. He's a con man and a carny and a little dictator and an exotic bird, a schoolteacher, ballerina, pimp, a clown and a buffoon and a president and a trash collector. He makes good spaghetti . . . very Italian, Francis Ford Mussolini. I love him dearly."

Coppola himself remained enchanted by Waits, as a character, a per-former, and a composer – citing him affectionately as "the prince of melancholy".

In the end, despite everyone's best intentions, neither *Rumble Fish* nor *The Outsiders* managed to tap into the mid-Eighties teenage zeitgeist – and both bombed at the box office, leaving Coppola, once again, as a gun for hire. Initially, he was called in just for a quick re-write of Mario Puzo's original script for *The Cotton Club*. But then, with the creators of *The Godfather* reunited again, someone scented box-office magic – and so Coppola was hauled aboard to write and direct.

The Cotton Club had all the hallmarks of greatness, and all the potential for cinematic disaster. It was almost as if Coppola's very presence on set were enough to set the budget spiralling out of control.

Robert Evans had been at loggerheads with Coppola over 10 years before, when he produced *The Godfather* ("You shot a great film, Francis, where the fuck is it? In the kitchen with your spaghetti?"). But by 1980, Evans' career was rollercoasting as precariously as Coppola's. It seemed that for every *Chinatown* or *Marathon Man,* he was doubling up with a *Players* and a *Popeye*. Evans now needed a hit as badly as his nemesis – and with *The Cotton Club* he was sure he had found it: "*The Godfather* with music!"

This was one of those dream projects that had something for everyone . . . Situated on Lennox Avenue, between Manhattan and Harlem, the Cotton Club was where the chic crowds of the Twenties and Thirties went to put on the Ritz. The club was New York's premier showcase for black talent between 1923 and 1936, boasting a jaw-dropping list of performers: Duke Ellington, Lena Horne, Cab Calloway, Bill 'Bojangles' Robinson . . . And all of them playing to strictly white-only audiences. The celebrities of the time flocked downtown, and on any one night you might see Charlie Chaplin or James Cagney, Fanny Brice or Cole Porter checking out the "mahogany talent".

Such exceptional talent drew in rich crowds; and the rich crowds would often include those who were reluctant to reveal their real names to the authorities. As the Cotton Club boomed, gangsters like Dutch Schultz and Lucky Luciano grew hungry for a slice of the action. The strap-line for *The Cotton Club* was "where crime lords rub elbows with the rich and famous"; but the project promised so much more.

Robert Evans was convinced that *The Cotton Club* was the one that would bring him back from the brink. So confident of success, that he even had the poster designed before a word of dialogue had been written. "Gable and Tracy; a buddy flick," Evans enthused, "great music, plenty of shoot-'em-up, great dancing, plenty of man and woman stuff. You name it. They were gettin' it."

Then shooting began, and the trouble started. Coppola banned Evans from the set. At one time there were an estimated 40 separate scripts in circulation. The budget rocked from $20 million to $48 million. Richard Gere couldn't handle Coppola's insistence on improvisation. The other actors sat around waiting . . . and waiting . . . Bob Hoskins told *New York* magazine: "I gained 20 pounds waiting around for something to happen."

Waits too endured a lot of hanging around on set ("it was like being Shanghaied"); and despite being cast as the club's cigar-chewing manager, Irving Stark, barely a dozen or so of his lines ended up in the finished film. For the most part, the shoot entailed Waits standing around for months on end in a tuxedo, while the script was re-written on an hourly basis – but the film did expand his acting palette by allowing him to deliver some of his lines through a bullhorn.

In the end, Waits came away with one particularly fond memory of working on *The Cotton Club* – the friendship he forged with Fred Gwynne, still remembered (revered!) as television's Herman Munster. "He was a good friend of mine," Waits told Jonathan Valania in *Magnet*. "We worked together on *The Cotton Club*. We used to talk all the time, very deep guy. We rode to work every day in a van; we'd hang out for hours and hours. Sweet guy. Head bigger than a horse. I don't think they added any plaster when they made him up as Herman . . . He said once: 'I feel like there is a battle going on all the time between light and dark, and I wonder sometimes if the dark has one more spear.'"

Evans and Coppola were once again locked into meltdown over *The Cotton Club* – and in his entertaining memoir, *The Kid Stays In The Picture*, Evans leaves little doubt as to where he thought the blame lay (clue: the guilty party's surname ended in a vowel). But as Evans himself was so fond of quoting: "There are three sides to every story: yours . . . mine . . . and the truth."

Maybe after running his own studio Coppola resented being under the thumb of yet another Hollywood producer, particularly as it happened to be the man who Coppola felt had tried to hijack his earlier triumph with *The Godfather*. Accustomed to being ringmaster, lion tamer, and high-wire walker at Zoetrope, Coppola was now once again at the behest of producer and studio finance – and he didn't much like it.

But while *The Cotton Club* demanded the hard-edge of a Bogart, Cagney or Edward G. Robinson, and a spin on the classic Thirties Warner Bros gangster pictures; what it got were the soft-centred Eighties equivalents. *The Cotton Club* should have sparkled like the champagne – which, legend has it – poured endlessly throughout the Jazz Age. Instead it was 128 minutes long, flat and tepid.

Guns should have blazed and passions poured over. But the onscreen romance between Gere and Diane Lane, Gregory Hines and Lonette McKee, lies stillborn; the Faustian pact between Gere's Dixie Dwyer and

James Remar's Dutch Schultz never really catches fire; and the film's take on racial prejudice is leaden. Richard Gere was unremarkable as the cornet-playing hero, and you kept expecting Bob Hoskins and Fred Gwynne's mugging gangsters to burst into 'Brush Up Your Shakespeare' . . .

The bloated *Cotton Club* ended up as a cumbersome cross between *Once Upon A Time In America* and *Guys And Dolls* – without the charm of either. Its pedigree promised so very much more – but *The Cotton Club* is not *The Godfather*. It's not even *Chicago*. In truth, and at a fraction of the cost, Woody Allen's *Bullets Over Broadway* captures the fun and fizz of the Jazz Age far more effectively than Coppola.

Coppola and Puzo – the dream ticket – had signally failed to rekindle the magic of their initial collaboration on *The Godfather*. Instead, *The Cotton Club* came across as an ineffectual mix of tap-dancing set-pieces and gang warfare. You could sense Coppola attempting to warm up his *Godfather* soufflé at the end of the film, as Hines' Sandman frenetic tap-dance routine is crosscut with the assassination of Dutch Schultz. But as with so many elements of this painfully drawn-out farrago, it just doesn't work.

Saddest of all, *The Cotton Club* seemed to have been stripped of all its racy glamour. The smoky whiff of danger and drama never crosses the footlights, and at the end of two hours, you cannot help but wonder just where those 50 odd million dollars actually went. As Waits' character remarks at one point in the film: "these are the times sent to try men's souls".

From the moment of its release, the scale of the failure of *The Cotton Club* was never in doubt. The film fell face-down into the quagmire of huge losses that seemed to haunt the movie industry during the Eighties. Having begun badly with the precedent of Michael Cimino's spiralling *Heaven's Gate*, the decade continued unabashed with such notorious (and hugely expensive) clunkers as *Revolution*, *Howard The Duck* and *Ishtar*. At least it meant *The Cotton Club* was not alone in juggling bloated budgets and egomania, only to wind up with lifeless, empty artifacts.

The reviews were predictably damning, with *Variety* finding it "uneven and . . . unfocused"; while in retrospect John Walker, writing in *Halliwell's Film, Video & DVD Guide 2005*, singled *The Cotton Club* out as "a prime example of the careless extravagance which all but killed the film business".

Waits was eminently watchable in a small but pivotal role, and there really should have been more of club owner Irving Stark – but with

Coppola frantically juggling dozens of different scripts, it's no wonder Stark got lost in the morass. One contemporary American review singled out "Hoskins and Gwynne who are a sheer delight whenever on screen . . . and singer Tom Waits as the club's Maitre'D."

On its release in 1984, *The Cotton Club* died. Jazz fans, recently invigorated by *Bird* and *Round Midnight*, felt ill-served by the Coppola film which managed, somehow, to surgically remove all of the musical vibrancy that the real-life Cotton Club once offered. Like the man said: "Jazz? Delicious hot, disgusting cold."

Coppola and Waits nevertheless went on to work fruitfully together over the next decade. There was one project that was particularly close to both men's hearts, but which – like so many Zoetrope projects – remained unrealised. In 1968 Coppola had obtained the film rights to Jack Kerouac's seminal text, *On The Road* – and more than once over the years, Coppola has announced a film . . . One version was to have been scripted by Michael Herr (*Apocalypse Now*, *Full Metal Jacket*); another by Russell Banks (*The Sweet Hereafter*, *Affliction*); and at one point, Jean Luc Godard was scheduled to direct. But remarkably, despite being one of the most influential of all post-war novels, and despite the encouragement of vociferous Kerouac fans like Waits and Johnny Depp, *On The Road* remains unfilmed.

In 2005 however, it was announced that Walter Salles and Jose Riviera, who had enjoyed such success with *The Motorcycle Diaries*, were to work with Coppola on bringing *On The Road* to the screen. The initial casting was intriguing: Colin Farrell, who needed a hit after his disastrous outing in Oliver Stone's *Alexander O'Great*, was set to play Dean Moriarty; while the versatile Billy Crudup (*Almost Famous*, *Stage Beauty*) was down for that of Sal Paradise (the Kerouac character).

Prior to *The Cotton Club*, Waits' film work had been sporadic. His song 'Invitation To The Blues' was heard over the end credits of Nic Roeg's 1980 *Bad Timing*; and with his acting hat on, Waits had appeared in *Wolfen*, a 1981 oddity that starred Albert Finney as – wouldn't you know it – a maverick detective with a drink problem. Future *Cotton Club* co-star Gregory Hines also appeared in *Wolfen*, making his film debut as Finney's jive-ass buddy.

A bizarre tale of werewolves menacing contemporary New York, *Wolfen* was *very* Eighties – plenty of cocaine-sniffing and a CEO making telephone calls *from his car*! The ubiquitous Steadicam drew comparisons with *The Shining*, while the story had overtones of *An American Werewolf*

In London. But *Wolfen* also juggled necromancy, cannibalism, voodoo and lupine horror . . . a truly whipped-up *mélange*. It's all a bit over-egged, but satisfactorily menacing, nonetheless. Bizarrely, *Wolfen* was the only other film ever from director Michael Wadleigh, the man responsible for the marathon 1970 documentary *Woodstock*.

Waits had a blink-and-you-miss-him scene as a bar pianist: Finney and love interest Diane Venora take refuge in a run-down bar after a shocking encounter in the South Bronx – and Waits is hunched over an upright piano performing his own 'Jitterbug Boy'. "Who's that?" asks a baffled Venora. "He owns the place," replies a no-nonsense Finney. And that's that.

Waits went on to appear in the rarely seen 1982 drama *The Stone Boy*, which starred Robert Duvall, and featured an early appearance from future bunny-boiler Glenn Close. Opinion was divided as to its merits ("quiet, sensitive film . . . director Chris Cain shows enormous talent . . . *The Stone Boy* pulls no punches," wrote one critic on release; "Duvall and Close . . . hold back their emotions in the over-emotional fashion that is the norm for this sort of tear-jerker," wrote another.) But one thing was certain: Waits' role hadn't stretched him and his name above the title would have to wait. In *The Stone Boy*, he was identified simply as "petrified man in carnival".

NOTE

1 Brian Case, *Melody Maker*

CHAPTER 22

THERE was to be a five-year hiatus between the album of *Frank's Wild Years* and Waits' next album of songs, *Bone Machine*. But the singer-songwriter-actor was not idle: asked later how he had occupied himself between albums, Waits informed his loyal audience that he had been "building a compost heap".

Besides his gardening activities, Waits was busy consolidating his standing as an actor – appearing in no fewer than 10 films between 1987 and 1992. He also undertook a world tour, appeared on two tribute albums, recorded a film soundtrack, and appeared in an all-star tribute to Roy Orbison. Meanwhile, his extra-curricular activities included helping bring up his two children; winning a multi-million-dollar law suit for plagiarism; and sporadic collaborations with the rock'n'roll elite.

When *Bone Machine* finally appeared in 1992, Tom's special new friend, Rolling Stone Keith Richards was once again in attendance. When the pair had first worked together on *Rain Dogs* in 1985, many of the interviews of the time dwelt on how Tom had persuaded Keith to appear – and Waits was typically diligent in replying to these queries: "We're relatives, I didn't realise it," he told Gavin Martin. "We met in a woman's lingerie shop, we were buying brassieres for our wives . . . No, he's been borrowing money from me for so long that I had to put a stop to it."

For Waits, a long-time, dyed-in-the-wool Stones fan, the opportunity to work with Keith was simply too good to miss. For while the Stones' standing in the mid-Eighties was far removed for their iconic twenty-first-century status, they were already acknowledged as one of the fundamental building-blocks of rock'n'roll.

Keith's reputation as "the most elegantly wasted man in rock'n'roll" obviously preceded him when he came to work with Waits, but the reality still came as something of a surprise. When he first appeared, on the song 'Union Square', which Waits was struggling to salvage for *Rain Dogs*, he made an immediate impression. "He came in – on the clock he stands with his head at three and his arm at 10. I said how can a man stand like that without falling over unless he has a 200lb test fishing line suspending him from the ceiling? It was like something out of *Arthur*."[1]

Twenty years later, Waits recalled the preamble to this first meeting, while talking to Sylvie Simmons for *Mojo*: "I'd moved to New York. I remember somebody said, 'Who do you want to play on your record?' and I said, 'Keith Richards – I'm a huge, huge fan of The Rolling Stones.' They said, 'Call him right now.' I was like, 'Jesus, please don't do that, I was just kidding around.' A couple of weeks later he sent me a note: 'The wait is over. Let's dance. Keith.'"

Clearly, the wasted one also got something out of the experience, and he invited Waits to appear on the album the Stones were recording in New York at the time. Unfortunately for Waits, his association with his favourite band came at a low point of their career: of all the Stones' 20-odd studio albums over 40 years of recording, 1986's *Dirty Work* still ranks as perhaps the least favoured.

Significantly, the lead single from *Dirty Work* was a cover of the old Bob & Earl favourite, 'Harlem Shuffle'. As the first non-original Rolling Stones single in 22 years, this was an unmistakable indication of the dissatisfaction in the Stones' camp – but it was also the track Tom Waits was asked to appear on. Today it is hard to discern Waits' contribution to 'Harlem Shuffle', even in its remastered CD form; but he is thanked on the sleeve, so he must be in there somewhere.

"The Glimmer Twins" (aka Jagger and Richards) were at each other's throats during the making of *Dirty Work*: Mick and Keith weren't writing songs together, and the fissure led to the most serious split in the band's history. For three years, the Stones' future hung in the balance. Keith was incensed at Mick's determination to pursue a solo career in preference to the Stones. "If Mick tours without us, I'll slit his throat," he gently remonstrated. But as it happened, the relative failure of Jagger's solo albums soon saw Mick back in the fold.

During the Stones' hiatus, Keith cut his solo debut album, *Talk Is Cheap*, in New York – and on the sleeve on the 1988 release, Keith thanked Waits for his "spiritual encouragement". Certainly by the mid-Eighties, Tom Waits was moving into the upper echelons of the rock aristocracy. Along with Dagmar Krause, Lou Reed and Van Dyke Parks, Waits had appeared on the 1985 tribute album to Kurt Weill, *Lost In The Stars*, singing 'What Keeps Mankind Alive' from *The Threepenny Opera*. Waits and Krause also intended collaborating on another musical exposition of the Weimar Republic, *Tank Battles: The Songs Of Hans Eisler*, but when the time came, Waits was away filming *Cold Feet*.

In 1988 Waits participated in another glossy project, this time alongside Ringo Starr, James Taylor, Michael Stipe and Sinead O'Connor on Hal

Willner's *Stay Awake – Various Interpretations Of Music From Vintage Disney Films*. Waits elected to cover 'Heigh Ho (The Dwarfs' Marching Song)', but his was an . . . idiosyncratic interpretation. The familiar bright and breezy version from the Disney animated classic *Snow White and The Seven Dwarfs* was translated, in Waits' hands, into a gruff, chain-gang style, call and response. But Hal Willner remained philosophical, reasoning that Waits' cover was: "a protest song. I think that Tom felt that the dwarfs really didn't *want* to go to work and his version reflected that."

Waits included the only live performance of 'Heigh Ho' so far recorded, at a 1990 New Year's Eve gig at the Orpheum Theatre in San Francisco. Other intriguing material that night included 'Broken Bicycles' (a live debut for the *One From The Heart* ballad); 'I Left My Heart In San Francisco'; and, natch, 'Auld Lang Syne'.

Around the time *Stay Awake* was released, Waits' praises were routinely being sung by U2 ("the great talent of the last 10 years"), The Pogues, R.E.M., Bruce Springsteen, Nanci Griffith ("*such* a great storyteller") and Elvis Costello. The latter particularly took a shine to the man from Pomona. "I've always admired Waits," Costello told me. "We used to stay in the motel he lived in in LA, a nodding acquaintance literally, as he'd be passing by with his groceries."

Waits was one of Costello's choices as Master of Ceremonies for his 1987 Wheel Of Fortune tour: "The whole idea of the Spinning Wheel tour," Costello told me later, "was that I have a very large repertoire, and you can never satisfy the demands of your audience, even if you play three and three-quarter hours! I had in mind various people for the character of Napoleon Dynamite the MC. Over the course of the tour, we had the Italian Samantha Fox, Roberto Benigni, magicians Penn & Teller, Buster Poindexter . . .

"We began the Wheel shows in LA, and I asked Waits to come and co-host with me. He was remarkable; he coined a lot of expressions which ended up in the show. We had a roving spotlight and he was prowling around the front of the stage and picked out this voluptuous girl in the audience and growled, 'I knew you were out there, baby', then went on with some story that she was a dancer he knew from Vegas!"

Years later, recalling the Spinning Wheel experience, Costello wrote: "We were assisted in this endeavour by a series of guest MCs, the finest of which by far was Tom Waits. He had both the animal magnetism and the lion-tamer's charm to entice and corral our most outstanding contestants."

The tour, which I saw in London – sadly without Waits – was Costello at his most charming. A large wheel on stage was divided into 38

The Eyeball Kid. (ADRIAN BOOT/RETNA)

A rare shot of Waits with his
wife Kathleen, 1984. (CORBIS)

Separated at birth? Waits with
Jim Jarmusch, 1985. (DEBORAH FEINGOLD/CORBIS)

'Made it Ma, top of the world…'

(AARON RAPOPORT/CORBIS)

Live on stage, Rotterdam, November, 1985.

(ROB VERHORST/REDFERNS)

And for my next trick... (LFI)

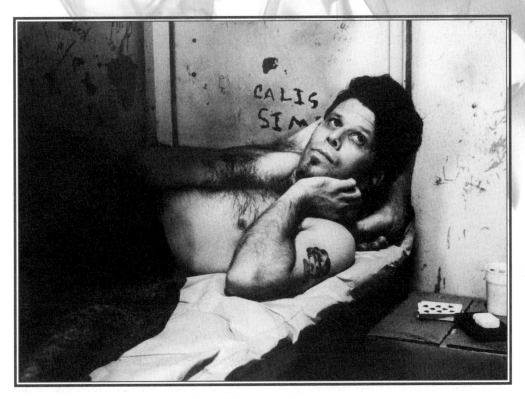

Down By Law, 1986. (ISLAND PICTURES/THE KOBAL COLLECTION)

On stage, 1988. (CORBIS)

Sally Kirkland, Keith Carradine and Tom Waits in *Cold Feet*, 1989. (AVENUE PICTURES/THE KOBAL COLLECTION)

Waits at the premiere of *Wild At Heart*, LA, August 1990. (JIM SMEAL/WIREIMAGE)

Recording *Bone Machine,* with the aid of a loud hailer, 1992. (JAY BLAKESBERG/RETNA)

The piano *has* been drinking, 1992. (JAY BLAKESBERG/RETNA)

Nighthawk at the diner, 1993. (ED KASHI/CORBIS)

With Lily Tomlin in *Short Cuts*, 1993. (FINELINE/EVERETT/REX FEATURES)

On stage in California, 1994. (KELLY A. SWIFT/RETNA)

Would *you* buy a used car from this man? (JAY BLAKESBERG/RETNA)

Earth dies screaming, 1999. (TS/KEYSTONE USA/REX FEATURES)

segments, each representing a different singalong Elvis favourite. Recalling the variety shows familiar from Costello's childhood, the guest MC would invite an audience member up on stage to "spin the wheel" – and depending on where the arrow came to rest, Elvis & The Attractions would tear into the requisite choice.

Costello's most accomplished biographer, Graeme Thomson, wrote of the tour: "Replete with bowler hat, the gruff Waits in particular was a master stroke, hollering out the evening's entertainment with an intrinsic understanding of the ringmaster's art. He set an impossibly high standard for the rest of the tour."

Waits' influence could still be heard on Costello's 1989 album, *Spike*, and after witnessing "two mind-bending concerts in Paris" he later went on to "poach" guitarist Marc Ribot and percussionist Michael Blair from Waits' band. "I heard things in [Tom Waits'] music," Costello told me, "that I recognised in my own imagination. But it was to do with the players he had, as much as what he was doing with them . . ."

At the *Wheel Of Fortune*'s 1987 Los Angeles show, Waits and Costello had duetted together on 'I Forget More Than You'll Ever Know' (popularised by Bob Dylan on *Self Portrait*); and they were due to collaborate again – on record this time – for the *NME*'s imaginative charity album, *Sgt Pepper Knew My Father*. The big stars of 1988 (Sonic Youth, Wet Wet Wet, Billy Bragg) would each recreate, in sequence, a track from the 1967 Beatles' classic. Waits and Costello were keen to team up on an acoustic version of the album's climactic 'A Day In The Life', but sadly, schedules clashed, and the task fell instead to The Fall.

The following year in Los Angeles, while Costello was doing the promotional rounds for *Spike*, and Waits was appearing downtown in the play *Demon Wine*, the pair were brought together in print by *Option* magazine.

It was a fascinating opportunity to eavesdrop on two of the most articulate men in the music industry. Waits, particularly, was at his most lucid when describing the songwriting process: "It's like translation. Anything that has to travel all the way down from your cerebellum to your fingertips, there's a lot of things that can happen on the journey. Sometimes I'll listen to my records . . . and I think, 'God, the original idea for this was so much better than the mutation we arrived at.' What I'm trying to do now is get what comes and keeps it alive. It's like carrying water in your hands. I want to keep it all, and sometimes by the time you get to the studio, you have nothing."[2]

The mutual admiration continued when Costello performed with The Brodsky Quartet during the early Nineties, and one of the select few covers they included in performance was Waits' 'More Than Rain'. In 2001 Costello went on to produce an album by opera singer Anna Sofie Von Otter, *For The Stars*, for which Elvis selected a couple of Waits songs ('Broken Bicycles', 'Take It With Me'). Unfortunately, their inclusion proved particularly problematic. "Any song that Tom Waits sings is difficult for me to imagine that I could sing," the mezzo-soprano admitted with admirable candour.

When it came to the 2004 re-release of his 1995 album *Kojak Variety*, Costello clearly remained impressed by Waits. The bonus tracks included a lovely, lilting version of the Waits song 'Innocent When You Dream'. On the sleeve, Costello noted that he had been in touch with one of his many idols, the great country singer George Jones, who had originally recorded one of Costello's biggest hits, 'A Good Year For The Roses'.

"I had been frustrated and disappointed," Elvis wrote, "by the inferior songs that he had sometimes been obliged to record . . ." Costello then spent a day bashing out demos of a dozen songs which he thought might lend themselves to Jones' inimitable style. As well as 'Innocent When You Dream', the selection included Paul Simon's 'Congratulations', Dylan's 'You're Gonna Make Me Lonesome When You Go' and Springsteen's 'Brilliant Disguise'. Diplomatically, Costello noted: "It didn't seem as if George had been doing much broad listening, as he had apparently never heard of some of the composers, let alone their songs."

The only way Tom Waits could have got on the stage at 1985's Live Aid was by offering to sweep it. However, his presence was requested at another particularly star-studded night in September 1987. *Roy Orbison, A Black & White Night* was one of those fabricated, but nonetheless entertaining, evenings beloved of the record industry at the time. Perhaps Eighties record executives already suspected that current chart favourites Bros, Lisa Lisa & Cult Jam and Belinda Carlisle may not have much staying power, and so it would not be a bad idea to honour those enduring names who had paved the way. There were similar events held around this same time to honour Chuck Berry, Bob Dylan and Carl Perkins – but this was the night when Roy Orbison was duly celebrated.

Long fascinated by his operatic-style vocals, Waits remembered a conversation he once had with Orbison, in which he had asked him to explain that peculiarly plaintive quality in his singing voice. Orbison explained that it was simply a result of growing up in the dry, flat Texas of the Thirties. As a child, he said, he had heard the bands playing at distant carnival shows. The lonely music came from far, far away – up to 300 miles Orbison claimed – drifting plaintively across the flat, featureless, Texas plains . . .

As well as Waits, those who turned out to pay homage to The Big O included Bruce Springsteen, Elvis Costello, Jackson Browne, Jennifer Warnes, Bonnie Raitt, k.d. lang, James Burton and T-Bone Burnett. It was a fitting testament to a man who began his recording life alongside Elvis Presley; went on to headline over The Beatles in the Sixties; and ended his days as a Traveling Wilbury, playing alongside Bob Dylan.

The Roy Orbison tribute show was filmed at the Coconut Grove of the Ambassador Hotel in Los Angeles, close by the kitchen where, in 1968, Robert Kennedy had been assassinated. ("Place was like something out of the fucking *Shining*," Elvis Costello remembered.)

As with all those stellar tribute events, initially there was a lot of political manoeuvring between managers, labels and PRs. But Waits, like Costello, Springsteen, et al., was simply humbled and honoured to be in the presence of The Big O. Among those in the audience for that Black & White Night were Leonard Cohen, Dennis Quaid, Harry Dean Stanton, Richard Thompson and Billy Idol.

Orbison was, of course, well used to walking with giants, but this star-studded evening was nevertheless a timely tribute to the man whose career was a virtual history of rock'n'roll itself. Orbison's recording career coincided with the dawn of rock'n'roll – when, way back in the Fifties, along with Elvis Presley, Jerry Lee Lewis and Johnny Cash, he had cut his early records for Sam Phillips' legendary Sun label. Over the next decade, Orbison produced a seamless run of powerful pop masterpieces. Orbison was almost operatic in his intensity, and hits such as 'Only The Lonely', 'Running Scared' and 'It's Over' were somewhat at odds with the frivolity of early Sixties pop. But, unlike many of his less talented, more fabricated contemporaries, Orbison did not fall from grace in the aftermath of The Beatles.

The Fabs themselves had always been in awe of The Big O, even after the group were bumped up the bill and had to headline over Orbison. "It was terrible following him," Ringo remembered. "He'd slay them and they'd scream for more." Even John Lennon was forced to admit that that first Beatles number one, 'Please Please Me', was directly inspired by Roy Orbison.

A decade later, an equally star-struck Bruce Springsteen testified that the ghost of Orbison had hovered over his breakthrough album, *Born To Run*. But despite all the glowing testimonials, there were quite a few years in the wilderness before Orbison was brought centre-stage again during the Eighties. The new phase of his career started in 1980 when Don McLean reached number one with Roy's 'Crying'; and in 1986, David Lynch's use of 'In Dreams' in his film *Blue Velvet* brought Orbison's work to a whole new generation. To cap it all, in 1987, The Big O was inducted into the Rock & Roll Hall Of Fame.

But that same year, Orbison found himself in even more exalted company when – during his fourth decade in the business – he joined his very first group. The Traveling Wilburys were convened in 1987 when George Harrison was short of a song for a B-side. He called up Jeff Lynne, who at the time was busy producing an Orbison album. The ex-ELO man also recommended using Bob Dylan's home studio – and Bob was only too happy to tag along. On their way, Harrison stopped by to borrow a guitar from Tom Petty, who couldn't resist joining in either. Before long, that George Harrison B-side had grown into a whole album, and the long-dead idea of a "supergroup" was given an exciting new lease of life.

The Wilburys enjoyed a surprising degree of success on both sides of the Atlantic. And maybe because they could hide behind silly pseudonyms and their fellow band members, Dylan and Harrison went on to produce some of their best work of the decade. Together, the Wilburys brought a much needed air of light relief back to the pompous, overblown Eighties – but all the other Wilburys were in awe of standing, and singing, alongside the mighty Roy Orbison.

To bring his renaissance right up to date, Orbison invited U2 along to guest on his Lynne-produced comeback album, 1989's (posthumously released) *Mystery Girl* – for which Elvis Costello had re-written his song, 'The Comedians'.

Rewinding to September 1987, *this* was the man being honoured that night at the Coconut Grove. Given the track record of those all-star occasions, Orbison's *Black & White Night* was a real triumph. All the stars were clearly delighted to be there, and Orbison himself was on fine form. His voice was soaring and sublime and age had not withered the songs either: those timeless teen ballads from the Sixties still sounded like they could move mountains.

Given the company he was in, Waits' role in the proceedings was inevitably fairly low key. At the time, Bruce Springsteen's standing was at its peak; Bonnie Raitt, Jackson Browne and Elvis Costello were undergoing career revivals; and Jennifer Warnes was basking in the chart glory of '(I've Had) The Time Of My Life'.

On the evening itself, Waits was confined to a sideman's role on organ and guitar – but his role in the *Black & White Night* is still worth seeking out, if only for the look of incredulity on guitar maestro James Burton's face as Tom takes an unorthodox solo on 'Ooby Dooby'. Waits would later recall with amusement that when Orbison fluffed a note in rehearsal, rather than curse or swear, the sunglass-shrouded singer would simply murmur a trademark "mercy" . . . !

Tragically, "Lefty Wilbury" tasted only a brief creative rebirth. In December 1988 Orbison died of a heart attack, aged only 52. And on his passing, Waits wrote a touching testimonial for *Rolling Stone*: "Roy Orbison's songs were not so much about dreams, but more like dreams themselves, like arias. He was a ghost coming out of the radio. His songs will not be diminished by his passing, for he was a rockabilly Rigoletto, as important as Caruso, in sunglasses and a leather jacket. Roy's songs always sounded like they were trying to reach out to you from far away. When you were trying to make a girl fall in love with you, it took roses, the Ferris Wheel and Roy Orbison. His songs will haunt us always."

NOTES

1   Gavin Martin, *NME*
2   *Innocent When You Dream*, Ed. Mac Montandon

CHAPTER 23

AS you might expect, when asked to name his favourite films over the years, Waits has produced a motley list, including Fellini's *La Strada* and *8½*; Kurosawa's *Ikuru*; Disney's *Snow White* . . . and Stanley Baker's *Zulu*. When pressed, he will list Peter O'Toole and Jack Nicholson among his favourite actors. And as for directors, Waits has singled out Hitchcock, Scorsese, Coppola . . . and Jim Jarmusch.

Four years younger than Waits, Jarmusch attended New York University Film School, where he studied under the legendary and truculent Nicholas Ray, director of *Rebel Without A Cause*. Jarmusch's own feature debut, 1984's *Stranger Than Paradise*, attracted favourable attention, and won a prize at that year's Cannes Film Festival.

Jarmusch went along to see Waits perform three times during the Chicago run of *Frank's Wild Years*, and the two subsequently formed a friendship. In trying to bring *Frank's Wild Years* to the screen, Waits was much encouraged by Jarmusch's enthusiasm and they set about fashioning a screenplay, which Jarmusch would direct. But, as ever, finance proved a problem, and the project never got beyond the planning stage.

John Lurie of the avant-garde New York act the Lounge Lizards was Jarmusch's choice for the leading role in *Stranger Than Paradise*, and he was already in place for Jarmusch's next feature project. During 1985 the director also got Waits on board for the film *Down By Law*.

It was to be Waits' biggest role to date. *The Cotton Club* had been a far more prestigious project, but Waits' role had been all but lost in the edit. Now, *Down By Law* offered the 36-year-old a real opportunity to make his mark in the movies. He was nervous, though, wary of the size of his role – and its intensity. Prior to *Down By Law*, he admitted, "Most of the parts I had were just a couple of lines"; this time, however, Waits would be firmly centre-screen. At the time though, Waits swore blind that the real reason he took on the role of Zack, the down-at-heel disc jockey in *Down By Law*, was that he got to wear a hairnet.

Jarmusch was happy to keep the hairnet in as an enticement, and when he spoke to Q about his new star, it was clear that he had genuine admiration for Waits' talent: "Tom is a very contradictory character, in that he's potentially violent if he thinks someone is fucking with him, but he's gentle and kind too. It sounds schizophrenic, but it makes perfect sense once you know him. He's a fine actor, too. I learned a lot from him, and yeah, he really likes to get dressed up, which is good, 'cos he puts on different clothes and becomes a different person."

When Waits spoke about his director to Henry Beck and Scott Mehno in the *East Village Eye*, it was clear the admiration was mutual: "Jarmusch is the guy who came to the party with his shirt inside out . . . He's got all these Russian films coming out under his hat. He's very funny, like Buster Keaton."

Down By Law has Waits as a DJ, and Lurie as a pimp. It opens with moody, monochrome shots of New Orleans, and of Waits' character, Zack, getting seven different types of shit knocked out of him by Ellen Barkin, then hot off *Diner* and *The Big Easy*. Zack is a burnt-out, broken-down disc jockey, the cinematic equivalent of Harry Chapin's character in 'WOLD', whose dream is to get back on air. But you just know that this guy is as likely to get his own show as Michael Moore is to host the Oscars.

In many ways, Zack is like a character out of one of Waits' own songs: a dreamer, rootless and questing, hat perched precariously, as he sets off tilting at windmills. He's a loser, who's destined to ebb away, hearing the streetcars rattle through the soft, mint-julep night on their way to Desire Boulevard. He's condemned to a lifetime of *listening*.

Escaping from the terrifying Barkin, Zack is asked to deliver a car to the other side of town. There he is, cruising quietly, singing along to Roy Orbison's 'Crying' on the car radio, when he's flagged down by the cops. And in the boot, instead of the customary spare tyre and wheel jack, there's a hard-to-explain, still-warm stiff.

Once inside the slammer, Waits shares a cell with Lurie, and a tiny Italian played by Roberto Benigni. You could call *Down By Law* Benigni's English language debut, were it not that his use of the language was limited to the undeniably useful, but conversationally restricting, "hello".

Down By Law came a good decade prior to Benigni sweeping the Oscar haul, for 1994's *Life Is Beautiful* – a wartime comedy/drama that divided opinion about the morality of making jokes about the Holocaust. But despite the controversial nature of its subject, *Life Is Beautiful* went on to become the most successful foreign language film released in America up to that point. It also won Benigni a fireplace full of awards – his enthusiastic acceptance speeches for which, were deserving of an award of their own.

Benigni's monosyllabic vocabulary had certainly expanded since the days of *Down By Law*. Picking up his statue from BAFTA, Benigni enthused: "This is my first prize in England. I am full of joy like a watermelon. I will explode. I cannot restrain this joy." At the Oscar ceremony, when he heard that he had won the award for Best Actor, Benigni vaulted over rows of seats to get to the podium.

At the time of *Down By Law* Benigni was little known outside his native Italy, but it was still his presence that elevated the film. "Ees a sad anna beautiful world," Benigni tells Zack, slumped over a bottle, a bad liver and a broken heart. "Buzz off," Waits tersely responds. "Buzza off. Thank you very much. Buzza off. It's a pleasure."

"Benigni is filled with hope," Waits told the *NME*. "He takes off his hat and all the birds fly out of his head. He still believes in songs and things he saw in movies. He walks between the raindrops." It was an astute judgement – and one that could also perfectly describe Benigni's character in *Life Is Beautiful*.

Waits claims to have been inspired by Benigni informing him while filming *Down By Law* – in one of those idle, endless, conversations people have to fill in the long hours between takes – that Michelangelo never washed while he was painting. This led to Waits' later claim that he doesn't change his clothes when he's making a record (though, he admitted, "it doesn't make me terribly popular at home").

Meanwhile, back on screen, the three unlikely cell-mates make a break together, and head off across the bayou. "Just like they do in American movies," Benigni suggests – and indeed, prison breaks have been better handled in movies like *I Am A Fugitive From A Chain Gang*, *Cool Hand Luke* and *Sullivan's Travels*. Even Woody Allen got a good laugh out of convicts escaping "linked together like a giant charm bracelet" in *Take The Money And Run*. Best of all though, the Coen Brothers got terrific mileage out of the formula in *O Brother, Where Art Thou* – managing at the same time to create a unique blend of bluegrass and Homer's *The Odyssey*.

Certainly, whatever their personal circumstances, the jail-break has a deep resonance for prisoners everywhere. Once, talking to *Mojo* about "the power of song", Waits fancifully recalled an occasion when "a singer at a prison concert sang the song 'Home Sweet Home', it was so moving that seven of the prisoners escaped the same night and were arrested in their homes the next day".

Despite its powerful theme, *Down By Law* was a deeply and fundamentally flawed film. Jarmusch was just too reliant on letting his principals find their own way out of situations, allowing his camera to dwell on them in the hope of something – anything! – interesting happening. There was no real sense of development or progression. And without the necessary structure, the interaction of the characters was simply not enough to maintain an audience's attention.

John Lurie composed the score for *Down By Law*, although Jarmusch did find room for 'Jockey Full Of Bourbon' and 'Tango Till They're Sore' from Waits' recent *Rain Dogs*. In the end, Benigni was a delight; Waits did look fetching in a hairnet; and, as for the fabulously named Rockets Redglare – well, with a name like that, what more do you need?

Critics also felt that Jarmusch showed promise as a director: "The Jim Jarmusch penchant for off-the-wall characters and odd situations is very evident," opined *Variety*. "The black-and-white photography is a major plus, and so is John Lurie's score, with songs by Tom Waits. Both men are fine in their respective roles, but Benigni steals the film."

On release though, *Down By Law* was largely ignored by audiences. Mind you, it was a curious time for cinema. Waits' old acting buddy Sylvester Stallone was among those knocking 'em dead (quite literally) with *Rambo: First Blood, Part II*. Despite its cumbersome title, the film set a record on its opening in 1985, by being shown simultaneously in over 2,000 American cinemas. For the industry, this was a canny move: a sure-fire way of making a massive impact, synchronising advertising, and also getting straight to the biggest audience possible, before the damning reviews appeared.

Despite *Down By Law*'s lukewarm reception, Waits' film career was now on a roll. *Candy Mountain* (1988) was a feature directed by Robert Frank, who was a noted photographer during the beat era. He had also shot the cover for Waits' favourite Rolling Stones album, *Exile On Main Street*; and was later responsible for the controversial, and largely unseen, documentary of the Stones' legendarily debauched 1972 American tour, *Cocksucker Blues*.

"I love Robert Frank," Waits told Chris Roberts in *Melody Maker*. "He's a visionary. He was a close friend of Kerouac's, and he changed the face of photography forever." It was Frank who shot the back cover photo of *Rain Dogs*.

The *Candy Mountain* screenplay was written by Rudy Wurlitzer – the maverick talent who, in 1973, had been responsible for writing the elegiac *Pat Garrett & Billy The Kid* for that other well-known maverick, Sam Peckinpah. This was the film that featured Bob Dylan, in his best acting role to date, as the enigmatic 'Alias' ("What's your name, boy?" "Alias." "Alias what?" "Alias whatever you want.")

Wurlitzer must have had a thing about rock stars. He also wrote *Two-Lane Blacktop*, a road movie that featured the only acting appearances of Beach Boy Dennis Wilson and singer-songwriter James Taylor. In 1987 he wrote the Alex Cox-directed *Walker,* for which Joe Strummer provided the music. And Waits was only one of a number of musicians cast in *Candy Mountain,* including Dr John, Leon Redbone and Joe Strummer.

The film's story concerned a young musician, Julius Book (Kevin J. O'Connor), who goes in search of the legendary Les Paul-type guitar maker, Elmore Silk (Harris Yulin), travelling all the way from New York to "the last town on the last street in North America". Along the way he encounters all manner of music industry characters, and by the end of his odyssey he has learnt that "life ain't no candy mountain".

Waits enjoys a cameo as Al Silk, a wealthy mogul with a big cigar, a house in New Jersey, and a penchant for golf. "At one point," Waits proudly told *NME*'s Jack Barron, "I turn to the kid and tell him 'Listen, you're young. You should be playing golf. You should be playing a *lotta* golf.' That's my big line."

Although denied a UK opening, or even the kudos of "cult favourite" by its limited American release, *Candy Mountain* was nonetheless selected as one of the films of the year by the influential *Village Voice*. "A film of off-putting attitude and unobtrusive, wintry splendour, this beautiful, mannered ridiculously hip, sad, funny road movie marks the end of the road, the end of America and even the ends of Endsville."

Next up was *Cold Feet,* a comedy drama with an elaborate plot, which involved smuggling emeralds across the Mexican border, using a horse with a hollow leg. And, if the tagline was anything to go by, this one was just made for Waits: "A comic fable about greed, lust and high-fashion footwear."

Scriptwriter Thomas McGuane had earlier penned *The Missouri Breaks,* arguably the oddest role Marlon Brando ever played. This time, Waits played Kenny, a Florida hit-man ("with a great wardrobe"). He was up there with the splendidly named Rip Torn (*Larry Sanders'* fearsome producer Artie), and Keith Carradine, winner of the Best Original Song for his 'I'm Easy', from Robert Altman's 1975 *Nashville*.

On location in Arizona, Carradine kept Waits and other cast members entertained with theatrical anecdotes gleaned from his family: "So this tenth-rate actor is doing *Hamlet,* and he's so bad that by the time he gets to the soliloquy, the audience is booing, throwing vegetables at him. Finally, halfway through the soliloquy, he stops and turns to the seats and says 'Hey, look, I didn't *write* this shit . . . !' "

While on location for *Cold Feet,* Waits shared his thoughts on movie-acting with Mark Goodman: "Movies are done in such small segments that you have to be very careful about preparation in order to stay in character, to be ready; you can't really sit around and watch the world news. It's like a very large orchestra, and you're one of the members; and since it's a director's medium, he's the conductor, the one you have to trust. You don't ever sincerely leave the ground the way you do in a performance onstage."

Worthwhile as Waits felt they were, few were watching his films. Instead, audiences flocked to see FX feasts and star turns in *Batman*, *Fatal Attraction*, *The Untouchables*, *Beverly Hills Cop*, *Ghostbusters* and *Die Hard*; while *Top Gun* pressed all the right, high-flying jingoistic buttons. But with his recording career on hold, Waits was determined to persevere with the acting.

And though he may have been quietly disillusioned with all the hanging around that constitutes film acting, Waits could take comfort in being one of the few "rock stars" to have successfully bridged the gap between musical success and film stardom. Indeed, he could pass time during those longeurs, by casting an eye over his shoulder at the long line of cinematic corpses that littered the highway . . . Mick Jagger (*Ned Kelly*), David Bowie (*Just A Gigolo*), Roger Daltrey (*Lisztomania*), Paul McCartney (*Give My Regards To Broad Street*), the Bee Gees (*Sgt Pepper's Lonely Hearts Club Band*), Bob Dylan (*Hearts Of Fire*), Chesney Hawkes (*The One And Only*) . . .

Waits' strength was that, by and large, he took below the title cameos. He could never be a traditional film 'star', his face was just too . . . *odd* for that. His elongated chin was born for a goatee; and, at times, and at certain angles, Waits looked like he was hewn from oak, like the battered figurehead from HMS *Oddball*. And he knew he was not leading-man material; at best, Waits was someone to be relied upon in times of trouble. Onscreen, he may be the hero's best friend, but he had to leave the heroics to the star.

On acting, as in life, Waits was pragmatic: "It's a lot of standing around," he told Neil McCormick. "It's very tedious and time consuming. It's not immediately rewarding. It's really a director's medium. Unless you're controlling the images, you're his paint."[1]

For his next role though, Waits was happy enough to be controlled. And he found himself in unusually exalted company, this time out brushing up against multi-Oscar winners Jack Nicholson and Meryl Streep.

NOTE

1 *Hot Press*

CHAPTER 24

WILLIAM KENNEDY won a 1983 Pulitzer Prize for his novel *Ironweed*, the concluding part of his "Albany Trilogy". Set amid a world of drifters and derelicts, at the time of the Great Depression half a century before, the focus of *Ironweed* is Francis Phelan (played in the film by Jack Nicholson).

Phelan is an alcoholic, one-time baseball player, haunted by the death of his baby son, who died as a result of his drunkenness – and it's that tragedy that sets him off on the road of penitence. On the bum, in and around Albany during the Thirties, he encounters other low-life compadres, such as failed singer, Helen Archer (Meryl Streep), and "hopeless hobo", Rudy the Kraut . . . played by Tom Waits.

In 1984, the year following the publication of *Ironweed*, Kennedy went on to receive a screen credit for *The Cotton Club* screenplay – which is where the novelist first encountered Tom Waits. Both Dennis Hopper and Harry Dean Stanton had been tested for the pivotal role of Rudy the Kraut, but William Kennedy had his own idea about who should play the part.

After their experiences together on the sprawling *Cotton Club*, the writer and sometime actor kept in touch. "I ran into him again at a black tie affair in San Francisco," Waits recalled to Ann Scanlon in *Sounds*. "He said to me, 'Boy, you oughta play Rudy.' And I said, 'Well, Goddam, but I don't know. They're probably thinking of some big shot for the part, somebody with more experience, and I'm very unconventional . . .'

"I went to New York, met Nicholson and read with him. I had some toast and an old toothbrush sticking out of my pocket, hadn't shaved, my hair was all messed up and I guess the director and everyone liked it pretty good. They even gave me the costume when the film was wrapped up – so I got a new suit out of it."

After a spell drifting round Europe, where he had worked as an extra on Spanish spaghetti Westerns, Argentinean director Hector Babenco had made a startling impact in the States with his 1981 film *Pixote*. Babenco was soon invited to Hollywood, where his first English-language film – 1985's much-lauded *Kiss Of The Spider Woman* – won William Hurt an

190

Oscar, and saw Babenco nominated as Best Director. It was an arresting arrival in the film capital.

For his next film, Babenco was drawn to *Ironweed*: "This film is about American culture – the importance of the home, the need for the road, and the use of alcohol to kill anguish. But it's also about a collective soul, anonymous vagabonds. About the courage and beauty of people who we don't usually think of as having deep and complex emotions."

Based on a Pulitzer Prize-winning novel, with a director hot off an Oscar win, plus the esteemed Jack Nicholson and Meryl Streep on board . . . *Ironweed*, despite the bleakness of its characters and plot, was shaping up to be one of the prestige movies of 1987.

By the time filming began, both lead actors were reigning royalty in the film acting fraternity. From an unpromising beginning (*Ensign Pulver, Hell's Angels On Wheels*) Nicholson developed into one of the leading actors of his generation, with era-defining roles in *Easy Rider*, *Five Easy Pieces*, *Chinatown* and *One Flew Over The Cuckoo's Nest*. Streep's career had been less visible; with stealth and without evident flamboyance, she had quietly established herself as the most intense and versatile actress of the decade, with remarkable performances in *The Deer Hunter*, *The French Lieutenant's Woman*, *Sophie's Choice* and *Silkwood*.

Together they made an intriguing combination: Nicholson, the engaging joker, full of brio; and Streep, the introspective, intensely private individual. Jack made it all seem such *fun*; while Streep made it all seem too *easy*: her *Silkwood* co-star Cher called her "an acting machine". Now acting together for the first and, so far, only time, great things were expected from the Nicholson and Streep pairing.

But, like *Ryan's Daughter*, *The Last Tycoon* and *Ishtar* – all of which had looked, on paper, as though nothing could possibly go wrong – *Ironweed* arrived on screen, only to flop with a resounding crash.

At the time of its release, audiences were riding high on the heady wave of Reaganomics and Thatcherism – and it was films celebrating those same values that they flocked to see. Films like *Wall Street*, released around the same time as *Ironweed*, with characters like Michael Douglas' venal Gordon Gekko, exulting that "Greed is good!" It seemed that Eighties cinema-goers wanted to relish the cut and texture of Armani suits, as their stars swanned around in plush Manhattan penthouses. They certainly did *not* want to watch as the scruffy, scabrous – almost unrecognisable – Jack and Meryl grubbed around in garbage tips. (Surely, one of the more redundant screen credits in the entire history of the movies had to be that for "Ms Streep's Costumer" in *Ironweed*!)

But in spite of the clear preferences of the paying public, there was obviously something in the air that suggested this was the moment for the Hollywood *demi-monde* to go slumming. As well as *Ironweed*, 1987 saw the release of the dreary *Barfly* – Barbet Schroeder's film, based on the writings of beat icon Charles Bukowski, which cast another pair of screen icons, Mickey Rourke and Faye Dunaway, as distinctly down-market bar-room bums.

In *Ironweed*, Waits provided valuable support as Rudy – Nicholson's partner in the skid-row flop houses. Waits looks, and sounds, the part and the film ranks as his best performance to date – in fact, you'd never guess that this wasn't his day job. And though his public image as a Boho bum meant that it didn't appear much of a stretch for him to slip into Rudy's grubby suit, that denies the real creative effort Waits invested in the role.

Rudy also provides some much needed light relief during the 135 minutes of undiluted gloom that is *Ironweed*. Even though we know he's dying of cancer, the audience is gripped by who'll go first: Rudy, or his shoes. Whatever the flaws of the film, Waits excels, investing Rudy with a dignity which enables him to rise above mere caricature – and, in so doing, proves himself a real match for Jack and Meryl.

Author William Kennedy was enthusiastic about Waits' contribution to the film: "Rudy is a crazy character, a kind of lost soul who has pickled his brains in whiskey and wine, and Tom was perfect for the part. From the way he wears his hat to the way he sits around, he can play the crazy, loopy bum wonderfully well. He tried out in the presence of Jack Nicholson, and everyone realised what great chemistry there was between these two guys. Tom's a natural; a terrific actor."[1]

Kennedy and Waits got on so well that they collaborated on a song for the film. 'Poor Little Lamb' – for which Waits supplied the music and Kennedy the lyrics – was inspired by an inscription the writer remembered seeing on a visit to a hobo shelter: "Poor little lamb, wakes in the morning, his fleece so cold . . ." Waits' version finally appeared 20 years later on his *Orphans . . .* collection.

In the film's press kit, Tom Waits was introduced as a "Popular singer, composer and actor . . . In *Ironweed*, Waits adds another dramatic credit to his growing list of film roles and brings to the part the same funky honesty and wit that characterise his music." Incidentally, *Ironweed* also marked the film debut of Nathan Lane, who went on to later triumphs in the stage and film musical of *The Producers*.

For all its many – *many* – flaws, there are some nice redeeming moments in the finished film of Kennedy's novel. Babenco's handling of the night-time raid on the hobo camp is flawlessly shot and fluently edited, and the scenes where Nicholson attempts a reconciliation with his estranged family are undeniably moving. Streep, too, is flawless as ever – but by this stage of her career, that was simply what you expected from this most versatile of actresses.

Ultimately though, too little actually *happens* in *Ironweed* – making it feel like a very long two and a quarter hours. The audience may marvel at the authenticity of Streep and Nicholson's wardrobes, but it's difficult to be concerned about the characters they are portraying. Hector Babenco wanted to rub his audience's noses into the grime, and he succeeded; but he also endeavoured to make *Ironweed* into *The Grapes Of Wrath*, in colour, and in this he failed.

Initially nervous to be among such exalted company, Waits got along well with his distinguished colleagues during filming. He particularly appreciated Nicholson's support, but was under no illusion about the competition he was up against. Much later, Waits likened acting opposite Nicholson to "trying to catch a bullet with your teeth".[2]

"Jack's real, he's very worldly, very wise." Waits said at the time of the film's release. "One minute he's like a captain of industry, and the next he talks like a railroad bum . . . He'll eat out of a can, but he also enjoys watching dog shows . . . Meryl Streep? Gothic and devastating . . . She's very fine . . . She can move into imaginary circumstances with complete honesty and truthfulness. If she wasn't an actress, she'd probably be in a state hospital for the criminally insane. She works without a net . . . There was great chemistry, because he's mostly mischief and she's mostly discipline, so it makes a little old-fashioned relationship."

Nicholson, too, was quietly impressed with Waits: "At rehearsals, Tom Waits looked like any moment he might break at the waist or his head fall off his shoulders on to the floor. I once saw a small-town idiot walking across the park, totally drunk, but he was holding an ice-cream, staggering, but also concentrating on not allowing the ice-cream to fall. I felt there was something similar in Tom."[3]

Looking back, Waits had fond memories of his famous co-star: "Nicholson's a great American storyteller," he told Bill Forman. "When he tells a story, it's like a guy soloing, he's out there, you know? Very spontaneous, thinks on his feet. I remember he said, 'I know about three things: I know about beauty parlours, movies, and train yards.'"

Nicholson and Streep were, naturally, Oscar-nominated. *Ironweed* was Crazy Jack's ninth nod from Uncle Oscar, and he had already landed two statues (for *One Flew Over The Cuckoo's Nest* and *Terms Of Endearment*).

Streep was equally illustrious – out of six nominations, she'd also landed two (*Kramer vs Kramer* and *Sophie's Choice*).

Waits, though, had to wait. Aside from his nomination for the score of *One From The Heart*, he has yet to get the nod from the Academy Of Motion Picture Arts and Sciences. But, true to form, he didn't seem unduly bothered: "I'm not big on awards," he told *Playboy*. "They're just a lot of headlines stapled to your chest, as Bob Dylan said. I've only gotten one award in my life, from a place called Club Tenco in Italy. They gave me a guitar made out of a tiger eye. Club Tenco was created as an alternative to the big San Remo Festival they have every year." (There is a grain of truth in this; Waits did actually perform at San Remo's Tenco Festival in November 1986). "It's to commemorate the death of a big singer whose name was Tenco and who shot himself in the heart because he'd lost at the San Remo Festival. For a while, it was popular in Italy for singers to shoot themselves in the heart. That's my award!"

Now on his ninth film, Waits had certainly grown in confidence – but he understood that he still had some way to go before he would be fully accepted by his peers: "I guess great actors work in the same way as writers, in the sense that that you compose a character from different parts of yourself: somebody else's limp, your grandmother's dentures, your brother-in-law's posture and your catechism teacher's dialect."[4]

In the event, come Oscar-time, *Ironweed* simply disappeared. Nicholson was knocked out by Michael Douglas' star turn in *Wall Street*; while Streep lost out to surprise winner Cher, for *Moonstruck*. Meanwhile, Tom Waits kept his powder dry, put his acting on hold, and set his sights high. Approaching 40, from third billing on *Ironweed*, Waits was out to get his name above the title. This boy was going straight to the top – *Big Time* . . .

NOTES

1 Ann Scanlon, *Sounds*
2 *NME*
3 *NME*
4 *Sounds*

CHAPTER 25

LOOKING back on a career that had begun at the dawn of the twentieth century, and had gone on to embrace the stage, cabaret, television and – legendarily – film, Groucho Marx was asked to define showbusiness: "We were playing a small town in Ohio, and a man came to the box office and said, 'Before I buy a ticket, I want to know one thing: is it sad or high kicking?' To me, that's it – sad or high kicking!"

With *Ironweed* in the bag, and plans for a proper film of *Frank's Wild Years* abandoned, Waits was determined to enshrine at least something of his pet project on celluloid. With his growing aversion to touring, a concert film would also offer Waits the opportunity to do it once – and then stay at home with the wife and kids.

And so it was that during 1987 he embarked on a concert tour which drew heavily on his Island trilogy of *Swordfishtrombones*, *Rain Dogs* and *Frank's Wild Years*. The shows in Los Angeles, San Francisco, Dublin, Stockholm and Berlin were filmed and recorded, for a live album and concert film which Waits ironically titled *Big Time*.

This was a traditional stopgap measure in the world of rock'n'roll, where "the Live Album" was all too frequently a filler or an easy way to fulfil contractual obligations. For fans, it was a souvenir of the concert tour; for the artist, a way of treading water until the creative juices started flowing again.

Rock concert films were an even riskier project. At their best, they could serve as a fly-in-aspic reminder of a tumultuous moment in a band's career arc: say, The Rolling Stones' *Gimme Shelter*; Prince's *Sign O' The Times*; or U2's *Rattle And Hum*. At worst, they were over-inflated, bombastic examples of cinematic self-indulgence: what Neil Tennant likened to a band's "imperial phase". The Rolling Stones' *Let's Spend The Night Together*; T. Rex's *Born To Boogie*; and – again – U2's *Rattle And Hum* spring to mind.

Big Time was, at once, both "sad and high kicking". Waits and director Chris Blum clearly had fun, and enjoyed fiddling with the formula. For example, *Big Time* did not open with the traditional shots of the audience filing in and then rapturously greeting their idol. In fact, throughout *Big*

Time, the audience are never even glimpsed. The camera remains locked on Tom Waits, transfixed by the endless parade of Waitses proceeding before it.

Chris Blum had previously directed jeans adverts for television, and *Big Time* threw up some particularly striking images, which seemed to come straight from the quick-cut world of commercials: for example, Waits singing '9th & Hennepin' from beneath a blazing umbrella, or crooning as the film print appears to disintegrate around him. Up close, Waits cuts a terrifying figure, his forehead glistening as he commands the stage. And when he sings, the intensity of that performance is inescapable – the veins on his neck standing out, like rivers on a large-scale map of South America.

You could even freeze-frame *Big Time*, allowing you to emulate your idol in the comfort of your own home . . . and do The Tom Waits Dance. For this, you have to grasp the microphone stand firmly with both hands, then crouch, like a presidential candidate ducking a bullet, and stamp your right foot repeatedly, really, *really* hard.

Of course, this is not Tom; this is Tom as Frank . . . Tom is Frank, but confusingly there are a variety of Franks: there's the huckster theatre usher ("wanna buy a watch?"); there's 'Frank as Crooner' ("I feel closer to you than my whole family"); and then there's the final shot of Frank, singing 'Innocent When You Dream' from inside a shower on a Los Angeles rooftop – surely a cinematic first this?

As Frank the Crooner, Waits is at his most slimily convincing. The merest trace of a pencil-thin moustache suggests the base nature of the man: this, clearly, is the sort of guy who'd auction his own children as a tax-loss. The white tuxedo is visual shorthand for the insincerity of a self-centred star, the kind of shameless celebrity who'd make out an auto-graph: "With sincere best wishes to my very good friend . . ." and then ask: "What was your name again?"

Big Time catches Waits as performer at a certain point in his career. The inebriated raconteur is long gone, and here instead is someone capable of taking centre-stage and holding your attention for the duration. His acting roles had perhaps strengthened his confidence, but whatever the reason, Waits is assured and commanding throughout. On 'Way Down In The Hole', he dispenses lines like saliva from the mouth of a Hellfire preacher. On 'Straight To The Top', his pastiche of a Las Vegas entertainer relishes and exposes the vacuity and hypocrisy of the type. I particularly like it when he encourages the invisible audience to sing along to "the old favourites, like 'There's A Leak In The Boiler Room'".

At times during *Big Time*, Waits' movements are as weird as a mangled mazurka; at others, he's as fluid as a chiffon scarf on a breeze. Sometimes he sounds like a worn-out reel-to-reel slowly winding down; then he'll reach out and tug at your heart strings with a perfectly poignant reading of 'Johnsburg, Illinois'.

During the live version of 'Hang On St Christopher', your mind may drift off to take in the other saints Waits has cited in his holy lexicon: "St Moritz, the patron saint of all hotel night clerks; Susan St James; St James Infirmary. There's '*The* Saint', Roger Moore, of course . . ."

Onstage, illuminated only by a cheap lightbulb on a set that's seen better days, Waits wields his bullhorn like a baton, marshalling his troops. He looks rather older than his 39 years, but then ever since he began performing, Waits has somehow always looked, and sounded, like he was just stopping off on his way to the retirement home.

As to the rest of the troupe assembled for *Big Time*, David Sinclair writing in *Q*, identified: "a magically loose ensemble sound which seems to have been coaxed from a drum kit built out of the contents of a plumber's yard, guitars with cheesewire for strings and a wind section using instruments borrowed from a rag and bone man's cart!"

Visually though, *Big Time* left a lot to be desired. If it had aimed to be more than a simple document, intended to serve as a keepsake of a concert tour, had it incorporated more of Waits' visual flair and genuinely witty onstage patter, *Big Time* would have made a more compelling film and helped enrich his filmography. As it was, shot in murk, and with songs chiefly drawn from familiar recent releases, *Big Time* begged for more: not least, an explanation of what lay behind that very mysterious end credit "featuring Gertz the Monkey"?

Big Time remains worthwhile for the priceless fragments of Waits as word-in-your-ear confidant: "I think the question I'm asked most, it happens a lot, enough that I would remark on it, a lot of people come up to me and say, 'Tom, is it possible for a woman to get pregnant without intercourse?'"

As the star of his own project, Waits had a clear image of himself, which the reality of the finished film didn't always match: "I see things about myself and the show I don't like. I thought I was much taller, for example. I thought I looked like Robert Goulet or Sean Connery. It was really shocking to see this old guy, sweating, bending over and scratching his head. It was a rough night." Eventually though, Waits became reconciled to his on-screen image, and continued: "I realise now why they were thinking of me as the only man capable of replacing James Bond."[1]

Of the songs on the *Big Time* soundtrack, 'Cold Cold Ground', 'Train Song' and 'Time' were exemplary, while 'Underground', '16 Shells From A 30.6' and 'Gun Street Girl' took their usual hammering. 'Way Down In The Hole' worked up a feverish, congregation-rousing fervour, while 'Rain Dogs' was spun into a veritable frenzy. Only two new songs were included: a strained studio recording of a rather leaden-sounding country ballad, 'Falling Down'; and the beguiling Kurfurstendamm meets Clonakilty turbulence of 'Strange Weather'.

Written by Waits and Kathleen, 'Strange Weather' was a song with an intriguing history. Marianne Faithfull was an Island labelmate of Tom's and 'Strange Weather' wound up as the title track of her 1987 comeback album. The original concept had been intriguing: Waits had suggested the whole of *Strange Weather* have a Storyville theme, which would have fitted Faithfull's fractured Eighties vocal style perfectly. Storyville was the New Orleans district celebrated as the birthplace of jazz, until the authorities closed it down during World War I because of the neighbourhood's disruptive influence on troops on shore leave.

In her autobiography, Marianne remembered "a phone friendship" with Waits, and his views on her album: "Tom's concept was quite different from mine. His idea was to do an album around the theme, 'the whore's revenge'. . . . In Tom's view of it, I would be bawling out raunchy songs in a pair of fishnet stockings and a suspender belt . . . Much as I'd love to believe that sexpot image, I don't really see myself as an unrepentant hooker belting out blues from the bordello.

"A project like this requires weeks and weeks of sitting around listening to old records and tapes, and the person you usually end up working with is the one who has the time. Tom wanted to do it, but he was busy living his life: getting married, having children, making records. What came out of our conversation was the album's title song, 'Strange Weather', which Tom had written with his wife Kathleen."[2]

Despite its undeniable charms, sadly, *Big Time* didn't progress Waits' career as much as he, or his faithful audience, might have hoped. It certainly confirmed him as one of the most idiosyncratic and original talents of recent years, but the whole enchilada was simply preaching to the converted, with neither album nor film demonstrably expanding his following.

"As is frequently the case in films such as this, the scope and impact are limited, with Waits' raucous vocals unlikely to attract anyone other than hardcore followers," sniffed Didier C. Deutsch in *Video Hound's Soundtracks.*

In mitigation, Waits claimed that *Big Time* had been shot in a day, for a total cost of $100 – maybe, if they could have afforded the Rangoon gladiator battles, and incorporated the underwater ballet sequences, a whole new audience might have flocked in. And had his scenes with Faye Dunaway made it into the final cut, it would certainly have been a different film – least ways, that's the way Waits told it in his defence.

Out on the stump to promote it, Waits had his own, quite distinctive, views about the finished film: "*Big Time* is a kind of action–adventure movie. One guy in Chicago said piano teachers will be shocked; someone else said it looked like it was filmed in the belly of a very sick animal."

Island paid up for a promo video to help Waits get out there and sell himself. The finished product was predictably quirky, with the artist being chauffeured round while musing on such diverse topics as clocks, confetti and where exactly did barbers get *their* hair cut? Wayne, the chauffeur, was given hell by his passenger, as Waits sat cradling Mario, a seedy looking poodle, while responding to an unseen interrogator: "Five words to describe yourself?" "No left turn!" "Favourite country?" "St Louis!" "Future plans?" "I live for adventure, and to hear the lamentations of the women."

Big Time was Waits' fourth album for Island, and to help celebrate the label's silver anniversary in 1988, he sent a taped message to Chris Blackwell, expressing his gratitude – and his delight that Blackwell had given up the midget wrestling outfit and gone into showbiz!

But, in retrospect, even Waits recognised the inherent flaw of *Big Time*: "It's difficult to retain what happened at that moment and preserve it. You don't want to kill the beast while you're trying to capture it. Also, the moment after it's completed, you'd love to go back and change something. Like watching my underwear come out of the back of my pants."[3]

Recalcitrant underwear or no, *Big Time* divided opinion. The film certainly had its fans: *Time Out* enthused about "this magnificent movie"; while *Melody Maker* found it "rather like reading a novel by Nelson Algren with every other page missing. Not a disagreeable sensation." The album, however, found fewer fans: "*Big Time*, the record, is, of course, only half the story, half the picture. It's also about half as inspiring as his previous perfumed nightmares," *Melody Maker* concluded. While *NME* considered that "overall it's an unnecessary experiment, hardly a companion to the movie and pretty insubstantial as a soundtrack . . . better seen than heard."

Like *Nighthawks At The Diner*, its predecessor over a decade before, *Big Time* had failed to capture the essence of what made Waits such a mesmerising live performer. Frustratingly single-minded in its focus, *Big Time* only made you wish that the more ambitious *Frank's Wild Years* had made it to film.

NOTES

1 *Melody Maker*
2 *Faithfull*, Marianne Faithfull and David Dalton
3 *Sounds*, Jonh Wilde

CHAPTER 26

THE next episode of Tom Waits' brilliant career, would find him deserting the recording studio, film set and concert platform for his strangest arena yet: the courtrooms of the world. As ever, Waits was keen to keep on keepin' on, and with the Big Time behind him, this time around Waits would find himself locking horns with some of the most powerful of global corporations.

The Rolling Stones' triumphant 1981 tour of America was, to date, the most financially successful rock tour ever. Significantly, it also came to us courtesy of Jovan perfume, making it the first rock'n'roll tour ever to be sponsored, thus helping to offset the constantly spiralling costs of touring.

Until then, concert tours had largely been loss-leaders, designed to incite audiences to go out and purchase new product – rather than to make any real money at the box office. The Stones' tour changed all that, at a stroke – and the remainder of the decade would see rock stars eagerly courting corporate sponsorship.

The spectacle of major rock acts rushing shamelessly to align themselves with corporate America was not a comfortable sight. But, in what many saw as an unseemly obeisance to Mammon, it became commonplace to see stars of the stature of Michael Jackson, Tina Turner, George Michael and Madonna accepting sponsorship, apparently happy to endorse pretty well any big-money product. The artists defended their actions, claiming that it was a way of keeping touring costs down and thus ensuring cheaper tickets for fans. But, somehow, ticket prices continued to rise inexorably upward and for many, it was flying in the face of what made rock'n'roll originally so inspiring.

The late Eighties also proved a boom time for the commercial pillaging of the music's history: 'Great Balls Of Fire' was used to sell batteries; 'Chantilly Lace' alerted people towards a certain theme park; and 'Turn! Turn! Turn!' (a song originally adapted from the Bible) now sold magazines. Rather more relevantly, classic songs by Sam Cooke, Marvin Gaye and Percy Sledge were used to market a certain brand of jeans – thus introducing their music to a whole new audience.

The Beatles themselves always remained above the murky world of advertising and sponsorship, but shockwaves were felt when Michael Jackson licensed the previously inviolate Fabs' material. In 1985 Jackson acquired the lucrative ATV Music which incorporated Northern Songs, The Beatles' music publishing company, and after consultation with Yoko Ono he permitted the sports outfitter Nike to use 'Revolution' in a 1987 TV commercial, making $500,000 in the process. McCartney and Harrison were not amused and Apple issued a lawsuit. "The song was about revolution, not bloody tennis shoes," said McCartney.

Waits was suitably dismissive about the whole unsavoury trend. In interview, he was scathing about rock stars who took their 30 pieces of silver. And even those that nipped off to another continent to sell their wares did not slip under the Waits radar: "I really hate the people that do them," he told Ted Mico. "I've been asked to endorse everything from underwear (lightning resistant) to cigarettes. I turned them all down. They cut bacon off your back before the pig is a ham. A lot of people go to Japan to do it, as though you can shit in the desert and no one will know. The lines are drawn, they have to be, as advertising is aligning itself with new counter-cultures . . . The idea is to be sovereign, independent and not have to work on Maggie's Farm . . . !"

It seemed unlikely that either Pepsi or Coca Cola would be rushing to sign Waits up to promote their frothy product. Mind you, stranger things have happened . . . Who'd have thought that the services of "punk poet", and Nico's ex-partner, John Cooper Clarke, would one day be seen promoting breakfast cereal on children's television? Or that the songs of such "underground" icons as the Nick Drake, Velvet Underground and Iggy Pop would be linked with corporate advertising?

But with advertising's relentless passion for piggy-backing on pop history, it seemed that everything and everyone was now up for grabs. "Corporations are hoping to hijack a culture's memories for their product," Waits cautioned.

Given such heartfelt and well-publicised antipathy towards "The Man", Waits was understandably incensed when, in 1988, Salsa Rio Doritos Corn Chips began a series of radio commercials using a character sounding too much like Tom Waits for comfort. Some might have been flattered. But if it profits a man nothing to give his soul for the whole world . . . then for corn chips?

Waits responded immediately, with a $2 million lawsuit alleging that the company had "wrongly and without justification, appropriated [his] singing style and manner of presentation". But the law would not be hurried. Waits' suit had echoes of Bette Midler's case against the Ford

Motor Co's ad agency, which had used a Midler soundalike without her approval. In the end, Waits' old duetting partner had won her case, but it had taken her four years.

The Waits case finally came to court in Los Angeles in April 1990 – and with it, elements of the trial scene from *Alice Through The Looking Glass*. Waits was pitted against the corn chip manufacturers Frito-Lay, and their advertising agency Tracey-Locke. The agency testified that they were looking for a "bluesy after-hours nightclub atmosphere" for their radio spot. But both the client and their agency admitted that their jingle ("it's boffo, boffo, bravo, gung-ho, tally-ho, but never mellow. Try 'em, buy 'em, get 'em, got 'em!) was based on Waits' 1977 song 'Step Right Up'.

Waits was "shocked" and "angry" when he heard soundalike singer Stephen Carter enthusing about the benefits of Salsa Rio Doritos Corn Chips on the radio, claiming that the commercial had put words of endorsement into his mouth. Waits also believed that if his fans heard the spot, aired on over 250 radio stations, they would believe he'd "sold out".

To add insult to injury, Frito-Lay based their defence on the contention that "Waits' voice is not as distinctively known as Midler's". The company also called in a phonetics expert, their very own Professor Higgins, who was there, rather bizarrely, "to testify that Waits cannot claim to his own voice". The company's defence also alleged that Waits' own singing style was simply an imitation of a style made popular by, among others, Louis Armstrong.

Waits was understandably incensed: "I've never heard anybody that I felt was doing or being me. Everybody stakes out their own territory in this deep world." Even soundalike Stephen Carter was embarrassed: "I have just about all of Tom Waits' albums," he confessed.

In the end, Waits was vindicated. He emerged from the court in 1993 in triumph, and Frito-Lay and Tracey-Locke had to fork out substantial damages. Waits was awarded a sum in excess of $2 million, which was put to excellent use. "Spent it all on candy," he later claimed.

With his individuality formally upheld by the courts, Waits now kept a weather eye open for future trespass. And even his avowed fondness for rap ("All those guys flunked English," he told Adam Sweeting in the *Guardian*. "It's so beautiful that it's words that have given them power and strength and courage to articulate the things they're talking about, the anger and the braggadocio and their years of exile and slavery") didn't stop Waits suing rappers 3rd Bass for sampling 'Way Down In The Hole' on their *Cactus Album*. "They probably think I'm a real prick," he acknowledged, "but you didn't take like boom-ching-boom, you took a *whole song*."

In 1993 Screamin' Jay Hawkins enjoyed his only sniff of UK chart action. The man who had electrified the Fifties with his chilling 'I Put A Spell On You', recorded two Waits songs ('Ice Cream Man' and 'Heartattack & Vine') for his 1991 album, *Black Music For White People*. Screamin' Jay had been managed by Waits' original manager, Herb Cohen, and went on to appear in Jim Jarmusch's 1989 Memphis triptych *Mystery Train*, which also featured Waits as an unseen DJ.

Released as a single, Screamin' Jay's 'Heartattack & Vine' reached number 42, on the back of its use in a television ad. But Waits, predictably, was far from happy, and soon became embroiled in another law suit. Some people would have been delighted to have their song aired in 17 countries on a Levi's commercial. Not so, Mr Waits. He was upset that any song of his had been sanctioned for use in a television advertisement.

The composer sued in 1993, and was rewarded in 1996 with a series of grovelling full-page ads from Levi's: "Tom Waits is opposed to his music, voice, name or picture being used in commercials. We at Levi Strauss & Co. have long admired Mr Waits' work and respect his artistic integrity including his heartfelt views on the use of his music in commercials . . . We meant no offence to Mr Waits, and regret that 'Heartattack & Vine' was used against his wishes and that the commercial caused him embarrassment."

On another occasion, Waits went to court to protest about his song 'Ruby's Arms' being used to promote a shaving cream in a series of advertisements on French television. The judge awarded Waits $20,000 "for embarrassment and humiliation sustained by him". And in 1994 he was awarded a "six-figure sum" in damages from his former music publishing company, who had licensed his music for use in commercials without the artist's consent.

In March 2004 Waits did the whole "no further questions m'lud" courtroom shuffle once again, this time over an Audi commercial, aired on Spanish television. The advert used a song "with an identical structure" to Waits' own 1987 'Innocent When You Dream', sung by a vocal impersonator – and given Waits' unique vocal styling, there's no shortage of *them*. Waits won again, and the Barcelona court awarded him compensation for the violation of his copyright and moral rights.

You had to admire Waits' single-minded tenacity, at a time when rock'n'roll was selling its soul. But he was not entirely alone. Bruce Springsteen – who turned down an eight-figure sum to licence 'Born In The USA' for a car campaign – recently joked: "I was at home, doing one of my favourite things, tallying up all the money I passed up in endorsements over the years and thinking of all the fun I could have had with it . . ."

Waits vociferously backed John Densmore in his refusal to sanction use of the Doors' music for television commercials. The drummer had used his veto over fellow surviving band members, Ray Manzarek and Robbie Krieger, to refuse permission for the use of 'Break On Through' and 'Light My Fire' in $20 million campaigns to help promote Cadillac cars and Apple computers.

"Corporations suck the life and meaning from the songs," Waits wrote in a letter to *The Nation*, "and impregnate them with promises of a better life with their product." He also provided a glimpse into the future of this brave new world of rock'n'roll: "Eventually, artists will be going onstage like race-car drivers covered in hundreds of logos."

Waits' dystopian vision of the future no longer seemed so distant, or so far-fetched, when in 1999 Moby's *Play* became the first album ever to have had *all* of its tracks licensed to adverts, TV stations and movies. Within a year, an estimated 470 separate licences had been granted. And just when you thought things couldn't get any worse in the unholy alliance between the creatives and the corporate suits . . . in 2004, McDonald's started offering financial incentives to rap acts who inserted mentions of the company's products in their lyrics.

Amid the plethora of product placement that marks out the twenty-first century, Waits increasingly stands alone. But just to prove that he isn't really a curmudgeon . . . testifying during the great Salsa Rio Doritos Corn Chip court-room battle, Tom did admit that, yes, he *had* once made a commercial, 10 years before . . . for dog food. "I was down on my luck, and I've always liked dogs," he swore – under oath.

CHAPTER 27

VANITY FAIR described Robert Wilson, in 2003, as someone who has "charged through contemporary music's obtuse-artperson firmament working with Tom Waits, Lou Reed, David Byrne and Laurie Anderson on theatrical projects of epic scale, visual and sonic audacity, and often punitive length . . . [an] inscrutable Texan-born stage director who has made a career of cooking up difficult but rewarding quasi-operas and musical happenings, usually at the Brooklyn Academy of Music or in some German city where people go for that sort of thing."

"Some German city?" Well yes, that would be Hamburg, Europe – which, coincidentally, is where Waits relocated to during the spring of 1989, in order to work with Robert Wilson. With his bank account nicely in the black, courtesy of Frito-Lay and Bruce Springsteen, and with his critical reputation secure, Waits set off for the north German city where Wilson's reputation as the Andrew Lloyd Webber of the avant garde had been secured in 1976, when he staged a four-and-a-half-hour production of Philip Glass's *Einstein On The Beach*.

Waits and Wilson came together to adapt *The Black Rider*, with a little help from librettist William S. Burroughs. Taken from the folk tale on which Carl Weber had based his 1821 opera *Der Freischutz* (*The Freeshooter*), it is the story of a clerk, in love with a forester's daughter. But her father will only allow the marriage to go ahead if the clerk proves he can shoot as well with a gun as he can wield a quill.

A chance meeting with a character called Pegleg proves fortuitous, as Pegleg turns out to be the Devil. It is perhaps worth bearing in mind that, as Waits had written earlier, "There ain't no Devil, there's just God when he's drunk." Wilhelm the clerk makes a Faustian pact with the Devil, accepting the gift of some magic bullets that will enable him to win the heart of Kathchen, his true love, in a shooting contest.

But, hey, wouldn't you just know it, Pegleg – being the Devil – passes Wilhelm bullets which, besides never missing their target, have other less obvious properties – including the power to keep anyone who accepts the Devil's gift, forever in his thrall.

On his wedding day, Wilhelm takes aim with his magic bullets, but

206

instead kills his bride. "The clerk [ends] up in an insane asylum, stark raving mad and joined by all the other lunatics in the Devil's carnival." *The Black Rider* radiates obsession, magic, addiction, insanity and death. Fertile territory indeed for William Seward Burroughs and Thomas Alan Waits.

After the initial approach Waits seemed to be in two minds about the collaboration, admitting to being "intrigued, flattered and scared". But in the end, flattery won out. "There'll be seven principal players," Waits revealed while he was still writing the score for *The Black Rider*, "all the rest will be carrying spears. It's a little oblique."

Waits was attracted to the project first and foremost because of Wilson's reputation. He had been impressed by *Einstein On The Beach*, which he had seen at the Brooklyn Academy of Music, and which had left him completely dazzled: "I had . . . been pulled into a dream of such impact and beauty. I was unable to fully return to waking for weeks. Wilson's stage images had allowed me to look through windows into a dusting beauty that changed my eyes and ears permanently." Subsequently, Wilson had been one of the first directors Waits approached to help him stage *Frank's Wild Years*.

Being asked aboard *The Black Rider* also gave Waits the opportunity to work with a legitimate living beat-idol, William S. Burroughs. "He was Bull Lee in *On The Road*," Waits proudly told Barney Hoskyns. (Burroughs was also "Frank Carmody" in *The Subterraneans* and "Bill Hubbard" in *Desolation Angels*). "He was the one that I guess was more like Mark Twain with an edge . . . He seemed ideally suited to the position of Poet Laureate. He seemed to have an overview, and one of maturity and cynicism."

Along with Kerouac and Allen Ginsburg, Burroughs had been one of the founding fathers of the Beat Generation; and he was now one of few living writers who could legitimately be described as "legendary". Waits was first introduced to Burroughs in New York in 1975, at a party to launch a beat memoir, *Tales Of Beatnik Glory*, when he was still young and hungry. Now the two men could meet again and work together as equals.

For all his impeccable beat credentials, Burroughs' background gave few clues as to his bohemian future. Born William Seward Burroughs in 1914, he came from a prosperous St Louis family. His grandfather had invented the adding machine, which ensured the young William a secure future and a conservative upbringing. But Bill soon fell among thieves. And a peripatetic existence in Harvard, Vienna and Chicago found Burroughs end up, aged 30, with a hat permanently stuck on his head, all in with the beats.

It was Burroughs' controversial novels *Junkie* (1953) and *The Naked Lunch* (1959) which brought him wider notoriety. While the other beats ranted and raged, and *looked* the part of wild, drug-crazed bohemians, Burroughs' conservative appearance did much to mask his true nature. Never seen without a suit, tie and hat, Burroughs appeared to have been born middle-aged. But from early on, he was addicted to hard drugs, and subsequently lived life through a needle. No stranger to liquor either, Burroughs killed his wife by shooting her through the temple, while drunkenly demonstrating his "William Tell act".

In terms of literary influence on rock'n'roll, it was Burroughs' notorious "cut-up" technique that assured his reputation. David Bowie, Brian Eno and Kurt Cobain were among the musicians who felt their work too could benefit from the random, dissociative technique Burroughs had pioneered in 1960's *Minutes To Go*. But in other ways too, the novelist's wiry, ascetic figure would come to shadow much of the rock'n'roll era.

The phrase "heavy metal", used to describe the pile-driving, riff-based musical style that emerged in the late Sixties, came from Burroughs. The Soft Machine and Steely Dan were just two of the bands who took their names from his works. Patti Smith palled up with him, and the Velvet Underground commemorated the venerable writer as 'Lonesome Cowboy Bill' on their final album, *Loaded*.

Some years later, David Cronenberg's 1991 film of *The Naked Lunch* helped renew interest in Burroughs' life and work, and the writer remained creatively active until his death in 1997, aged 83.

But for Waits, in 1989, the opportunity to work alongside the frail 75-year-old on *The Black Rider* was simply too good to miss. Following an initial meeting, along with Robert Wilson, at the Roosevelt Hotel in Hollywood, Waits hung out with Burroughs at his Kansas home ("very learned and serious" Waits recollected).

"For me," Waits told Sylvie Simmons, "working with him was a chance to go up on the wire without a net, and you really find out what resources you have. Because you're with someone who has a whole *community* inside of them. It was heavy."

Looking back on his experience of working with Burroughs, Waits was impressed with what the author had unearthed in *The Black Rider*: "Burroughs found branches of the story and let them grow into metaphorical things. In all our lives every day [there are], in fact, deals with the Devil that we've made. What is cunning about those deals is that we're not aware we've made them. And when they come to fruition, we are shocked and amazed."

After nearly 20 years working in isolation, or with his wife Kathleen, the collaborative process of *The Black Rider* was in itself a learning experience. Burroughs, after all, was a veteran literary innovator, and Wilson an experienced and venerated stage director. But flattered though he was to be asked, working in such exalted company presented Waits with something of a challenge.

One From The Heart was the best part of a decade behind him; the stage show of *Frank's Wild Years* had never made it out of Chicago; and now here he was transplanted to a strange new environment, far removed from his homeland. All of which left Waits feeling understandably, undeniably nervous.

Hamburg was the city where, nearly 30 years before, The Beatles had come as teenagers to "mak show", by playing eight-hour sets to an audience of drunken sailors, prostitutes and gangsters. Hamburg had always had a louche, seedy reputation. And though, by the time Waits came to reside there, much of the seediness had gone, there was still enough of a sassy edge to lend the city its decadent lustre. But it was "the rainy streets, church bells and the train station", that made up Waits' abiding memories of the city.

Along with Burroughs and Wilson, Waits also took musical succour from his long-time bassist and musical collaborator, Greg Cohen: "Greg helped me grow musically and had an endless supply of ideas with (long hours, cold coffee, hard rolls and no place to lie down.)"

As well as the libretto, Waits and Burroughs collaborated on three songs for *The Black Rider*. "Every day at about three o'clock," Waits told Sylvie Simmons, "he'd start massaging his watch, like he was trying to get the big hand to move with the heat of his fingers, because around . . . four o'clock it's cocktail time. We went to his house and hung out for a couple of days. I saw some of his shotgun paintings – he puts up plywood and shoots it – and we'd talk about the story . . . From Burroughs I learned a lot about reptiles and firearms."

His collaboration with Burroughs on *The Black Rider* also re-awakened Waits' interest in the music of Kurt Weill, and – more widely – that of the crumbling Weimar Republic. Between the Armistice of 1918 and the Nazis' electoral victory of 1933, Germany became a melting pot of artistic and sexual licence. "Released from the oppressive rule of the Kaisers, deprived of its social standards and restraints, eager to drown the memory of the horrors of the Great War, many of the survivors plunged blindly into a frantic quest for pleasure," wrote Anthony Read and David Fisher in their comprehensive *Berlin: The Biography Of A City*.

Once free of hyper-inflation (at one point, a single US dollar was worth 2.5 *trillion* marks) the Germany of *Grand Hotel* and Sally Bowles lifted its skirts and let its hair down. Probably best evoked by Christopher Isherwood's *Goodbye To Berlin*, later popularised in the film and musical *Cabaret*, Weimar Germany was notable for its thriving nightclubs and satirical revues.

One of the key works of the era was the 1928 Bertolt Brecht and Kurt Weill collaboration, *The Threepenny Opera* – best remembered today for giving the world 'Mack The Knife'. But after the Nazi victory of January 1933, began the slow, inexorable march towards the nightmare years of the Third Reich. And within weeks of Hitler assuming power, Kurt Weill had left his native Germany, and relocated to Hollywood.

"I didn't really know that much about Kurt Weill," Waits told Barney Hoskyns, "until people started saying, 'Hey, he must be listening to a lot of Kurt Weill.' I thought I better go and find out who this guy is. So I started listening to *The Threepenny Opera* and *Mahogany* and all that . . . macabre, dissonant . . . expressionistic music." Waits particularly admired Weill's ability at blending the unappealing lyric with the enticing melody: "I like to hear a beautiful melody telling me something terrible."

With echoes redolent of nineteenth-century romantic opera, the cabaret music of pre-Nazi Germany, the howl of the Fifties Beat Generation, the fractured instrumentation of rock'n'roll and the electric grind of rhythm and blues, *The Black Rider* was finally premiered at Hamburg's Thalia Theatre on March 31, 1990. The Beats, the Bohos and the Avant Garde met up that night by the Baltic, but the world outside that Hamburg theatre would have to wait a further three years to hear the results.

CHAPTER 28

FORGING ahead into a new decade, preparing for his own new album, the success of his collaboration on *The Black Rider* still fresh, Waits was disconcerted by the unexpected release of an album during 1991 – *Tom Waits: The Early Years*.

For fans, it was equally disconcerting to hear Waits sounding that *young*. Circa 1991, Waits was pummelling percussion, howling at the moon, making hitty-hitty-bang-bang music; but the younger Tom Waits heard here was a lachrymose, astonishingly sweet-voiced singer. The songs were undeniably those of a songwriter looking for an identity; 'Midnight Lullaby' and 'When You Ain't Got Nobody', in particular, spoke of a young man trying to sound mature beyond his years. But, for all their fledgling faults, those early songs were undeniably intriguing – certainly none of Waits' contemporaries among the early Seventies avocado mafia were writing songs like 'I'm Your Late Night Evening Prostitute'.

Four of the songs here ('Virginia Avenue', 'Ice Cream Man', 'Midnight Lullaby' and 'Little Trip To Heaven') were familiar from Waits' Asylum debut, *Closing Time*. Of the rest, the engaging 'Looks Like I'm Up Shit Creek Again' is archetypal outlaw country and western, with Waits bitching, on solo acoustic guitar. It is affectionately accomplished, in the world-weary style of Merle Haggard – a singer of whom Waits was particularly fond: "I always hear a train in his voice. His songs are made of wood and steel; tender, rough and wise. Want to learn how to write songs? Listen to Merle Haggard."[1]

'Goin' Down Slow' is jaunty, and uncharacteristically features a pedal steel guitar and smooth electric piano. 'Poncho's Lament' is melancholic country, with the boy Tom toying with a spoken interlude – and sounding unfeasibly young. 'Had Me A Girl' is one of those place-name songs, with the 23-year-old Waits confidently listing his conquests across the globe. The unconvincingly bluesy 'So Long I'll See Ya', signposts the start of a lifelong fascination with automobiles, its refrain dryly running: "I got them so long I'll see ya 'cos my Buick's outside waitin' blues." But perhaps most significant of all these early efforts was the short and simply titled 'Frank's Song'?

On its release, Edsel promised that *The Early Years* offered "a glimpse of what Waits was performing in clubs and dives all over California and how he would develop over the next few years into one of the world's most popular 'cult/underground' artists."

Reviewing *Tom Waits: The Early Years* in Q, Andy Gill was quietly impressed: "a fascinating glimpse of a now well-known character and style . . ." Though Terry Staunton in *NME* remained underwhelmed: "For those who only caught onto Tom after 1983's *Swordfishtrombones*, this will seem particularly ordinary fare, like Jackson Browne taking a stab at the comedy scene and ending up as funny as Leonard Cohen at a redundancy party."

While the world was still reflecting on the startlingly young Tom Waits of *The Early Years*, the old growler of 1991 was busy collaborating with cult San Francisco band Primus. "The vast majority of reviewers can generally agree on one word to describe Primus," wrote the authoritative *Encyclopaedia Of Popular Music,* "weird." No wonder Waits was drawn to them. He appeared as guest vocalist on 'Tommy The Cat' on their *Sailing The Seas Of Cheese* album – which also graced the soundtrack of *Bill & Ted's Bogus Journey.*

A second volume of *Tom Waits: The Early Years* followed in 1992. Six of its 13 tracks (including 'Ol' 55', 'Shiver Me Timbers' and 'Old Shoes') had made their way onto Waits' first two albums – and the remainder were little more than another collection of tentative efforts, although 'Diamonds On My Windshield' sounded fully formed, and the otherwise unreleased 'So It Goes' showed undeniable promise. Like the artist himself though, most critics considered these demos to be unnecessary echoes from an earlier time – particularly as the best of this early work had been more fully realised on his first few albums.

While Waits, and many aficionados of his work, were dismissive of *The Early Years*, the mere fact of their release was testimony to the growing interest in his music. It was clear that he had long since left the ghetto of cult act – and while mainstream chart success was never really on the cards, he had at last made it onto the music industry's A List.

Proof if it were needed had come in 1990 when the rock music community banded together to do what it could to help alert its constituency to the growing menace of AIDS. Imaginatively lighting on the work of Cole Porter, the organisers gathered together the top stars of the time to do justice to the work of a past-master – the result was the double album *Red Hot + Blue.*

The real coup was getting U2 to contribute to the project: 1987's *The*

Joshua Tree had established the Irish quartet as the biggest rock band on the planet – and there had been no album of original material since. So, as well as raising the bar, their swamp rock, jungle voodoo take on Porter's 'Night and Day' raised the odd eyebrow.

Waits was certainly in exalted company, and it wasn't just U2 – Annie Lennox, Deborah Harry, Iggy Pop and The Pogues were just some of those involved. Waits contribution was 'It's Alright With Me', which came complete with a Jim Jarmusch video. Cole Porter had written the song for 1953's *Can Can*; but when Lena Horne lifted it, upped the tempo, and enjoyed a contemporary hit, Porter *hated* it. God alone knows what the sophisticated Cole would have made of Waits' interpretation.

Clearly U2 could afford to wait four years between albums, but Waits upped the ante even further, with a five-year hiatus between *Frank's Wild Years* and 1992's *Night On Earth*. However, between albums, Waits found himself involved in a number of side-projects. (Incidentally, to date, Kate Bush still holds the record with a 12-year gap between *The Red Shoes* and *Aerial*.)

The failure of big budget films such as Coppola's *One From The Heart* in the Eighties had sent shockwaves through an industry usually inured to such failure. Symptomatic of the flops was *Revolution* in 1985, a singularly ill-conceived War of Independence drama, which fell from such a height that it kept the great Al Pacino off the screen for a full four years.

Pacino's return came with the punchy serial-killer drama *Sea Of Love* in 1989. Tom Waits was an odd choice to record the title song, a startling reworking of the drippy 1959 hit (for Phil Phillips in America and Marty Wilde in the UK) given that Robert Plant (as The Honeydrippers) had enjoyed a 1985 hit with the very same 'Sea Of Love'.

Waits had also popped up at the Los Angeles Theatre Center early in 1989, performing in *Demon Wine*, a play by Thomas Babe. Waits' co-stars included the baby-faced Bud Cort, star of the cult *Harold And Maude*; Carol Kane, Oscar-nominated for her 1974 debut in *Hester Street*; and a young Bill Pullman, later to become a hard-hitting US president in *Independence Day*. Waits' straight-acting, no music stage debut picked up a fistful of good reviews, and attracted healthy audiences, including *Ironweed* co-star Jack Nicholson, and the young Sean Penn.

For Waits, 1989 was turning out to be a very busy year. He was also heard, though not seen, as the spectral late-night DJ in Jim Jarmusch's *Mystery Train*. Taking its title from Elvis's final Sun Records single, Jarmusch's feature takes place in the Arcade Hotel in Memphis, and deals with a pair of Elvis-obsessed Japanese tourists. Joe Strummer and Screamin' Jay Hawkins are in there too.

Jarmusch's next film was the episodic *Night On Earth* (1992): a portmanteau made up of five vignettes of five taxi drivers and their passengers in five different cities – with a score by Tom Waits. The Los Angeles segment featured Winona Ryder and Gena Rowlands; New York, Armin Mueller-Stahl and Giancarlo Esposito; Paris, Beatrice Dalle and Isaack De Bankole; Rome, Roberto Benigni; and Helsinki, Matti Pellonpaa.

Much of the interest in *Night On Earth* centred on Winona Ryder, who played Corky, the snappy, chain-smoking cabby in the opening segment ("Men? Can't live with 'em, can't kill 'em."). The fascination was not so much piqued by her performance, as by the fact that the 19-year-old actress had just broken off her engagement to Johnny Depp.

To get over it, Winona stayed in nights, smoked cigarettes, and played Tom Waits albums over and over again. But her work didn't appear to suffer and in the event, her role in *Night On Earth* was one of the best in the film. Gena Rowlands' casting agent is keen to get Corky on her books, but the cab driver responds: "Look lady, I know the movies and all, I see you're being serious, but that's not real life for me."

Waits' score for *Night On Earth* was suitably atmospheric, with lots of plucked bass, lonely trumpet, moody sax – but it was, after all, just a soundtrack, with only three vocal tracks. Nevertheless, the fact that it was the first new Tom Waits album in five years got the critics salivating. The press release proudly boasted that Waits' *Night On Earth* soundtrack "resonantly illuminates" Jarmusch's film, but the critics ventured to disagree. In his *NME* review, David Quantick found that "the songs here, all variants on a slow and moody theme, are Waits-by-numbers, reasonably memorable, but hardly guaranteed to make the listener shout: 'Good God! Tom Waits has taken popular music by the scruff of the neck and thrown it into the flames of excitement!'"

Q singled out "Squiffy time signatures and dustbin-lid percussion [which] apply a deadbeat arty patina to the sleazy jazz and cheesy waltz interludes . . . this is fairly tedious fodder." *Empire* admired Jarmusch's work, but still found *Night On Earth* wanting: "a highly entertaining and thoroughly oddball collage celebrating the typically inconsequential nature of most daily encounters. Nothing much really *happens* of course, but as the man himself is fond of pointing out '*Life* has no plot'."

The shock-haired director and singing actor had kept in touch since *Down By Law*. And Jarmusch recalled one appropriate taxi-cab moment with his soundtrack buddy: "I was in this cab with Tom," Jarmusch told

John Naughton in 1992, "and he's singing this song 'Motel Girl' which he's written for Keith Richards ('with her half-assed curls and her Woolworth pearls, she's my motel girl'). The cab driver, who was Turkish, turned to Tom and said, 'Hey man, that's a really nice song, but man, you should get someone else to sing it because your voice is really fucked up. You have some problem with your voice, you should get some cough medicine.' Tom just laughed and said, 'Yeah, you're probably right.'"

Jarmusch and Waits remained close over the years, and membership of a semi-secret society, The Sons of Lee Marvin, was whispered. This close-knit community was limited to those who looked like the Oscar-winning star of *Cat Ballou*. Interestingly, it was Marvin whose portrait glowered over Jack and Meg White during their scene in Jarmusch's 2003 *Coffee And Cigarettes*.

Inexplicably, 1991's *Queens Logic* – a 30-something drama set in and around the New York borough of the title – never received a UK theatrical release. Waits only appeared fleetingly, but above the title were such star names as John Malkovich, Jamie Lee Curtis, Joe Mantegna and Kevin Bacon. Critics praised it as "an ensemble piece well worth rooting out on video". But few bothered.

Clearly it was now time for Waits to target the commercial mainstream – so where else would he turn but to the experimental composer Gavin Bryars, with whom he set about collaborating on a project snappily entitled *Jesus' Blood Never Failed Me Yet*?

Bryars explained the genesis of the project: "In 1971, I came across a tape of an old tramp singing a fragment of a religious song. I made a long orchestral piece out of it and this was recorded in 1975. For the 1993 recording I added many other instruments as well as Tom Waits to the ensemble. Some years ago, Tom contacted me because he had lost his recording of the original version, which he said was his 'favourite recording'. Accordingly, when I developed the new piece, I decided to ask Tom if he would like to join in."

The song has Waits "accompanying" the unknown tramp. Together, the two duet on the repeated phrase "Jesus' Blood Never Failed Me Yet", as Bryars' lavish orchestration lends the rendered line a dignified poignancy. The effect is hypnotic and quite dislocating, like the final track the Bonzo Dog Band ever recorded together, 'Slush', which was one irritating, staccato laugh, endlessly, terrifyingly, repeated, as a lush orchestra played beneath it.

Writing in *The Sunday Herald* in 2004, Gavin Bryars recalled the 1993 'Jesus' Blood . . .' session with Waits: "He sang to headphone playback, head close to the microphone, with just me in the room. It was like being in the company of a great blues singer from the past. He sang, eyes closed, constructing sequences of the phrase, maybe five or six repetitions, until he moved immediately to a new idea. Some were subtle and tender, some very powerful and even angry . . . Throughout the recording I could witness at close quarters his musical strengths: impeccable timing, beautifully focused intonation, an instinctive musical intelligence and diction as clear as Frank Sinatra's . . ."

Waits had grown to love the original version of that down-and-out's pathetic song long ago, but he cherished a particularly fond, more recent, memory of hearing the piece at a birthday party for his wife Kathleen; the tramp singing 'Jesus' Blood . . .' came out of a radio as the party wound down, and Tom and Kathleen sat holding hands as the song "settled like dust on the evening".

Unbelievably, the new version of 'Jesus' Blood Never Failed Me Yet', on which Waits duets with the long-forgotten tramp, was released as a single in 1993. However, it did not chart. Amazingly though, the album was nominated for the 1993 Mercury Music Award, although it lost out to Suede.

A decade later, 'Jesus' Blood Never Failed Me Yet' was included on the album *Gavin Bryars: A Portrait*, and was subsequently nominated for the Grammy Award for Best Male Rock Vocal Performance. Honestly, you couldn't make it up . . . (However, once again, it did not win.)

For years, Waits has occupied a permanent apartment situated somewhere out near Left Field, in a personal musical universe full of black holes and obscure satellites. For years, 'Jesus' Blood Never Failed Me Yet' was rarely off the Waits turntable; and Agnes Bernelle was another family favourite, with her irresistible opening line: "Father's lying dead on the ironing board, smelling of Lux and Drambuie." Frequently, when asked to name his favourite record, Waits would return, having plucked an album from the shelf labelled "Obscure". And when repeatedly questioned as to who he had recently been listening to, Waits would give the stock answer: The Romiyiana Monkey Chant!

Journalists scratched their collective head, and left little the wiser, but Waits would helpfully elaborate: "This guy went into the jungle and found a group of natives that sat ritually in concentric circles and did what has come to be known to millions as the Romiyiana Monkey Chant, where they relive their own tribe being saved by monkeys . . . These monkeys, apparently, came down out of the trees and killed an attacking tribe. Romiyiana. Ask for it by name. Accept no substitutes."[2]

And always, *always*, there were those memorable one-liners. Eminently quotable, dripping with wit and vinegar, Waits' public utterances are rightly cherished, his every interview an opportunity for set-piece routines and droll one-liners. Call them what you will, fans relish them as . . . Waitsisms.

"I'd rather have a bottle in front of me than a frontal lobotomy."

"There ain't no Devil, there's just God when he's drunk." (Robin Williams liked that one enough to include it in his live routines.)

"I don't have a drink problem, 'cept when I can't get a drink."

"Everybody I like is either dead, or not feeling very well."

"I'm so broke I can't even pay attention."

"You have to keep busy, after all, no dog ever pissed on a moving car."

"I don't care who I have to step on on my way down."

And, best known of all, the most widely quoted Waitsism of all time: "Champagne for my real friends, real pain for my sham friends." Waits actually never claimed this one as his own, but it did become inextricably linked to him. In 1998, quote master Nigel Rees identified the genesis of the gag as: "an Edwardian toast that the Irish-born painter Francis Bacon . . . acquired from his father".

Ironically, given the paucity of contemporary wit and wisdom, Waits is largely absent from the dictionaries of quotations. There is a frequent, conspicuous, Tom Waits-sized gap in such collections, right there between the poets John Wain and Derek Walcott. Although two of Waits' lines – the dog and moving car observation, plus the drink problem reflection – did manage to hustle their way into *The Pan Dictionary Of Contemporary Quotations.*

Despite the disappointing critical response to his *Night On Earth* sound-track, the mere fact that a new Tom Waits record had appeared, was enough to send out signals – and the album's release, in May 1992, marked the definite stirrings of . . . a Tom Waits *cult*.

While never as organised as the Mormons, or as committed as the People's Temple followers of the "Reverend" Jim Jones in Guyana, devotees were quietly fanatical in their pursuit of the great Waits. The development of the Tom Waits Cult was rooted in that man's polymath activities. But membership of the TWC was furtive, its procedures arcane and its purpose extremely uncertain.

Over lightly frothed cappuccinos, or perhaps while sipping a preprandial sherry, cult members would sift through the entrails of a career now enter-ing its third decade. In that innocent pre-internet era, yellowing press cuttings were handled as reverentially as shavings of the true cross and crackly black-and-white performances were watched on bulky video recorders. Viewed through a haze of static, with Waits' arms flailing and jerking across long-forgotten stages, it was like watching a very old basketball match through a snowstorm.

Audience members of long-ago concerts were revered as true disciples . . . While Waits' witticisms were endlessly revisited . . . Frequently Asked Questions were answered ("Was that Tom Waits in *Alien: Resurrection*, *City Of Lost Children* and *The Name Of The Rose*?) A fair question . . . though it was in fact Ron Perlman, who shares a strong facial resemblance to Waits. Perlman went on to become a star in TV's *Beauty And The Beast* – and not as the Beauty.

And all the while, the object of their affection kept on moving: onward, upward, forward; sometimes way out on a limb; but *always* reluctant to look back.

Waits offered up a skewed and frequently original take on the word and the world. His weapons were a ready wit and a large shot of cynicism; his ammunition, a peerless lexicon and a mind full of arcane knowledge. Best of all, everything was fair game in Waits' shooting gallery.

Finally, following the release of *Night On Earth* in 1992, there came official news. A press release stated baldly that: "Songs from *The Black Rider* form the basis of a new album, to be released in the spring of 1993. It will be preceded, however, by an as-yet-untitled collection of new songs this autumn."

The anticipation was tangible. Waits was certainly an acquired taste, but he was now becoming known for reaching the parts others did not dare to approach. Traditional "rock" acts had found themselves increasingly marginalised by the explosive interest in dance, garage and hip-hop; and in the age of sampling, the barriers were down and the dander was up. But because of his wayward detours and wilful determination, there remained an abiding interest in a quirky craftsman like Tom Waits.

NOTES

1 *Songwriters On Songwriting*, Paul Zollo
2 *Playboy*

PART III

Straight To The Top

CHAPTER 29

ALL Tom Waits' determination to push ahead, broaden his musical boundaries, and stand unfettered as an artist . . . were fortunately built upon a sound commercial foundation. For all his wilful single-mindedness, there was no denying Waits' ability to pen a tune which many would pay to hum.

While his public profile is demonstrably lower than that of singer-songwriting contemporaries such as Bruce Springsteen or Neil Young, Waits basks in a warm and comfortable alcove in the celebrity bear pit. Like his English peer Richard Thompson, whose songs have been recorded by, among many others, R.E.M., Bonnie Raitt and The Corrs, Waits has an enviable track record, but remains a shadowy figure.

Over the years, Waits has accrued an impressive collection of cover versions, perhaps most lucratively when Springsteen chose to cut 'Jersey Girl'. Early in 1990 though, he acquired another – less likely – champion, when Rod Stewart found himself undergoing one of his periodic chart rebirths, this time courtesy of Tom Waits. Rod's take on 'Downtown Train' was a number three hit in America, his biggest hit there since 1976's 'Tonight's The Night'. While in the UK 'Downtown Train' reached a very respectable number 10.

It was label boss Rob Dickins who had alerted Stewart to the potential of Waits' work: "A few years ago, I started suggesting songs which I thought [Rod] should cover," Dickins told Paul Gorman in *Music Week*. "The biggest gamble was 'Tom Traubert's Blues'. I played it to Rod, expecting him to hate it, and we got halfway through and he said, 'I love it. Let's do it. It'll be a brave thing to do.'"

Following his success with 'Downtown Train', Rod went on to cover two further Waits songs. 'Tom Traubert's Blues' was helpfully bracketed "(Waltzing Matilda)" when he made it into a hit in 1992. There were even those who tipped Stewart's maudlin cover as the surprise UK Christmas number one – though, in the event, it stalled at six.

Before he embarked on the wholesale plundering of *The Great American Songbook* (Volumes 1–99), Stewart had already more or less given up on songwriting, preferring to cover other people's material. His 1995 album

A Spanner In The Works featured songs by Bob Dylan, Chris Rea and Tom Petty; there was also an intriguing take on Waits' own 'Hang On St Christopher' – with producer Trevor Horne allegedly employing more than a hundred drums and effects on every verse.

Despite the benefits of these collaborations for both parties, Waits and Stewart never met. Talking to Nick Johnstone for *Uncut*, Rod enthused: "Tom's brilliant . . . when I did 'Downtown Train', he said he put a swimming pool for his kids in his back garden and I paid for it!"

Covers by such high calibre acts ensured a healthy income for Tom, Kathleen and all the little Waitses. Bruce Springsteen's inclusion of 'Jersey Girl' on his 1986 live box-set alone, would have paid for a whole clutch of swimming pools; the fact that he also chose 'Jersey Girl' as the B-side to 'Cover Me', was an added bonus.

There may not have been a very long queue to cover 'Dave The Butcher', 'Jockey Full Of Bourbon' or 'Telephone Call From Istanbul' . . . But certain songs, particularly those from Waits' early career, have lent themselves to being covered by a gratifying, if bewildering, array of artists over the years.

From early on, Waits' material was mined. The gruffer his voice grew, the less casual punters bought into his career; but fellow artists were quick to recognise the inherent quality of the material the grizzled troubadour was producing.

Even early on, however, Waits was stinting in his gratitude. Hell, these guys were doing him a favour – but that's not how it looked from where old grumble-pants was sitting. Among the earliest to cover a Waits song ('Ol' 55' in 1974) were his Asylum labelmates, the Eagles. As mentioned earlier, the composer's views on his contemporaries were at best withering; his considered opinion being that all Eagles albums were good for was "keeping the dirt off your turntable".

And it wasn't just the Eagles . . . In his first decade as a professional songwriter, Waits' work had seen service in many hands, among them ex-Fairport Convention singer Iain Matthews, Bette Midler, Manhattan Transfer, Tim Buckley, Dion and Eric Andersen – an American singersongwriter whom Brian Epstein had once expressed an interest in managing. And in later years, acts as diverse as Meat Loaf, Mary Chapin Carpenter, Jonathan Richman, Shawn Colvin, Paul Young, Marianne Faithfull, Everything But The Girl and Nanci Griffith . . . have all enriched Waits' standing – and bank account – by recording his songs.

At the turn of the new millennium, Hootie & The Blowfish included 'I Hope That I Don't Fall In Love With You' on their *Scattered, Smothered &*

Covered album – and while the band's popularity has never really extended beyond North America (and a mention on *Friends*), at home they were massive. Anyone whose song was included on an album by Hootie & The Blowfish was guaranteed to send the kids to school with shoes on their feet.

Fans may still chafe at Waits' lack of real commercial success. But they really needn't worry. Impressed by Norah Jones' multi-platinum debut *Come Away With Me*, Waits sent her a new song, 'Long Way Home', which she included on her 2004 follow-up, *Feels Like Home*. Inclusion on a number one album by one of the decade's brightest hopes, brought not only the customary financial boost, but also ensured that Waits' work reached out to a whole new audience.

Bob Seger by his own admission, came "really late" to Waits. But the gritty Detroit rocker ended up covering two of his songs ('Blind Love' and 'New Coat Of Paint') after bumping into the composer in Los Angeles. "I met him once in my whole life, driving my Mercedes . . . I've got a Hawaiian shirt on . . . it's real hot outside, 90 degrees. I see Tom Waits, all in black, long-sleeved shirt, cowboy boots. . . ." Seger told *Rolling Stone*. "So I pull up next to him and I say, 'Tom!' I've got sunglasses on, he probably thought I was with the CIA – car phone and everything – and he says, 'Heh?' and looks real startled, so I say, 'It's Bob Seger.' He says, 'Oh, hi, Bob.' He jumps in the car, and we start talking. I asked him what he was doing, and he says, 'Uh, I'm walkin'.'

"I've loved his stuff down through the years so I started asking him all these dumb questions about his songs. I said in 'Cold Cold Ground' Tom, you say, 'The cat will sleep in the mailbox.' Yesterday I went out and bought my cat one of those fuzzy mailboxes. Is that what you're talking about? He looked at me like I was from Mars. 'No, no. My cats sleep under the house.' So it goes on, this strange interlude, for about 15 minutes. Finally, I asked if I could drop him somewhere and he says, 'Tell you what, take me back to right where you picked me up . . . and, uh, I'll just keep on walking.'"

Round up other Waits admirers, and you'll have corralled a right motley crew: thriller writer Ken Follett ("I'd love to meet him and ask him what his lyrics are about"); insurance fraudster Lord ("Call me Charlie") Brocket ("some of Tom's songs are beautiful, but he has ended up sounding a bit like an old town crier"); the illustrator Raymond Briggs and presenter Graham Norton each selected a Waits song as one of their *Desert Island Discs*; as did Colin Firth, because 'Heartattack & Vine' reminded him of bedsit squalor in Chalk Farm. For Bonnie Raitt, he's "a true original . . . a window on the scene we never got close to"; P.J. Harvey admires a man who "doesn't care and is not interested in making money. He explores all different avenues, like writing film music, acting, doing music for theatre"; while K.T. Tunstall, finds him "one of the best in the world at doing his own thing".

Man of the moment Russell Brand, recently enthused: "Tom Waits, the carnivals in that man's mind are just astonishing." While an even more unexpected testimony came from TV historian Simon Schama, who found Waits' 'Ol' 55': "the single most beautiful love song since Gershwin and Cole Porter shut their piano lids".

The Pixies' Frank Black is inspired to the extent that "when I listen to a Tom Waits record, I want to go out and make a record"; while the actor Robert Carlyle named his Rain Dog Theatre Company in his hero's honour. And whereas Josephine Hart (the other Mrs Saatchi), organiser of London's most prestigious poetry readings, was attracted by the "pure poetry" of Waits' lyrics, weathergirl Sian Lloyd just loves the voice.

Among the many others who have sung Waits' praises over the years are Jack Nicholson, Elvis Costello, Johnny Depp, Norah Jones, Thom Yorke, Katie Melua, Bruce Springsteen, Winona Ryder, Nick Cave, Jamie Cullum, Dave Matthews, Keith Richards, Marianne Faithfull, Kim Wilde, Rod Stewart, Jerry Hall, Don Black, Chris Eubank . . . Bands such as U2, Coldplay, Starsailor, Muse, Depeche Mode, Travis . . . All in all, not a bad Christmas card list. No small wonder that in a recent profile, *Hot Press* singled Waits out as "the coolest man in the known universe".

Celebrity fans in the Age of Celebrity . . . All those years ago, when Andy Warhol forecast that "in the future, everyone will be famous for 15 minutes", everyone thought: wow, how cool. Now, in the febrile, fast-food, soundbite culture of the early twenty-first century, that quarter of an hour can seem like an *awfully* long time.

Yet Tom Waits has endured. By keeping a constantly shifting veil between himself and his audience, he has consolidated an air of inscrutability, which you don't get by endlessly plumping up the sofa cushions with Richard & Judy. By pulling on his various "Tom Waits" personae, and indulging in a judicious amount of shape-shifting, he has helped ensure a degree of personal privacy, while providing his audience with plenty of fodder for the imagination.

It's always nice to have your songwriting ability appreciated, and as someone who prefers remaining at one remove, Waits must be doubly gratified when his songs are recorded by others. Such homages are not only financially satisfying, they also stand as a formal acknowledgement by your peers. But isn't it just typical: you wait ages for one Tom Waits tribute album to turn up, and then bizarrely, 1995 saw two coming along together!

Towards the end of the last century, there was a vogue for such testimonials, the stars of today acknowledging the work of their predecessors. Among those "we are not worthy" collections, were homages to Syd Barrett, Richard Thompson, Nick Drake and – twice! – Leonard Cohen, all of whom were celebrated with lavish, star-studded tribute albums.

Step Right Up: The Songs of Tom Waits gathered together the likes of 10,000 Maniacs ('I Hope That I Don't Fall In Love With You'), The Wedding Present ('Red Shoes By The Drugstore'), Pete Shelley ('Better Off Without A Wife') and Violent Femmes ('Step Right Up') – all of them doing the bending at the knee bit.

It was a nicely packaged set, with a cover shot of Waits' old home, the Tropicana Motel. And the sleeve notes for *Step Right Up* also included comments from the artists about their reasons for wanting to take part; viz. Pale Saints, who tackled 'Jersey Girl', because: "Tom Waits is not content to be just a great songwriter, instead he continually explores digging into the darkest corners to unearth new inspiration and the means to express it. A rare artist who has the conviction to do exactly what he wants, and the dress sense to carry it off."

The only archive track was Tim Buckley's 1973 cover of 'Martha'. His tour manager, Robert Duffey, recalled: " 'Martha' was recorded for Tim's album *Sefronia*. In about 1973, Tim and Tom knew each other, and even played together on a record company softball team. Tim heard 'Martha' on *Closing Time*, and wanted to record it immediately. Tim talked about how visual Tom's songs were." As someone whose idea of exercise was tugging the ring-pull on a can of Bud, the idea of Tom Waits striking out for the Asylum softball team sets the mind reeling.

Temptation was the other 1995 Waits tribute, a solo effort which gathered together 17 Waits compositions by Canadian chanteuse Holly Cole, who treated such Waits favourites as 'Jersey Girl', '(Lookin' For) The Heart Of Saturday Night' and 'Soldier's Things' in a smoky jazz style. Enjoyable as the tribute was, equally entertaining was the accompanying press release, in which we learnt that: "Tom Waits is, along with Leonard Cohen, Randy Newman and Joni Mitchell, one of the greatest lyricists in contemporary pop music. His words are an inspired melange of surrealist imagery and hard-boiled street talk. His music reflects influences as diverse as ragtime, jazz, gospel, country, swing and Igor Stravinsky.

"There is an irony in all of Tom Waits' songs, due to the constant tension between Tom – the urban primitive, and Tom – the sophisticated avant-gardist. This in turn makes the material ideal for Holly Cole, who is herself a designer of split-level musical mansions, constantly seeking out the subtext in an apparently straightforward lyric."

At the other end of the spectrum, locked in an LA studio in late 2006, the actress Scarlett Johansson announced that she too was cutting an entire album of Waits' songs. ("Bring on her version of 'Earth Died Screaming'," slavered Q magazine.)

On occasion, one of these covers would even come to supersede the Waits original. From *Bone Machine,* The Ramones lifted 'I Don't Wanna Grow Up' – and whereas Waits' original sounded like a drunken sea shanty recorded at the bottom of a hulk by grumpy midgets, The Ramones turned it into a trademark thrashing romp. 'I Don't Wanna Grow Up' appeared on the seminal punk quartet's final album, *Adios Amigos* – fitting neatly into The Ramones' predominantly negative firmament, alongside early songs such as 'I Don't Wanna Go Down The Basement' and 'I Don't Wanna Walk Around With You'. Of course, once the Prozac took hold, the band soon became much more positive in their outlook on life, with a notable 'I Wanna . . .' sequence ('I Wanna Sniff Some Glue', 'I Wanna Be Your Boyfriend', 'I Wanna Be Sedated' . . .)

In his sleeve notes to The Ramones' own *Anthology*, David Fricke wrote: "'I Don't Wanna Grow Up' was an isolationist variation on the Peter Pan dream of eternal youth, a prayer to be taken away from war-torn matrimony, suck-city television, a world in mad, black flux. The Ramones saw plenty of themselves in there: 'I don't wanna be filled with doubt/ I don't wanna be a good boy scout/ I don't wanna have to learn to count/ I don't wanna have the biggest amount/ I don't wanna grow up . . . !'"

The admiration was evidently mutual, with Waits obviously finding some resonance in The Ramones' relentless two-chord barrage; and in 2003 he appeared alongside U2, Kiss, Red Hot Chili Peppers, Green Day and The Pretenders on *Tribute To The Ramones*. Waits chose to cover 'The Return Of Jackie & Judy' from *The End Of The Century*: "Jackie is a bookie, Judy's taking loans, they both came up to New York just to see The Ramones . . ." Weirdly, after years of neglect for his own work, this cover earned Waits a Grammy nomination for "Best Rock Vocal Performance". But even in the twenty-first century, the Grammys couldn't go *that* far out on a limb, and the award eventually went to . . . Dave Matthews.

While the proceeds of all cover versions were presumably welcome, it was particularly gratifying for Waits when an act he had long admired paid him the compliment of recording one of his compositions. Waits had been proud to appear alongside Roy Orbison at 1987's Black And White Night; and was now delighted by The Big O's Sun labelmate Johnny Cash recording a version of 'Down There By The Train' for his triumphant 1994 *American Recordings*.

Cash had been wandering in the wilderness for a decade or more, churning out lacklustre albums for an increasingly apathetic label. Until in 1986, after the best part of 30 years with the same company, Columbia Records let Johnny Cash go. Dwight Yoakam was not alone in his outrage: "What kind of decency is that? He built the building, man."

To the amazement of everyone – not least the Man In Black – it was maverick producer Rick Rubin who threw him a lifeline. In the early Eighties Rubin had co-founded Def Jam Records, and through the label's endorsement of acts such as Run DMC, LL Cool J, Public Enemy and the Beastie Boys, had effectively introduced rap into the mainstream. But running parallel with his pioneering rap productions was Rubin's abiding love of heavy metal, and by the time he came to Johnny Cash, Rubin had produced albums by AC/DC, Slayer and Red Hot Chili Peppers.

Even in the give and take, sample-and-be-damned style of the mid-Nineties, the alliance between Rick Rubin and Johnny Cash was improbable enough to raise the odd eyebrow. But it turned out that what Rubin wanted from Cash was just a very simple guitar, vocal album – in effect taking Cash right back to his pioneering roots at Sun Records, 40 years before.

American Recordings put Cash firmly back on the map. His first solo show in 30 years took place at the trendy Viper Room in Los Angeles, where he was cheered on by the likes of Johnny Depp, Juliette Lewis and Sean Penn. A headlining appearance at Glastonbury in 1994 was equally well received. Suddenly Cash had become trendy. But it was his old friend Kris Kristofferson who best understood and described Cash's iconic status: "He stands out in any bunch . . . just by the heart and soul of his music. It's like watching an old coyote walk through a poodle party."

For Cash, this was an album of "sin and redemption". And deep in the mix – among the songs by Leonard Cohen, Loudon Wainwright, Kris Kristofferson and the Man In Black himself – was Tom Waits, distinguishing himself with 'Down There By The Train': which *Time* magazine saw as "a heavenly train for wrongdoers seeking righteousness". Cash sounds magnificently gnarled and grizzled, as he sings Waits' song of a train, bound for the gates of hell.

American Recordings was garlanded with praise on its release: "an epochal American recording," *Billboard*; "unquestionably, one of his best albums," *Rolling Stone*; "Johnny Cash has ascended a new musical peak with his finest album," *Time Out*.

"Rick Rubin told a lot of writers that I was listening out for songs," Cash told Terry Staunton in *NME* in 1994. "He did ask a few people to write specially for me. That's how I got the Tom Waits song 'Down There By The Train'. I'd heard his name before, and that was about it, but I went out and bought some of his albums afterwards. He's a very special writer, my kind of writer. It's really inspiring to know that there are so many great writers out there."

"Somebody said, 'You got any songs for Johnny Cash?'" Waits remembered in a 2006 interview with Mick Brown for *The Word*. "I just about fell off my chair. I had a song I hadn't recorded, so I said, 'Hey – it's got all the stuff that Johnny likes – trains and death, John Wilkes Booth, the cross . . . OK?'"

American Recordings gave Johnny Cash the fillip his career needed, and for the remainder of his life, his status as an American icon was assured. When Cash died in September 2003, that 1994 album was frequently cited as the beginning of his third career – and Tom Waits was particularly proud to have been associated with that well-deserved rebirth.

It was Nick Lowe who won first prize in the *American Recordings* sweepstake, for the pithy rhyme: "Patently unclear, if it's New York or New Year". But by linking the betrayer of Christ with Lincoln's assassin, Waits did come up with a killer couplet of his own: "There's no eye for an eye/ There's no tooth for a tooth/ I saw Judas Iscariot carrying John Wilkes Booth."

CHAPTER 30

HIS name was being dropped in all the right circles, his songs recorded by the great and good, and his own records receiving rapturous receptions but, for much of the early part of the Nineties, Tom Waits decided to concentrate on his career as a film actor.

Film "star" would be pushing it – after all, many of the roles Waits undertook were little more than cameo appearances. But they were eye-catching cameos, in high prestige productions. There were, for example, few more eagerly anticipated films than 1990's *The Two Jakes*. Nearly 20 years in the coming, this found Jack Nicholson reprising one of his best-loved roles, as private eye Jake Gittes, who had made his first appearance in *Chinatown*.

Soon after it opened in 1974, *Chinatown* was established as a classic. It had everything: heavy on Forties atmosphere; Roman Polanski's assured direction; Robert Towne's spider's web of a script; a plethora of stylish costumes; the sultry mystery of Faye Dunaway; the cloying menace of John Huston . . . And, of course, Jack, at the top of his game.

For many years, there were rumours of a *Chinatown* sequel. Yet, even by the convoluted standards of film-making Hollywood-style, *The Two Jakes* was in a league of its own. Nicholson was still basking in the glow of *Batman*'s success, which was hurtling the film to the top of the all-time box-office greats. But not only had Jack agreed to star in the *Chinatown* sequel, he was also due to undertake one of his rare directing forays.

The second Jake was to have been played by the film's producer, Robert Evans. Evans had begun his movie life as an actor (*The Fiend Who Walked The West*), but by this time he hadn't been in front of a camera for over 30 years. Though from behind the camera, he'd had a hand in producing a number of films over the years – you might have seen some of them, like *Love Story*, *The Godfather* and *Chinatown* . . .

Scriptwriter Robert Towne was down to direct, but he couldn't take Evans as an actor. Then Towne fell out with his buddy Nicholson. And so it was, that over the years *The Two Jakes* limped along in development limbo, until Nicholson finally took the plunge.

Whereas *Chinatown* forced its audience to wade through a watery and complex plot, *The Two Jakes* was truly opaque. The intrigue, this time involving land deals, was just too complex. Forty years before, even Raymond Chandler didn't understand the plot of *The Big Sleep* – and he wrote it! But the story of *The Two Jakes* was as dense as the oil it appeared to be about. The film did, however, have its moments: the spirit of *Chinatown* subtly haunted its sequel, with Gittes glimpsing the ghosts of the Mulwray family and acknowledging that "the footprints of the past are everywhere". Nicholson was easily as compelling as the first time around, and more lizard-like than ever. This time Jake Gittes was a war hero, but his laconic edge hadn't been dulled by combat: "People like him don't get arrested," Jake cautions at one point, "they get streets named after them."

When it was eventually released, in 1990 – five years after the first scenes were shot, the film's reception was muted. *Variety* found it "jumbled" and "obtuse", but the UK critics were generally kinder: "a film . . . which shoots for the moon and which, if it misses, does so in quite magnificent style," judged *Empire*. In the event, *The Two Jakes* just couldn't escape from beneath the shadow of *Chinatown*, and it later found itself marginalised and overshadowed by the far more assured *LA Confidential*.

Waits, playing a sneering cop, was glimpsed only in one brief scene, attempting to literally put the boot into Nicholson's Gittes. Tom looked as if he enjoyed his big nasty moment, and he certainly looked the part, nattily clad in 1948 wardrobe and happily reunited with his *Ironweed* co-star.

Alongside such prestige productions as *The Two Jakes*, Waits also appeared in the hard-to-find and rarely screened *Bearskin: An Urban Fairytale*. He was cast as a "Punch & Judy man" in this 1990 production, which sounded only marginally more appealing when it was released in Portugal as *Na Pele do Urso*.

Despite boasting a credible cast (Nicolas Cage, James Coburn, Peter Fonda) in a complexly plotted scam film, written and directed by one Christopher Coppola (nephew of Tom's old mentor, Francis Ford – whose other nephew, Cage, and sister, Talia Shire, also appeared), *Deadfall* was another Waits outing that disappeared almost immediately after release. Sold under the tagline: "You Don't Know Who To Trust . . . What To Believe . . . Or Where To Run . . . The Ultimate Con", *Deadfall* centred on an elaborate diamond heist, but failed to find an audience.

At Play In The Fields Of The Lord was one of the prestige projects of 1991. Hector Babenco's much-anticipated follow-up to *Ironweed* was an ecological thriller, which dealt with a group of American mercenaries who become involved with the plight of an Amazonian tribe. Perhaps it was all down to Sting's desperate determination to alert audiences to the plight of the rainforest . . . But like the contemporaneous *Medicine Man*, *At Play In The Fields Of The Lord* ended up as just another Hollywood vehicle attempting to jump aboard the Amazon bandwagon. Even the combined weight of Waits, Daryl Hannah, Tom Berenger and Kathy Bates couldn't save it. And *Empire* magazine's observation that "the Amazonian tragedy is surely not best served by three hours of tedium", neatly summed up the general consensus.

Better by far, and for all concerned, was Terry Gilliam's *The Fisher King* – in which Waits appeared in an uncredited role as a kind of down-on-his-luck Vietnam vet, slumped in New York's Grand Central Station. Following *Brazil*, one of the key movies of the Eighties, Gilliam plunged headlong into *The Adventures Of Baron Munchausen* (1988) – the first of his ambitiously chaotic, big-budget flops. *The Fisher King* (1991) was his next outing, and the first that Gilliam had no hand in originating. Working from an existing script by Richard LaGravenese, Gilliam admitted: "I made the film to discover whether or not I was a film director . . . I saw myself as a film maker, not a film director. The directing bit was just one of the jobs along the way to getting the idea from brain to script to budget to film to final cut to cinema audience to, finally, out of my hair."

Set in contemporary New York, *The Fisher King* gave Robin Williams and Jeff Bridges two of their best roles, in a drama that blended romance, redemption, shock-jocks, and the Holy Grail . . . "It had wonderful characters, it was emotionally powerful," Gilliam explained when asked what attracted him to *The Fisher King*, "and it had a Holy Grail in it . . . and I've had some experience with films with Holy Grails!"

The most striking scene in *The Fisher King* comes soon after Bridges has literally bumped into Waits' character. A glitter ball plays over thousands of commuters, who cease flocking through Grand Central Station, and suddenly pair-off to begin waltzing around its Art Deco charms. It is a startling, eye-catching moment, a brief moment of film magic, which ends with the commuters reverting to their trudge homewards.

Slumped by a pillar, holding an outstretched cup to catch any proffered small change, Waits looks and sounds the part of an embittered war veteran. This is a man who has outlived his usefulness, returned to an ungrateful nation that desperately wants to forget about him, and all his ilk. Waits gets to deliver a nice little speech about how he acts as a "moral traffic light". He's the guy who recognises that the commuters blindly rushing past have their nuts in a vice, and will soon end up puckering up, and kissing the boss's ass. "They're paying so they don't have to look down," he spits from his wheelchair. Waits invests his brief role with a canny appreciation of his character's circumstances, and a tangible bitterness at the hordes passing him by.

The Fisher King is illuminated by Gilliam's ability to make the ordinary appear *extra*-ordinary: the medieval Red Knight, horsebound, and clattering in full armour down 5th Avenue; the wonderful waltz around Grand Central Station; and the romance between the tragedy-touched Robin Williams and the hapless Amanda Plummer, which is both deft and touching. Mercedes Ruehl rightly won an Oscar as Best Supporting Actress, for supporting Bridges' vain and selfish DJ, whose fall from grace is convincingly handled. ("I can't believe I'm on first name terms with these people," he gasps out loud, at one point on his long journey down among the down-and-outs.)

You can see exactly why *The Fisher King* appealed to Waits . . . At his lowest ebb, Jeff Bridges' character, Jack Lucas, is given a Pinocchio doll (and remember, Pinocchio was cited as one of Waits' formative role models); and throughout, Robin Williams serenades antagonists with 'How About You' (the one that goes "I like a Gershwin tune . . ."), another element which would surely have resonated with the young Tom.

Despite the brevity of Waits' *Fisher King* appearance, Gilliam and he obviously made some sort of connection – and as a result, the Waits' song 'Earth Died Screaming' was heard prominently during Gilliam's next film, 1995's *Twelve Monkeys*.

Well-received as *The Fisher King* was, it was – as so often with Waits' movies – clearly out of kilter with what the vast majority of cinema audiences required from their movie-going during the early Nineties. With a core audience of predominantly 16–24-year-old American males, there was unlikely to be massive interest in a magical and touching film about desperation, derelicts and redemption. A reality that was spelt out by the film director character in Alan Alda's satire on the film industry, *Sweet Liberty*: "What the kids want today is three things: nudity, defiance of authority, and destruction of property!"

Audiences at the time were flocking in droves to romantic comedies like *Ghost* and *Pretty Woman*, and to special-effects fests such as *Total Recall* and *Universal Soldier*. And, as ever, sex and violence also sold, witness the box-office triumphs of *Basic Instinct* and *The Silence Of The Lambs*. But a love story that was part-fantasy and part scathing indictment of how marginalised the underclass has become? With the addition of acerbic comment on shock-jocks, and a consideration of the difficulties in running a video store?

Even without the Waits' jinx, it was hardly the recipe for a box-office triumph. Still, *The Fisher King* deserved a better fate. It was a touching and thoughtful tale, in which the fantastical elements were woven seamlessly into the sadness and seediness of real life.

Waits himself has rarely been more convincing onscreen. And the film also reminded you of just what a consistently fine actor Jeff Bridges is, while signalling that, in the right circumstances, even Robin Williams can still rekindle some of that *Good Morning Vietnam* chemistry. As the four-some are walking back from their first date, Bridges makes a disparaging remark about romantic novels. "There's nothing trashy about romance," Williams gently chastises.

CHAPTER 31

THERE are certain career options which grow more appealing only with the passing years – and film-making is one of them. Following the millions which spilled from the farrago that was *The Cotton Club*, in any other profession Francis Ford Coppola would have been bypassed, blackballed and blacklisted. But hey, this is the movies. So Coppola just went on. And on. And on . . .

The remainder of Coppola's Eighties output was, as ever, intriguing: 1987's *Peggy Sue Got Married* played with the fascinating idea of the 43-year-old Kathleen Turner returning to 1960 – and to her teenage-self. With the benefit of hindsight, she could appreciate just how adolescent choices affect your future life. If you knew then, what you know now . . . was a fascinating idea, but the film suffered, coming on the heels of *Back To The Future*.

Gardens Of Stone, also released in 1987, had Coppola revisiting the Vietnam conflict he had made his own with *Apocalypse Now,* eight years before. This time around, his film centred on the Marines who guard the military graves at Arlington National Cemetery, solemnly standing watch over the Tomb of the Unknown Soldier. Set in 1968, *Gardens Of Stone* portrayed the war in Vietnam as a dark and distant force. Coppola was now interested in the career soldiers and their orchestrated manoeuvres, rather than the Grunts in their meandering jungle haze. It was an honourable and powerful film, at odds with the times, but it quickly disappeared.

Tucker: The Man And His Dream (1988) was visually dynamic, but fundamentally flawed. The ever-reliable Jeff Bridges played Preston Tucker, a visionary Forties car manufacturer whose dream was to market the affordable and family-friendly "Tucker Torpedo" – until the car giants of Detroit got wind of his plan, and ruthlessly crushed his dream.

"Tucker is the great American success story, rags to riches, pull yourself up by your boot straps," Waits told me enthusiastically in London, a good five years before Coppola began filming. "He took on all the major automobile companies of the time. He was eventually dragged through the muck, but his car, the Tucker, had disc brakes, rack-and-pinion steering and automatic transmission. It could do 60 miles to the gallon, rear wipers, sun roof. . . I think Francis wants it to be a metaphor for his own life; as an artist working in America, being up against Ford, Chevrolet . . ."

Despite his avowed fondness for, and knowledge of, the American automobile, there was no space for Waits on board *Tucker*. But you get the feeling that if Coppola were ever to plan a movie about shoes, Waits is up there, near Napa Valley, just waiting for the call.

All of Coppola's films – even the sprawling failures – have their moments. And in *Tucker . . .*, it came with the spectral encounter between the endlessly optimistic Bridges and a twitchy Howard Hughes, played with ghostly presence by Dean Stockwell. That one scene somehow said more about that paranoid tycoon's vaulting ambition than the whole of Scorsese's overblown portrait in *The Aviator*.

Visually alluring, thanks to Coppola, and held together onscreen by Bridges' boundless energy, *Tucker* also celebrated the power of dreams and imagination in a genuinely winning, Capra-esque manner. But late Eighties audiences and critics remained utterly unmoved by one man's vision of 40 years before, and his dream of building "The Car Of Tomorrow – Today!"

Back on the ropes again and facing up to his 50th birthday, by 1989 Coppola was badly in need of a bona fide hit. Though mired in personal tragedy (his son Gian Carlo had died in a boating accident in 1986), Coppola knew that to salvage his reputation, and fortune, he had to come up with the goods at the box office. It had been nearly 20 years since his last hit, and the pressure was on . . . it was time to put the director back on nodding terms with the Corleones.

To everyone else it felt like an idea whose time had come, but the director himself entertained considerable doubts. For Coppola, *The Godfather* had become a shadow which hung over him – like that of The Beatles over Paul McCartney, or *Citizen Kane* over Orson Welles. And before the official announcement was made, Coppola had shrugged the idea off: "I'm not really that interested in gangsters."

In 1990, as today, there were few certainties in the world of cinema. But the allure of Francis Ford Coppola finally wrapping up the long and bloody saga of the Corleone family in the third and final part of *The Godfather* did seem to guarantee a certain degree of box-office success. Trouncing even expectations of *The Two Jakes*, *The Godfather, Part III* became the most keenly anticipated film of the year – and possibly the decade.

During the 18 or so years since the original film, *The Godfather* and its sequel had taken on a near-mythic status. All the original discoveries

(Pacino, De Niro) were now established stars – and any appreciation of post-war American cinema routinely cited *The Godfather*. There were rules you lived your life by, that emanated from the script of *The Godfather*; there were films which endlessly parodied or referenced *The Godfather*; and there was the knowledge that *The Godfather*'s all-consuming triumph at the box office had launched a whole era of lesser "event movies".

Above all, though, there was the realisation that in its depiction of America through the eyes and deeds of the Corleones, Coppola, Mario Puzo and Robert Evans had together fashioned a truly timeless film. As long as there are ways for it to be seen, be they plasma screen, television set or mobile phone, there will always be *The Godfather*.

With *The Godfather, Part II*, Coppola had upped the ante even further. It remains the only sequel ever to win a Best Picture Oscar, and it also stands as – arguably – the only sequel to better its predecessor. With stakes this high, Coppola understood that once he announced plans for the third and concluding instalment of *The Godfather*, all the critical knives would be sharpened and at the ready. And if he flopped this time, his fall would be mighty – possibly even fatal. If *The Godfather, Part III* failed to bring in the crowds, there would be nobody left to indulge the cinematic whims of Francis Ford Coppola.

Bringing *The Godfather, Part III* to the screen was as tortuous and elaborate a process as organising a Corleone family wedding. For $5 million, Al Pacino agreed to reprise the crucial role of Michael; Diane Keaton was brought back as the long-suffering Kay, and Talia Shire as the feckless Connie. Unable to make good his demand that Tom Hagen be the financial equal of Michael Corleone, Robert Duvall was regrettably absent; his place taken by the suave George Hamilton.

Fresh blood was, quite literally, provided by Andy Garcia, Joe Mantegna and Bridget Fonda. But by far the most controversial casting in *The Godfather, Part III*, came with the loss of Winona Ryder, who had agreed to play Michael's daughter, Mary. However, physically stretched after coming straight off *Mermaids*, Ryder had collapsed from exhaustion. And holed up in Rome, with a temperature of 104, it was apparent that there was no way the young actress would be fit enough to undertake such a gruelling shoot. In desperation, Coppola cast his own daughter Sofia – and even before filming began, the smell of blood was in the air.

There was no way *The Godfather, Part III* could ever match the impact of the original. But on its release in 1990, opinion was – as ever with Coppola – sharply divided. Critics sniped that he had taken the easy option, by returning to the scene of former glories, while supporters praised his bold decision to build on past successes by closing the Corleone book once and for all.

"Oddly enough, Michael [Corleone] seems to shrink in stature as the picture proceeds, and the Lear-like tragedy at which Coppola aims is not realised," reflected Philip French in the *Observer*, while *Variety* judged that *The Godfather, Part III* matched its predecessors "in narrative intensity, epic scope, sociopolitical analysis, physical beauty and the deep feeling for its characters and milieu". *Empire* wrote that: "Fans of the first two instalments are likely to find *The Godfather, Part III* an unworthy heir to the tradition." On balance, though, *Rolling Stone* got it just about right: "It's still *The Godfather* and some of it's deeply affecting."

In the event, *The Godfather, Part III* proved a box-office success. It was also nominated for Best Director and Best Picture at the 1990 Oscars, but lost out when Kevin Costner's *Dances With Wolves* swept the board. While never matching the returns generated by its predecessors, *The Godfather, Part III* nonetheless pulled Coppola safely back from the brink.

Now, keen to match the financial success his contemporary Martin Scorsese was enjoying with his 1991 thriller *Cape Fear* – which, incidentally, remains Scorsese's only genuine box-office smash – Coppola started casting his eye round for a feature that would consolidate the success of *The Godfather, Part III*, but would also guarantee him financial security. In the current climate, he knew that was the only way he would ever be able to make the pictures he wanted, rather than those dictated to him.

The answer came from an unlikely source. Scouting around for a new part, following her withdrawal from the role of Mary Corleone, Winona Ryder had been beguiled by a retelling of the Dracula legend, an original script by James V. Hart, entitled *The Untold Story*. Hart had begun the script back in 1977 – and a few years later narrowly avoided Fleetwood Mac adapting it into – gasp! – a rock musical. Now, many years on, Ryder was enchanted by the way Hart had taken the character of Bram Stoker's Count Dracula back to its dramatic roots.

Ryder had originally intended developing the project with British director Michael Apted. But, eager to appease Coppola after dropping out of *The Godfather, Part III*, she decided to take the script up to his Napa Valley property. "I never thought he would even read it," Ryder later recalled, "I thought he would be too busy, or not interested, but he was the ideal choice. On my way out the door, I handed it to him.

"I think Francis and I liked the same things about the script, which was very romantic and sensual and epic, a real love story that was very passionate . . . This is the story of Dracula. It's not really a vampire movie. To me, it's more about the man Dracula, the warrior, the prince. He is unlike any other man – he's mysterious and very sexual – attractive in a dangerous way."

One of the first books Coppola remembers reading as an impressionable nine-year-old, was *Bram Stoker's Dracula*. And the fact that Hart's script rescued Dracula from post-ironic camp, and instead took the Count back to his foggy, wolf-howling, Transylvanian home drew him further in. This project would also give Coppola an opportunity to revisit the horror genre, something he hadn't done since 1963, when he wrote and directed his first feature, *Dementia 13*, for producer Roger Corman.

The newly pragmatic Coppola also recognised the reality of his situation: "I really wanted to solidify a new working base with the Hollywood companies," he told Chris Heath. "It was really a decision to strike while the iron was hot and while I was still in their good graces after *Godfather III*, to solidify it with a real mainline kind of movie and, by doing that, so set up American Zoetrope for the next few years."

At the time Coppola came to read Hart's script, the writer had just seen his first ever screenplay realised. *Hook* (1991) was another of those "(on paper) this just can't fail" projects. Here was Steven Spielberg – a past-master at bringing childish imagination to life on screen, filming *Peter Pan*, with a cast led by Robin Williams, Dustin Hoffman, Julia Roberts – and in her film debut – Gwyneth Paltrow. Well, aside from Hoffman's gleeful Terry-Thomas take on the title role, *Hook* stank – and sank.

Undeterred by the reception accorded *Hook*, Coppola found himself as impressed as Winona Ryder by the vibrant sexuality and crimson carnage of Hart's *Dracula* screenplay. Here was a sexy Count, up against a bunch of worthy adversaries, all played out against the visually dramatic backdrop of a highly codified Victorian world.

With the lashing he received for using daughter Sofia in *The Godfather, Part III* still fresh in his mind, Coppola understood that for his next production, casting was more crucial than ever. As a "thank you" for alerting him to Hart's script in the first place, Coppola cast Winona Ryder as the female lead, Mina Murray. And for the key role of Renfield, Coppola immediately contacted Tom Waits, then working on the album which would eventually be released as *Bone Machine*, who was only too happy to oblige.

Although he was committed to his first new album in over five years at the time, Waits was also aware that his film career was in danger of being marginalised. Besides, he and Coppola had enjoyed a fruitful relationship over the years, and Waits was permanently indebted to his friend for helping him escape from the career slough he had endured immediately prior to *One From The Heart*.

The two men remained close, and when we met in London Waits told me about a Coppola family moment at which he had been present. The acclaim which awaited the future director of *Lost In Translation*, still lay some years ahead . . . "Francis' daughter Sofia was about seven years old, and wrote something on the wall of the family home in crayon. Her mother was all: 'Oh boy, are you gonna get it when your father gets home . . .' and Sofia sits waiting, shaking. Francis comes in: 'I hear you've been writing on the wall? I *never* want you writing on the wall again. From now on, you put it down on paper and we *publish* it!' "

Like Coppola, Waits knew that as diverting and rewarding as his recent roles had been, *Bearskin: An Urban Fairytale*, *Queens Logic* and *At Play In The Fields Of The Lord* weren't really tapping into the jugular of mainstream cinema. But, like Coppola, he could see that a sexy re-telling of the Dracula legend, directed by the man who made *The Godfather* – well, that might just do it . . .

Written by Irish author Bram Stoker, and originally published in 1897, *Dracula* had helped renew interest in the Gothic novel, unleashing a whole slew of vampire novels and early films. For all Anne Rice's post-modern spin, and for all the cinematic indignities heaped upon his caped head, just say "vampire" – and "Dracula" still comes back as an echo.

In cinema iconography, Dracula remains second only to Sherlock Holmes as the most filmed fictional character of all time. The Transylvanian Count with the distinctive teeth has been seen in over 160 films to date: a true cinematic immortal. The first release was F.W. Murnau's 1922 silent masterpiece, *Nosferatu*, but the vampire is still perhaps most closely identified with Bela Lugosi, the sinister Hungarian star of 1931's Universal classic, *Dracula*. "Listen to them," Lugosi famously hisses, as the wolves howl, "children of the night, what music they make!" So closely did Lugosi come to identify with Dracula, that he even had himself buried in the count's cape.

In the wake of Lugosi, Dracula drew back into the darkness for 30-odd years, until in 1958 he was revived, in all his gory glory, when the British studio Hammer shot a series of *Dracula* films starring Christopher Lee as the aristocratic vampire – in which, for the first time, the blood flowed in colour.

The Count had proved to be an almost bottomless cinematic pit: George Hamilton's *Love At First Bite*; *Countess Dracula*; *Dracula's Dog*; *Dracula Is Alive And Well And Living In London* and *Blacula* were only some of the films that had escaped from the dungeons under Dracula's castle. And by the time Coppola came to Transylvania, the genre was ripe for a revival. The Hammer series had eventually spun out of control with sequels such as *Dracula AD 1972*, but the success of upmarket horror fests such as *The Exorcist* and *The Omen* during the Seventies, and 1980's *The Shining*, suggested the existence of a young edge-of-the-seat crowd, impatient for another audience with Count Dracula.

After just about *everyone* else (Antonio Banderas, Gabriel Byrne, Daniel Day-Lewis, Viggo Mortensen, Andy Garcia . . .) had been considered, Gary Oldman eventually stepped into the Count's cape. And not for the first time . . . the south London star of *Sid And Nancy* and *JFK* remembers entering a fancy-dress competition at Butlin's in 1963 dressed as Dracula, in a crepe cape his mum had made for him.

Aware that the version of *Dracula* most audiences were familiar with was derived from the Twenties stage version, Coppola delighted in Hart's fidelity to the original novel. He was also keen to incorporate the legend on which Stoker had based his most famous creation, that of the fifteenth-century Hungarian despot, Vlad the Impaler.

Despite memories of his experience with *One From The Heart* a decade before, Coppola decided the best way to give his *Dracula* a unique look would be by shooting everything on a studio set. Filming began in October 1991, with Dracula's castle all cobwebs and strange, and the pace of the film dictated by the quick cross-cutting of the ubiquitous MTV.

Lining up alongside Waits, the final cast now included Anthony Hopkins, Keanu Reeves, Richard E. Grant and Winona Ryder, and throughout the studio-bound three-month shoot, Waits kept them amused during the longeurs of filming, entertaining them with songs like 'Tom Traubert's Blues' played on a piano kept permanently on set.

But once the cameras started turning, Waits became Renfield – who is seen only as the inmate of a long-term institution, banging at the walls and howling at the moon. "I worked for about five days and all my stuff was screaming in Romanian, wearing a straitjacket that made me look like a moth," Waits, the Method Actor, told Stuart Bailie.

In Bram Stoker's novel, Renfield is described by Dr Seward as a man of "59, sanguine temperament . . . morbidly excitable; periods of gloom ending in some fixed idea which I cannot make out . . . a possibly danger-ous man . . ."And in the original 1931 film, Renfield had been played by Dwight Frye, laconically described by the late Leslie Halliwell as an "American character actor who made a corner in crazed hunchbacks".

It is the solicitor Renfield who first visits the Count in Transylvania, and on his return, suffers a complete breakdown. His place in Transylvania is then taken by Keanu Reeves' Jonathan Harker, but Renfield is alerted to the arrival of Count Dracula in London – and gets all in a twitch at the prospect. Waits delivered a strong and physically compelling performance, arguably his best to date – and the sight of Renfield going into spasm at the onset of the visitation is truly chilling. Waits' elongated face, at times eerily reminiscent of Lyle Lovett, lends Renfield the air of a genuinely haunted, Victorian oddball.

Renfield's big set-pieces in the film consist of his snacking on canapés of flies and worms. But these are only small fry; when Renfield requests a kitten for company ("my salvation depends on it . . ." Waits leers to Richard E. Grant), you just know it's not going to be a big role for the cat.

Despite the stellar cast around him, Waits distinguished himself. His English accent, in particular, was better than that of Keanu Reeves – not to mention Gary Oldman's mangled attempt at Transylvanian ("our vays," Oldman primps, in a mittel-European accent as grating as nails on a blackboard, "err not your vays").

As Renfield, Waits managed to avoid the trap of appearing like a man suffering from excruciating stomach cramp, to suggest a more subtle sort of demonic possession. He made it seem as though Renfield's very soul was in danger of eternal damnation. Waits even managed to lend his character an unexpected touch of humanity; unlike Anthony Hopkins, who, hair flowing as he storms around in a strop, comes across as more Van Halen than Van Helsing.

In the publicity for *Bram Stoker's Dracula*, Waits was described as: "internationally known as a composer, singer, performer and actor . . ." with a style that "combined a kind of bohemian word-jazz with a bit of the blues". Unfortunately, even with that CV, he didn't get to sing the *Dracula* theme, 'Love Song For A Vampire', which was written and sung by Annie Lennox.

The early industry buzz had Coppola "apparently after a mainstream hit that will add lucre to genius". But by the time of the previews he was juggling with an estimated 37 different cuts of the film, and audiences confessed themselves baffled by the narrative, the eroticism, and the violence. In the end, after graciously declining the studio's suggestion that the finished film should be retitled *Francis Coppola's Dracula*, the director unleashed his neck-sucker onto the American public – as *Bram Stoker's Dracula*.

Of course, this was the era when synergy and marketing became almost more important than the making of the film itself; with the studio eager to cross-pollinate The New Big Film with everything from burgers to haute couture. *Bram Stoker's Dracula* did, naturally, present some problems with marketing (one imagines that neither Burger King nor McDonald's were much interested in a Vampire Burger). But in the event, the merchandisers came through, with spin-offs that, according to the trade paper *Screen International*, included "coffin-shaped handbags . . . gargoyle earrings, bloody logo-laden T-shirts and glow-in-the-dark nightgowns. The campaign also boasts a video game . . . Winona Ryder lookalike figures and Bloody Mary spirit mixes."

Soon, everyone was happy . . . On its American opening in 1992, *Bram Stoker's Dracula* scored a palpable hit. In the studio hyperbole, it was noted that Coppola's film achieved the "Number 1 Opening Weekend in Columbia Pictures history, ahead of *Ghostbusters II* . . . the Number 1 Non-Summer Opening Weekend in Movie History, ahead of *Back To The Future II* . . . the Number 2 Non-Sequel Opening Weekend, behind . . . *Batman* . . ."

Within weeks, *Bram Stoker's Dracula* had amply recouped its $40 million budget, and Coppola was back on course. But it wouldn't last for long . . . with his very next film – *Jack* with Robin Williams – he was straight back down the dumper. "An unbelievably bad, totally risible movie . . . it represents a regrettable infantile regression by its director and star," noted *Halliwell*, more in sorrow than anger.

Even *Bram Stoker's Dracula* had not met with universal approval. It had efficiently captured exactly what the studio was looking for: "the MTV audience . . . teenagers and young adults in the 17–25 range, slightly skewed towards males . . .", but some of the reviews were damning. Writing in the *Guardian*, Derek Malcolm found the film "a fairly comprehensive and often vulgar mess". He went on to reflect rather prophetically: "The whole somehow seems to sum up what people want from cinema nowadays: style hinting at content but gradually drowning it out with pyrotechnics." *Newsweek* too, observed that *Bram Stoker's Dracula* had "drowned in a tide of images".

The young cast was also lacerated, Adam Smith finding Keanu Reeves "armed only with an English accent that finally had Dick Van Dyke heaving a sigh of relief!" But Waits was singled out for praise by *Variety*, among others, who described his performance as "compelling". While in *Empire*, Angie Errigo dismissed Oldman's Dracula as bringing to mind "Alistair Sim in drag" and "Ryder and Reeves" as "distinctly out of place as mock Victorians", before concluding . . . "Surprisingly, it is Tom Waits who proves the scene-stealer as the maggot-munching maniac Renfield."

CHAPTER 32

BACK at the coal face, the lovable old maggot-muncher was busy finishing off his new studio album, *Bone Machine*. And anticipation was high: *Night On Earth* had reminded people of Waits' existence; while *Bram Stoker's Dracula* had significantly raised his profile. Now, after a five-year sabbatical, it was back to the day-job.

When asked about the title, Waits was typically cryptic: "Hmmm, *Bone Machine* . . . Just trying to take two things and bring 'em together, which is what you try and do with music: take something and make it work with something else . . . What's a *Bone Machine*? Most of the principles of most machines developed in the machine age were principles that would be found in the human body.

"Originally, I was going to take sounds of machines I'd recorded and add a really strong rhythmic sense; I was going to try to build songs out of the rhythms. But then it didn't really develop that way. The stories kind of took over. So it's more bone than machine. *Bone Machine* . . . we're all like bone machines, I guess. We break down eventually, and we're replaced by other models. Newer models. *Younger* models. *Bone Machine* . . . sounds like a superhero doesn't it?"

Bone Machine is a dark and brooding album, a record that reflects deeply on love and mortality. Death – viewed from both the inside and the outside – is writ large over all its length. Salvation and redemption are stirred in too, along with the blood and bones; sinew and muscles; eyeballs and singed hair . . . All of them bobbing around in that devilish cauldron.

The opening track 'Earth Died Screaming' is, even by Waits' pile-driving standards, a love song that's right off the scale, citing shredded skin, skulls, raining mackerel, three-headed lions and ladder-climbing monkeys "while I lay dreaming of you". Waits himself felt the song drew from "one of the lost books of the Bible: the Book of Rudy"; while Andy Gill in Q, likened the song to "the apes bashing bones around the monolith in *2001* – the parabola of civilisation plummeting back to square one for this apocalyptic howl".

Richly studded with hangmen and Heaven, a gallows pole, Cain and Abel, sinners, Ophelia and Anthony Franciosa, brine and raining fish, a

243

blood-stained Bible and prosthetics and driven by mighty percussion (courtesy of a drummer called "Brain"), *Bone Machine* sounds like the Day of Judgement in stereo. The album benefits too from Waits' own powers of invention: "the Conundrum . . . looks like a big iron crucifix, and there are a lot of different things that we hang off it: crowbars and found metal objects that I like the sound of."

The opening lines of 'All Stripped Down' sound like Waits has been listening to Bob Dylan's 'When The Ship Comes In' – and is it just a coincidence that the sleeve photography came to us courtesy of Bob's eldest son Jesse? One of Bob's other boys, Jakob, later of The Wallflowers, was a staunch Waits fan, who took great pleasure in introducing Tom and Bob.

Bone Machine's 'Jesus Gonna Be Here' is curiously warped gospel ("Hollywood be thy name"), with the singer equally interested in the coming of the Lord and a brand new Ford . . . The title of 'Murder In The Red Barn' brings to mind that great broadsheet ballad, 'The Murder Of Maria Marten'. But in Waits' hands the song seems like the love-child of that nineteenth-century tabloid drama and *The Blair Witch Project* . . .

'All Stripped Down' was described in the album's press kit as "a kind of Mardi-Gras-in-Purgatory that explains dress code for the Rapture" . . . 'The Ocean Doesn't Want Me' goes full fathom five, an eerie spoken word reflection from "deep down in the brine" . . . 'In The Colosseum' marries Ancient Rome with the 1992 Bush Senior versus Bill Clinton election . . . while 'Goin' Out West' opens with a *Dragnet*-style guitar, and continues with the extraordinary sound of Tom Waits rocking out.

The album concludes with 'That Feel', a "duet" between our Tom and the only vocalist alive who sounds even more ragged than he does, Keith Richards. The two old reprobates come together on a twisted love song, about how you can lose your pants, your shoes, your glass eye . . . but the one thing that never gets lost is that feeling for the one that you love.

Sifting through the detritus of *Bone Machine*, there are still some songs that recall the "old Waits": 'Who Are You' is a guitar ballad which asks the disquieting question: "Are you still jumping out of windows in expensive clothes?" 'A Little Rain' features piano, plaintive pedal steel and a melancholy Irish feel. Waits' vocal here is fragile and affecting, but the subject matter is strangely disturbing, involving a German dwarf, teenage runaways and the vanishing of children.

'Whistle Down The Wind' (not, you will be surprised to learn, a cover of the 1983 Nick Heyward song of the same name) is without doubt, the most effective track on the album. It sounds like an out-take from *Small*

Change, with Waits on piano, singing an unaffected ballad, accompanied by Los Lobos' David Hidalgo's violin and accordion and David Phillips' pedal steel. The title is taken from the incomparable 1961 Bryan Forbes film; the reference to "the Marley Bone Coach" from Dickens' *A Christmas Carol*; and the sentiments, from the heart. 'Whistle Down The Wind' was dedicated to the memory of Tom Jans, a folk-singing contemporary of Waits, who was the partner of Mimi Farina (Joan Baez's sister) in the early 1970s, and went on to record a series of solo albums. An exact contemporary of Waits, Jans had died in 1984, aged only 35.

Sounding like *The Night Of The Hunter* scored by a demented inventor of dangerous percussion, *Bone Machine* was as incongruous as a pitcher at a Test Match – and about as comfortable as sleeping on a bed of nails. With his first album of new material since *Frank's Wild Years* in 1987, Waits was swimming defiantly against the tide. This was the dawn of the compact disc age, with the recording process growing ever more technical and remote; but *Bone Machine* had more in common with the field recordings made by Alan Lomax 60 years before.

Those primitive tapes of field hands, blues singers, prisoners and hillbillies had captured a more honest and authentic sound – and best of all, a more textured and interesting sound. They were, Waits explained "like listening to a big open field. You hear other things in the background. You hear people talking while they are singing. It's the hair in the gate."[1]

With Waits, you always got the hair, and the bark and husk, the creaking chair on the porch, the rustle of the scarecrow . . . While everyone around him was heads down and hell bent on the future, Waits was trudging doggedly in the opposite direction, forging a solitary path back to the past.

Talking to Jonathan Valania in 2004 Waits admitted that those Lomax records were still an influence, and he spoke with great fondness of the effect they had on him, and his music: "When I listen to those old field recordings, maybe you'll hear a dog barking way off in the background. You realise the house it was recorded in is torn down, the dog is dead, the tape recorder is broken, the guy who made the recording died in Texas . . . even the dirt the house sat on is gone – probably a parking lot – but we still have this song."

To help promote *Bone Machine*, Waits made a promo video of the title track. Shot in a studio that looked more like a foundry, Waits in welding goggles, tramped around, roaring. A berserk blues, it's the sort of song you could imagine Renfield cutting – if he'd been allowed an electric guitar in his asylum, rather than a kitten.

Some aficionados claimed that Waits was providing the missing link between Howlin' Wolf and Captain Beefheart. Yet at times on *Bone Machine*, Waits' familiar growling-in-a-bucket-of-gravel vocal is replaced by a falsetto, that verges on the irritating. When spinning yarns, as on 'Black Wings', he is simply spellbinding; but thrashing around, screaming, looking for a way out, he becomes just grating.

Bone Machine was, as ever, a family affair: besides Kathleen, 'The Ocean Doesn't Want Me' featured a little help from Waits' youngest, Kellesimone, who contributed the word "strangels" to the song. Writing in *NME*, Terry Staunton duly noted: "Tom's old lady, Kathleen Brennan, was all over the record, having co-written eight of the 16 tracks. Now, usually, this would be a bad thing. If you think of Yoko or Linda or Cait or Courtney, D-A-M-E can only spell trouble, but on *Bone Machine* Kathleen's little word games helped to flesh out the already instantly recognisable Waits sound."

Even Tom's mum had a finger in the pie. *NME*'s Stuart Bailie was shown some religious tracts that Mrs Waits, unhappy with the title *Bone Machine*, had dispatched to her errant son. Her son tugged out one in particular, with the cautionary threat: "There's Nothing The Devil Hates More Than A Singing Christian." Apparently he filed that one away for future use.

Although free of the tour-album-promotion syndrome for the past five years, Waits was growing increasingly weary, and wary, of it. But, however reluctantly, he did break cover to talk up *Bone Machine*. After a two-hour drive from the family home – presumably calculated as just far enough to keep the journalistic enemy at bay – he submitted to some good-natured probing. Settling down in a San Francisco diner, appropriately called the Limbo, Waits kept an eye on the door, and proceeded to spill the beans over cola and coffee.

He admitted to Stuart Bailie that yes, he had been re-reading his Bible for *Bone Machine*; and yup, there was good and bad in all of us. Quotable as ever, Waits confirmed: "I'm just tryin' to find that Jerry Lee Lewis meridian, between the arms of Jesus and the silk sheets of Delilah . . ."

To Adam Sweeting in the *Guardian*, Waits confided that he lived "in a little cow town . . . over that way. There's a couple of other people living there, and I'm trying to get rid of them. Put the evil eye on 'em." Intriguingly though, Waits bridled at Sweeting's suggestion that, thanks to his continuing dallying with the likes of Robert Wilson, he was in danger of being hijacked by the highbrows. "Hey, highbrow, low-brow, y'know . . . I'm the Oddball Kid . . . I love words. Every word has a particular musical sound to it which you may or may not be able to use. Like for example 'spatula', that's a good word. Sounds like the name of a band. Probably *is* the name of a band."

In cold print, *Bone Machine* attracted the sort of reviews that appeared written into Waits' contract. In his four-star review of the album for *Q* ("Excellent. Definitely worth investigation."), Andy Gill acknowledged Waits' audacity, calling him "a formidable talent . . . in an era when even the fringes of cultural enterprise, in music as much as movies, are becoming increasingly dominated by market pandering, his is the bravest of stances."

Ann Scanlon was unreserved in her praise in *Vox*, hailing *Bone Machine* as "another masterpiece . . . a series of black-and-white stills, lit by splashes of blood red . . . By retaining a child-like imagination and unlearning things as well as learning them, Tom Waits has become one of the most reliable guides to the joys, sorrows and mysteries of this world. Let's hope he never grows up."

But only Terry Staunton in *NME* followed Waits' lead and went the shoe-route . . . "*Bone Machine* . . . seemed as if nothing much had changed, it was like rediscovering a favourite pair of boots that had been at large in the bottom of the closet for a while."

In the summer of 1992, Waits paused in Paris, where he undertook a family holiday – interrupted only by a round of European press interviews. There was also a sprint to Spain, where a new production of *The Black Rider* was being developed. And later that year, 16 of his albums – from *The Early Years*, right up to *Night On Earth* – were made available on CD.

Andy Gill swallowed them whole, eloquently identifying the unifying theme: "In all his work, the theme of lowlife redemption, of escape, is ever-present: characters are always moving on to another entry in one of the most impressive gazetteers of American songwriting, from Nebraska or Philadelphia to New Orleans or Baton Rouge, feeding from the myth of escape that such a huge country encourages. But . . . Waits, the itinerant hobo auteur came to realise that those places from which his characters fled were each in their own way as interesting, with their own peculiar immigrant traditions, as the places to which they flew. He learned to celebrate the diversity of a perpetual immigrant culture whose incomers are drawn by the same dreams of escape that fuelled the pioneers, the beat poets and Waits himself."[2]

In 1993 Waits landed his first-ever Grammy, when *Bone Machine* won the award for Best Alternative Music Album. And later that same year, after a wait of three years, audiences who couldn't make it to Hamburg,

New York or Seville, finally got the chance to hear how *The Black Rider* sounded on album. However, those who hadn't seen the production at the Thalia Theatre or the Brooklyn Academy struggled to find cohesion in the record's clunky narrative.

Even though the libretto is supplied, so that you can learn all about the pact with the Devil and the shooting contest, as a stand-alone disc, *The Black Rider* hardly leaves you spinning. It opens promisingly enough, with Waits as a carny barker shouting up a storm at Harry's Harbour Bizarre, pulling in the prurient on the midway. You pays your money, and you takes your choice from "the German midget . . . Mortando, the human fountain . . . a three-headed baby . . . Hitler's brain . . . Sealo the seal boy . . . Radion, the human torso . . .". It's a freak show for the intelligentsia; Tod Browning's *Freaks* come to life . . .

While Waits was mixing *The Black Rider* with Biff Dawes in Hollywood, he allowed *Spin* magazine's Mark Richard a rare glimpse of him at work in the studio. Waits appeared to have little interest in the technical side of the process ("Put a little more hair on that, will you Biff?"). Though occasionally, surely in the knowledge he was being observed, Waits proffered some more intuitive guidelines: "Try and get the feel of a Bahia slave galley leaving the Amazon loaded with molasses and sugar cane."

Leaving aside his evident delight in winding up hapless hacks, Waits clearly has a picture in his head that he wishes to communicate to the listener. But he is far from a purist when it comes to recording his music, and *The Black Rider* was no exception. Audio perfection is never sought – creaking chairs and ringing telephones, for example, are wilfully included. And for the inquisitive, Waits has dusted down some of his "found" instruments for inclusion: the waterphone, for example, described as "two pizza pans welded face together with a length of rope-wrapped muffler pipe fitted to the centre. Varying lengths of steel rods are staggered around the edges. When water is poured down the muffler pipe into the pizza pans, you rap the rods with a mallet or draw a bow across them to achieve deep-sea, science-fiction-movie sounds."[3]

All the ingredients are there, but as a finished album *The Black Rider* just doesn't hang together. The impressionistic songs have little cohesion; the narrative plot appears to bear little relation to the 20-odd tracks; and throughout, the album is pervaded by a rather weary sense of Waitsian déjà vu. There are moments though: I, for one, am always glad to hear a musical saw employed, and knowing what we know of his background, it's engaging to hear William Burroughs sing about taking off your skin and dancing round in your bones.

As to the songs themselves . . . 'The Briar And The Rose' is starkly affecting, with Waits once again drawing from the deep, deep well of the folk tradition to combine a melody drawn from 'Scarlet Ribbons' with imagery that was heard way back on the traditional 'Barbara Allen'. As popularised in the Sixties by Joan Baez, this seventeenth-century song has been called "the veritable *Romeo and Juliet* of Anglo-American balladry". Waits was certainly familiar with this tale of two true lovers, buried alongside each other: from the grave of one sprouts a rose; from the other, a briar – and where they join, they are linked together for all eternity. ("All these songs about roses growing out of people's brains," Bob Dylan enthused, way back in 1966, "and lovers who are really geese and swans that turn into angels – they're not going to die.")

'I'll Shoot The Moon' is a modest and engaging little love song, with Waits promising to be the "pennies on your eyes". The image is typical of Waits, but not many love songs incorporate such macabre references: the tradition of placing coins on the eyes of the dead came from Greek mythology, where it was thought necessary to pay the boatman Charon for carrying a corpse safely across the Styx, the River of the Dead.

'Gospel Train' has more of that syncopated, distorted gospel, borrowing heavily from the old railroad lament, 'Bound For Glory'. Ralph Carney's bass clarinet makes train noises; Waits sounds eerily distant. Otherwise, it's pointed, jagged music, determined to stick out at weird angles, rather than drawing a comfortable circle.

'The Black Rider' itself has the composer putting on the type of German accent you thought went out with *Hogan's Heroes*. While 'Lucky Day' finds Waits keeping the in-laws content with a poignant piece of prime Irish balladry. Although quite what the doings of Waits' Miss Kelsey and Johnny O'Toole have to do with the determinedly German goings-on of *Der Freischutz* is, frankly, baffling.

During a break from mixing *The Black Rider*, Waits had lunch with his father – and Waits' memories of this encounter, which he later relayed to Mark Richard, give a fascinating insight into the dynamics between Waits Senior and Junior: "We were reading a menu at a restaurant and he said, 'Jeez, they have a skinless chicken here, Tom, and I just imagine how *painful* it was for him to grow up.' And I said 'Yeah, but what about the *boneless* chicken, such an *unimaginable* life!' "[4]

Reviewing the album for Q, Giles Smith wrote of "some . . . songs, with tunes and everything, some of them brief instrumental fragments which sound like several different bands warming up while a train goes past . . . Waits' crabby voice, in tremendous condition here, i.e., he still sounds like someone who enjoys flossing their vocal cords with a brillo-pad on a stick."

More positive affirmation came from Danny Frost, writing in *NME*: "Unlike pop's myriad pretenders to 'cinematic' status (Clapton, Knopfler . . .) he's not a mere dealer in soundtracks. Waits' music has always been filmic, drawing from a palette of few words and found instruments to lovingly daub his vibrant cast of freaks, dwarves, losers and psychos on the blank page of the listener's consciousness." Frost went on to liken the album's 'Gospel Train (Orchestra)' to "the Portsmouth Sinfonia conducted by Charles Manson from the top of a rickety pile of chairs".

Ultimately, although it seemed to have everything going for it, *The Black Rider* did not translate particularly effectively onto disc, coming across as a grand piece of self-indulgence for Messrs Burroughs, Waits and Wilson, but a bit of a thankless struggle for outsiders. Maybe you just had to be there . . .

NOTES

1   *Observer* Music Monthly
2   Q 73
3   Mark Richard, *Spin*
4   Mark Richard, *Spin*

CHAPTER 33

SAILING fearlessly towards middle age, and with Coppola's film of *Bram Stoker's Dracula* having provided him with a bona fide box-office smash, Waits' career was in pretty good shape. Prior to the release of *The Black Rider* album, he had been flattered to be asked to join the cast of a film by another American *auteur*.

Robert Altman had come out of World War II only to find there wasn't much work for bomber pilots – and, after a spell studying engineering in his home town of Kansas City, the 32-year-old Altman began making movies.

In 1957 he lashed together *The James Dean Story*, which was rushed out to cash in on the cult that was growing up around the late actor. While fashioning the documentary, Altman found himself being stalked by a tenacious young tearaway who had just arrived in Hollywood. Elvis Presley was convinced he could authentically recreate James Dean in the film's dramatised portions but, in the event, Altman stuck with a straightforward documentary, and then went into television limbo (*Bonanza*, *Alfred Hitchcock Presents*) for a decade. And as for Elvis . . . well, sadly, *GI Blues* was no *Rebel Without A Cause*.

As with Coppola and *The Godfather*, Altman only got to direct his breakthrough smash, *M*A*S*H*, because no one else wanted to touch it. But Altman too struck lucky, and the scathing 1970 anti-war satire gave him the hit which started the ball rolling.

Although set in Korea, few of the hippies who flocked to see it were in any doubt as to which south-east Asian country the film was *really* about. *M*A*S*H* established Altman's trademark style of overlapping dialogue and deftly handled ensemble casts, while the air of anarchy and irreverence on screen found the 45-year-old Altman lionised by the Woodstock generation. It also made stars of Elliot Gould and Donald Sutherland, and led to a television series that ran for 11 years, and whose final episode was watched by the largest television audience ever recorded in America up to that point.

By the time the TV series ended in 1984, Altman (who had been paid "$75,000, period" for *M*A*S*H* the movie) was predictably scathing: "They took *M*A*S*H* . . . and turned it into the most insidious propaganda with that TV show," he told Cynthia Rose. "From art to commerce to corruption; it's always the way."

It may not have paid, but the box-office triumph of *M*A*S*H* had allowed Altman half a decade of self-indulgence (*Brewster McCloud*, *Images*, *Thieves Like Us*) – interspersed with the odd triumph such as *McCabe & Mrs Miller*, which made memorable use of Leonard Cohen's songs. But it wasn't until 1975 that Altman delivered his masterpiece, an informal bicentennial birthday present to America – the sprawling and masterly *Nashville*.

Then it was into the darkness again, with the critically and commercially unengaging *Buffalo Bill And The Indians*. *Three Women* and *Quintet* followed, before Altman sank without trace with the help of 1980's *Popeye*. Concentrating his efforts on filmed plays for the next decade, Altman became the forgotten man of Hollywood, until in 1992 he turned his steely eyes on the film capital.

The Player was the film which restored Altman's reputation. Madly over-praised on its release – films *about* films always appeal disproportionately to film critics – *The Player* nonetheless proved that Altman had not lost his touch, as he marshalled the huge cast (Tim Robbins, Julia Roberts, Lyle Lovett, Whoopi Goldberg, etc.) through an engaging and multi-layered plot.

With the film world at his feet again, on the back of the *The Player*'s success, Altman remembered a collection of Raymond Carver short stories he had once read while flying home from Italy. Carver, once hailed as "the American Chekhov", died from cancer in 1988, at the age of only 50. But now Altman took over, relocating Carver's work from the Pacific north-west to the sprawling suburbs of Los Angeles. Eventually, he fashioned eight of Carver's stories (and one poem) into a 188-minute, 22-character film called *Short Cuts*.

Casting *Short Cuts* was a dream. After seeing how well his mix of ensemble casts and cameo appearances had worked on *The Player*, the Hollywood A-list was queuing up to work with Altman. Eventually, he marshalled Jennifer Jason Leigh, Tim Robbins, Julianne Moore, Jack Lemmon, Andie MacDowell, Matthew Modine and Frances McDormand into the freewheeling narrative of *Short Cuts*. Of the 22 lead actors in speaking roles, seven had been Oscar-nominated.

"The actors in *Short Cuts* weren't exactly a stock company," Altman reflected, "but there were certain actors I asked to be in it and I would just find them a part. Or create one. I like to bring new attitudes into a film – with somebody like Lyle Lovett we're going to see something new."[1]

Besides Lovett (then in tabloid hell following his marriage to Julia Roberts, who he had met on the set of *The Player*) and Tom Waits, *Short Cuts* benefited from another strange rock'n'roll addition: Huey Lewis, recruited as "technical advisor" for the fly-fishing scenes, who also ended up appearing on screen.

Altman was aware of Tom Waits' work before casting him in *Short Cuts*. Indeed, Waits had been credited as "music supervisor" on another of Altman's ensemble pieces: 1978's diverting *A Wedding*. Traditionally the music editor either co-ordinates the soundtrack, or selects outside songs to incorporate. But as the soundtrack for *A Wedding* was composed by John Hotchkis, and the only extra songs featured were Leonard Cohen's 'Bird On A Wire' and the standard 'Love Is A Many Splendoured Thing', Waits' duties can't have been too onerous that time around.

But maybe there was something in Waits' own work with which Altman identified. As Geoff Andrew wrote of the director's oeuvre: "He depicted losers, loners and dreamers struggling to cope with that country's sanctification of success, fame, money and aggressive ambition."

The official synopsis of *Short Cuts* noted its veering "in mood and intention between humour, romance and horror, a collection of cops, cello players, pool cleaners, make-up artists, chauffeurs, jazz singers, doctors, phone-sex specialists, TV commentators, fishermen, waitresses and incontinent dogs keep criss-crossing each other's paths, each unaware of the dramas unwinding on parallel tracks."

Waits came in as Earl Piggott, a chauffeur who was married to waitress Doreen (Lily Tomlin). The couple existed in an alcoholic haze, careering around in a lurid Hawaiian wardrobe, which certainly appealed to Waits. Described as "a drunken lout", it is implied that Earl had interfered with his step-daughter Honey (Lili Taylor). Honey is now married to Bill (Robert Downey Jr), a make-up artist who is friendly with Jerry (Chris Penn), who runs a pool maintenance service; but to make ends meet, his wife Lois (Jennifer Jason Leigh) operates a phone-sex business from the family home . . . You get the picture. Lives overlap and intertwine, then an earthquake brings the film to its conclusion.

While not in the same ambitious league as *Nashville*, *Short Cuts* benefits from universally strong performances. But as a film, it meanders; like life, it is sprawling, inconclusive and frequently frustrating. It records the minutiae of contemporary life in all its mundane details, but doesn't really know what to do with them. One of the film's most celebrated scenes – of Julianne Moore haranguing Matthew Modine – was largely memorable for Moore delivering her monologue naked from the waist down.

Coming hard on the heels of *The Player*, *Short Cuts* did much to re-establish Altman as a director with vision and a unique screen voice. Unfortunately, he proceeded to undo most of the good with the horribly over-dressed and laborious fashion satire, *Pret A Porter* in 1994.

Waits was excellent as the boorish Earl in *Short Cuts* – "a drunken, stupid pig" as his daughter characterises him. Looking unusually dapper while on chauffeuring duty, his scenes with Tomlin crackle. She's a hard-bitten hard-working waitress, not unlike the "spent piece of used jet trash [who] made good bloody Marys" of whom Waits sang on 'Frank's Wild Years'. Together, this pair of trailer-park refugees suggest a couple linked by convenience, liquor and little else. It was hardly a star turn – in a cast that vast, and that distinguished, he'd have been struggling. But Waits was firmly on track, proving himself adept as a character actor and supporting player, while distinguishing himself in another prestige production.

Musically, *Short Cuts* was as intriguing as its casting. One of the more affecting storylines in the film was the relationship between chanteuse Annie Ross and her cello-playing daughter, Lori Singer – the only characters that did not draw on Carver's writings.

"The cello that Lori Singer plays represents inner feelings," Altman revealed. "It's more internal and secret, and Annie Ross' jazz is what we express outwardly. I thought that somehow putting these things together, and melding them would work. Also, I think when you see somebody perform music, there is a certain amount of emotion and storytelling involved."

To oversee the soundtrack of *Short Cuts*, Altman enlisted Hal Willner, whom Waits had worked with on his Eighties Kurt Weill and Walt Disney tribute albums. Willner was keen for Ross to interpret contemporary songs on the soundtrack, but numbers by Tom Waits are curiously absent – although his long-time bassist Greg Cohen was in the film band, and Ross did get to try out new songs by U2, Elvis Costello, Dr John and Doc Pomus.

Of his character Earl's incessant drinking, the teetotal Waits admitted that he "improvised a lot". He got on well with Tomlin, respected Altman, and watched with relief as the reviews confirmed the cast's belief in the project – with *Rolling Stone* singling out Waits and Lily Tomlin as "sensational".

The *Observer*'s Philip French was equally impressed, finding it "a film with no dud line, flawed performance or slick piece of editing in all its 188 minutes . . . Only at a second viewing can one fully appreciate the magnificence of the film's grand design, which is the presentation of life as a mutually shared tragi-comedy."

It was hard to insert a cigarette paper between such an ensemble cast, and indeed, the International Critics Prize at the 1993 Venice Film Festival was awarded to the entire cast of *Short Cuts* for their performances. While the festival jury divided the Golden Lion award between *Short Cuts* and Kieslowski's *Three Colours Blue*, in a year of high-concept films (*Schindler's List*, *The Remains Of The Day*, *Howard's End*, *The Age Of Innocence*) *Short Cuts* nonetheless made its mark.

Following the film's release in 1993, Waits and Kathleen and their three offspring settled in Somona County, northern California. This was lush, wine-growing country, far removed from the motorway mêlée of Los Angeles and the turmoil of New York. Coincidentally, the Waits' new family home was not a million miles away from the 1,500-acre estate of Francis Ford Coppola in Napa Valley.

Another film project close to Waits' heart during the early Nineties, was Tim Robbins' *Dead Man Walking* (1995). Along with his partner Susan Sarandon, Robbins had come to represent the highly vocal, and highly visible, face of liberal Hollywood. Movie insiders joked that 60 years before, Fellow Travellers had volunteered to go to Spain to fight in the Civil War; today, it was Saturday night dinner with Robbins and Sarandon. The couple courted further controversy in 1993 when, as Oscar presenters, they used the platform to protest about the plight of Haitian Aids victims illegally detained at Guantanamo Bay.

Following star turns in *Bull Durham*, *Jacob's Ladder* and *The Player* (we'll draw a veil over *Howard The Duck*), Robbins had made an impressive directorial debut with 1992's *Bob Roberts*. Coming as he did from a politically active family, steeped in the folk revival, it was hardly surprising that his tale of the rise of a right-wing politician also displayed an innate grasp of the folk tradition. But so cleverly did his character subvert the songs to his own fascist ends that Robbins, concerned lest right-wing groups should miss the irony and use the songs as slogans, refused to allow the film's soundtrack to be released.

For his second stab at directing, Robbins stayed in the political arena; this time fuelling the debate on the death penalty. *Dead Man Walking* was based on the memoirs of Sister Helen Prejean, a nun who has spent her life counselling and comforting condemned inmates on Mississippi's Death Row.

In Robbins' film Sister Helen (played by Susan Sarandon) is drawn to

Matthew Poncelet (Sean Penn), who is awaiting execution for the rape and murder of a young girl. *Dead Man Walking* does not deal with Poncelet's guilt or innocence, but rather with the iniquity of a society which still claims the right to execute those it finds guilty.

Dead Man Walking strove to be even-handed: neither condoning nor seeking sympathy for Penn's character, while excoriating the system which sanctions capital punishment. As with all Death Row movies, *Dead Man Walking* presented the opportunity for both leads to do the Big Acting Thing with gloves off.

In the event it was Sarandon who scooped the Oscar, although Penn was also nominated, as was Robbins as director. Robbins' brother David was the musical supervisor on the movie, and both the Robbins were determined to ensure that the soundtrack gave *Dead Man Walking* an added dimension.

They tried laying gospel, cajun, Delta blues, and even the chanting of Benedictine monks onto rough cuts of the film, but nothing jelled. "They made it too regional," Tim Robbins wrote on the sleeve notes of the soundtrack. "This is a universal story so the answer lay in a meeting ground between, a mix of the South and the music of the world."

Later, Robbins decided that he "wanted to see what Sister Helen's experience would inspire if it were given to songwriters . . . I sent the film in its rough form along with a file of newspaper articles my office had been collecting. I sent them to songwriters whose music tells stories . . . All these songwriters come from a base of honesty and have inspired me in my own work. Bruce Springsteen, Tom Waits, Patti Smith, Lyle Lovett, Steve Earle and Eddie Vedder . . ."

Whether it was the seriousness of the subject matter, Robbins' manifest commitment to the project, or simply the spur of finding himself pitching against his peers, is unclear – but *Dead Man Walking* inspired Waits to fashion two of his finest songs to date for the soundtrack. Far removed from the ear-piercing howl of *Bone Machine* and the studied art-house machinations of *The Black Rider*, Waits' contributions to *Dead Man Walking* were substantial songs in their own right.

You could almost imagine 'The Fall Of Troy' slotting neatly onto the soundtrack of a John Ford film, just before they all gather for the consecration of the church, and the congregation sings 'Shall We Gather At The River'. There is a recognisable tune, and Waits feels no need to bark the lyrics through a megaphone. 'Walk Away' was upbeat gospel, short, effective and to the point; again there were no irritating vocal mannerisms or distracting "found" instrumentation, just Waits doing what he does very well – and that was something he hadn't done for a long, long time.

In fact, the whole *Dead Man Walking* experience with Robbins prompted a raft of leading songwriters to work triumphantly. Bruce Springsteen's 'Dead Man Walkin'' was Oscar-nominated, though it lost out in the end to 'Colours Of The Wind' from Disney's *Pocahontas*. Johnny Cash's 'In Your Mind' was a notable addition to the Man In Black's already glorious list of prison-related material. Suzanne Vega sounded like she'd been listening to Tom Waits; Eddie Vedder blended beguilingly with Nusrat Fateh Ali Khan; while Steve Earle's poignant contribution, 'Ellis Unit One', was further powerful evidence of the singer's lifelong commitment to opposing the death penalty.

It was a *Dead Man Walking* benefit concert at the Shrine Auditorium, in March 1998, that saw Waits returning to live performance. "Not In Our Name" was a benefit for the Murder Victims' Families For Reconciliation, a charity which aims to benefit the families of both murder victims and of those executed for their crimes. Besides Tom, the concert also featured Steve Earle, Eddie Vedder, Lyle Lovett and Michelle Shocked.

For this, his first Los Angeles show in six years, Waits played a 45-minute, seven-song set which included both his *Dead Man Walking* contributions, together with songs from *Rain Dogs* and *Frank's Wild Years*. Waits wrapped up his performance with 'Jesus Gonna Be Here' from *Bone Machine*, performed through his customary megaphone – and was followed onto the stage by Sister Helen Prejean, who admitted she had never heard of Tom Waits. The evening concluded with *les toutes ensembles*, including Tim Robbins, coming on to finish the show with a version of the Waits' song 'Innocent When You Dream'.

The release of the 23-track *Beautiful Maladies* later in 1998 marked the end of Waits' era on Island Records. Since joining Chris Blackwell's happy breed in 1983, Waits had seen Island absorbed by ever larger corporations: first as a part of Polygram, then of the Universal empire. The label had offered him sanctuary after his quitting Asylum, and given him the space to make experimental albums such as *Swordfishtrombones*. But after a fertile 15 years, albeit with numerous detours into film acting and stage production, Waits was now keen to move on. "For me, it's about relationships," Waits explained. "And when Blackwell pulled out and started his own company, I lost interest."[2]

There had been compilations before *Beautiful Maladies* – the 1981 round-up, *Bounced Checks*, released immediately after his departure from Asylum, was notable for the otherwise unavailable 'Mr Henry' (a *Heartattack & Vine* out-take) and barely discernible "alternate masters" of

'Jersey Girl' and 'Whistlin' Past The Graveyard'. There was also a reward-ing, live 'The Piano Has Been Drinking', incorporating Waits' inebriated take on 'The Lord's Prayer': "Our Father, hallowed be thy glass . . . forgive us our hangovers as we forgive them that continue to hang over us . . ."

In his *Q* review of *Beautiful Maladies*, Peter Kane wrote: "as part of a loose trilogy with *Rain Dogs* and *Frank's Wild Years*, this is music with its own crazed logic and agenda that's as obsessive, dysfunctional and plain scary as anything the Eighties could muster . . ." While Joe Cushley in *Mojo* compared the Waits to be found on *Beautiful Maladies* with Walt Whitman "nineteenth-century laureate of a burgeoning USA, so with Tom Waits, twentieth-century chronicler of its human detritus".

But despite their evident admiration, all the reviews noted *Beautiful Maladies* as a marking time exercise, a marker placed down to com-memorate the end of the second phase of Waits' career. And all looked to the first album of new material since *Bone Machine*, a gap that was already getting on for seven years.

NOTES

1 *Uncut*
2 Jonathan Valania, *Magnet*

CHAPTER 34

WITH his connections to a major label severed, Waits was now a free agent. As the twentieth century began winding down, he was facing 50, and once again at liberty.

Even with his uncommercial penchant for operating on the margins, Waits would have been quite a catch for any number of record companies – he was, after all, what the labels like to call a "trophy" act. But with the free-wheeling anarchy offered by Napster and the internet, the polarisation of pop, the mobility of music . . . major labels had less and less to offer "cult" acts like Tom Waits.

Back when Waits began, Asylum, as part of the Warner conglomerate, used their corporate muscle to push him out as a tour support. They could also co-ordinate single releases while negotiating radio and television appearances. But by 1999, all that support network had gone. To make it today, you had, effectively, to make it on your own . . .

Waits signed to Epitaph Records in the summer of 1998. "I like their taste in music, barbecue and cars," the label's latest star confirmed. While in the official announcement the record company described themselves as: "the Southern Californian label . . . best known for such artists as Offspring, Rancid and Pennywise". As Waits explained at the time: "Epitaph is a label run by and for artists and musicians, where it feels much more like a partnership than a plantation . . . We shook on the deal over coffee in a truck stop. I know it's going to be an adventure."

Another reason Waits was attracted to the independent label was that he used to live near what is now their office in Los Angeles . . . "I remember when it was a taxidermist," he told *Newsweek*'s Karen Schoemer, "and there was an enormous stuffed bear and a couple of decomposing reindeer that for years I used to remark on as I went by."

Waits reasoned it was better to be a big fish in a small pond than vice versa. And he may have had a point. After all the three most important things a major, international record label could offer an artist were: the opportunity to promote their singles; securing radio play for those singles; and getting them the platform of television appearance – and none of these was likely to apply to the defiantly left-field and increasingly wayward talent of someone like Tom Waits.

"The big companies are more like countries than companies," he griped to Jon Pareles in *The New York Times*. "Record companies are no longer interested in maintaining or nurturing or supporting the growth of an artist. They want you as a cash cow on the day you get there. And then, when you stop making milk, they want you on the barbecue right away."

But, as he was about to discover, there were disadvantages with a small label too . . . and some expense was certainly spared in the making of Waits' Epitaph debut. *Mule Variations* was recorded at Prairie Sun Recording Studios, a converted chicken coop in Sebastapol, northern California. Once installed, Waits and his crew recorded 25 songs ("a little too much material to digest") for the new album. Ever practical, for Waits one advantage of this particular studio was that "in between takes you can pee outside". Actually, this was becoming a familiar theme: the alfresco toilet arrangements were the same reason he gave to those who inquired as to why a notorious city dog had moved to such a rural retreat.

The first tracks for this album began life in the Waits family bathroom ("the acoustics are great in there"), but he found he could not re-create those same dynamics in the studio. It was much the same problem Bruce Springsteen had while recording what would become his sixth album, *Nebraska,* a decade before. Recorded initially on a tape machine at home, Springsteen carried round the cassette for months, but could never replicate that home-grown sound in the studio. So in a process which required as much 1982 technology as splitting the atom had, the original battered old cassette was cleaned up, mastered and subsequently released.

For the *Mule Variations* songs, Waits' solution was surprisingly similar – if even more low-tech: he simply dug out his own bathroom tapes and had the musicians play over them. Those musicians included esteemed harmonica virtuoso Charlie Musselwhite; blues guitarist and harp maestro John Hammond; bass player Les Claypool, on loan from Primus; ex-Beck guitarist Smokey Hormel; and long-time Waits associates, Ralph Carney, Greg Cohen (Waits' brother-in-law) and long-standing guitarist Marc Ribot. (It was Ribot who once memorably described working on a Tom Waits track as "like rock'n'roll, after America had been conquered by a small African republic".)

Waits' musical work-bench was also in evidence again on *Mule Variations*. He was still hammering away at his new percussive instrument, the conundrum; but also included an array of other instruments you would never see featured on a Simply Red sleeve: chumbus, douesengoni, chamberlin, optigon and bass boo-bams. The press release introduced "a cast of chain monkeys . . . roosters . . . birds in the chimney . . . chocolate Jesuses . . . Filipino Box Spring Hogs . . . Turkey-neck stews . . . riverside motels . . . pock-marked kids . . . Studebakers . . . peppertrees . . . scrap-iron jaws . . ." George Michael territory this was *not*.

Idiosyncratic, wilfully perverse, and spread over 70 minutes – at times, *Mule Variations* sounded like music beamed from another galaxy. And yet, it actually contained some of the most accessible songs Waits had made available in years. You could almost imagine some of this material ending up on a Rod Stewart album . . .

Mule Variations opens with 'Big In Japan', a steam-driven piece, featuring drums that sound like King Kong tap-dancing. 'Hold On' was a frail and affecting memoir of all the Mary C. Browns who still flocked to Hollywood with their "charcoal eyes and Monroe hips". On a soft guitar shuffle, Waits sings with touching immediacy, like he was staring out the window of the long-gone Tropicana Motel at the parade gone by ("you don't meet nice girls in coffee shops"). 'Hold On' was the nearest he had got in decades to the poignancy of *Closing Time* and the mean-street verve of *Small Change*. With the trademark gravelly timbre on hold, his singing voice on this song was strangely reminiscent of Bruce Springsteen.

A sense of brooding isolation and ghostly absence hovers over the entire set, like the wide-open spaces pictured on the album's cover; the self-explanatory 'House Where Nobody Lives', recalling the sombre mood of David Ackles' sonorous 1972 album *American Gothic*. For Waits, the 'House Where Nobody Lives' was clearly drawn from life: "seems like everywhere I've ever lived there was always a house like that . . . like a bad tooth on the smile of the street". There was the wide-ranging but ultimately home-loving 'Pony', which brought to mind the sentimentality Elvis loved on 'Old Shep'; the piano introspection of 'Take It With Me', made all the more effective by its evocation of plaintive, distant train whistles; and, most strikingly, the heart-wrenching 'Georgia Lee'.

The song was based around the real-life story of a 12-year-old runaway, Georgia Lee Moses, who was murdered near the Waits family home in northern California. As the father of teenage children, Waits was obviously particularly susceptible to their vulnerability, and to the age-old tragedy of the death of a child: "I guess everybody was wondering, where were the police? Where was the deacon? Where were the social workers? And where was I? And where were you?"

'Georgia Lee' wasn't going to make it onto the album: even with the space gained by squeezing everything digitally onto a compact disc, *Mule*

Variations was already bulging. But then Waits' firstborn, Kellesimone, pointed out how sad it would be if the song's subject "gets killed and not remembered, and somebody writes a song about it and doesn't put it on the record".

Maybe it was the rural setting, but *Mule Variations* came out as Waits' best stab yet at a blues album. The musical spirit of the Mississippi Delta and South Side Chicago were evident, particularly on 'Lowside Of The Road', 'Cold Water', 'Picture In A Frame' and 'Get Behind The Mule'. The blues was a form to which Waits had always been indebted: "I guess it's where I keep coming back to. As an art form, it has endless possibilities." But Waits explained that 'Get Behind The Mule' was specifically inspired by what Robert Johnson's father had said about his son, aka the King of the Delta Blues Singers: "Trouble with Robert is, he wouldn't get behind the mule in the morning and plough."

As with the rural communities that gave birth to the blues, on *Mule Variations*, gospel was also a part of the mix. And Waits delivers his own warped variety of church music on 'Chocolate Jesus', which came complete with real rooster crowing, right on cue!

The concluding 'Come On Up To The House' conjures a rousing riverside revival, while Biblical echoes reverberate ("In my Father's house are many mansions", John 14: 2). But to my mind, there on the horizon, for balance, also stands the sinister, stalking figure of Robert Mitchum – out after the two Harper children in *The Night Of The Hunter*. Waits even finds space to quote Thomas Hobbes (1588–1679) on the life of man as: "nasty, brutish and short".

There was less thunderous percussion here; more guitar, less grit in the voice, more melody in the material. They were songs that told stories, and they were stories you could hear. This was music you could listen to for pleasure, rather than out of some demented discographical duty.

'Eyeball Kid' was a return to the carnival territory of *Freaks*, a pounding and unsettling narrative about a sideshow exhibit. Significantly, this ocular oddity shares the same birthday (December 7) as his creator. It also marked a rare example of Waits revisiting a character other than Frank: Barney Hoskyns pointed out that the Eyeball Kid had been namechecked on *Bone Machine*'s 'Such A Scream', to Waits' evident bafflement ("I *did*? . . ."). The character would also crop up again a few years later in 'Hang Me In The Bottle' on *Alice*, where we learn more of his genealogy – "he was born alone in a petri dish . . .".

The Eyeball Kid was originally an Eighties comic-book character created by Eddie Campbell, and based on the Greek myths. But Waits was at pains to emphasise that his Eyeball Kid wasn't an oddity, to be scorned: "It's like a little show biz tune, about the perils of the business . . . a metaphor for people that get into show business, because they usually have some kind of family disturbance or are damaged in some way or another . . . There are obviously people with physical deformities and I'm not poking fun at that at all. I'm just taking the idea of show business to a ridiculous place. It's really more autobiographical than anything else."

Perhaps the most striking track on *Mule Variations* was the furtive whispered narrative, 'What's He Building?' Waits had never sounded more sinister, or more menacing, than on this spooky speculation. Inspiration could well have come from the chilling 1999 Tim Robbins' thriller *Arlington Road*, whose strap-line was "How Well Do You Know Your Neighbour?" But Waits conceded in interview that 'What's He Building?' also contained something of Boo Radley, the twitchy, solitary neighbour in *To Kill A Mockingbird*.

"We're all, to a degree, curious about our neighbours," Waits reflected. "We all have four or five things that we know about them. And with those things, we usually create some kind of portrait of their life . . . That dog has no hair in the back . . . His wife must be 16 . . . Where's he from, St Louis? . . . But he said he was from Tampa . . . And you never, ever introduce yourself. But he continues to develop like a film for you."

For Waits, *Mule Variations* signposted a new direction ("The original idea was to do something somewhere between surreal and rural. We call it surrural."). There were unashamed love songs to Kathleen; there was a real energy in his reworking of urban blues; and there were, once again, the moving ballads with which he had made his name . . . All in all, *Mule Variations* marked a return to the form many had thought missing from the apocalyptic mix which Waits had been fashioning for much of the preceding 15 years.

Out on the publicity trail for his new album, Waits was, as ever, reflective about the songwriting process: "You texture and layer them and turn the lights down inside the song . . . after a while, you do it by taking things away, and adding things, until you have just the right feeling for where you're going. It's like a room in your ears. It's like throwing a T-shirt over the lamp by the bedside to change the way the motel looks."

And as to that frustrating seven-year delay between albums . . . "I was stuck in traffic," deadpanned Waits.

Rather disconcertingly for the faithful fans who had followed Waits from his grubby beginnings, *Mule Variations* gained him wider acceptance than any of his previous outings. Its success moved him up a notch: for so long he had been the guy with his nose pressed up against the glass, this was the record that opened the French windows and ushered him indoors. In America, *Mule Variations* peaked at number 30 on the charts; and the album even landed Waits a second Grammy win, when it scooped the award for Best Contemporary Folk Album.

It was in May 1999 that Tom Waits landed his Big Hit. In the UK, in its first week of release, *Mule Variations* sold 14,000 copies, peaking at number nine in the UK album charts – as a new entry, over Ultrasound, B.B. King, Tom Petty, Hurricane Number 1, Beverly Knight and Fish.

Categorised as a "cult figure", for years Waits' UK sales had been hardly noticeable, but constant, like a well-fitted prosthesis. Prior to cracking the Top 10 with *Mule Variations*, Waits' biggest hit had been *Frank's Wild Years* which reached number 20.

The press campaign was carefully orchestrated this time round, with 36 European journalists flown out to interview Waits so he could talk up the album. But the success of Tom Waits and *Mule Variations* in the UK could be attributed to a number of other factors. The growing circulation of monthly magazines such as *Mojo* and *Uncut* testified to the increasing power of the "grey pound": they had identified an audience that had grown up in the Sixties and Seventies and were now mature, but still interested in contemporary music.

This generation had reached a point in life where their children had left home, the mortgage was all but paid off, and their disposable income was considerable. But with pop's increasing polarity, many felt there was little to interest them in the current music scene. And there were those who found it hard to reconcile the passing years: "I can't be a grandmother for Christ's sake," Dianne Wiest roared in *Parenthood*, "I was at Woodstock!"

These more mature music-lovers probably had a passing interest in Blur or Oasis, but as the years rolled by they felt little fascination for either current pop or rap. Instead, they stood by the lodestars of their youth. That was why, as the twenty-first century dawned, The Rolling Stones, the Eagles or Simon & Garfunkel could still play concerts where people paid up to £50 just to *stand* within hearing distance. And where the price of today's souvenir programme would have bought the two best seats in the house 20 years before.

With the onset of the new millennium, reunions such as Crosby, Stills, Nash & Young, Cream and The Who – which would have been unimaginable back when Waits last released an album – were proving that there was a real market for retrospection. Not that Tom Waits ever went the cosy nostalgic route; and, in any case, his reluctance to tour consigned him to the "cult" ghetto. But with consistent album sales and his name being dropped in all the right places by all the right names, it must have been nice to know there was an audience out there.

At century's end, *Mojo* selected *Mule Variations* as its Album of the Year, over such rookies as Fountains Of Wayne, Supergrass and The Chemical Brothers. The magazine found Waits' album "moving at a slower pace than today's shiny pop vehicles, its chrome pockmarked with the tarnish of generations past . . . a Route 66 record in a freeway world . . . another landmark album from one of modern music's most valuable talents – a man who, like one of his characters here, is 'a diamond that wants to stay coal'."

If they were lucky, the hacks who were shipped across the pond to probe Waits' psyche in Santa Rosa coffee bars and diners, also got to ride in his 1970 Coupe de Ville. And on their return, the new album received glowing reviews. For David Fricke, writing in *Mojo*, the music of *Mule Variations* "isn't quite music . . . but a sonata of fear and inquisition: rattling metal; things that sound like they're falling down stairs; the squeal of shifting radio frequencies. It's Harry Partch does Alfred Hitchcock – funny, creepy and wickedly real."

Nigel Williamson in *The Times* rated *Mule Variations* as "a quite dazzling return to the fray . . . the songs . . . have been finessed to an exquisite art, the poetry honed to its emotional core and a succinctness applied to the surreal narratives, like a Haiku with not a syllable wasted." While in *Q*, Danny Eccleston found "The clank, boom and steam of 1992's mortality-obsessed *Bone Machine* and the satanic polka of 1993's Teuton operetta *The Black Rider* are on hold, so the warmth and humour of *Mule Variations'* songs are allowed to shine through their lo-fi, bucolic blues skeletons."

Even *NME* came on board, with Stuart Bailie testifying to Waits' enduring influence: "Newcomers will maybe recognise bits of the style from Gomez, Beck, Shane MacGowan, Paul Heaton and Polly Harvey, all of whom owe plenty to Tom." The fact that, pushing 50, Waits could still secure reviews in the weekly inkies was a testament to his credibility. And the sad fact that they are a fast-disappearing breed – at the time of writing only *NME* survives – does not diminish the importance of a review in their pages.

In 1999 the *Guardian* decided to mark the end of the millennium by holding a poll of the Greatest Albums Ever Made. This time out though, the paper played a maverick card by deciding to exclude all the tired old favourites. For compiler Tom Cox, the usual suspects – *Sgt Pepper's*, *Pet Sounds*, *What's Going On* . . . "though good enough – are hugely overrated and far from the finest achievements of the artists concerned".

Instead, the paper selected a more thoughtful alternative list. Number one was Nick Drake's *Bryter Layter* (all three of the late singer-songwriter's works were included). While Waits was comfortably ensconced at number two with *Rain Dogs* ("not a flicker of daylight creeps in on this faultless, 18-track nightmare of rotting blues, last-orders boogie and low-life poetry . . . *Rain Dogs* . . . is a perfect example of how to make a mainstream album without being a mainstream artist.") Waits was also represented at number 50, with *The Heart Of Saturday Night*.

Alive and still kicking at century's end, Waits was duly shortlisted for induction into the Rock and Roll Hall Of Fame during 2000, along with Black Sabbath, Dick Dale and Lou Reed – though in the event, none of them made it.

Closing the book on his final album of the twentieth century, Waits was determined to let the truly trivial have the last word. He concluded his *Mule Variations* press release by informing interested parties that "a giraffe can go without water longer than a camel. And even though the neck is seven feet long, it contains the same number of vertebrae as a mouse's. Seven. And a giraffe's tongue is 18 inches long. It can open and close its nostrils at will. It can run faster than a race horse and make almost no sound whatsoever."

While the giraffe took centre-stage and acted as decoy, a more significant – if elusive – presence was, as always, that of Waits' wife Kathleen. Only two photographs have been seen of the shadowy Mrs Waits, and she steadfastly refuses all interview requests. But Kathleen is all over her husband's records, like a whispered prayer.

She shuns publicity and is known to loathe the media treadmill, but Waits is pragmatic about the media interest in their partnership, and in interview, regularly testifies to the spectral presence of his wife, and muse, of two decades. And on the release of *Mule Variations*, Waits delivered a touching testimonial to his partner. So far as the couple's working relationship was concerned, Waits conceded: "You need someone to tell you when you're full of shit, and I'd rather have my wife say it than someone in the newspapers."[1]

Outsiders are fascinated by the collaborative nature of Waits and his wife's working methods. While many husbands welcome the opportunity to flee the family nest during the working day, Mr & Mrs Waits – together since the De Lorean was tipped as the car of the future – have remained constant, in life and art.

"The way we work is Kathleen and I will write a line each and she'll say that's a terrible line, we've written that song 700 times before, why'd you keep writing the same damn song? I'll say what do you know? She throws a magazine at me. I'll shut up a while . . . She writes down in a journal all the time, a constant log of all things happening in the world, she has this enormous wealth of material, mixing dreams with the kids stories, magazine things and things you cut out of newspapers."

Normally, Waits sidestepped the "how do you collaborate?" question with practised ease and a natty quote, or three ("I'm the prospector, she's the cook"; "She says 'you bring it home, I'll cook it up'"; "Oh, y'know, one person holds the nail, the other one swings the hammer"). However in 1999, on the release of *Mule Variations*, Waits confided: "Most of the significant changes I went through musically and as a person began when we met. She's the person by which I measure all others. She's who you want with you in a foxhole. She doesn't like the limelight, but she is an incandescent presence on everything we work on together."

As Cath Carroll would later write of the partnership between Tom and Kathleen: "When measuring a rock'n'roll marriage, you have to count time like dog years, so that would be around 140 years of regular matrimony."

NOTE

1   Richard Grant, *Zembla*

CHAPTER 35

WHEN Mr and Mrs Waits weren't committed to a joint project, as ever in and around albums, Mr Waits busied himself with outside projects, guest appearances, acting and other extra-curricular activities.

For a number of years, Warner Strategic Marketing have been looking at the possibility of repackaging Waits' Asylum back catalogue. There were seven albums, spanning *Closing Time* to *Heartattack & Vine*, crying out for upgrading and the label was enthusiastic – eager to undertake a project along the lines of what they have already accomplished with their recent reissue series. Albums by Love, Grateful Dead and Emmylou Harris have all been remastered, with the original albums further enriched by freshly commissioned sleeve notes and contemporaneous, unreleased bonus tracks.

But despite persistent inquiries, and Waits' own avowed enthusiasm for the plan, he was always just "too busy". You can understand why. Although largely eschewing concert tours, there were still sporadic live appearances, such as the one in autumn 1999, when he guested at Neil Young's annual Bridge School Benefit. The all-acoustic, nine-hour concert was Young's thirteenth such charity event. Waits (described in one review as an "eccentric genius") appeared alongside The Who, Eddie Vedder, Emmylou Harris, Sheryl Crow, Brian Wilson – and Smashing Pumpkin Billy Corgan, who performed Waits' 'Ol' 55'. The composer himself dusted down "almost unrecognisable" versions of 'Gun Street Girl' and 'Jockey Full Of Bourbon' in a performance Jaan Uhelszki described as "more cinematic than musical".

Waits was also busy collaborating in the studio. In 1998 he joined Woody Guthrie's old sparring partner Ramblin' Jack Elliot, on his album *Friends Of Mine*. Despite being born the son of a dentist in Brooklyn, ol' Ramblin' Jack sang of an America the young Tom Waits could only dream of. Jack had begun rambling after witnessing a rodeo at New York's Madison Square Garden, and hitched up with Woody before paralysis claimed the great songwriter. Woody had nominated Ramblin' Jack as his heir and successor, until a certain young Robert Zimmerman hitched down from Minnesota to pay homage to the author of 'This Land Is Your

Land'. But Ramblin' Jack was always there to encourage the young Bob Dylan; for example, the original version of what is arguably Dylan's finest-ever song, 'Mr Tambourine Man', had begun life as a duet with Ramblin' Jack Elliott.

Friends Of Mine also included contributions from Emmylou Harris, John Prine and Nanci Griffith, but the number Waits and Ramblin' Jack collaborated on was a Waits original, called 'Louise'. It was a jaunty, country ballad, with a mournful accordion wailing in the background – and those two broke-down voices sounded like Butch and Sundance serenading each other around the campfire on the old Chisum trail. Waits' voice was also the last to be heard on the album, serenading Jack with a snatch of what sounds like an age-old frontier lament, 'That Old Time Feeling'.

Around the same time, along with Robert Plant, Beck and Robyn Hitchcock, Tom Waits also appeared on 1999's *More Oar: A Tribute To Alexander Skip Spence*. Skip Spence was the founder of Moby Grape, one of the archetypal Summer of Love bands which emerged from the San Francisco scene during 1967. But Spence was plagued by personal problems, and 1969's *Oar* proved to be his only solo album.

Oar was recorded in just four sessions, and figures suggest that total sales on its original release amounted to a mere 700 copies, but nevertheless, over the years, the album gained cult status. *Oar* bracketed Skip Spence "as a North American answer to Syd Barrett"; and, like the Pink Floyd founder, Spence suffered serious mental problems, exacerbated by his drug use. *More Oar . . .* had Skip Spence fans flocking to pay tribute although, prior to his death in 1999, Spence himself remained "mildly puzzled by all the hoopla surrounding *Oar*".

Another homage that year came when Waits appeared, singing 'Highway Cafe', on *Pearls In The Snow: The Songs Of Kinky Friedman*. Now established as a successful mystery writer, Friedman began life as a folk-cum-country singer who defiantly celebrated his Jewishness – a song such as 'They Don't Make Jews Like Jesus Anymore' gives a flavour. Waits was again in good company, with Lyle Lovett, Dwight Yoakam and Willie Nelson among those paying tribute.

The most substantial outside work Waits undertook around the turn of the century came when he produced an album by John Hammond. The two first met when Waits opened a Hammond show in Arizona in 1974, and they had subsequently kept in touch, with Hammond lending his distinctive harp to *Mule Variations*.

A lifelong blues enthusiast, Hammond was six years older than Waits – and he had an impeccable musical pedigree. His father, John Hammond

Senior, produced Billie Holiday's first session; nurtured the careers of Bessie Smith, Count Basie and Sister Rosetta Tharpe, before the war; he had even intended bringing Robert Johnson to New York to perform at Carnegie Hall, until a jealous lover got there first, and poisoned the King of the Delta Blues Singers.

Hammond Senior's ears didn't let him down after the war either. He brought Pete Seeger, Johnny Cash and Leonard Cohen to Columbia – and in 1961, to his eternal credit, he also signed Bob Dylan to the label. However, the sales of Dylan's debut album the following year were so paltry that for a while the singer-songwriter was known around Columbia's offices as "Hammond's folly". Then, in 1972, while his contemporaries were considering retirement, Hammond proved his ears were as acute as ever. He was once again blown away by a guitar-toting, harp-blowing kid with a head full of ideas – so when Bruce Springsteen auditioned for him, Hammond signed him on the spot.

Being the son of a father like that was a heavy burden to shoulder; but the young John Hammond knew where his musical loyalty lay. He made his debut while still a teenager in 1963 and has proselytised on behalf of the blues ever since: on record, in performance, and at festivals all over the world.

Waits had given Hammond a new song, 'No One Can Forgive Me But My Baby', for his 1992 album, *Got Love If You Want It*. Now, keen to explore Waits' work further, Hammond had decided to record an entire album of Waits' originals, produced by the master himself. "When John asked me I said yes, and then I gulped, having never done it except with my wife on my own records," Waits admitted. "Producing someone's record is kind of like spotting someone who is on the trapeze. John's sound is so compelling, complete, symmetrical and soulful with just his voice, guitar and harmonica, it is at first impossible to imagine improving on it."

Selecting a baker's dozen of Waits compositions from the 20 or so routined, Hammond put together an album which reinvented Waits' work as a simmering twenty-first-century blues chowder. *Wicked Grin* (2001) included muscular interpretations of 'Heartattack & Vine', 'Til The Money Runs Out' and '16 Shells From A 30.6'. In Hammond's hands, the more abrasive and intimidating elements of Waits' original versions were rounded-out, while his often-overlooked melodies were brought strongly to the fore.

Wicked Grin also included the hard to find 'Buzz Fledderjohn', and the previously unavailable '2:19' and 'Fannin Street' – a beguiling, world-weary country-styled rumination about a Houston thoroughfare. Waits' own versions of all three of these songs later appeared on 2006's *Orphans* . . . collection. On the final track of *Wicked Grin*, Waits and Hammond came together roaring on the spiritual 'I Know I've Been Changed'.

The producer of *Wicked Grin* was delighted with the result: "John has a blacksmith's strength and rhythm and the kind of soul and precision it takes to cut diamonds or to handle snakes," Waits enthused. On the sleeve of *Wicked Grin*, T-Bone Burnett, in his role as fan, waxed lyrical about the pairing: "This is the deep stuff . . . every note is original . . . This is music only a full-grown man can make. In this case, two of them . . . John Hammond plays the whole deal . . . Tom Waits. The Sheik of Risk. Performs difficult operations using only his mind . . ."

Following *Short Cuts* in 1993, Waits' return to film was subdued; mostly heard, but not seen. A new song, 'A Little Drop Of Poison', appeared on the soundtrack of Wim Wenders' "stylish" 1997 thriller, *The End Of Violence*, starring Andie McDowell and Gabriel Byrne, and scored by Ry Cooder.

When it came to reviving his acting career after a six-year absence, Waits chose to appear in 1999's tongue-in-cheek superhero satire, *Mystery Men*. The film was sadly ignored on release, probably because it chose to mock comic-book superheroes at a time when those two-dimensional characters were in cinematic vogue.

Based on the Dark Horse comic, *Mystery Men* featured "seven lame superhero wannabees". A glittering cast (Ben Stiller, Geoffrey Rush, William H. Macy, Lena Olin) appeared as such hapless and incompetent "heroes" as The Shoveller, The Spleen and The Furious. With great verve and wit, *Mystery Men* mercilessly took the rise out of *Batman, Superman, X-Men*, and the rest.

The superhero auditions (with applicants like The Waffler, Ballerina Man and The PMS Avenger) were alone worth the price of admission. Pitched against evil genius Casanova Frankenstein (Geoffrey Rush having the time of his life), the all-powerful Sphinx solemnly warns his motley crew: "To beat him, you will have to have more than forks and flatulence".

Waits appeared as Dr Heller, the quirky scientist ("he's . . . *eccentric*") who supplies these incompetents with their equipment; and even by Waits' standards, Heller is a singularly seedy character – *Mystery Men* opens with him trying to pick up a pensioner in a rest home. Home for Heller is a deserted fun-fair, where he lives with his inventions like The Can

Tornado, The Blame Thrower ("you aim it at people and they start blaming each other") and The Shrinker. "They all come with warranty," Waits cheerfully informs his not-so-super buddies.

On the subject of superheroes, Waits was reintroduced to their world for the first time since childhood, while working on Coppola's *The Cotton Club*. Hanging around together during shooting, and with time on their hands, Waits' co-star Nicolas Cage – a comic-book obsessive – took Tom back to the colourful fantasy land. Waits had fond childhood memories of comic-book characters like The Incredible Hulk and The Silver Surfer, and, of course, The Eyeball Kid found his way into several songs.

Nowadays, superheroes have been elevated from the pages of comics; they are instead the featured players in "graphic novels". During 2002, while undergoing the tooth-pulling process of Q&A, Waits cheerfully offered up his own idea for a superhero: "What I would like to do is have a special power to find things that were lost," he enthused to Ross Fortune. "People would come to me because they lost their purse in the Fifties . . . If they lost a pocket knife that they really loved, or toys from childhood, I would be the Finder Man. 'Let's get the Finder Man,' they'd say. Yeah, the Finder Man, that'd be me."

Once again, Waits' role in *Mystery Men* is little more than a cameo, but his distinctive personality and angular looks lent themselves particularly convincingly to the part of the mad scientist. And while on first release, *Mystery Men* seemed like merely a lightweight diversion; seeing it again in the aftermath of the ignoble *Catwoman*, *The Fantastic Four* and *Superman Returns*, puts it right up there alongside *Citizen Kane*.

Around the same time as he appeared in *Mystery Men*, Waits also contributed the forewords to two volumes by Bart Hopkins: *Gravikords, Whirlies And Pyrophones* and *Orbitones*. The books (described by *Billboard* as "fascinating") examined unusual and experimental musical instruments – so who else but the inventor of the conundrum could Hopkins have considered for the foreword?

"With the digital revolution wound up and rattling, the deconstructionists are combing the wreckage of our age," Waits wrote with fervour. "They are cannibalising the marooned shuttle to send us on to a place that will sound like a roaring player piano left burning on the beach."

Still enthused by his memories of working with Robert Wilson in Germany in 1990, and with *The Black Rider* album freshly minted, Waits returned to Europe during 2000 to embark on two further Wilson collaborations, *Alice* and *Woyzeck*.

Woyzeck was based on George Buchner's 1837 play, which in turn was used by Alban Berg as the basis for his 1925 opera, *Wozzeck*. In 1979 the story was also filmed, predictably bleakly, by Werner Herzog, with Klaus Kinski playing a private soldier in a nineteenth-century garrison town who, obsessed by his wife's infidelity, is driven to madness, murder and suicide. Adding further spice to the already gloomy mix, following the murder of his unfaithful wife, Woyzeck is ordered by his army superiors to undergo medical experiments to judge his sanity. You can see just what attracted Tom Waits to the piece.

Robert Wilson's production of *Woyzeck*, which would also form the basis for Waits' 2002 album *Blood Money*, premiered at Copenhagen's Betty Nansen Theater in November 2000. And, according to James McNair, one of the few critics who actually saw the production: "Waits' performance is limited to the singing voice of a sinister toy monkey in the opening scene, yet his personality dominates the work."

The production eventually transferred to London in 2002, where it was respectfully, if not enthusiastically received. Writing in the *Guardian*, Michael Billington found it "aurally and visually beguiling, [but] it ends up too much like a fashion-plate Versace show". Susannah Clapp in the *Observer* concurred: "Watching Robert Wilson's production of *Woyzeck* is like looking at a bad-taste fashion shoot: it's as if an exquisite, skinny model has posed in front of a famine-blasted land." However, both critics agreed on the quality of the music: "If the spirit of the playwright survives at all, it is in the Waits/Brennan songs, which hauntingly draw on a variety of popular traditions. There is more than a touch of Satchmo . . . the influence of Kurt Weill is all-pervasive."[1]

"Tom Waits' music and the lyrics of Kathleen Brennan weave a twenty-first-century version of *The Threepenny Opera*. There's undodgeable desolation in their heavy marching rhythms; loneliness in the stripped-back brass; lots of rasp and clangour – and an occasional injection of sweetness. Waits doesn't suffer by the comparison with Weill."[2]

As this was their second collaboration, Waits and Robert Wilson were already accustomed to the other's methods. By nature, they were opposites when it came to working techniques; but the wayward Waits was curiously drawn to the director's meticulous approach: "When I first met him, I felt I was with an inventor, Alexander Graham Bell or one of those guys. He's a deep thinker, a man who chooses his words very carefully and is not to be trifled with."[3]

Due to the pressure of his other commitments at the time, Waits' score for this play based on the *Woyzeck* story was not released until 2002 – by which time it had become *Blood Money*. As ever, the album was a full-blooded collaboration with Kathleen, and it was she who had suggested the new title, bearing in mind Woyzeck's role as a medical guinea pig.

Despite its long pedigree, the story of Woyzeck as conveyed by Waits on *Blood Money* just didn't click. He admitted that, "The songs aren't really a linear narrative; you couldn't understand the story from hearing them. They might have been part of a theatre piece to begin with, but if you are going to do a record, it has to stand alone. You have to get beyond the original concept; it's like making a movie out of a book."[4]

But with *Blood Money*, Waits had taken a step too far from the original concept, and a step right back with the music. Quite how a song such as 'Coney Island Baby', enchanting as it undeniably was, fitted in with the goings-on in a Polish garrison town during 1837 eluded many listeners. And how did a line like "I'd sell your heart to the junk man, baby, for a buck . . ." connect with the character of Buchner's nineteenth-century soldier?

'Misery Is The River Of The World' came with some striking lyrical observations ("if there's one thing you can say about Mankind, there's nothing kind about man") while owing a lyrical debt to Benjamin Franklin. 'Starving In The Belly Of A Whale' had a nice suggestion that "man's a fiddle that life plays on". But there was, once again, a feeling of déjà vu on this disc. Vocally, Waits was pushing that emphysema-style delivery to the brink. Musically, *Blood Money* was a weary re-visit to the familiar landscape of seedy Weimar cabaret, welded onto Mississippi delta blues, and garnished with a light sprinkling of Captain Beefheart.

Overall, there was a more European feel to the albums of *Blood Money* and *Alice* – but no surprise there, given that both were commissioned, written and premiered in Europe. Neither offered any dramatic departure from Waits' existing formula, though the grim nature of the *Blood Money* narrative was unsettling. In a fit of quiet desperation, Waits even commissioned a video to accompany 'God's Away On Business' from *Blood Money*. The director was Jesse Dylan, who remembered it as an eventful shoot, with the star suggesting at one point: "This would be better with an emu!"

Reviewing *Blood Money* for *Record Collector*, James McNair found "Waits' vocal timbre somewhere between Captain Caveman and Lee Marvin as he rasps over a percussive backing track partly realised through the shaking of the Indonesian botang tree's giant seed pod. Not for Tom, it seems, the Akai sampler or the airbrushed twiddlings of a thousand

A Sight For Sore Eyes, 1999. (NEIL COOPER/IDOLS)

Waits listens intently to a Senate panel investigating record label accounting practices, 2002.

(AP PHOTO/LUCY NICHOLSON/EMPICS)

With Keith Richards backstage at Rolling Stones' 40 Licks show at the Wiltern Theatre, Hollywood, November 4, 2002.

(ALEX BERLINER/BEI/REX FEATURES)

On stage during the Healing The Divide peace and reconciliation concert, New York, September 21, 2003.

(ADAM ROUNTREE/STRINGER/GETTY IMAGES)

Smoking with Iggy Pop in *Coffee & Cigarettes*, 2003.

Waits as "a wanderer" with Keira Knightley, in *Domino*, 2005.

Doffing his hat around the time of *Real Gone,* 2004, US. (KIM KULISH/CORBIS)

Waits live at Carre, Amsterdam, November 20, 2004. (ELS DECKERS/RETNA)

Waits back on stage for his first European tour in 17 years, 2004

(SOEREN STACHE/DPA/CORBIS, ROBERT VOS/EPA/CORBIS, PAUL BERGEN/REDFERNS & LEX VAN ROSSEN/REDFERNS)

Waits in *The Tiger And The Snow*, 2005. (EVERETT COLLECTION/REX FEATURES)

On stage at the 'Big Apple To Big Easy' benefit concert for the Gulf Coast at New York's Radio City Music Hall, September 20, 2005. (SCOTT GRIES/GETTY IMAGES)

Guitar Institute of Technology graduates." Waits himself declared that what he was aiming for with *Blood Money*, was that it "should sound as though it's been ageing in a barrel and distressed".

Reflecting on his efforts in *Mojo*, Sylvie Simmons' review included words like "brutal . . . nihilistic . . . dark . . . visceral . . . discordant . . . clatter . . . blare". It's like the critics really *wanted* to like *Blood Money*, but were left confused by its general lack of narrative, melody and purpose.

Blood Money was one of a pair of albums Waits released simultaneously in 2002. ("You wait three years for a new Tom Waits album," *Mojo* head-lined, "and then two come along at once.") He had not pioneered the idea of releasing two albums on the same day – both Bruce Springsteen and Guns N' Roses had previously been down that road – but Waits did attempt to explain his reasons to Nigel Williamson. "One's chicken. One's fish. But if you're going to turn on the stove you might as well make dinner."

But cooking ahead can be a risky business. And as so often happens, one of the dishes ends up forgotten at the back of the fridge, while the other is welcomed with relish in the dining room. In Waits' case, it was *Blood Money* that was put to one side; in favour of the haunting and timeless story of the young Alice Pleasance Liddell . . .

NOTES

1   Michael Billington, the *Guardian*
2   Susannah Clapp, the *Observer*
3   Gavin Martin, *Uncut*
4   Gavin Martin, *Uncut*

CHAPTER 36

"ALL in the golden afternoon, full leisurely we glide . . ." On the afternoon of July 4, during the long vacation of 1862, a boat carrying three young children was rowed three miles along the Thames near Oxford. In order to distract and entertain his companions on this golden journey to Godstow, mathematician Charles Dodgson, the man at the bow, amused the young girls with his tale of another little girl.

Extemporising as he rowed, the 30-year-old Dodgson spellbound them with his tale of the girl who fell down a rabbit hole, and what she found there. On returning to Oxford, the middle child begged: "Oh Mr Dodgson, I wish you would write out Alice's adventures for me." On returning to his rooms in Christ Church, Dodgson spent the entire summer night doing just that.

The real-life object of the storyteller's affection was 10-year-old Alice Liddell. And that summer day was to prove, as W.H. Auden later wrote, "as memorable a day in the history of literature as it is in American history".

Three years to the day from that memorable river trip, Dodgson (under the pseudonym Lewis Carroll) published *Alice's Adventures In Wonderland*. Its publication in 1865 opened up a Freudian can of worms which, ever since, has fascinated – sometimes to the point of obsession – literary critics, social commentators, psychologists, historians, and artists.

The literary Alice (and her subsequent adventures *Through The Looking Glass* in 1871) gave the world the Cheshire Cat, the Mad Hatter, the White Rabbit, the Caucus Race, the Walrus and the Carpenter, the Mock Turtle, Jabberwocky, Tweedledum & Tweedledee, and Humpty Dumpty. It enriched the language with "curious and curiouser"; "off with her head"; "begin at the beginning . . ."; "the time has come, the Walrus said . . ."; "cabbages and kings"; "never jam today" . . .

In the course of Alice's fantastical adventures, Carroll also found time to parody such esteemed Victorian poets as Walter Scott, Tennyson and Wordsworth. He inverted logic and literally created a world in which both children and adults have revelled for nearly a century and a half. And it is a testament to Alice's enduring charms that, over the years, illustrators of her adventures have included Walt Disney, Arthur Rackham, Ralph Steadman, Mervyn Peake and Peter Blake.

Following his death in 1898, Lewis Carroll fell out of favour. But there was a renewal of interest in the *Alice* books during the Great War; perhaps, it was suggested, because *this* was precisely the image of England the troops were fighting to preserve. Although it seems equally possible that Wonderland came in those times to represent an escapist Eden, far removed from the carnage of the 1914–1918 conflict – a horrific war which claimed the lives of two of the real Alice's three sons. But the fictional Alice endured, and in the next war her story was used by Leslie Howard in *Pimpernel Smith* to baffle the Gestapo; while Mrs Miniver read Alice's adventures aloud, to soothe her children during a Nazi air raid.

From early on, the Freudian interpreters seized upon the *Alice* books. Rich in allusion, illusion and metaphor, they proved fertile territory for analysis. While the fecundity of Carroll's literary imagination; his penchant for photographing very young girls, frequently in various stages of undress; his bachelor status . . . all have fuelled the *Alice* controversy over the years.

Lewis Carroll – or rather Oxford mathematician and photographer Charles Lutwidge Dodgson – was far from unique in the world of mid-nineteenth-century scholarship. Those comfortable, prosperous Victorians frequently placed children on a pedestal; idealising the virginity, purity and innocence of childhood.

A shy, remote, austere scholar, Dodgson never married. But his rooms overlooking the garden of the Liddell children, allowed him to worship his idealised fantasies, literally from afar. He often saw Alice and her sisters at play, and through a camera lens, he could observe, without the necessity of involvement. It was, for Dodgson, an apparently innocent hobby, which brought him closer to the young girls who so bewitched him.

Comparisons have been made between Dodgson and *Lolita*. But while the hero of Nabokov's novel is sexually obsessed with his nymphet; it was precisely the absence of sexual threat that seemed to appeal to Dodgson, allowing him instead to idealise the young girl's innocence. But exactly what was the nature of Dodgson's relationship with Alice is a question that has fascinated scholars, critics and artists ever since she symbolically disappeared down the rabbit hole in 1865.

The Annotated Alice by Martin Gardner, is the most diligent and engaging examination of Lewis Carroll and his world (Gardner, for example, reluctantly reports that when he checked the Meteorological Office's records for that historic day of July 4, 1862, it was not the "golden afternoon" of Carroll's recollection, but "cool and rather wet".)

However, when it comes to the celebrated exchange between Alice and the Cheshire Cat, Tom Waits would doubtless take issue with Gardner's opinion: "Would you tell me, please, which way I ought to go from here?" "That depends a good deal on where you want to get to . . ." "I don't much care where . . ." "Then it doesn't matter which way you go . . ." Writing in 1960, Gardner noted sniffily: "These remarks are among the most quoted passages in the *Alice* books. A recent echo is heard in Jack Kerouac's forgettable novel *On The Road* . . . 'Where we going, man?' 'I don't know, but we gotta go.'" But such priggishness would win him few friends in the beat universe.

Tom Waits was not the first writer in the rock'n'roll orbit to be attracted to the *Alice* stories. The hallucinogenic nature of Carroll's prose was particularly attractive to Sixties "heads" who wanted an escape from materialism, civil strife and war. As a means of slipping back to childhood idylls, *Alice's Adventures In Wonderland* and *Through The Looking Glass* were required reading – along with *The Hobbit* and *The Wind In The Willows*. Alice, the pretty pill-popping heroine; Alice, expanding and diminishing in size; Alice, with all her warped logic and surreal juxtapositions . . . no surprise that the hippie culture embraced Carroll's heroine so enthusiastically.

Perhaps the most memorable precursor of Waits' *Alice* was Jefferson Airplane's 'White Rabbit', indelibly linked to the swirling sounds of 1967, along with Grace Slick's stern injunction to "feed your head". While in his exhaustive 2006 *Bob Dylan Encylopedia*, Michael Gray suggested some intriguing link between Lewis Carroll's work and Dylan's songs, specifically 'Drifter's Escape' and 'I Threw It All Away'.

Appropriately enough, for someone who was lionised during the Summer of Love, Dodgson himself believed that – despite all the genuinely inspired nonsense poems – his finest lines came from 'The Song Of Love', a sickly lament in the largely forgotten *Sylvie and Bruno*, in which the two fairies of the title coo to each other: "For I think it is Love/ For I feel it is Love/ For I'm sure it is nothing but Love!"

It was during 1967's Summer of Love that John Lennon fed his half-remembered memories of Carroll's characters the walrus and the carpenter, from *Through The Looking Glass*, into 'I Am The Walrus'. Lennon also had *Alice*'s Humpty-Dumpty in mind when he sang about his eggman . . . Goo Goo Ga Joo . . .

I also half-remember a song from the Seventies whose refrain ran: "cat's nose, dog's eyes, Lewis Carroll tells lies . . . !" And, lest we forget, it was in a 1954 school production of *Alice In Wonderland* that Paul Simon and Art

Garfunkel first met. Paul was the White Rabbit ("a *lead* role," he reminded audiences during the duo's 2004 reunion tour); while Art was the Cheshire Cat ("a *supporting* role," Simon helpfully pointed out).

Tom Waits' and Robert Wilson's *Alice*, based on the Lewis Carroll character, had been premiered at Hamburg's Thalia Theatre in December 1992. But, busy as he was clearing the decks, Waits waited over a decade before releasing his score as an album. Though Waits and Lewis Carroll had briefly brushed on disc before – on *Rain Dogs'* 'Singapore' Waits had sung "we're all as mad as hatters here", citing one of the best-known characters from the *Alice* books.

Rather than journeying through *Wonderland* or *The Looking Glass*, Waits' *Alice* looked instead at the relationship between Dodgson and the real-life Alice. Coming at the subject in the heightened climate created by the well-documented child abuse cases, internet pornography and paedophile scares of the early twenty-first century, Waits saw *Alice* as being about "repression, mental illness and obsessive, compulsive disorders".

The relationship between Dodgson and Alice had fascinated other artists over the years. In 1985 Dennis Potter scripted the film *Dreamchild*, in which Coral Browne played the elderly Alice Liddell, travelling to New York in 1932 to commemorate the centenary of Dodgson's birth, with Ian Holm as the author of *Alice*. It was a reflection on childhood innocence and the intimations of mortality which inevitably come with ageing.

These were subjects that also preoccupied Dodgson: one explanation put forward for his particular fondness for children was that he suffered from a lifelong stutter, which all but disappeared in the company of children. Another was that because Dodgson himself had enjoyed a happy childhood, it remained with him as a place and time he was only too pleased to return to, as both an adult, and as an author.

Intriguingly, when his childhood home in Cheshire was renovated in 1950, half a century after his death, beneath the floorboards in what had been his nursery, builders found a thimble, a white glove and a lobster shell! All perfect material for the future creator of *Alice In Wonderland*.

The full nature of Dodgson's relationship with young girls remains enigmatic: he only craved the company of girls ("I am fond of children," he once admitted in a letter, "except boys.") But once the girls had passed over into puberty, Dodgson's interest diminished. He once kissed a girl of 14; on discovering she was actually 17, Dodgson wrote an apologetic letter to the girl's mother. He received the frosty response "we shall take care it does not recur".

As with *Blood Money*, Waits and Kathleen used the Lewis Carroll originals simply as a basis for their album of *Alice*. What fascinated them was the precise nature of that celebrated relationship. There remains a tantalising mystery – Alice's mother sensed something unnatural in the relationship, and later burned all his early letters to her daughter. Further mystery surrounds Dodgson's diary entry for October 18, 1862, three months after that memorable boat trip, where he notes he has fallen out of Mrs Liddell's graces "ever since Lord Newry's business". To this day, scholars are baffled by precisely what his Lordship's "business" had to do with the rift between 10-year-old Alice Liddell and the man who made her immortal.

Recent evidence suggests that the 31-year-old Dodgson may actually have proposed marriage to the 11-year-old Alice Liddell. Future prime minister Lord Salisbury, later a friend of Dodgson's, wrote: "They say that Dodgson has half gone out of his mind in consequence of having been refused by the real Alice. It looks like it." Today, such a proposal would obviously be inconceivable, but in *The Victorians*, his exhaustive survey of those times, A.N. Wilson points out that "the 1861 census shows that in Bolton, 175 women married at 15 or under, 179 in Burnley".

Examining Lewis Carroll's fascination with young girls from the vantage point of today naturally raises worrying questions. But there is no evidence whatsoever to suggest that any of the relationships were ever of a sexual nature. In all likelihood, there was an element of naivety and innocence in his dealings with the girls, which today would simply not be countenanced.

The songs on Tom Waits' *Alice* have little direct reference to Dodgson, or his Alice; in Waits' world, however, 'Flower's Grave', 'No One Knows I'm Gone', 'Lost In The Harbour' and 'Fish & Bird' were welcome. There are, however, some jarring inconsistencies: how exactly does a song like 'Reeperbahn' fit into the cloistered world of nineteenth-century Oxford? Why include the German language 'Kommienezuspadt', when Dodgson's only trip outside England was to Russia? And 'Table Top Joe' cuts an incongruous figure, even in the topsy-turvy world of Wonderland.

Yet some slight echoes of Lewis Carroll can be detected: the lyric "Alice, arithmetic, arithmetock" on the title track has a nice mathematical Carrollian feel; 'Flower's Grave' contains references to the "pilgrim's withered wreath of flowers" which Carroll cited in his prefatory verse to *Wonderland*; and a certain "Mrs Carroll" crops up on 'We're All Mad Here' – the title of which is taken from the Cheshire Cat's observation to Alice.

On the title track, Waits deals thoughtfully with Dodgson's bittersweet obsession: "the skates on the pond they spell Alice"; "the branches spell Alice". While on 'Watch Her Disappear', he memorably evokes the image of the aloof, clinical Dodgson watching the young, sprightly Alice cavorting across the lawn outside. Innocent or knowing? Lascivious or tender? We will probably never know . . . Only that it proved an unbridgeable gap; and provided the world with one of fiction's most magical and enduring worlds.

In fairness, Waits had not set out to make a literal examination of Lewis Carroll, or Alice Liddell. If *Alice* were to be evoked musically, it would have to be to the sound of acoustic English pastoral, rather than smoky American jazz. But Waits' *Alice* does suggest the slow, stately steps of mortality: evoking wistful reflections on what has been, while contemplating what lies ahead. And, above all, the rueful acceptance that some things can never be.

Alice herself died in 1934. To the end of her life she was astonished by the enduring fascination with her life as a child during one Victorian summer. The child within her was equally baffled by the interest shown long-ago by the man who ensured her immortality.

And what of that curious genius Lewis Carroll: photographer, mathematician, lay preacher? All these and more, but it is as the creator of *Alice* that he is best remembered. It was not only his addition of new words to the English language ("chortle" and "galumph"); but the gallery of characters that flowed from his pen, creating a timeless world which never ceases to amaze and delight.

In the concluding poem of *Through The Looking Glass*, Lewis Carroll wrote some of his most haunting lines. As a mathematician and wordsmith, Charles Dodgson was naturally attracted by the challenge of an acrostic – a poem in which the first word of each line spells out the name of its subject . . . in this case Alice Pleasance Liddell. The poem wistfully concluded: "Ever drifting down the stream – Lingering in the golden gleam – Life, what is it but a dream?"

CHAPTER 37

TOGETHER, *Alice* and *Blood Money* put Waits back on the map. Of the two albums, Sylvie Simmons in *Mojo* preferred *Alice*: "Unhealthy obsession has rarely been this beautiful. But it belongs with its bloody, blasphemous counterpart . . . Get both and you have a photograph and its negative. Or, more precisely, a new negative of an old photograph . . ."

In *Uncut*, Chris Roberts wrote that "*Alice* bleeds with sorrow and longing . . . referencing an unholy host of eccentric characters that could be drawn from somewhere between *Under Milk Wood*, the Bible and *Barfly*, it's a work of literary grit and grandeur as well as musical invention."

For his Q review, David Quantick noted that Waits "seems never happier than when he is listing the grimness of existence and his tunes and rhythms are at their jauntiest. George Buchner, not a happy man, said that 'The individual is just foam on the wave, greatness is mere chance; genius a puppet-play.' With respect, on the evidence of these two extraordinary albums, he was wrong."

Waits confessed himself baffled as to why there had been a decade's delay between the staging of *Alice* and its release in album form. Indeed, it was so long lost, that the composer had to go out and buy a bootleg of his own *Alice* demos in order to refresh his memory for the official 2002 recording. It would prove to be a worthwhile investment.

On May 18, 2002, *Music Week*, the industry bible, noted that "Tom Waits sold more albums in the UK last week than he has sold in any other given week . . ." – although sales were split between *Alice* (number 20 in the chart; 8,753 copies sold) and *Blood Money* (number 21; 8,622). Still, combined sales, though less than those of The Jam (whose *Greatest Hits* collection was the highest entry on that week's chart), were more than the Bellrays, who had the highest new entry behind Waits during that particular week. In America, the combined first week sales of the two albums totalled 64,000, landing him a brace of chart positions just outside the Top 30.

Waits' long-time UK publicist, Rob Partridge, won *Music Week*'s "Niche Campaign of the Quarter" award for his promotion of the two

282

albums. "We knew his fan base was very solid, despite the fact he hadn't toured in this country for 15 years. He remains cool and is completely untouched by current notions of fashionability. He is also one of the few artists in his 50s still going forwards in his career and we knew that fans would be equally interested in both CDs."[1]

To keep visiting journalists entertained while he was doing promotion for the two albums, Waits set up a talking shop in Suite 101 at Santa Rosa's Flamingo Hotel, just a half-hour car journey from his home. Although it was already far removed from Orwell's Room 101, Waits brought along a variety of personal artefacts to give the room a more homely feel: Mahalia Jackson CDs; bags of chocolate raisins; a never-empty coffee pot; and in pride of place, a box-set of Charley Patton discs. He was also at pains to stock up his collection of weird and wonderful facts, just in case the conversation should dry up during the 60 minutes allotted to each European journalist.

Like so many others, Gavin Martin was intrigued by the collaborative process which went on chez Waits – and Tom's reply was rather less oblique than usual: "We do talk about what we're doing all the time. The way we work is like a quarrel that results in either blood or ink. You find you may not have known how you felt about a particular sound or issue or phrase or melody until you are challenged to expand or change it. If it's a successful collaboration, you end up with more things in there than occurred at the outside. But hell, we got kids. Once you've raised kids together, you find songs come easy, actually."[2]

Some time earlier, while preparing *Alice* and *Blood Money* for release, Waits had been recognised by ASCAP (the Association of Composers and Performers). Accepting the organisation's Founder's Award, for his "tremendous body of work", Waits kept the audience entertained with an acceptance speech which revealed that dish-washing remained his favourite job "because no one bothers you". Straightening up, the ever-eloquent Waits then compared his songs to vessels . . . because "when people migrate, they take with them their seeds and their songs. And I think essentially that's all you'll need when you get there. Well, I should amend that. There are other things you're going to need when you get there: a shaving kit and a change of clothes would be important. You get the point."

All that looking over your shoulder stuff was fine for a while, but Waits was still as keen as ever to edge his way forward. In person, even after 30 years hovering around the limelight, Waits actually remained quite a shy person. And despite all the chutzpah of his stage persona, and the beloved entertainer schtick he put on during interviews, Waits found the whole process rather taxing. In truth, rather like his erstwhile co-star Jack Nicholson in *Terms Of Endearment*, Waits "would rather stick needles in my eyes" than go repeatedly through the whole interview process.

For Tom then, the internet came as a welcome barrier. Waits' official site allowed for plenty of obfuscation and the perpetration of myth. While the unofficial sites took care of the many (and frequently tedious) "Frequently Asked Questions" . . . Is Tom Waits his real name? Why doesn't Tom like touring? Who is Harry Partch (and why is he saying all those terrible things about me)? What is a *Rain Dog*? . . .

By the end of the twentieth century, the internet was really humming; offering unlimited amounts of pornography, dubious knowledge, and anonymity . . . It could be anybody out there. For an artist like Waits, this was a canny way of keeping fans at arm's length, while giving the illusion of whispering in their ear. The internet could encourage dialogues and end arguments; it could settle scores and open up whole new cans of worms.

Waits relished the freedom, enjoying the fresh opportunities offered by cyberspace. It kept him in touch, but out of harm's way. While his official site alerted fans to new material, film projects and product availability; he could eavesdrop on message rooms, pretending to be somebody else – or if a query intrigued him sufficiently, descend into the bull pit himself.

One of the best examples of just how much an artist could relish this anonymous interplay came in 1999. A network of Bob Dylan fans were scratching their collective electronic heads over the true meaning of 'Blowin' In The Wind'. Then, out of cyberspace, came a message saying that it was simply "a naive political plea by a young man". "And how the fuck do *you* know?" "Because I'm Bob." "Yeah, right . . ." Forced to prove his identity, "Bob" agreed to play his never–ever–performed, 17-minute 'Highlands' onstage the next night. And sure enough, fifth song in, at the Coors Amphitheatre, Bob Dylan gave 'Highlands' its live premiere!

Of course, the internet also offered a whole new way to access music at the flick of a switch. All the music of the world was suddenly within reach. For Waits, and others of his generation, obtaining a favoured piece of music had meant a trip down to the record store. It necessitated buying (or sometimes even ordering) a fast revolving 45, or forking out more serious money for an LP. Although as the technology improved, it did become possible to swap tapes of your favourites with teenage chums – until the industry cautioned that "Home Taping Is Killing Music".

Even then, for those born before the limitless horizons of the internet, musical remained a *physical* reality. The record, the tape, the shiny disc or 8-track cartridge actually existed; it had sleeve notes, composer credits, acknowledgements, production details . . . it allowed you access to a closed room. In theory, the internet offered up a whole brave new world – and unfettered choice. In cyberspace, Tom Waits floated alongside Charley Patton and The Allman Brothers; Miles Davis nestled next to Tony Christie; Johnny Cash swam alongside Van Der Graaf Generator . . . and the opportunities for discovering and accessing music seemed limitless.

Like so many musicians, however, Waits was wary of downloading, and railed against having his music stolen by anonymous thieves. In 2001, along with Randy Newman and Heart, Waits took legal action against MP3.com. The $40 million suit alleged that the company's My.MP3 service allowed access to the artist's work – in Waits' case, songs from *Mule Variations* – without their permission. "People are excited about a breakthrough in new technology," Waits' attorney commented at the time, "forgetting that you have to put the law first."

One criticism frequently levelled at net surfers is that they should get out more. American fans of Tom Waits took this advice literally when they organised a convocation which they called "Waitstock". The yearly event took place in Poughkeepsie, upstate New York – which, prior to the Waits convention, was best remembered as the subject of Gene Hackman's surreal interrogation in *The French Connection*.

Waitstock actually sounds like an opportunity for aficionados simply to get bladdered in the company of like-minded souls. On their website, the organisers claim that: "Waitstock is about Tom Waits as much as bourbon is about oak casks!" But when it came to finding a venue for the event, which began in the mid-Eighties, things became very Waitsian indeed. Waitstock regularly took place at a location Waits himself would surely have approved of: Uncle Bob's Dead Battery Farm.

The organisers of Waitstock describe it as "a 24-hour party, infected with Waitsitis, a virus like Ebola, but instead of your insides melting down by an accidental infection, this is something you do to yourself willingly. Vomit optional."

Waits himself was understandably wary about this latest tribute. Asked exactly what happened at Waitstock, the idol responded: "I don't know. It's just what I imagine . . . incantations, speak in tongues, wake up at six in the morning and have whiskey and eggs, walk around in their undershirts . . . it's just some attempt at worshipful homage."[3]

Grappling with such unhinged tributes, and with one eye always open to the future, Waits briefly allowed the past back on the scene. In June 2004 the first English language production of *The Black Rider* opened at the Barbican Theatre in London as the centrepiece of its *Bite:04* season. Critics were particularly wary of the production, as the term "rock musical" now came with an automatic public safety warning: predecessors such as Dave Clark's *Time*, the Rod Stewart homage *Tonight's The Night* and Queen's *We Will Rock You* having already rung the warning bells.

The casting of Marianne Faithfull as Pegleg, the Devil, for *The Black Rider*'s three-week run helped ensure sell-out performances. But there were still those who found Robert Wilson's elaborate theatrical events (such as his seven-hour silent piece, *Deafman Glance*) pretentious and over-powering; and I, for one, breathed a sigh of relief that the Wilson/Waits adaptation of a Samuel Beckett play remains mercifully stillborn.

Waits himself, however, remains effusive about Wilson and his work: "He's like a scientist, medical student or an architect . . . In theatre, he's developed a whole language for himself and those he works with . . . right down to the way he has people move. He's compelled to create a world where everyone conforms to his laws of physics. He has everyone move real slow, because you can't grasp the full drama of a movement onstage that happens in real time. It won't register with you. It makes you think about the simplest movement, the act of getting out of a chair or reaching for a glass."[4]

And Wilson was equally enamoured of Waits, once describing their relationship as "grandiose, touching and elegant". Asked a specific question about the staging of *The Black Rider*, Wilson was once heard to comment: "it's OK, if it's OK with Tom". Following his decade-long collaboration with Waits on *The Black Rider*, *Alice* and *Woyzeck*, Robert Wilson stayed in the rock'n'roll orbit, to work with Lou Reed on *Time Rocker*, a 1996 adaption of H. G. Wells' *The Time Machine*.

The Black Rider was rapturously received during its London run. Writing in the *Sunday Telegraph*, Ben Thompson began unpromisingly: "Few people would deny that grizzled old soak Tom Waits has written music of extraordinary beauty. On the downside though, the tireless gene-splicer of Bavarian oompah and junkyard avant-blues has also been responsible for some of the most unlistenable records ever made . . . but now that British audiences can at last hear these [*Black Rider*] songs in the theatrical setting for which they were originally intended, their human virtues shine through."

His colleague, the notoriously hard-to-please theatre critic of the *Daily Telegraph*, Charles Spencer was even more enchanted: "Shows don't come more achingly hip than *The Black Rider* . . . The heart of the piece . . . is Waits' superb score, a wheezy, clanking variation of Weimar cabaret, with echoes of Brecht/Weill, gospel and blues. The band features such unusual instrumentation as the musical saw, the glass harmonica and the didgeridoo, and its rancid carnival atmosphere really gets under your skin.

"This is a show with a divinely decadent whiff of sulphur and brimstone, and all those involved display exactly the required touch of satanic majesty."

NOTES

1 *Music Week*
2 *Uncut*
3 Jonathan Valania, *Magnet*
4 Gavin Martin, *Uncut*

· CHAPTER 38

AFTER its triumphant London run at the Barbican came to an end in 2004, *The Black Rider* played to similar acclaim in San Francisco and Sydney. But for all the diversionary tactics, fascinating side projects and nicely judged guest appearances, Tom Waits aficionados still had plenty of questions:

(1) When was the dinner fork introduced into England?
(2) When is Tom Waits going to tour?
(3) Who said: "All the things I really like to do are either illegal, immoral or fattening"?
(4) When will there be a new Tom Waits album?

Well . . . (1) 1608; (2) Who knows? (3) Alexander Woollcott (4) Very soon . . .

Following the double whammy of *Alice* and *Blood Money* during 2002, Waits himself was eloquently evasive about his new album: "There are songs about politics, rats, war, hangings, dancing, automobiles, pirates, farms, the carnival and sinning, mama, liquor, trains and death. In other words, the same old dirty business."

By this stage of his career, Waits' songs could pretty much be split into two distinct categories, which Kathleen wryly identified as "grand weepers or grim reapers". When it finally came out in 2004, *Real Gone* – originally entitled *Clang, Boom & Steam* – proved rich in both.

When Jonathan Valania of *Magnet* confessed himself curious about some of the characters who populated *Real Gone*, Waits explained: "if there was a Jesus of Nazareth, there had to be a Mike of the Weeds and a Bob of the parking lot . . . Poodle Murphy was a girl from Funeral Wells' knife act . . . Joel Tornabene's in the concrete business, a Mob guy . . ." The motley cast also included Bowlegged Sal; Knocky Parker; Piggy Knowles; Zuzu Bolin; Yodelling Elaine, the Queen of the Air; Mighty Tiny; Horse Face Ethel; Saginaw Calinda; Bum Mahoney; and not forgetting one-eyed Myra (in her Roy Orbison T-shirt). Thanks to Waits, all of them were on nodding terms with a bargain-basement Greatest Show On Earth, with just a little help from Damon Runyon and Fellini.

Waits' first all-new album of the new century came in hard and heavy in a post 9/11 world. His old compadre Bruce Springsteen had tapped into the zeitgeist with his reflective *The Rising*. But in the idiosyncrasies and poignancy of *Real Gone*, Waits sought solace from his homeland, while casting open arms to a wider world. At one point he sings: "I want to believe in the mercy of the world again" – a line he borrowed from a Bob Dylan interview.

The absence of piano on *Real Gone* was frequently remarked upon. Ever since *Heartattack & Vine* Waits had switched between piano and guitar, but he was still most frequently pictured at the keyboard. Waits did have a piano in the studio for *Real Gone*, but it wound up being used as "the end table", covered with coats and drinks and other detritus. It was like Waits had taken his instrument of choice and torched it; and as it blazed, the piano man bid his final goodnight to old Broadway.

But *Real Gone* marked another kind of departure for Waits. Perhaps unsurprisingly, given that it had been written in the aftermath of the Twin Towers atrocities and the subsequent war in Iraq, and was recorded with the election of 2004 looming, this was the most overtly political album of Waits' career. Besides the standout song on *Real Gone*, 'Day After Tomorrow', a political dimension was also evident on 'Hoist That Rag' and 'Sins Of My Father'.

It should have come as no surprise that as one of America's most articulate songwriters, Waits would feel compelled to comment on the upcoming presidential elections, his country's slow drift to the right and the terrible reality of the ongoing war in Iraq. "I guess saying absolutely nothing is a political statement all of its own. I want to get Bush out of there, but I don't know if Kerry is the answer. I think we really have a one-party system with two heads on it."[1]

'Day After Tomorrow' was the album's best song, and the one on which Waits' indignation shone most brightly. It also featured his most sensitive and affecting vocal, making it the song that critics immediately picked up on when reviewing the album. It was a poignant classic – a style of which Waits is a past-master, but to which he has lately seemed reluctant to return. Whatever the reasons, there is no denying that 'Day After Tomorrow' is the strongest song he has written in years.

The plaintive epistle contained within the song; the young soldier's fears of life, and death; the yearning for home from a faraway war . . . all informed the song. But 'Day After Tomorrow' also evoked a sense of cosy family familiarity which recalled 'Rocking Chair', a long-forgotten song on the second album from The Band, and Robbie Robertson's touching inquiry: "Wouldn't it be nice just to see the folks, and listen once again to the stale ol' jokes?"

Waits sings fondly of such mundane pleasures as shovelling snow and raking leaves, but inevitably, given its subject matter, the song also touches on the bigger questions, such as "How does God choose/ who's [sic] prayers does he refuse?" The result is strength and fear, cosiness and horror, in equal measure; and an achingly intense scar of a song, timeless and evocative – which speaks of a real life being lived, long after the song itself has finished.

The power of 'Day After Tomorrow' clearly owed much to the fact that Waits' own son Casey had come of age at the time of the Iraq war. "My son and all of his friends are draft age and they are all heading into the world, and it's looking like the whole world is at war." But Waits' song also held echoes of his own adolescence, growing up near the military base in San Diego, and coming of age during the Vietnam War.

Plaintive and pleading, 'Day After Tomorrow' was a soldier's letter home, desperately hoping that he wouldn't let his buddies down. Waits indignation was apparent and heartfelt: "These ads for the Army, they're ridiculous. They all play rock'n'roll . . . Do you think that a senator sleeping in a nice warm bed looks at a soldier as anything more than a spent shell casing?"[2]

In a strange reversal of the norm, in the rebellious, youth-dominated world of rock'n'roll, it was, for the most part, middle-aged men like Tom Waits who were openly speaking out against the war in Iraq. Along with Bruce Springsteen, John Fogerty and Steve Earle, Waits was one of the few famous voices raised in protest. With the notable exception of Green Day, it was as if the young pretenders were too terrified of losing T-shirt sales and tour sponsorship to risk raising their heads over the parapet. And on a practical level, they were probably right. Just think of the stink that followed The Dixie Chicks' throwaway criticism of President Bush made on stage in Shepherds Bush – a furore which quickly echoed round the world. The trio's new album *Home* was subsequently removed from radio playlists all over America; and, in certain states, copies of the CD were ceremonially burnt.

The shock America felt following the impact of 9/11 reverberated around the world and tested Bush's new-found presidency to the limit. To his credit, Tony Blair did attempt to sound a cautionary note in the immediate aftermath, warning Bush against a global scorched-earth policy against anyone who wasn't shot through with the red, white and blue. But Bush went ahead regardless, and soon soldiers and civilians alike were dying daily.

When the weapons of mass destruction failed to materialise, warning bells began to ring, and it became obvious that we had been taken to war, at best under a flag of deceit; at worst, on the wilful lies of our leaders.

For all the horrors of Saddam Hussein's regime, people around the world were chary of the military muscle being flexed against Iraq. And – young, middle-aged and old – they came out onto the streets in their millions to protest. Waits was only one of many who was mistrustful of his president's motives and intentions.

Seeking a second term in such a highly charged climate, the 2004 presidential debates between Bush and his Democratic opponent, John Kerry, were instructive: if an alien had arrived, been placed in front of a television set, and asked which of the two men looked and sounded most presidential, Kerry would undeniably have swung the ET vote.

By all accounts, Kerry had already won the rock'n'roll community over – and they were now doing their level best to broaden his appeal. It was Bruce Springsteen, R.E.M., Pearl Jam and John Fogerty who in a 2004 tour asked the American electorate to Rock The Vote. Waits himself was not on board, he did, however, donate 'Day After Tomorrow' to a fund-raising anti-Bush compilation, *Future Soundtrack For America*, on which he appeared alongside R.E.M. and Blink-182.

'Sins Of My Father' from *Real Gone* made mention that "the game is rigged", leaving the listener in little doubt about which state and which result it was referring to. But the song's leisurely 10-minute stroll also found space for reference to Stephen Foster's Jeannie (with the light brown hair) as well as the Tyburn jig.

It was typical of Waits to write about the dance that the condemned did at the end of a rope. Up until 1783 Tyburn Tree, which stood near the site of the present Marble Arch, was where public hangings took place. Victims with sufficient means paid the hangman a guinea to ensure a quick and painless death, otherwise they might be left half-alive, dancing "the Tyburn jig". For the hanging of "Spring-Heeled Jack" (Jack Shepherd) in 1714, a crowd of 200,000 gathered at Tyburn. It was the hangman's habit after an execution to sell off the rope – for 6d an inch! This was precisely the sort of arcane information that Waits relishes, and which he cheerfully used to deflect and bamboozle those bothersome interviewers.

Sailing past 50, Waits was still busy competing against himself, fending off competition, and striving against the horrors of repetition or predictability. "Fighting against decay," he admitted, while conceding that "old trees produce the best fruit". With his three children now teenagers, this was also a good moment for Waits to reflect on his role as a parent: "Your kids are not your fans, they're your kids. The trick is to have a career and have a family. It's like having two dogs that hate each other and you have to take them for a walk every night."[3]

As a parent, Waits never ceases to marvel at his children's imagination. Talking once to Pete Silverton in *Vox*, he remembered a trip to Graceland with Casey: "My little boy said, 'I wish they'd dig him up and take all his teeth out so I can make a necklace.' I don't think anybody had thought of that yet: Elvis' teeth necklace!" The child has obviously inherited those weirdly macabre genes from somewhere . . .

Real Gone, for all its laudable attempts at diversity and innovation, quite often sounded like variations on Lee Dorsey's 'Working In The Coal Mine' – particularly on 'Don't Go Into That Barn'. Or perhaps Tom had been drifting off to sleep, with the fractured rhythms of Sam Cooke's 'Chain Gang' still ringing in his ears.

He even impressed himself with 'Metropolitan Glide', "a dance number" which, for Waits, evoked long-ago memories of the Twist, the Mashed Potato, the Stomp and the Watusi. Though quite what the kids of today would think about taking to the dance floors and whipping the air "like a Rainbow Trout", or braying "like a calf", is perhaps best left to the imagination.

'Dead And Lovely' was a stately minuet, a poignant reflection on one of those strange "what on earth do they see in each other?" relationships. 'Circus' was the sound of Tom Waits just like you'd want him to be, were you to bump into him at a bus stop or in a bar: gravelly, worldly wise and with a slew of stories, each as good as a royal flush in Texas Hold 'em. But the tone changes starkly on 'Green Grass' . . . there is no mistaking the voice here, this is Waits as stalker rather than suitor. And that's one of the artist's charms: he doesn't need to be liked in his work, he wants the songs, and their weird and warped characters, to stand on their own.

'How's It Gonna End' is an intriguing portmanteau observation, involving fragments of people's lives: the wife who walks out; the murder victim; the catcher in the rye. And what we want to know, what Waits *needs* to know, is just that: how is it going to end? Will we make it through the night? Or see tomorrow . . . which as any fule kno, is another day. And the day after that . . . the day after tomorrow?

Real Gone may not have carried the emotional resonance of *Mule Variations*, but in a world of wretched talent shows, tragic cover versions and pinched lack of imagination, it continued to mark Waits out as an individual voice. That indignant roar against conformity and lazy music still raged loud and hard.

Chapter 38

The UK playback for *Real Gone* took place in Fitzrovia, a rakish territory, neither Soho, nor Bloomsbury; an artistic haven in the West End, and an appropriately bohemian enclave. One summer evening, a hundred or so hacks gathered for warm beer and the opportunity to eavesdrop. It was rather like a school assembly. Rows of chairs were laid out in lines, the album was relayed through speakers, but there was nothing to look at – no lyrics, no visuals. Just the sight of a host of heads bent to try and catch Waits' words as they spilled out. Then at the end of the first hour (there were 72 minutes of *Real Gone* to sit through), eyes meandered around the studio's baffled walls . . . and notes were made . . . Attention must be paid . . .

That familiar growl filled the room with deranged gospel, unsettling spirituals, a rhumba from beyond the grave, a guitar figure that sounded like the musical equivalent of a monkey tapping out Chekhov on a typewriter . . . This is the soundtrack to the twenty-first century, the soundtrack to Armageddon, cracked voices and dislocated melodies scratched out against desolate cityscapes and a ravished countryside . . .

Real Gone is the sound of a shotgun wedding between Alan Lomax and 50 Cent . . . Spiders webs and Miss Havisham inhabit antebellum mansions, but in the distance there are plangent echoes of 57th Street walk-ups and previous occupants . . .

Here are field hollers and hip hop. Tangos and tarantellas. Blues and bossa nova. It is ironic – but somehow wonderful – that, in 2004, with digital remastering the norm and all that technology available at the flick of a switch, Tom Waits is still working hard to make every record sound as scratched and worn as a cracked, but much-loved 78.

Waits himself was to recall that wilfully retro sound with fondness when he came to talk about *Real Gone*. He remembers the illicit thrill that came with the vinyl bootlegs he obtained during the Seventies, particularly Dylan's legendary *Basement Tapes*: "I like my music with the rinds and the seeds and pulp left in . . . so the bootlegs I obtained . . . where the noise and grit of the tapes became inseparable from the music, are essential to me."[4]

Real Gone came rich in resonance. Like Tom asks, in the end, and at the end: how's it gonna end? And even if *Real Gone* isn't up there in any list of favourite albums; even if you don't take to any of Tom Waits' records; even if you think he's just an overblown and inflated talent, a critics' favourite . . . You just can't help but *like* ol' Tom.

Tom's the drunken uncle who livens up the dreary and predictable family Christmas; the weird relative that makes every funeral memorable.

Tom's the guy who nails you with his needle eye and tells you tales, weaves his words, spins you yarns . . . And he has a turn of phrase as tight as the lock of a London taxi.

The reviews for *Real Gone* were for the most part effusive. "Compared to this, Waits' 1992 racket *Bone Machine* was well-oiled chamber pop," reckoned David Fricke in *Mojo*; while Pat Long in *NME* found *Real Gone* "not by any means easy listening. It is, though, possibly a new type of music. And how often can you say that?" The *Independent* was positive and unqualified: "Album of the week, any week of the year."

Elsewhere though, there was an uneasy sense that perhaps this time round Waits was ploughing an all-too-familiar furrow. In *Tracks*, R.J. Smith wrote: "Tom Waits has made a great Tom Waits album that doesn't amble off in any new direction so much as it digs deeper into his familiar affectations."

Long-time Waits watcher Barney Hoskyns also struck a cautionary note in *Uncut*: "Since it's hard – and possibly verboten – to say a bad word about Tom Waits, unholy shaman of whacked-out Americana, I'll content myself with expressing a few mild reservations . . . with 2002's *Alice* and *Blood Money*, it seemed he was veering off into wilfully art-wank . . . territory . . . A whole album on the vein of 'Day After Tomorrow' might be the most radical thing Tom Waits could do next. One from the heart, in other words."

NOTES

1 *Uncut*
2 Jonathan Valania, *Magnet*
3 Jonathan Valania, *Magnet*
4 *Observer* Music Monthly

CHAPTER 39

TO ensure *Real Gone* received its due attention (and save our hero the trouble of leaving town), the world's press were once again bussed out to California. This time, the venue was the Little Amsterdam restaurant (described, politely, as "ramshackle") where Waits held court, while the owner looked on in bafflement. A retired Dutch sailor with a penchant for bullfighting memorabilia, he had little knowledge of, or interest in, his celebrity guest: "Never heard of Tom Wait . . ."

As ever though, the visiting inquisitors were nimbly fended off whenever Waits felt they were getting too close. Typical was Richard Grant, writing for the *Daily Telegraph*: "How are things at home? How would he describe the basic dynamics of his family?" the journalist politely enquired. "He clears his throat with a sound like a pneumatic drill and clomps over to the coffee pot with a loop of underwear caught up in his belt. He sits back down and says, 'Do you know what the girls use for hair mousse in jail? They use Jolly Ranchers [a popular brand of boiled sweet]. They melt it in a spoon and slick back their hair with it. Sets solid and tastes good.'"

Waits is obsessive in the collecting and hoarding of all matters trivial ("You know there's a device that they invented during World War II that could print 4,000 words on a surface the size of a piece of rice?"). It's a useful smokescreen, which he uses deftly to deflect interviewers, and it also provides him with a wealth of spurious information which one day may, or may not, feature in a song. You get the impression that he's the kind of guy, had he the serious money required, who would be up there alongside Michael Jackson, bidding for the Elephant Man's skeleton. Except, knowing Waits, he'd end up using it as an umbrella stand.

Lurking in the limelight for over 30 years now, Tom Waits has become adept at storytelling – and at telling tales of the shaggy dog variety. Journalists talk of his inbuilt defence mechanism; of how, when the questions get too close to home, Waits will arch an eyebrow and peer intimidatingly over his half-moon glasses. Pausing, he will wander off on a tangent, or make some oblique connection. More likely, he will throw up a smokescreen of trivia, culled from *Ripley's Believe It Or Not*. It is done partly to delight ("Louis XIV owned 413 beds"), but also, ultimately, to keep the international inquirer at arm's length.

Courteous, but distant, Waits retreats like a tortoise back into its shell as soon as anything approaching a personal inquiry about himself, his wife or family hoves into view. He may be reluctant to give much away, but time spent with Tom is rarely wasted. And though it may be just another way of obfuscating, his technique is vastly more entertaining – even charming – than the straightforward grumpy stonewalling employed by others (mentioning no names . . .).

Journalists spend a large portion of their working lives sequestered in hotel suites, while this or that "artiste" blathers on at length about their current product. The subject steadfastly ignores all links or references to earlier work, while the same PA who promised a good three-quarters of an hour, starts making urgent windmilling motions 15 minutes into the interview. At worst it can be like Chinese water-torture; at best a numbing and desultory experience. But when the thumbscrews are applied, Waits can squeeze a lot of juice from the interview satsuma.

One lucky representative of the fourth estate learned all about a book Tom had been reading called *Manifold Destiny*: "It's about all of the different things you can cook with the engine of your car . . ." But fascinated as you may be by that, or indeed by the mating habits of scorpions, what you really long to know is just how the creative partnership of Mr and Mrs Waits actually *works*. Inevitably you are more curious about how Waits now regards his early boho image, or how he looks back on his mid-Eighties Frank . . . trilogy, or which film roles he now regrets declining.

But however subtle your technique, you're soon up against the Waits Wall: "I'm not Zsa Zsa Gabor. I'm not Liberace. I'm not a showbiz animal," he insisted to *Time Out*'s Ross Fortune. "My life is different from my career. People will only pry as far as you allow them to . . . I'm very careful about what I allow to be public and what I allow to be private."

It was a distinction he was determined to maintain. After meeting Waits in 1992, Adam Sweeting wrote in the *Guardian* that, "questions aimed at provoking career analysis or self-assessment get Waits measuring the distance between himself and the exit". In fairness though, Waits is rarely truculent, and almost always gives very good interview – though it may not be the interview your editor sent you to get. Like Bob Dylan who, when asked how an interview was going, complained: "OK, but he keeps asking me *questions* . . .", Waits simply mistrusts the formality of the whole interview process: "I don't like direct questions," he told Sweeting later, offering a concise insight, "I like to *talk* . . ."

And talking is something he's *very* good at. No rock star, save perhaps Bob Dylan at his mercurial mid-Sixties peak, ever gave such good copy as Tom Waits. Even responding to those tediously predictable question-naires, Waits managed to bring something fresh to the encounters. (Which words or phrase do you most overuse? "Do as I say and no one will get hurt"; What do you most value in your friends? "Jumper cables and a tow chain"; On what occasion do you lie? "Who needs an occasion?")[1]

Waits once clarified his elliptical approach to the interview process: "Always answer the question you *wish* they'd asked you . . ." Next thing we know he'll be running for office . . .

Having observed Waits first-hand over the years, the UK writer and journalist Barney Hoskyns thinks he has worked out what really upsets him about interviews: "I think he resents the banality of the questions. You watch a parade of earnest Germans and Danes parading through, all asking the same questions about jazz and the beats. With Waits, you sense his frustration at the lack of reciprocity. There's a fascinating mix of hard-earned wisdom and simmering anger. And that cantankerous side is channelled into humour."

For nearly a quarter of a century Waits has retained the same UK publicist, Rob Partridge, who admits: "If he were being honest, I'm sure Tom would say he prefers not to give interviews, but he recognises the benefits. Whether his stories are all true though, it's a matter of conjecture.

"Some of the more bizarre ones that people assume are invented turn out to be true. A few years ago he told a journalist about a cucumber slug festival in his home town during which the local population would cook up these slugs and eat them. Everyone thought he was making it up, but it was true. On the other hand, he didn't send his children to military academy . . . !"[2]

It was at the London playback of *Real Gone* that Rob Partridge was finally able to give the long-awaited positive response to that second Most Frequently Asked Question in Waitsworld: Is Tom going to tour? Well, yes, up to a point . . . Tom Waits' 2004 UK "tour" was at last confirmed – it would consist of a single date.

"You want to make sure that your demand is much higher than your supply," Waits cautioned *The Times*. It was sage advice: Waits had donated the best years of his life to touring, and it had taken its toll. Working with Coppola on *One From The Heart* had been recuperative, and restorative. His subsequent marriage had given him a real sense of home, and three children – all blessings to be savoured.

At the time he quit touring, Waits explained that "the uncontrollable urge to play Iowa has finally left me". With fatherhood, that urge had become non-existent. "These long tours make me even more grumpy," he told David Sinclair. "I leave home and my family. I'm dealing with tickets and cabs and theatres. And hotels. Four walls, a TV and an ice machine. I used to like it, but now I really have had it after two weeks."

This aversion to prolonged absences also explained Waits' recent reluctance to accept acting roles. But, maybe, just maybe, with daughter Kellesimone away at college, and the prospect of his other children quitting the roost, Waits might feel more inclined toward extra-curricular activities in the not too distant future.

The rarity value of Tom Waits in concert certainly lent a real air of frenzy to his November 2004 London show – ironically, the only similarly anticipated London gig I can recall was Bruce Springsteen's appearance at the same Hammersmith venue almost 30 years before.

Prior to the show, the excitement was almost tangible. An autographed copy of *Real Gone* was sold online for £265: less than a signed Jennifer Lopez T-shirt, but nonetheless a respectable sum for someone not blessed with such a memorable figure. *Record Collector* reported vinyl copies of Waits' *Bone Machine* and *The Black Rider* exchanging hands for up to £120; but warned "to play it safe, I'd have to say that your records are worth what you paid for them, but they could go for a lot more, as long as this brief flurry of interest in Waits continues."

Time Out ran a competition to win signed copies of *Real Gone* leading up to the London shows. "Inundated? You don't know the meaning of the word . . ." the magazine breathlessly reported. Entrants had to describe – in no more than 20 words – Tom Waits' voice. Among the five lucky winners were: "A wasp trapped in a box, content often to ghost around but prone to suffering bouts of lucid frustration" (Mark Terry); "A house brick being scrubbed up and down with a cheese grater" (David Guy); and "It sounds like riding a rusty merry-go-round at two in the morning in some time-forgotten coastal town" (Michael Lam). Waits himself recently likened his own tubes to "the sand in the sandwich".

For years critics and fans had existed on a diet of Chinese whispers, second-hand accounts and rumours of Tom Waits in concert. Here at last was the weird made flesh – and Waits' forthcoming concert date was greeted with barely subdued hysteria among the chattering classes. It had been 17 years since Waits last played London. Indeed, many of that 2004 audience, salivating at the prospect of witnessing the wizened wizard in performance, had still been at primary school the last time Waits hit town.

Chapter 39

As soon as the date was announced, there were 78,000 ticket applications for the 3,700 or so available seats; Waits would have had to play nearly a month of dates to satisfy the demand in full. Tickets for the November 23 date sold out within 20 minutes, though some of them changed hands later for up to £900.

Tom Waits was the hot ticket that autumn night – mere mortals rubber-necked as Jerry Hall, Thom Yorke, Johnny Depp, David Gray, Norman Cook, Zoe Ball, Jamie Cullum, Tim Burton and Helena Bonham-Carter briefly became ordinary people as they filed in to witness the show.

The pre-show tape came from another time: music from the Alan Lomax collection and the Carter Family wafted over the beautiful people as they delicately picked their way through the decades-old chewing gum and sticky lager of the auditorium floor. Today, it may well be branded the Carling Apollo Hammersmith, but to anyone with a shred of rock'n'roll in their sinews it will always be the Hammersmith Odeon.

Part of Waits' delay in returning to England's green and pleasant, he claimed, was due to the lack of a suitable venue. So, Bjork had played the Royal Opera House; Brian Wilson had made it down to the Eden Project in Cornwall; and Tony Bennett had cropped up in a Somerset field . . . but Tom Waits had waited 17 years to be sure of getting the Hammersmith Odeon?

Coming on promptly just after eight, dressed all in black, Waits *looked* like a down-on-his-luck undertaker touting for trade. But he swept on more like a fire and damnation preacher, ranting, railing and roaring, against the sins of the flesh.

The waiting piano was studiously ignored; instead Waits wielded maracas like he was trying to shake the brains out of an irritating budgie. He grasped the microphone stand with both hands, as if to throttle it. And then, to a cheer, out came the megaphone. It was, it struck me, a strange way for a father of three to occupy his evenings.

But this was a family show, with son Casey back of stage, fiddling turntables, pounding percussion, keeping an eye on the old man. ("It's kind of inevitable," Waits Senior confirmed, "if you go into the family business. I told him, if you want to be an astronaut, I can't help you.") Dad, meanwhile, was making like a sombre marionette, twisting and turning, jerking spasmodically like a *Thunderbird* puppet. (Which of the Tracey brothers does Tom Waits most resemble?) After all those years away, and all the years Waits has under his belt, there was still a surprising *physicality* to the performance. You can actually *feel* the boot-stomping, hard-sweating, hand-wringing manual effort, which leaves an indelible impression when you witness it at first-hand.

It is almost as though Waits gets rid of a lot of his anger in performance. As if in that hammering, stamping, churning, pounding . . . *grinding* work-out, he achieves a type of catharsis that stops him committing unspeakable acts. ("Sometimes when I'm really angry at somebody," Waits once told Mark Rowland, "I try to imagine people that I want to strangle. I imagine them at Christmas in a big photograph with their families, and it helps. It's kept me from homicide.")

The music was junkyard-techno: hammering hollers, yelps of pain, howls of delight – leavened with a sprinkling of percussive throwbacks and clattering glimpses of future shock. He played *real* heavy on *Real Gone*; made occasional forays back, but not too far ('Alice', 'Straight To The Top', 'Jockey Full Of Bourbon', 'Eyeball Kid'); but the best-received song was 'Day After Tomorrow'. Delivered in a plaintive, stark confessional performance, it dwarfed everything that came before.

Novices had heard that he was funny live, and Waits didn't disappoint. He apologised for his absence ("I know it's been 17 years, I know . . . But *you* look good"). Strengthening the bond, Waits explained to his 3,700 new best friends about the "Three Ages of Man: youth, middle-age, and . . . You're looking good!"

He stayed on stage for over two and a half hours, and along the way shared his enthusiasm for a picture of the Virgin Mary that appeared on a grilled cheese sandwich, before digressing into a little natural history: "The male spider spends all night working on his web, and when he has completed it, he uses an appendage – some say his leg, though I am not so sure – to strum it lightly. That sound is irresistible to the female spider. And this . . ." confided Waits, tugging on his guitar, "is the male spider's chord . . ." You certainly don't get that kind of useful detail at a Keane concert.

Waits snaked out for the encores, waving to the front rows, and leering out over the stalls as if he were planning to molest them. An upright piano was wheeled out – and even the *piano* got an ovation. Then the troubadour was back with 'Invitation To The Blues' and 'Johnsburg, Illinois'. As the applause rose, he invited us to 'Come On Up To The House', before concluding with 'The House Where Nobody Lives'. Then he was gone. Hands were clapped raw. Heads were scratched. Just who *was* that masked man . . . ?

Some were frankly baffled, Tim de Lisle in the *Mail On Sunday* described the star as "a man in his mid-fifties who looks like a wino, moves like a hunchback and sings like a dog". But the reviews were generally ecstatic, like this was a second coming. Perhaps the appeal for some lay in never having seen Waits before, and simply feeling privileged to be sharing the same space as the great man . . . Whatever the reason, Tom Waits, London 2004, got the sort of notices he'd normally have to pay someone to write for him.

"Few artists of any note have remained at the peak of their powers for as long as Waits," wrote David Sinclair in *The Times*. "To say that there was a sense of occasion in the auditorium would be putting it mildly. Waits did not disappoint . . . In between songs, Waits regaled us with unlikely anecdotes and tall narrative yarns, leavening the show with his engaging and sometimes macabre touches of vaudeville humour . . . Sitting down at the piano . . . he ended this master class in bohemian rhapsody with an unbelievably poignant rendition of 'The House Where Nobody Lives'. The audience left, seduced and spellbound."

"In 20-plus years of London gig-going," wrote James McNair in *Mojo*, "I have never seen a crowd so rapt. Every mobile has been silenced, people seem lost in personal, Waits-induced reveries, and the great man's charisma is such that you simply can't look away . . . Waits is one of a dying breed; a canny old buzzard who knows that the strict rationing of his live shows helps facilitate irresistibly gung-ho performance when he does come out to play . . ."

The Observer Music Monthly selected Waits' as the gig of the year ("roll on 2021 . . ."); while *Time Out* had it at 52nd in their list of the best London gigs *of all time* – sandwiched between Blur at Alexandra Palace, 1994 and Marvin Gaye, Royal Albert Hall, 1976. ("Waits was haunting, askew, smoky, rattled, beautiful, broken and violent.")

Asked at the end of a remarkable 2004 to look back on "the best thing I've heard all year", Waits was suitably opaque, selecting *Shakin' The Rafters*, an album by Alex Bradford & The Abyssinian Baptist Church Choir ("Tony Bennett said this was the greatest rock'n'roll record ever recorded . . . Astonishing, awesome. You will be saved.")[3]

Rolling on into 2005 on a wave of renewed interest, Waits was nominated as 'Best International Male Solo Artist' at the 2005 Brit Awards, alongside Eminem, Brian Wilson, Kanye West and Usher (he lost to the artist formerly known as Marshall Mathers).

While the buzz surrounding his return to live performance overshadowed all other activities, there was a residual interest in his acting career. Waits, after all, was one of the few "rock stars" to have made a decent fist of film acting. By now, he had been away from the screen for half a decade, but he didn't seem to be missing the bright klieg lights. "Acting is not something that I really pursue," he told Jonathan Valania in 2004, "I like to say that I'm not really an actor but I do a little acting. I'm not really looking for something, but if something came along that I really loved, I would do it."

Waits was resigned about his film acting career. He knew that he was not leading man material, and he didn't have the commitment to pursue a serious career as a character actor. Besides, with a regular income from his songwriting, there was little real incentive for him. "I have fun with it," he told Dave Fanning in *Hot Press*, "I meet interesting people and go to weird places."

Talking earlier, Waits had suggested that he was actively looking for roles that would expand his repertoire – "an attorney, a certified public accountant". But following his appearance as Renfield in Coppola's *Bram Stoker's Dracula*, Waits extraordinarily angular face and off-kilter personality had casting agents filing him firmly under "eccentric". What he did get offered, and regularly, were "drunken Irish piano players . . . and Satanist cult leaders".

Jim Jarmusch's *Coffee And Cigarettes* – finally released in 2003, though filming had begun a decade earlier – did feature a Waits cameo. He and a gnarled, but nonetheless engaging Iggy Pop shared a booth, getting jiggy over who's more famous, while squaring up to a packet of left-behind Marlboro. Waits stumbles in, trying to convince Iggy that he combines a career in music with one of medicine ("there's nothing worse than road-side surgery"). Everything gets Waits' goat: the quality of the coffee, the absence of his records on the jukebox, and Iggy's suggestion that he recruit a professional drummer.

The downside was, that with nothing to do but sit in a booth with Iggy, drinking coffee and smoking cigarettes, Waits got hooked back on nicotine, 20 years after quitting. And quitting is *tough*. I once asked Lou Reed which was hardest to give up, heroin or nicotine? Cigarettes affirmed the man in black emphatically, but even then, after many years away from the weed, Reed characterised himself as still "in mid-quit". "But hey," Waits joked in 2004, "it takes a real man to quit *twice*."

Coffee And Cigarettes was 93 minutes of inconsequential chat, lapped up eagerly by those who should know better. Aside from Tom'n'Iggy, Jarmusch's black-and-white ennui was momentarily enlivened by a bum-clenching cameo from Alfred Molina and a supercilious Steve Coogan. These were shaggy-dog stories, anecdotes and lectures, all without a purpose, and most withering without an ending. Unsurprisingly, it was panned by the mainstream press, with the *Daily Telegraph*'s take being fairly typical: "a flimsy grab-bag of vignettes . . . Bill Murray, Iggy Pop, Tom Waits, Steve Coogan et al., whose characters trade barbs and banter, imagining they're cool, but invariably proving to be anything but".

Though he was keeping film appearances in abeyance, Waits could now be *heard* all over the big white screen. Mr and Mrs Waits wrote 'The World Keeps Turning' to play over the end credits of *Pollock*, Ed Harris' 2000 Oscar-winning biopic of the abstract artist Jackson Pollock – or "Jack the Dripper" as he was known. That same year, Waits contributed a new song, 'Puttin' On The Dog', to the soundtrack of Barry Levinson's Baltimore coming-of-age drama, *Liberty Heights*.

In 2002, two new bluesy Waits songs ('Long Way Home' and 'Jayne's Blue Wish') appeared alongside R.L. Burnside and Tom Verlaine on the soundtrack of *Big Bad Love*. The film was directed by actor Arliss Howard, who had appeared in Kubrick's *Full Metal Jacket* as well as *The Lost World: Jurassic Park*. The tale of a Vietnam veteran, *Big Bad Love* also starred Angie Dickinson – and, making a return to the screen after a long absence, Debra Winger (aka Mrs Arliss Howard). All these songs would eventually appear a few years later, on Waits' catch-all collection *Orphans* . . .

The DVD premiere of *One From The Heart* during 2004 attracted considerable interest. Looking back, Coppola himself admitted "it may be a bit wacky . . . [but] there is, I hope, a charm of its own." Enthusing in a five-star review for *Uncut*, Chris Roberts opened: "It does for love what *Apocalypse Now* did for war . . . Now it's ripe for reappraisal: open your heart and let the neon flood in."

After a six-year absence, Tom The Actor did eventually reappear in Tony Scott's 2005 biopic, *Domino*, which stared Keira Knightley as the real-life daughter of film star Laurence Harvey, who became a bounty hunter. Quite what made Waits choose *Domino* for his cinematic return is frankly baffling. Shot in a contemporary style that would make an MTV video look like *The Birth Of A Nation*, *Domino* is the type of twenty-first-century film where the costume designer is known simply as "B" and every other word in the script is "fuck". Nastily crafted, *Domino* revels in its gore: in a grisly homage to the ear-lopping of *Reservoir Dogs*, an arm is gorily amputated to the strain of 'Mama Told Me Not To Come'.

Besides Keira Knightly (whose incongruous, perfectly rounded vowels can be heard pronouncing "This ain't Sunset Boulevard!"), *Domino* assembles one of the weirdest casts of recent years: Jacqueline Bisset, Mo'nique, Christopher Walken, Macy Gray, Lucy Liu and – never mind the botox – it's Mickey Rourke!

Waits is at first heard, rather than seen, when 'Cold Cold Ground' plays as Domino flushes her pet goldfish down the toilet. He makes his appearance later in an appropriately battered Cadillac in the middle of a desert after the bounty hunters crash their coach because their coffee was spiked with mescaline . . . Oh, really, don't ask . . .

Ironically, Waits' performance as a Bible-waving preacher is resonant. At one point he gleefully informs Domino and her lawless compadres that they "will all die contorted, and you will die unforgiven"; and he also gets to mouth off on a fire-sacrifice motif, and a colourful "blood of the lambs" riff.

Dismal as *Domino* was, it was probably no worse than most of the multiplex mediocrity currently on offer. "We are dealing with an audience that is primarily under 25 and divorced from any literary tradition," the acerbic Billy Wilder once griped. "They prefer mindless violence to solid plotting; four-letter words to intelligent dialogue; pectoral development to character development. Nobody *listens* any more. They just sit there, waiting to be assaulted by a series of shocks and sensations." And Wilder was moaning about the state of cinema in *1975*!

Just before Christmas 2005, posters appeared all over Paris advertising the new Roberto Benigni film, *La Tigre e la Neve* (*The Tiger and The Snow*), "avec le participation de Tom Waits". Based in Iraq just before the American invasion, the film stars Benigni as Attilio, an Italian poet, and features Waits as a singer . . . well, himself really. Unfortunately, at the time of writing, the film has yet to secure a UK release, but Waits' song from the film, 'You Can Never Hold Back Spring', is included on his 2006 *Orphans* collection.

At around the same time, *Variety* announced that *Hamlet* was "to be remade as a Modern-Day Indie film", set in east Texas in the late Eighties and entitled *Texas Lullaby*, in which "a young man is tortured by the mysterious death of his father. He's trying to figure out how it happened and why his mother is now married to his dad's brother, the town sheriff." Waits is mentioned in the proposed cast, headed by Josh Hartnett, John Malkovich, Ellen Barkin and Alison Lohman.

Waits' name also features in the cast of the tantalising-sounding *Wristcutters: A Love Story*, whose tagline describes it as "an offbeat comedy, a love story, a road movie – but everybody's dead!" Although premiered at the 2006 Sundance film festival, the movie has yet to be given a full UK release.

A reunion with Meryl Streep was also planned, in Robert Altman's 2006 film of Garrison Keillor's *A Prairie Home Companion,* which would turn out to be Altman's last film, but in the end clashing commitments had Waits reluctantly decline.

His film appearances may now be more sporadic, but Waits' court appearances continue unabated. Legally, it seems, Waits just won't let it lie. Early in 2005, the self-confessed "really grumpy guy" was further riled by Opel Cars' use of a soundalike in a German TV advert. He got to hear about that one thanks to keen-eared Scandinavian fans. And Waits was incensed. "This is the third car ad, after Audi in Spain and Lancia in Italy. If I stole an Opel, Lancia or Audi, put my name on it and resold it, I'd go to jail."[4]

He did have a point. But at times, like The Rolling Stones back in 1967, Waits seemed to be spending more time in court than in the recording studio. "I have a long-standing policy against my voice or music being used in commercials and I have lawyers investigating my options. They hire impersonators. They profit from the association. And I lose time, money and credibility. What's that about? It's painful and humiliating . . . Commercials are an unnatural use of my work . . . it's like having a cow's udder sewn to the side of my face. Painful and humiliating."

Working up a full head of steam, Waits railed: "Apparently, the highest compliment our culture grants artists nowadays is to be in an ad – ideally naked and purring on the hood of a new car. I have adamantly and repeatedly refused this dubious honour. Currently accepting, in my absence, is my German doppelganger. While the court can't make me active in radio, I am asking it to make me radioactive to advertisers."[5]

In *The Word*, David Hepworth quoted "the words of an ad man who once offered Waits a Diet Coke commercial 'you never heard anyone say no so fast!'" In a world where large corporations wield tremendous power, and there really is no business like BIG business, you have to admire Waits' steadfast refusal to let his material be hijacked. Composer Gavin Bryars recalled Waits' last words to him after their collaboration. "He said, 'If ever some bastard comes up with a wine called Jesus' Blood, don't let them use the piece for a commercial.' Nobody has. But I wouldn't."

Early in 2006, it was announced that a Spanish court had awarded Waits "several thousand euros" in compensation from Volkswagen-Audi. The Barcelona ruling found that the car manufacturer had breached the artist's copyright when they used an impersonator and altered the lyrics of his song 'Innocent When You Dream' to help promote their cars. It was a landmark in Spanish legal history: the first time ever that a court there had upheld an artist's moral rights in a copyright case.

"Now they understand the words to the song better," Waits commented. "It wasn't 'Innocent When You Scheme', it was 'Innocent When You Dream'." The fight, however, continues and at the time of writing, Waits has just reached a legal settlement with Adam Opel AG and their advertising agency in the German courts.

It isn't just a question of the cash. Waits has a deep respect for his own moral rights – and, not unreasonably, he expects them to be respected by others. Financially though, Waits need never worry again. By now he must have enough put by to see the kids through college, and to keep him in dog food, shoes and trivia books for life.

Money also comes in regularly from a number of successful soundtrack albums. Among others, space was found for Waits material on the wonderfully titled Andy Garcia vehicle *Things To Do In Denver When You're Dead* ('Jockey Full Of Bourbon'); George Clooney's *The Perfect Storm* ('The Heart Of Saturday Night'); *Fight Club* ('Goin' Out West'); and, amazingly, the 2003 teen rom-com *The Prince & Me* ('I Hope That I Don't Fall In Love With You'). Even *Shrek 2* found a little Waits room, and filled it with 'A Little Drop Of Poison'. The soundtrack of that, plus the concomitant CD and DVD releases, should ensure a modicum of financial stability for some time to come.

With the financial pressure off, Waits could afford to indulge himself. He donated a song ('Picture In A Frame') to Willie Nelson's 2004 album, *It Always Will Be*, and also contributed to Eels' *Blinking Lights And Other Revelations*. Mark Everett, (aka E, who is Eels) was particularly keen to involve his hero ("Maybe I'll grow old gracefully like Tom Waits. He's one of the few who will always be a class act . . . He doesn't have the Mick Jagger problem where it starts to look a little silly after a certain age.").

Talking to Andrew Harrison in *The Word*, E explained that when he invited Waits to appear on 'Going Fetal', he had suggested "collapsing on the floor under life's pressure and curling up as if you're getting back into your mother's womb". Waits' typically deadpan response was: "I always wanted to do a dance number." E also had in mind an instrumental solo; but when Waits returned the tape, it had him howling like an angry baby . . . "Then I realised, this is just what I should have expected, and it was exactly right. I pictured him onstage at *American Bandstand*, sliding to the front of the stage on his knees and going 'Waaaaah!' So I added screaming girls. You're never sure if they're screaming in delight or horror." Sounds like the story of Waits' life, so far . . .

Although, in truth, screaming girls have never been a major problem for our hero – as he disarmingly admitted back in the Seventies: "I've never met anyone who made it with a chick because they owned a Tom Waits album," he cracked to anyone who'd listen. "I've got all three, and it's never helped me!"

The see-saw of delight and horror, the dichotomy of "that Jerry Lee Lewis meridian" has always been an integral part of Waits' enduring appeal. Even today, as a happily married, middle-aged father of three, his image precedes him: and people remain convinced that the shambling figure they see on stage really is a drunk, stumbling through, and getting by on bourbon.

But then audiences, particularly rock audiences, have always relished living vicariously. They devour, with glee, accounts of the copious drug intake of their idols. They read with relish of the wanton trashing of hotel rooms. They delight in imagining the groupies and orgies and other priapic antics. It's like . . . the life of a civil servant or stockbroker isn't really that glamorous, and the nearest many of us ever get to a life lived to excess is to by pressing our noses up against somebody else's window.

Over the years, Waits has carefully fashioned his own alter ego. At the beginning, he was the barfly who had stumbled out of an Edward Hopper painting, drunk on dictionaries and loaded on Kerouac. He was the madcap, laughing and waving a bottle of Bushmills as he tugged your heartstrings with a ballad. Waits got right under your skin and left you scratching. Part idiot-savant, and part just plain old-fashioned idiot; he was both beat writ large, and a sensitive soul cast low.

Waits addressed this dilemma when talking to Mick Brown: "Most of us expect artists to do irresponsible things, to be out of control. Somehow we believe that if you're way down there, you're going to bring something back up for us, and we won't have to make the trip. Go to hell with gasoline drawers on and bring me back some chicken chow-mein while you're at it . . . The dice is throwing the man, instead of the man throwing the dice."

NOTES

1   *Vanity Fair* 2004
2   *Music Week*
3   *Mojo*
4   *The Times*
5   *Uncut*

CHAPTER 40

IN an entertainment industry fuelled by celebrity and gossip, and driven by tired unimaginative formulae, Tom Waits stands out as defiantly individual. And in a world swamped by mediocre machine-made music, his songs bear the tell-tale flaws and rare beauty of a real craftsman.

There is so much, in so many fields, worth admiring in Waits' activities over the past quarter of a century. Artistically, he rages hard against the dimming of the light. He refuses to bask in former glories, and instead forges wilfully ahead. But, unlike some others of his generation, he does not needlessly court modern fads and favours, nor have his name linked to fashionable producers. Above all, he *absolutely* will not accede to commercial pressures of any kind.

Tom Waits has fought hard and consistently against the hijacking of his music for commercial purposes. No other artist of his era has fought so persistently against exploitation – and in a world increasingly dominated by passionless Pop Idols and dreary corporate rock'n'roll, that is an admirable stand to take.

For years, Waits has been scathing about the commercial links between artists and advertisers: "If Michael Jackson wants to work for Pepsi," he suggested, "why doesn't he just get a suit and an office in their headquarters and be done with it?"

There are many who find hope in the work of artists like Tom Waits: a lone voice, howling in the wilderness – but a strangely comforting and important voice for all that. And though some of his more avant-garde work may not make for easy listening, there is something very affecting about an artist who remains so defiantly at odds with an industry where blandness and homogenisation are on the march. As the man himself recently observed: "Contemporary music is like processed cheese – not a lot of nutrition."[1]

The enduring appeal of Tom Waits in the twenty-first century owes much to the vivid, if sometimes uncomfortable, idiosyncrasy of his work and his character. We live increasingly in a world where risk-taking is rare; a world where the young grow up inured against reality; where a whole generation drifts, swaddled in iPods and Bluetooth earpieces. Texting has replaced talking; conversation takes place in anonymous chatrooms; and surfing the net has replaced the walk to the shops. Never have there been so many opportunities for communicating; and never has so little been said.

Couples and friends walk alongside each other, together in name only, each chatting to an unseen third party on the ubiquitous mobile, glued to their ear. Any attempt at a face to face conversation cut short by restless, fidgety thumbs. See them as they drift sullen and self-obsessed through the malls: they could be anywhere in the developed world, the products, the shops, the look, the brand names and logos . . . all exactly the same.

But Waits takes pride in being different. Despite all the disguises and dissembling, he – like the jester in a medieval court – can be relied upon to see through the bullshit. In his review of a 1999 Waits show, for *The New York Times*, Jon Pareles noted: "He looks back to an era before strip malls and multinational branding, when hobos rode the rails and pitchmen set up on street corners instead of Web sites." And it is this doggedly wayward path he has chosen to walk, that makes Waits such a rare and valuable talent.

Writing in 2002, Andy Gill skewered the singular appeal of Waits' work: "Through it all courses a lust for life, in all its myriad forms, that shames the paltry ambitions of lesser artists."

Two years later, in breathless anticipation of his London show, *Time Out* commented: "Of those left standing, probably only Bob Dylan, Randy Newman, Elvis Costello and Nick Cave come close to Waits in stature or gift, and none is ageing quite so gloriously or with such savage mystery and sheer aplomb." (Though I'd quite like to add Richard Thompson and Bruce Springsteen to that list.)

In 1965, Robert Aldrich made *The Flight Of The Phoenix*. It was a gritty, *Boys' Own* tale of the unquenchability of the human spirit. Aldrich gathered together some vintage Hollywood names (James Stewart, Ernest Borgnine, Dan Duryea) and a smattering of others to lend international appeal (Richard Attenborough, Peter Finch, Hardy Kruger) in a yarn sufficiently memorable to be forgettably remade 40 years later with Dennis Quaid.

The original film told of a plane crashing in the African desert (for the convenience of Hollywood, all Africa becomes one enormous desert). Marooned and isolated, the passengers moan, argue and bicker. Then, and here's the clincher, they bond, come together, and manage to rebuild the plane. And in the end – spoiler warning! – they fly out of the desert to safety.

The Flight Of The Phoenix is unifying and life-affirming; it also happens to be one of Tom Waits' favourite films. He uses it as a metaphor for his own life, and profession. And as he has yet to be asked to select his *Desert Island Discs*, we must make the most of this candid confession about how he would cope with the inevitable isolation: "If this was *The Flight Of The Phoenix*," he hold Richard Grant, "and our plane crashed in the middle of the desert and we had to make it fly again, I might be able to successfully compose a ballad about the events once they were over, but during our struggle, I would be radically useless."

While he may not be of much practical use in such an unlikely scenario, as a songwriter Waits has time and again, for over 30 years, proved his mettle. But as with many of his contemporaries, when it comes to discussing the actual mechanics of songwriting – *where* the ideas come from and *how* they are then conveyed in song – Waits is as baffled as anyone.

Yet whenever the subject comes up in interview, Waits is pleasantly discursive, richly imaginative, and thoroughly dramatic in his description of the mysterious process: "Every song is special, they're like birds, you send them out there: some of them get blown out of the sky on the first day, some of them come back, some go across the country . . . My music is kinda like Tabasco, you can use it on fish, fowl or poultry . . . it's kinda like a shipwreck, with all these things floating on the water . . . Some songs you have to hit over the head, drag home, skin, cook and eat . . . Songs are kind of like hats, I look good in this now, maybe I won't tomorrow . . ."[2]

Over the years, Bill Flanagan has extracted some illuminating comments from songwriters on their craft, and Waits was no exception: "There's one song, 'Time', that I can't even play any more. It happened that one time and I haven't been able to get it back . . . Any attempt to recreate that moment is like showing pictures of your family. The pictures never really capture what happened: 'Here I am with Mrs Chalmer. You'd love Chalmer, he's here with Evelyn. And there's Elwood! You can't see all of Elwood, he's behind Ruby. And here's Howard . . .' Well, you had to be there."[3]

For all his glib responses, there is no denying how seriously Waits takes his writing; and beneath all the tongue-in-cheek metaphors, when he talks of his craft, it can offer, however obliquely, an insight into the whole mystifying process. To Bill Flanagan again: "When you're writing, your life is like an aquarium. Some things float and some things don't. Some things breathe and some drown. Some look better and some worse. That's the moment I know I'm writing – when I've filled the room with water!"

When I interviewed him, Waits described his approach to songwriting as making "dangerous choices . . . where to take it, whether to keep it, whether to abandon it. I write sometimes 20 songs and put 12 on the record. The process is . . . *excruciating*."

From Napoleone's Pizza Parlour to his own substantial property, way up the Napa Valley, Tom Waits has dreamed hard and long. An established raconteur and wit; a celebrated songwriter and performer; a screen actor with an impressive CV . . . It's been a long, strange trip. Professionally and personally rewarding, Waits has bided his time.

Reflecting on his musical mood swings, Waits was once asked how he viewed the seismic changes between albums: "The songs were more out of focus, I was trying to give them nervous breakdowns . . ." And in what could act as a definition of a musical odyssey now entering its fourth decade: "I'm trying to take a hammer to what happened. Don't hold a mirror up to it. Hit it with a hammer. Take my advice."

Just when you think Tom Waits has gone as far as he can go, he'll be eyeing that rug and seeing just when, and how far, he can tug it from beneath your feet: "I wrote an orchestral piece once for a squeaky door, a Singer sewing machine and washing machine set on a spin cycle," he cheerfully confided recently to Richard Grant in *Zembla* magazine.

Waits has travelled a long way from that lonesome derelict who used to hang around the Tropicana Motel. Now rural and retiring, for Tom Waits the boozing is nothing but a decade-old memory; the cigarettes consigned unsmoked to the trash can. A Grammy award-winning musician, acclaimed by his peers and his public, he no longer has to endure punishing promotional tours to promote his records. These days, the world comes to Tom Waits – or it does without.

With a loving wife and family, a regular income from cover versions, film soundtracks, record sales and law suits, Waits can look forward to a comfortable future. He's at a place now that few, himself included, figured he'd ever reach. The alcohol abuse, poor diet, chain-smoking and incessant touring took their toll. But he survived. And for Tom Waits now, "on the road" means driving the kids to school, the dump or the corner store.

"I love what I do," Waits marvelled in 2004, "I got the three cherries, y'know. I pulled the handle, and all the quarters came out."[4]

Though notoriously reluctant to look back, if he did, he'd find his name widely dropped, his work acknowledged, his reputation secure. But to his credit, Waits keeps on keeping on, pushing forward, toward an unknown future, where the things he can no longer remember inform the things he will never be able to forget . . .

And so to end . . . As ever, we must return to the beginning . . . When he was celebrating the birth of his first child, daughter Kellesimone, way back when Reagan was in the White House, Waits was asked by Kristine McKenna: "Any advice for your daughter?"

"That you can dream your way out of things and into things," the proud, first-time father replied, as if reflecting on his own life, then entering its fifth decade. "I think you can dream yourself out of some place and into another place that's better for you. To dream hard enough; I hope I can teach her how to do that."

On into the twenty-first century, now edging 60, with the kids leaving home for college and his reputation as a maverick enshrined, Waits like all his contemporaries, is nearer the end than the beginning. But, as he was once so fond of saying: "That's the beauty of showbusiness . . . it's the only business you can have a career in when you're dead."

Mind you, he's not ready to leave the building yet . . . This most quotable of artists and engaging of songwriters was recently asked by *Vanity Fair* "How would you like to die?" And, answering for all of us, Tom Waits responded gravely: "I don't think I would like that very much at all."

NOTES

1   *Time Out*
2   *Time Out*
3   *Written In My Soul*, Bill Flanagan
4   *Time Out*

EPILOGUE

BUT the train kept a-rollin' . . . Like a rusty locomotive on an old Southern Pacific branch line, Waits built up a full head of steam and managed to deliver three discs of flotsam and jetsam. The 54-song, three-hour-plus *Orphans: Brawlers, Bawlers & Bastards*, trundled into view just before Christmas 2006, hauling a snaking cargo of ones that almost got away – and a cornucopia of earthly delights for Waits aficionados.

As he shunted into the fourth decade of his career, Waits seemed to be wilfully meandering off the map, striking out for that uncharted territory marked "Here Be Dragons". Not for him contentment and middle-aged complacency. In the gloaming of his years, Waits was still awash with surprises, and the new material had him pulling 'em out, like rabbits from a hat. "If a record really works at all," Waits confided at the time of the release of *Orphans* . . ., "it should be made like . . . a good woman's purse with a Swiss army knife and a snake bite kit."

Of this latest collection, no fewer than 30 were new songs, while others were culled from soundtracks and tribute albums. There were some out-takes from *Mule Variations*, and some others that were new songs, written while Tom and Kathleen were on a roll from 2004's *Real Gone*.

Here at last were the hard-to-get tributes: 'What Keeps Mankind Alive', 'Books Of Moses', 'King Kong', 'Danny Says'; the long-deleted soundtrack songs: 'Sea Of Love', 'The Fall Of Troy', 'Poor Little Lamb'; the Bukowski, Kerouac and Leadbelly covers; and the songs Waits had let others have: 'Fannin Street', 'Louise', and, of course, 'Down There By The Train' . . .

Orphans: Brawlers, Bawlers & Bastards naturally came with its fair share of new Waitsisms ("I smoked my friends down to the filter", 'Little Drop Of Poison'; "Were you drying your nails, or waving goodbye?", '2:19'; "I want to look in the mirror, and see another face . . .", 'Walk Away'); and the set also introduced some new characters who will always be guaranteed a welcome *chez* Waits: Jockey La Fayette, Big Eyed Al, Peoria Johnson, the 44 Kid, Nimrod Cain . . .

For the first time, *Orphans* . . . contained a namecheck to Waits' longtime muse – on 'First Kiss', a rambling reminiscence of a maybe romance, which ends with a little trill 'bout "my little Kathleen". The concluding song on *Bawlers* saw Waits tackling Sinatra's 'Young At Heart'. It was a straight and poignant reading of a song which Waits would have remembered from his teenage years when, apparently electing to be middle-aged, he was actually trawling round looking for a father – anybody's father.

'Home I'll Never Be' was particularly intriguing: a posthumous collaboration between Waits and Jack Kerouac, on which Waits sets a Kerouac poem to music. And perhaps appropriately, the final track of the whole, reflective collection was another Kerouac/Waits fusion. Kerouac was, after all, the man who had first set Waits off on the road, so hearing Waits croon Kerouac's own 'On The Road' seemed like a very fitting conclusion to such a sprawling, career-embracing collection. (Actually, there are also a couple of – literally – shaggy dog stories as hidden tracks, but why spoil a good conclusion?)

One of Waits' regular collaborators cropped up again on *Orphans* . . . Harmonica virtuoso Charlie Musselwhite had started out by sitting in with Muddy Waters in Memphis. He laid floors for a time, but soon discovered that moonshining paid better, if less regularly . . . When I caught up with him late in 2006, Charlie had just bought the Wholesale Store in Clarksdale, Mississippi, right next door to Morgan Freeman's renowned blues club, Ground Zero. Charlie was a neighbour of Tom Waits': "We first met when we were drinking, so neither of us can remember *when* we first met! But he's quite a character, Tom . . . I hear a lot of the blues in Tom's music . . . The blues is closer to the bone, it nailed the truth . . . The blues is too tough to die."

Blues is just one of the threads that runs through *Orphans* . . . there's also Fifties rock'n'roll ('Lie To Me'); gospel ('Take Care Of All My Children'); fractured country ('Bottom Of The World'); nursery rhyme ('Jayne's Blue Wish'); Irish traditional ('Widow's Grove'); even – surprisingly – some jaunty pop. With the help of a following wind, you could almost imagine 'Long Way Home' as a hit for whichever 15-minute fame-junkie becomes the next *Pop Idol*. Then there's the *just plain weird*, comin' straight atcha from Planet Tom. The spoken-word recitation 'Army Ants' was culled from all over ("*The World Book Encyclopedia* . . . reliable sources . . . the naked eye . . .") and is precisely the kind of wordy weapon Waits commonly uses to keep the inquisitive at arm's length ("if one places a minute amount of liquor on a scorpion, it will instantly go mad . . .").

But it was the jagged ballads that brought the most delight. For all the creative punching above his weight, surely few would listen to Waits' roaring rants, set against a backdrop of staccato hubcap percussion and telegraph wire guitar, for *fun*. It was, after all, Waits the storyteller, the heart-tugger, the eye-moistener, that first made him a family favourite. The ballads on *Bawlers* (significantly, the longest of the three albums), like 'Bend Down The Branches', 'World Keeps Turning', 'Louise', 'If I Have To Go' . . . and many more, all provided fresh fodder with which to cement his reputation. Frail and smoky-voiced; intimate and enticing; this was where Waits got right back into his stride: keeping those plates spinning on his sticks, as he marshalled his bruised and battered cast.

Perhaps though, the most striking of all the 54 songs was the unflinchingly political 'Road To Peace'. Waits had put down his marker with the anti-war protest 'Day After Tomorrow' on 2004's *Real Gone*, but this song was as specific as it was heartfelt: a seven-minute extrapolation on what motivates teenage suicide-bombers in the Middle East. Waits highlights both the suffering and the waste, while pointing the finger at Israeli militarism. But the Middle East conflict has defeated strategists, politicians and bombers for over 60 years, since the formation of Israel, and it is unlikely that any song – even one as good as this – will propel it to a satisfactory conclusion. But Waits accepts his limitations with good grace: "I don't really know what a song like that can achieve," he told Sean O'Hagan in the *Observer*, "but I was compelled to write it. I don't know if meaningful change could ever result from a song. It's kind of like throwing peanuts at a gorilla."

Over the length of the set, Waits' voice – once described as "that of a drunken hobo arguing with a deli owner over the price of a bowl of soup" – reaches sublime new depths. "At the centre of the record is my voice," Waits told Mick Brown, "I try my best to chug, stomp, weep, whisper, moan, wheeze, scat, blurt, rage, whine and seduce. With my voice, I can sound like a girl, the boogieman, a theremin, a cherry bomb, a clown, a doctor, a murderer . . ."

The *Orphans* . . . booklet boasted snapshots of Tom with some of his famous friends: Keith Richards, John Lee Hooker, Fred Gwynne, John Hammond, Nicolas Cage, Roberto Benigni . . . Also reproduced were a handful of the sort of fascinating facts with which Waits delighted in wrong-footing interviewers: "Queen Elizabeth was annoyed by a red nose. Her attendants were accustomed to powder it every few minutes to keep it presentable." And then there were reprints of some of the "famous last words" which Waits so cherished, such as Pitt the Younger's unimpeachably patriotic: "My country! Oh how I love my country" – although less sentimental historians have asserted that the precocious prime minister's final utterance was the rather less resounding: "I think I could eat one of Bellamy's veal pies."

During its first week of release, *Orphans . . .* made a respectable UK chart debut at number 49, below The Beatles, U2, Oasis and – duh – Westlife; but coasting in over the heads of *Greatest Hits* collections by the Carpenters, Gloria Estefan, and The Corrs – and a full five places higher than *Michael Bolton Swings Sinatra*!

In its familiar, elliptical showbiz style, *Billboard* wrote of the album: "Waits swings for the fences and scores on this set . . . vast in scope, rich in trope and full of hope." Other reviews too were uniformly ecstatic: "A boundlessly fascinating treasure trove . . ." (*Uncut*); "an astounding musical creation . . . that nods to almost every known genre of American music, and some that have yet to be named." (*Observer Music Monthly*); "*Orphans . . .* encompasses something like the full breadth of Waits' vision – songs that uplift, entertain and utterly bamboozle, and stuff straying far beyond the frontiers of music." (*Daily Telegraph*); "Tom's victory of style over substance is actually a singularity of vision rather than an artist's egotism. With his unfussy brushstrokes, umber hues and humanely honest delight in warts and all, he is the Rembrandt of modern music." (*Mojo*).

Inevitably, the deaths of Johnny Cash and Ray Charles and the recent passing of James Brown signify that the survivors of that golden age are now a dwindling number – Willie Nelson, Jerry Lee Lewis, Chuck Berry . . . Which means that the spotlight now turns more than ever onto their successors, those they inspired to pick up the baton and run with it into defiant middle-age and beyond . . . Bob Dylan, still in pursuit of something, whether on his Never-Ending Tour, or in the Cairngorms; Pink Floyd, and the nine-figure offers on the table for a reunion tour in the wake of Live 8; and the Stones, still regularly rolling into the record books (their 2006 *A Bigger Bang* dates raked in $437,000,000, making it "the top-grossing tour ever") . . . And then, a little lower down the food chain, there is Tom Waits.

The intensity of interest in Waits' live performances testifies to the loyalty and devotion of his audience. In August 2006 for example, when Waits returned to live performance in Nashville, Tennessee, after a 30-year absence from the state, tickets for his show at the historic Ryman Auditorium sold out in an incredible *three* minutes! And the reason for this return? "I needed to go to Tennessee to pick up some fireworks, and someone in Kentucky owes me money," Waits explained. A rare and welcome performance of 'Tom Traubert's Blues' was trumped by the encore of 'Day After Tomorrow': "one of the most stunning and moving performances to ever grace the stage of Nashville's Mother Church," wrote Lydia Hutchinson in *Performing Songwriter*.

Like the ol' Shep of popular music, Tom Waits just always seems to have been there, a nagging, dissonant, spellbinding presence. The man has been making records for over 30 years; and if it's true that a week is a long time in politics, then three decades is a lifetime in popular music. If it came to talking about singers who were working 30 years before Waits' own career began, you'd be namechecking Glenn Miller, Harry James or Tommy Dorsey.

Waits is seemingly immune to passing fads and fashions; and he effortlessly transcends both genres and generations. At the first-ever Loughborough Folk Festival in October 2006, when Spiers & Boden announced to a capacity crowd that they were going to do a Tom Waits song, the groan was nervous rather than anticipatory. But a heartfelt 'Innocent When You Dream', accompanied by violin and accordion, soon got the folkies singing along, and I was struck by how well a Waits song had slotted into that tradition.

But when it comes to actually engaging with the music business, Tom Waits has consistently kept himself at one remove from the process. The two interviews to promote *Orphans* . . . were undertaken, as per usual of late, at the Little Amsterdam restaurant. Waits was as engaging as ever ("Writing songs is like capturing birds without killing them, sometimes you end up with nothing but a mouthful of feathers"), and as wary as ever of any personal intrusion ("Well, if it matters to anybody other than *me* . . .").

Of an age now when his kids are fleeing the nest and grandchildren may be just over the horizon, Waits doggedly persists in keeping himself to himself. Happy to let his records do the talking, he retreats ever further from the limelight. I remember all those years ago, how surprised I was after spending an afternoon with Waits, just how *shy* he seemed to be. I had always believed that anyone who spent time on stage and in the spotlight would be buoyed up by self-belief and confidence. But despite all the probing, and all the searching for the skull beneath the skin, Waits still prefers to keep himself to himself. What was Marlene Dietrich's epitaph on Orson Welles in *Touch Of Evil*? "He was . . . some kind of man . . ."

Rarer than hen's teeth, or a politician with a hinterland, it seems that Waits may just be that all but extinct specimen: a rock star with a real *life* . . . Yet, despite all the showbiz things he shies away from, Waits still rattles along, picking up passengers at every stop. But then trains have always appeared to preoccupy the writer, and the man. Talking to Sean O'Hagan in 2006, Waits recalled: "When I was a kid and we went on a car trip, it seemed like we had to stop and wait for a train to go by every two miles. Seemed like there were train crossings everywhere, nothing but train crossings."

And you can see why trains would matter to a small-town frontiersman, a rambling American, like Tom Waits. For a whole generation of baby-boomers, they have acted as a symbol of the lost innocence, the Eden before Vietnam and Watergate, Iraq and Guantanamo. For visitors too, they remain the sound – and spirit – of the true America. To stand in, say, Clarksdale, Mississippi, and wait while a freight train lumbers through. And wait . . . and wait . . . as those endless box-cars shake, rattle and roll on their way. Or to be sitting out on the stoop at twilight, and to hear somewhere, way, *way* off, that lonesome whistle blow.

"That's the thing about train travel," Waits explained to Mark Rowland in *Musician*, "at least when you say goodbye they gradually get smaller. Airplanes, people go through a door and they're gone."

"It was a train that took me away from here" Waits once sang, but with weary resignation, he also recognises that a train can never bring him home. Never can. Never will.

Because it's true: you never can go home again. A train can't take you there, nor a car; but maybe, just maybe, a memory can . . . Perhaps a memory inspired by a song – a song that takes you back to a particular time or a certain place. A song that takes you back to a girl, or to the time when first you heard it. And not just any song, but a song that's crafted and which endures. A song whittled by one of a dying breed, like Thomas Alan Waits. A true original. An American original.

Over four decades now, he has defiantly forged ahead in his own shambling, idiosyncratic way. Like Charley Varrick, Walter Matthau's character in the film that appeared the same year Waits made his debut, the singer-songwriter remains "the Last of the Independents". Waits works in his own way, in his own time, to his own ends – and the rest of us, if we know what's good for us, are happy to wait.

DISCOGRAPHY

CLOSING TIME (1973)

Ol' 55; I Hope That I Don't Fall In Love With You; Virginia Avenue; Old Shoes (And Picture Postcards); Midnight Lullaby; Martha; Rosie; Lonely; Ice Cream Man; Little Trip To Heaven (On The Wings Of Your Love); Grapefruit Moon; Closing Time

THE HEART OF SATURDAY NIGHT (1974)

New Coat Of Paint; San Diego Serenade; Semi Suite; Shiver Me Timbers; Diamonds On My Windshield; (Looking For) The Heart Of Saturday Night; Fumblin' With The Blues; Please Call Me, Baby; Depot, Depot; Drunk On The Moon; The Ghosts Of Saturday Night (After Hours At Napoleone's Pizza House)

NIGHTHAWKS AT THE DINER (1975)

Emotional Weather Report; On A Foggy Night; Eggs & Sausage (In A Cadillac With Susan Michelson); Better Off Without A Wife; Nighthawk Postcards (From Easy Street); Warm Beer And Cold Women; Putnam County; Spare Parts I (A Nocturnal Emission); Nobody; Big Joe & Phantom 309; Spare Parts II

SMALL CHANGE (1977)

Tom Traubert's Blues (Four Sheets To The Wind In Copenhagen); Step Right Up; Jitterbug Boy (Sharing A Curbstone With Chuck E. Weiss, Robert Marchese, Paul Body And The Mug And Artie); I Wish I Was In New Orleans (In The Ninth Ward); The Piano Has Been Drinking (Not Me) (An Evening With Pete King); Invitation To The Blues; Pasties & A G-String (At The Two O'Clock Club); Bad Liver And A Broken Heart (In Lowell); The One That Got Away; Small Change (Got Rained On With His Own .38); I Can't Wait To Get Off Work (And See My Baby On Montgomery Avenue)

FOREIGN AFFAIRS (1977)

Cinny's Waltz; Muriel; I Never Talk To Strangers; Medley: Jack & Neal/ California, Here I Come; A Sight For Sore Eyes; Potter's Field; Burma Shave; Barber Shop; Foreign Affair

BLUE VALENTINE (1978)

Somewhere; Red Shoes By The Drugstore; Christmas Card From A Hooker In Minneapolis; Romeo Is Bleeding; $29.00; Wrong Side Of The Road; Whistlin' Past The Graveyard; Kentucky Avenue; A Sweet Little Bullet From A Pretty Blue Gun; Blue Valentines

HEARTATTACK & VINE (1980)

Heartattack & Vine; In Shades; Saving All My Love For You; Downtown; Jersey Girl; 'Til The Money Runs Out; On The Nickel; Mr Siegal; Ruby's Arms

BOUNCED CHECKS (1981)

Heartattack & Vine; Jersey Girl; Eggs & Sausage; I Never Talk To Strangers; The Piano Has Been Drinking; Whistlin' Past The Graveyard; Mr Henry; Diamonds On My Windshield; Burma Shave; Tom Traubert's Blues

ONE FROM THE HEART (1982)

Opening Montage (Tom's Piano Intro; Once Upon A Town; The Wages Of Love); Is There Any Way Out Of This Dream?; Picking Up After You; Old Boyfriends; Broken Bicycles; I Beg Your Pardon; Little Boy Blue; Instrumental Montage (The Tango; Circus Girl); You Can't Unring A Bell; This One's From The Heart; Take Me Home; Presents
[The 2004 reissue included two "previously unreleased bonus tracks" – Candy Apple Red; Once Upon A Town/ Empty Pockets

SWORDFISHTROMBONES (1983)

Underground; Shore Leave; Dave The Butcher; Johnsburg, Illinois; 16 Shells From A 30.6; Town With No Cheer; In The Neighbourhood; Just Another Sucker On The Vine; Frank's Wild Years; Swordfishtrombone; Down, Down, Down; Soldier's Things; Gin Soaked Boy; Trouble Braids; Rainbirds

ASYLUM YEARS (1984)

Ol' 55; Martha; Rosie; Shiver Me Timbers; San Diego Serenade; Diamonds On My Windshield; (Looking For) The Heart Of Saturday Night; The Ghosts Of Saturday Night (After Hours At Napoleone's Pizza House); Small Change; Tom Traubert's Blues; Step Right Up; Burma Shave; Foreign Affair; Mr Henry; The Piano Has Been Drinking (Not Me); Potter's Field; Kentucky Avenue; Somewhere; On The Nickel; Ruby's Arms

RAIN DOGS (1985)

Singapore; Clap Hands; Cemetery Polka; Jockey Full Of Bourbon; Tango Till They're Sore; Big Black Mariah; Diamonds And Gold; Hang Down Your Head; Time; Rain Dogs; Midtown; 9th & Hennepin; Gun Street Girl; Union Square; Blind Love; Walking Spanish; Downtown Train; Bride Of Rain Dogs; Anywhere I Lay My Head

FRANK'S WILD YEARS (1987)

Hang On St Christopher; Straight To The Top (Rhumba); Blow Wind Blow; Temptation; Innocent When You Dream (Barroom); I'll Be Gone; Yesterday Is Here; Please Wake Me Up; Frank's Theme; More Than Rain; Way Down In the Hole; Straight To The Top (Vegas); I'll Take New York; Telephone Call From Istanbul; Cold Cold Ground; Train Song; Innocent When You Dream (78)

BIG TIME (1988)

16 Shells From A 30.6; Red Shoes; Underground; Cold Cold Ground; Straight To The Top; Yesterday Is Here; Way Down In the Hole; Falling Down; Strange Weather; Big Black Mariah; Rain Dogs; Train Song; Johnsburg, Illinois; Ruby's Arms; Telephone Call From Istanbul; Clap Hands; Gun Street Girl; Time

TOM WAITS, THE EARLY YEARS (1991)

Goin' Down Slow; Poncho's Lament; I'm Your Late Night Evening Prostitute; Had Me A Girl; Ice Cream Man; Rockin' Chair; Virginia Avenue; Midnight Lullabye; When You Ain't Got Nobody; Little Trip To Heaven; Frank's Song; Looks Like I'm Up Shit Creek Again; So Long I'll See Ya

BONE MACHINE (1992)

Earth Died Screaming; Dirt In The Ground; Such A Scream; All Stripped

Down; Who Are You; The Ocean Doesn't Want Me; Jesus Gonna Be Here; A Little Rain; In The Colosseum; Goin' Out West; Murder In The Red Barn; Black Wings; Whistle Down The Wind; I Don't Wanna Grow Up; Let Me Get Up On It; That Feel

NIGHT ON EARTH (1992)

Back In The Good Old World (Gypsy); Los Angeles Mood (Chromium Descensions); Los Angeles Theme (Another Private Dick); New York Theme (Hey, You Can Have That Heartattack Outside Buddy); New York Mood (A New Haircut And A Busted Lip); Baby I'm Not A Baby Anymore (Beatrice Theme); Good Old World (Waltz); Carnival (Brunello Del Montalcino); On The Other Side Of The World; Good Old World (Gypsy Instrumental); Paris Mood (Un De Fromage); Dragging A Dead Priest; Helsinki Mood; Carnival Bob's Confession; Good Old World (Waltz); On The Other Side Of The World (Instrumental)

TOM WAITS, THE EARLY YEARS, VOLUME 2 (1992)

Hope I Don't Fall In Love With You; Ol' 55; Mockin' Bird; In Between Love; Blue Skies; Nobody; I Want You; Shiver Me Timbers; Grapefruit Moon; Diamonds On My Windshield; Please Call Me, Baby; So It Goes; Old Shoes

THE BLACK RIDER (1993)

Lucky Day (Overture); The Black Rider; November; Just The Right Bullets; Black Box Theme; 't'ain't No Sin; Flash Pan Hunter (Intro); That's The Way; The Briar And The Rose; Russian Dance; Gospel Train (Orchestra); I'll Shoot The Moon; Flash Pan Hunter; Crossroads; Gospel Train; Interlude; Oily Night; Lucky Day; The Last Rose Of Summer; Carnival

BEAUTIFUL MALADIES: THE ISLAND YEARS (1998)

Hang On St Christopher; Temptation; Clap Hands; The Black Rider; Underground; Jockey Full Of Bourbon; Earth Died Screaming; Innocent When You Dream (78); Straight To The Top; Frank's Wild Years; Singapore; Shore Leave; Johnsburg, Illinois; Way Down In The Hole; Strange Weather; Cold Cold Ground; November; Downtown Train; 16 Shells From A 30.6; Jesus Gonna Be Here; Good Old World (Waltz); I Don't Wanna Grow Up; Time

MULE VARIATIONS (1999)

Big In Japan; Lowside Of The Road; Hold On; Get Behind The Mule; House Where Nobody Lives; Cold Water; Pony; What's He Building?; Black Market Baby; Eyeball Kid; Picture In A Frame; Chocolate Jesus; Georgia Lee; Filipino Box Spring Hog; Take It With Me; Come On Up To The House

USED SONGS: 1973–1980 (2001)

Heartattack & Vine; Eggs & Sausage (In A Cadillac With Susan Michelson); A Sight For Sore Eyes; Whistlin' Past The Graveyard; Burma Shave; Step Right Up; Ol' 55; I Never Talk To Strangers; Jersey Girl; Christmas Card From A Hooker In Minneapolis; Blue Valentines; (Looking For) The Heart Of Saturday Night; Muriel; Wrong Side Of The Road; Tom Traubert's Blues

BLOOD MONEY (2002)

Misery Is The River Of The World; Everything Goes To Hell; Coney Island Baby; All The World Is Green; God's Away On Business; Another Man's Vine; Knife Chase; Lullaby; Starving In The Belly Of A Whale; The Part You Throw Away; Woe; Calliope; A Good Man Is Hard To Find

ALICE (2002)

Alice; Everything You Can Think; Flower's Grave; No One Knows I'm Gone; Kommienezuspadt; Poor Edward; Table Top Joe; Lost In the Harbour; We're All Mad Here; Watch Her Disappear; Reeperbahn; I'm Still Here; Fish & Bird; Barcarolle; Fawn

REAL GONE (2004)

Top Of The Hill; Hoist That Rag; Sins Of The Father; Shake It; Don't Go Into That Barn; How's It Gonna End; Metropolitan Glide; Dead And Lovely; Circus; Trampled Rose; Green Grass; Baby Gonna Leave Me; Clang Boom Steam; Make It Rain; Day After Tomorrow

ORPHANS: BRAWLERS, BAWLERS & BASTARDS (2006)

Brawlers: Lie To Me; Low Down; 2:19; Fish In The Jailhouse; Bottom Of The World; Lucinda; Ain't Goin' Down To The Well; Lord I've Been Changed; Puttin' On The Dog; Road To Peace; All The Time; The Return Of Jackie & Judy; Walk Away; Sea Of Love; Buzz Fledderjohn; Rains On Me
Bawlers: Bend Down The Branches; You Can Never Hold Back Spring; Long Way Home; Widow's Grove; Little Drop Of Poison; Shiny Things;

World Keeps Turning; Tell It To Me; Never Let Go; Fannin Street; Little Man; It's Over; If I Have To Go; Goodnight Irene; The Fall Of Troy; Take Care Of All My Children; Down There By The Train; Danny Says; Jayne's Blue Wish; Young At Heart

Bastards: What Keeps Mankind Alive; Children's Story; Heigh Ho; Army Ants; Books Of Moses; Bone Chain; Two Sisters; First Kiss; Dog Door; Redrum; Nirvana; Home I'll Never Be; Poor Little Lamb; Altar Boy; The Pontiac; Spidey's Last Ride; King Kong; On The Road

FILMOGRAPHY

Paradise Alley (1978)
Wolfen (1981)
One From The Heart (1982)
The Outsiders (1983)
Rumble Fish (1983)
The Cotton Club (1984)
The Stone Boy (1984)
Down By Law (1986)
Ironweed (1987)
Big Time (1988)
Candy Mountain (1988)
Cold Feet (1989)
Bearskin: An Urban Fairytale (1989)
Mystery Train (1989)
The Two Jakes (1990)
Queens Logic (1991)
The Fisher King (1991)
At Play In The Fields Of The Lord (1991)
Bram Stoker's Dracula (1992)
Deadfall (1993)
Short Cuts (1993)
Mystery Men (1999)
Coffee & Cigarettes (2003)
Domino (2005)
La Tigre e la Neve (The Tiger and The Snow) (2005)
Wristcutters: A Love Story (2006)

BIBLIOGRAPHY

The Annotated Alice: Alice's Adventures In Wonderland And Through The Looking Glass by Lewis Carroll, Edited by Martin Gardner (Anthony Blond, 1960)

Berlin: The Biography Of A City, Anthony Read and David Fisher (Pimlico, 1994)

The Bob Dylan Encyclopedia, Michael Gray (Continuum, 2006)

Complicated Shadows: The Life & Music Of Elvis Costello, Graeme Thomson (Canongate, 2004)

Coppola: The Man And His Dreams, Peter Cowie (Andre Deutsch, 1989)

Faithfull, Marianne Faithfull and David Dalton (Michael Joseph, 1994)

David Geffen: A Biography Of New Hollywood, Tom King (Hutchinson, 2000)

The Glory And The Dream: A Narrative History Of America, 1932–1972, William Manchester (Michael Joseph, 1975)

Halliwell's Film, Video & DVD Guide 2005, Edited by John Walker (Harper Collins Entertainment, 2004)

Hotel California: Singer-Songwriters And Cocaine Cowboys In The LA Canyons, 1967–1976, Barney Hoskyns (4th Estate, 2005)

Innocent When You Dream; Tom Waits: The Collected Interviews, Edited by Mac Montandon (Orion, 2006)

Jack Kerouac: King Of The Beats, Barry Miles (Virgin, 1998)

The Kid Stays In The Picture, Robert Evans (Faber & Faber, 2003)

The Mansion On The Hill, Fred Goodman (Jonathan Cape, 1997)

Nick Drake, The Biography, Patrick Humphries (Bloomsbury, 1997)

Rock Lives, Timothy White (Omnibus, 1991)

Songwriters On Songwriting, Fourth Edition, Paul Zollo (Da Capo, 2003)

To The Limit: The Untold Story Of The Eagles, Marc Eliot (Little Brown, 1998)

Tom Waits, Cath Carroll (Unanimous, 2000)

Waiting For The Sun: The Story Of The Los Angeles Music Scene, Barney Hoskyns (Viking, 1996)

Written In My Soul: Conversations With Rock's Great Songwriters, Bill Flanagan (Contemporary Books, 1987)

Zappa: Electric Don Quixote, Neil Slaven (Omnibus, 1996)

Frank Zappa, Barry Miles (Atlantic, 2005)

ACKNOWLEDGEMENTS

To Thomas Dylan Brooke, for growing up . . . and Laura-lou for arriving just in time.

Thanks go to Fred Dellar, as ever, the man who knows; Colin and Anita for the heart of Saturday night; Angie Errigo, for films, videos . . . and ain't freelancing a bitch? Dan French, for Austin 1978; Peter K. Hogan, Ellie and Quinn, for what's been and what lies ahead; Barney Hoskyns, for the geography lessons; Ken Hunt, for cuttings and encouragement; David Taylor, for what he doesn't know about film; Tina, for biscuits and coffee; and to Bill, Josie, Ellie, Harry and Ben for keeping us going.

Thanks also to Chris Charlesworth for commissioning this (again) – and having the patience to see it through; to Johnny Rogan for an invaluable index and painstaking proofing; and finally, to Sue, for the title, the first cut and so much, much more . . .

INDEX

Singles releases are in roman type and albums are in italics

09/07(63236)